Mercer Commentary on the Bible

Volume 6

The Gospels

Mercer University Press

Mercer Dictionary of the Bible
July 1990; 4th and corrected printing July 1994

Mercer Dictionary of the Bible Course Syllabi
July 1990

Mercer Commentary on the Bible
November 1994

Cover illustration: *The Evangelists* (by Fr. Gregory Kroug, 1909–1969), Royal Doors, Nosily-le-Grand, France. Photograph by Andrew Tregubov, in *The Light of Christ Iconography of Gregory Kroug* (1990). By permission of St. Vladimir's Seminary Press, 575 Scarsdale Road, Crestwood, New York 10707.

Mercer Commentary on the Bible

Volume 6

The Gospels

GENERAL EDITORS
Watson E. Mills, Richard F. Wilson

ASSOCIATE EDITORS
Roger A. Bullard, Walter Harrelson, Edgar V. McKnight

MERCER UNIVERSITY PRESS EDITOR
Edd Rowell

WITH MEMBERS OF THE
National Association of Baptist Professors of Religion

MERCER UNIVERSITY PRESS
March 1996

ISBN 0-86554-511-1 MUP/P138

Mercer Commentary on the Bible: Gospels
Volume 6 of an 8-volume perfect-bound reissue of
the *Mercer Commentary on the Bible* (©1995).

Printed in the United States of America
First printing, March 1996

The paper used in this publication meets the minimum requirements
of the American National Standard for Information Sciences—
Permanence of Paper for Printed Library Materials, ANSI Z39.48-1984.

Library of Congress Cataloging-in-Publication Data

Mercer commentary on the Bible.
Volume 6. The gospels /
general editors, Watson E. Mills and Richard F. Wilson;
associate editors, Walter Harrelson . . . [et al.].
l+226pp. 6x9" (15x22cm.).
1. Bible—commentaries. I. Mills, Watson Early. II. Mercer University Press.
III. National Association of Baptist Professors of Religion.

**CIP data available from Library of Congress
and will appear in subsequent printings.**

Contents

Preface

This volume includes the commentaries on the canonical Gospels from the *Mercer Commentary on the Bible* (MCB) plus several appropriate articles from the *Mercer Dictionary of the Bible* (MDB). This MCB/MDB portion is for use in the classroom and for any other setting where study focuses on the Gospels and where a convenient introduction text is desired. It is number 6 in the series of MCB/MCB portions or volumes.

1. Pentateuch/Torah (Genesis–Deuteronomy)	Isbn 0-86554-506-5 P133
2. History of Israel (Joshua–Esther)	Isbn 0-86554-507-3 P134
3. (Wisdom) Writings (Job–Song of Songs)	Isbn 0-86554-508-1 P135
4. Prophets (Isaiah–Malachi)	Isbn 0-86554-509-X P136
5. Deuterocanonicals/Apocrypha	Isbn 0-86554-510-3 P137
6. Gospels (Matthew–John)	Isbn 0-86554-511-1 P138
7. Acts and Pauline Writings (Acts–Philemon)	Isbn 0-86554-512-X P139
8. Epistles and Revelation (Hebrews–Revelation)	Isbn 0-86554-513-8 P140

That these divisions—and their titles—are arbitrary is obvious. These divisions originate in the classroom as convenient and provisionally appropriate blocks of text for focused study during a semester- or quarter-long course of study. Other divisions are possible, perhaps even desirable (combining Acts with the Gospels, for example, rather than with Paul), but the present divisions seem appropriate for most users.

Regarding the use of this and other MCB/MDB portions, please note the following.

A bracketed, flush-right entry at the head of each MDB article and MCB commentary indicates the original page number(s): for example, "Gospel" [MDB 342]; and "Matthew" [MCB 939-74]. The text of both MDB and MCB is essentially that of the original, differing only in format; that is, it is redesigned to fit a 6x9" page (the page size of both MDB and MCB is 7x10").

References to other MDB articles are indicated by small caps: for example, KINGDOM OF GOD in the fourth paragraph of the article on "Gospel" refers to the article in MDB on "Kingdom of God"; MAGI and HEROD in the third paragraph of the commentary on Matthew refer to those articles in MDB. In addition, the "See also" sections at the end of the MDB articles indicate other articles in MDB that are appropriate for further study.

(Observe, however, that small caps are used also for B.C.E. and C.E., for certain texts and versions [LXX, KJV, NRSV], and for the tetragrammaton YHWH.)

In addition to the *Mercer Dictionary of the Bible* and the *Mercer Commentary on the Bible*, a booklet is available of sample course syllabi that includes actual outlines of courses in which a Bible version and MDB are the required texts. (Regarding this booklet, please contact the Mercer University Press marketing department.)

For abbreviations, see the lists in either MDB or MCB. Regarding the editors and contributors, please see both MDB and MCB. The *Course Syllabi* handbook has a complete listing of MDB articles (pp. 73-80). MDB includes a complete listing of articles arranged by contributor (pp. 989-93).

We intend that these texts be available, appropriate, and helpful for Bible students both in and out of the classroom and indeed for anyone seeking guidance in uncovering the abundant wealth of the Scriptures. Your critical response to these and other texts from Mercer University Press is most welcome and encouraged.

March 1996 *Mercer University Press*

Introduction

Gospel Studies

New Testament as Literature [MDB 611-14a]

•**New Testament as Literature.** NT writings follow the rules or conventions not only of the Greek language but also of secondary literary "languages." Biblical scholars in general have discovered the value of viewing the Bible as literature, and NT scholars are sharing in this discovery. This essay will first of all survey the literary conventions of the NT writings and then discuss broader implications of viewing the NT as literature.

Literary Conventions of the NT. A beginning point in examining the nature of the NT as literature is the distinction between narrative and nonnarrative discourse or didactic material. The four Gospels, Acts, and the Book of Revelation (to a large extent) are in narrative form and follow the conventions of narrative. The remaining material follows various epistolary and rhetorical didactic conventions. The narrative of the Gospels is to be read differently than didactic epistolary works.

Identification of the specific genre of each writing is important, for each genre has its own conventions. The Book of Revelation is an apocalyptic writing and it may be appreciated by seeing it in relation to apocalyptic sections of the NT. But the conventions of the apocalypse are best seen by comparing it with the OT Book of Daniel and various nonbiblical apocalypses. It is helpful to note the common characteristics of the four Gospels and to read each Gospel in light of those conventions. But distinction must also be made between the conventions shared by the first three Gospels and those unique to the Gospel of John. In a sense, each Gospel (and each NT writing) is unique and demands reading in light of its unique nature, but attention to common characteristics is important as a beginning point.

The epistolary material of the NT follows the conventions of ancient letters. Of course, care must be taken to distinguish between the genuine letters which follow the conventions in a standard fashion and those following the letter form in a more or less creative fashion. Paralleling the epistolary conventions are Greco-Roman rhetorical conventions which were followed in composition of speeches and letters.

Smaller forms are to be found within each of the larger units. These range from figures of speech to extended literary units. Best known are the forms which have been identified by NT form critics following the distinction between narrative and discourse. The PASSION NARRATIVE is an intermediate form standing between the gospel genre and the smaller forms. To determine conventions to be followed in reading and interpreting a passion narrative, the passion narratives of the four Gospels may be compared and then passion stories outside of the Gospels may be utilized. Pronouncement stories are short stories which tell of isolated events in the life of Jesus and which contain pronouncements suitable for sermons. Miracle stories in the NT follow the style of similar stories from ancient to modern times, giving the history of the illness, the technique of the miracle, and finally the success of the miraculous act. Miracle stories may be compared with other miracle stories and with pronouncement stories which use accounts of miracles as the narrative framework for a pronouncement. Legends are religious narratives of saintly men and women, and myths are narratives which describe the many-sided interaction between transhuman persons. Discourse material includes the PARABLES and sayings such as proverbs, prophetic and apocalyptic sayings, and laws and community regulations.

The form critics combined historical and literary interests when they studied the Gospel tradition. They were concerned for those forms which could be connected with a particular life setting. A literary approach is less concerned with a sociological or historical life setting and more concerned with the literary form and function of the unit. A literary approach, then, will examine the smaller forms in light of their relationship with each other within the larger literary unit. It places the units within larger literary complexes. Miracle stories in the Gospel of Matthew and pronouncement stories in the Gospel of Mark, for example, combine to form larger literary units. Parables and sayings of Jesus have been combined into larger literary units in the well-known five discourses of the Gospel of Matthew.

A literary approach to a particular book of the NT is not content with specifying genre and examining the individual units and their combinations in light of literary affinities. It is concerned with examining the literary coherence of the entire unit. The beginning point of the contemporary literary contextualizing of biblical writings may be seen as the emphasis upon the literary work as a unity to be understood essentially in terms of that literary structure. In literary studies in America, this emphasis resulted from New Criticism, which desired to explain a work by considering it as an autonomous whole with a significance and value determined apart from any external reference. When the new critical principle is applied to biblical literature, the biblical text is interpreted as a structural unity, with each part seen as integral to the whole and as modifying the meaning of the whole. Interpretation, then, involves bringing all parts of the texts into a meaningful relationship to the entire text. This involves the linear (or syntagmatic) relationships within a text. But it also involves metaphoric (associative or paradigmatic) relationships. Whenever possible, that is, one unit in the text is seen as standing in a metaphoric relation to other units and to the total work. A literary approach, therefore, does not begin by dissecting a book of the NT into different sources, but considers the book as a unity. Each part of the text is studied in relation not to the historical setting and activity of the author or editor but on its own in relation to other parts. With narrative, for example, plot is important. Plots are arrangements of events into a beginning, a middle, and an end, which together form a completed whole. The events in the plot move toward the resolution of some conflict, and plots are often characterized by the sort of conflict (physical, character, and moral and spiritual) that is resolved in the story. Ingredients of stories are characters (even when the conflict is not essentially between characters), settings, and the strategies for moving the story along in an interesting way and involving the reader in the story.

A literary approach to the Gospel of Mark, for example, will attempt to discern some plot developing from a beginning to a ending. It will attempt to discern relationships of significance between and among the units. Readers who have been influenced by the form-critical attention to the individual units may attempt to escape the ambitious task of relating the series of actions in Mark 1:4–3:35 to each other. The conclusion of the story of Jesus' healing on the Sabbath ("The Pharisees went out, and immediately held counsel with the Herodians against him, how to destroy him" [3:6]), however, encourages the reader to organize the segments into a story which will conclude with the passion. The early stories of Jesus' success in chaps. 1–3 serve as motivation for the plot of his enemies against Jesus recounted in chap. 3. The chapter on parables (4) with its emphasis on the "secret" of the Kingdom of God relativizes such a passion-directed processing. The reader may even despair of making any sense of the materials as a whole. Later on in the Gospel, moreover, the reader is encouraged once again to tie segments together as the author specifies relationships. In Mark 8:19, the Jesus of the Gospel of Mark questions the disciples about events recorded earlier in the Gospel: "When I broke the five loaves for the five thousand, how many baskets full of broken pieces did you take up?" They said to him, "Twelve." "And the seven for the four thousand, how many baskets full of broken pieces did you take up?" And they said to him, "Seven." And he said to them, "Do you not yet understand?"

Readers are encouraged by the Jesus of the Gospel of Mark to see metaphoric relationships. In the stories of feeding, the remaining broken pieces serve effectively as a symbol for the abundance of bread. But the question of Jesus indicates that another meaning is to be discerned as well. The reader who wants to discover that meaning must see metaphoric relationships between different episodes. The text refers the reader back to the stories of miraculous feedings (6:35-44; 8:1-8). But by means of the repetition in 8:18 of the quotation about seeing but not understanding (which came first in 4:12), the reader is invited to re-examine and find deeper meaning in the parable of the seed in 4:3-9. The reader may see connections between this parable and the miraculous feedings which had escaped detection at first.

But the reader must go further, for to make sense of these relationships is to overcome the failure to understand Jesus' identity. The reader continues to read the Gospel in light of this perspective. Immediately after the discussion in the boat, comes the central part with Jesus' own answer to the question of who he is (8:27-29). The threefold announcement of his arrest, execution, and resurrection as the completion of his way of life is connected with the theme of seeing and understanding by the framework of the two stories relating the healing of a blind man in Mark. The theme of the first story (8:22-26) is the development of "seeing" into "looking intently" and movement from seeing men that "look like trees" to "seeing everything clearly." The story suggests various ways of seeing, a way of seeing which causes one to misinterpret what one sees and a way of seeing which is both clear and comprehensive. The theme of the second story (10:46-52) is the connection between seeing on the one hand and following Jesus on the way on the other.

Literary Study of the NT as a New Paradigm. The study of the NT as literature must be seen as something new in the history of interpretation. It may be compared and contrasted with the study of the NT as dogma and as history. With the dogmatic approach of the ancient and medieval church, the essential character of the Bible was its nature as a sign of God, a communication intrinsically far above the pitch of human minds but available as a sign. The critical and historical approach resulted from a transformation of world view in the Enlightenment. The historicality of literary documents and of other cultural phenomena replaced the framework provided by the theological conceptualization of the ancient and medieval world. Cultural documents and artifacts are bound up not with a preexisting world, of which the artifacts are an exteriorization. They are to be understood precisely within the temporally and spatially limited context of their origins.

Literary approaches are not satisfied with the reduction of biblical texts to "causes" in the Neoplatonic and historical-critical perspectives. Texts are viewed in light of linguistic and literary relationships, but there is no attempt to reduce texts to linguistic and literary systems. Instead of a simple one-to-one cause and effect model, literary critics emphasize the multiplicity of relationships and interdependence or mutual "causation."

When the NT is viewed as literature, historical and dogmatic factors are not ignored. The historical factors, however, are seen as circumstances of origin, and the discovery of such circumstances is not seen as the ultimate goal of NT study. The dogmatic aspects are not ignored, but they are coordinated not with an ancient or modern dogmatic system. A contemporary literary approach is concerned with translating doctrinal emphases into terms which are relevant for the modern reader and consistent with the nature of the NT text as literature.

The practical use of the biblical texts in ancient and modern times does not mean that a literary approach is impossible or inappropriate. At one period in literary study, the view of literature separated it from other uses of language. The reality of literature was seen as a world of its own. Literature, then, was essentially independent of historical, social, and economic realities. The aim of literary study was to explain why a particular work of art was beautiful. Judged in light of this particular literary ideology, the Bible could not be approached as literature. But this ideology is no longer self evident in literary criticism. All sorts of texts may be read as literature regardless of their original functions. Moreover, literary and nonliterary functions coexist. Giving attention to aesthetic, emotive, and conative functions of biblical texts does not deny that biblical texts had particular practical functions and continue to have such functions. In the real life of a culture, texts must often carry out different functions at the same time in order to be effective. In order for an icon to be perceived as a religious text, it must also be a work of art. The reverse is also true. In order to be perceived as a work of art, the icon must have the religious function that is proper to it. Placing the icon in a museum, in a certain sense, violates the effect of the unity of the two functions.

From the perspective of the literary paradigm in its broadest sense, the question as to the role and function of the NT arises. With the dogmatic approach, the function of the Bible was to provide doctrine, and the NT was the ultimate source of doctrine. The OT was preliminary. With the historical approach, the Bible provided historical answers to historical questions. The development of an evolutionary approach reinforced the significance of the NT over against the OT. A role and function of the NT consistent with a literary view of the Bible will begin with the Bible as a whole. It is possible to see the entire Bible in literary terms as kerygmatic. That is, the Bible as a whole and in its individual units is proclamation and actualization of a good news.

The question of function is related to the matter of genre in terms of the Bible as a whole. The biblical writings (OT and NT) share a common narrative plot at the most profound level. This common plot may be perceived by utilizing the four-fold organization of basic motifs, or "pre-generic elements of literature," at work prior to the development of ordinary literary genres. (The four seasons of the year have been used in explicating the motifs.) These elements are comedy (the mythos of spring), romance (the mythos of summer), tragedy (the mythos of autumn), and irony and satire (the mythos of winter). The Bible contains stories that reflect all of these plots and their modifications and combinations. Romance is the successful quest, and the complete form of the romance has a preliminary stage of a perilous journey with its minor adventures, a crucial struggle in which either the hero or his opponent or both must die, and the exaltation of the hero who has proved himself to be a hero even if he does not survive the conflict. But the thrust of the Bible is in the direction of the comic. The standard shape of comedy is a u-shaped pattern in which the action is first of all brought to a low point by a series of misfortunes and then sent to a happy conclusion by some fortunate twists in the plot. The normal pattern of action for comedy the desire of a young man for a young woman, resistance of this desire by some opposition, and a twist at the end of the plot, which enables the hero to have his will.

The comic pattern is obvious in the stories of the failure, captivity, and redemption of the people of God. An essentially comic perspective is evident in the narrative accounts of Israel and Jesus Christ. It is also evident in nonnarrative material of the Bible. A literary approach to the NT allows use of the resources of the OT in a different fashion than did the dogmatic and historical approaches. The biblical writings as a whole present a view of the world which is at odds with the view of life as romance, as a quest in which the universe is the creation of humankind. The Bible is the epic of the creator, not of the creature.

The question of the sacred is an important question which must be raised in a literary approach to the NT as literature. With the world view which operated with the dogmatic approach, there was no question concerning the divine. The divine was essential. With the Enlightenment, a view of the world developed in which the criterion of reality is the order of nature as the source of sense experience. This view of the world has resulted in what is known as the "death of God." There is no criterion in the natural world which can serve as the basis of judgment of the sacred. It is possible that with the new world view operating with a literary approach to the Bible, God may be conceptualized once again. The world which is disclosed in the biblical texts, in fact, involves a sacrality which enables human experience to be fulfilled. But the sacred is not approached as a "thing" as would be required in the critical approach growing out of the Enlightenment. John Macquarrie's suggestion that Exodus 3:14 be translated as "I let be what I let be" allows us to conceive of the sacred which is related to the world but which is not to be reduced to the world. God *is* in a dynamic and creative sense. The very fact of God is the condition that there are any beings or properties of beings. We may speak of the experience with the sacred as grace is so far as it supports and strengthens human existence and helps the overcoming of the fragmentariness and impotence of this existence. The sacred is judgment as it lays claim on humans and exposes the distortions of their existence. As it brings new understanding of ourselves and of the wider life within which we live, we may call this "revelation." The Bible approached as literature discloses a world in which the sacred makes sense. It invites its readers to share such sense and such a world.

When the Bible is seen as a kerygmatic offering of such a world, as the proclamation of this good news in the comic genre, the reader's interaction with the Bible is seen as an essential factor in biblical literature. The reader's interaction may result in a special kind of knowledge. This knowledge is not essentially dogmatic information. It is not essentially historical data. It is a "knowledge" which affects relationships of individuals with other individuals, of individuals with themselves, and of individuals with the sacred. The emphasis on the role of biblical literature in the life of the reader does not mean that the text is minimized. On the contrary, the text is taken just as seriously as before. But taking the text seriously in a reader-oriented literary approach does not mean distancing the text so that it becomes and remains ancient and strange. It means situating the text in a fashion that it is able to speak to the reader in his or her contemporary idiom. Readers come to texts and are able to make sense because there is some correlation of textual factors and factors in the reader's world. Characters, events, and situations in the text are not unlike those in the reader's world. But the text often challenges the conceptions and ideologies with which the reader begins, and the reader modifies or recreates his world ideologically. Since world and self do not exist in isolation, however, the reader's self is being redefined in the process. Experience with the text is an experience which alters needs and possibilities.

The sort of knowledge which is provided by the Bible as literature is expanded. This knowledge is not simply knowledge of facts which can be determined from the biblical narrative and discourses, detached from the texts, and then reattached to dogmatic and historical systems of the reader's own day. The knowledge gained is the kind that is obtained by viewing biblical texts in light of their integrity as linguistic and literary creations and by examining the world disclosed in the texts and the world of values and meanings presupposed by the world of the text. The sacred is experienced in creative interaction with the biblical text. This experiential knowledge may influence the reader more intimately than convention biblical knowledge. A sensitive reader may, in fact, be "creating" a new world in the process of reading.

See also APOCALYPTIC LITERATURE; APOPHTHEGM; BIBLE AND WESTERN LITERATURE; BIBLE IN AMERICA; EPISTLE/LETTER; FORM/GATTUNG; GENRE, CONCEPT OF; GENRE, GOSPEL; INTERPRETATION, HISTORY OF; LITERARY CRITICISM; LITERATURE, BIBLE AS; MIRACLE STORY; PARABLES; PASSION NARRATIVE; PROVERB/RIDDLE.

Bibliography. M. H. Abrams, *The Mirror and the Lamp: Romantic Theory and the Critical Tradition*; R. Alter, *The Art of Biblical Narrative*; R. Alter and F. Kermode, eds., *The Literary Guide to the Bible*; Augustine, *On Christian Doctrine*; G. B. Caird, *The Language and Imagery of the Bible*; B. S. Childs, *The New Testament as Canon: An Introduction*; F. Dreyfus, "Exégèse en Sorbonne, Exégèse en Eglise," *RB* 81 (1975): 321-59; R. M. Fowler, "Irony and the Messianic Secret in the Gospel of Mark," *Proceedings: Eastern Great Lakes Biblical Society* 1 (1981): 26-36; N. Frye, *Anatomy of Criticism: Four Essays, The Great Code: The Bible and Literature,* and *The Secular Scripture: A Study of the Structure of Romance*; S. A. Geller, "Were the Prophets Poets?" *Prooftexts: A Journal of Jewish Literary History* 3 (1983): 211-21; W. Iser, *The Act of Reading; A Theory of Aesthetic Response*; J. L. Kugel, *The Idea of Biblical Poetry: Parallelism and Its History* and "On the Bible and Literary Criticism," *Prooftexts: A Journal of Jewish Literary History* 1 (1981): 217-36; E. V. McKnight, *The Bible and the Reader: An Introduction to Literary Criticism, Meaning in Texts: The Historical Shaping of a Narrative Hermeneutics,* and *Postmodern Use of the Bible: The Emergence of Reader Oriented Criticism*; J. Macquarrie, *Principles of Christian Theology*; D. Robertson, *The Old Testament and the Literary Critic*; L. Ryken, *How to Read the Bible as Literature*; M. Sternberg, *The Poetics of Biblical Narrative: Ideological Literature and the Drama of Reading.*

—EDGAR V. MCKNIGHT

Gospel [MDB 342]

•**Gospel.** [gos′puhl] The English word "gospel" is derived from the Old English "godspell," an abbreviated form of "goodspell." The root meaning of "spell" was story. Hence, godspell and its later derivative referred to a good story, or good news. This is consistent with the Greek term used in the NT; the Gk. term (εὐαγγέλιον) is composed of a prefix (ευ) meaning "good" and a stem (ἀγγέλιον) meaning "message" which is derived from a word (ἄγγελος) meaning "messenger." The term (ἐυαγγέλιον) refers to the good news which is proper to a good messenger. "Gospel," "good news," and "glad tidings" have served appropriately since the Tyndale version as English translations of the Gk. noun. The verbal form which appears frequently in the NT is usually rendered, "to preach" or "to proclaim" the good news (gospel). Therefore, gospel indicates an announcement of a highly favorable experience or event. The verb, likewise, refers to the action of announcing such an event.

In the pre-Christian Greco-Roman world, the word translated "gospel" was used originally with reference to victory in battle. It was employed in two connections: (1) to designate the the actual good news of victory and its consequent deliverance, and (2) to designate a reward which was given to the messenger who delivered the good news after the announcement had been verified. For the adherents of the imperial cult the term acquired religious connotations as it was employed in reference to the birth, power, and pronouncements of the emperor-god.

The noun appears infrequently in the Septuagint (LXX), and a distinction is made between the good news itself and the reward for good news by using the singular form for the good news and the plural form for the reward. On the other hand, the verb occurs often in the LXX as a translation of the Hebrew word which denoted the good news of the great victory of Yahweh.

Jesus probably employed the Hebrew verb or its Aramaic equivalent to convey his belief that the KINGDOM OF GOD brought salvation, deliverance, and joy. Later Christian writers employed the Greek noun in order to describe Jesus and what he did and taught to accomplish the transformation of humanity. The good news of the Kingdom proclaimed by Christ became equated with the good news of Christ himself and what he accomplished through his life, death, and resurrection. Paul's use of the term focused on the death and resurrection of Jesus, but Mark confirms that others used the word to describe the entirety of Jesus' life, not just his message or death and resurrection.

During the centuries subsequent to the NT two major developments occurred in the usage of "gospel." Early Christian interpreters employed the term frequently to describe the entirety of the Christian scripture as distinct from the Jewish scriptures. All scripture was viewed as either Prophets (OT) or Gospel (NT). Gospel also became a technical term for the specific books which recorded the story of Jesus' life, message, and redemptive death. Anxious to contend for the singularity of the good news, the documents became entitled "The Gospel according to Mark, Matthew, Luke, and John."

See also EVANGELIST; SCRIPTURE IN THE NEW TESTAMENT.

Bibliography. G. Friedrich, "εὐαγγέλιον," *TDNT*; B. H. Streeter, *The Four Gospels*; K. Nickle, *The Synoptic Gospels*. —ROBERT M. SHURDEN

Gospel Genre [MDB 324a]

•**Genre, Gospel.** [zhahn´ruh] In literary terms, what is a GOSPEL? In the nineteenth and early twentieth centuries similarities between the canonical Gospels and Greco-Roman biographies were recognized and the inference drawn that the Gospels were biographies of the founder of Christianity (Renan, Votaw). In the 1920s a new position was staked out, contending that the canonical Gospels are not biographies, but are the apostolic kerygma (preaching) built up into a vivid narrative form (K. L. Schmidt, R. Bultmann). For nearly fifty years critical orthodoxy held that the Gospels are literarily unique, but by the 1970s a coalition of factors forced a reopening of the case. Chief among them was the recognition by critics that any text standing alone lacks meaning. Such reasoning led criticism to attempt to view the individual text or document in terms of a universal type or genre which is constructed on the basis of an inductive grouping of texts with common features. It is the particular text's participation in the genre that gives it a first level of meaning. A further way of saying something about the meaning of the document as a whole is to note the particular text's transformation of the genre. Recognition of this fact forced NT scholars to ask into what larger context the canonical Gospels fit. In the current discussion there are two very different conceptions of what is meant by genre. Some scholars use genre for classifications that have no necessary ties to a particular time and place: e.g., tragicomedy, parable, fantasy. Others speak of genre in the sense of a literary grouping tied to a particular time, place, and culture: e.g., romance, aretalogy, Greco-Roman history, ancient Mediterranean biography. Since the late 1970s there has been a growing consensus that the canonical Gospels are types of ancient Mediterranean biography, participants in the same large grouping as Philo's *Life of Moses* and Philostratus's *Life of Apollonius of Tyana.* If so, then the canonical Gospels can no longer be regarded as literarily unique. Participation in the ancient biographical genre does not, however, undermine the uniqueness of the canonical Gospels' content any more than the participation of Gen 1 in the genre of ancient Near Eastern creation myth detracts from its uniquely Hebraic witness to the Creator.

See also CANON; GENRE, CONCEPT OF; GOSPEL; GOSPELS, CRITICAL STUDY OF; HERMENEUTICS; LITERARY CRITICISM.

Bibliography. D. R. Cartlidge and D. L. Dungan, *Documents for the Study of the Gospels*; C. H. Talbert, *What Is a Gospel?*; C. W. Votaw, *The Gospels and Contemporary Biographies in the Greco-Roman World.* —CHARLES H. TALBERT

Critical Study of the Gospels [MDB 343a-46a]

•**Gospels, Critical Study of the.** Two very different objectives have governed the modern, critical study of the Gospels. One aim has been to reconstruct a picture of JESUS using modern, historical methodology. This quest of the historical Jesus has treated the Gospels as the soil containing the ore that, when refined, may yield the gold of reliable historical information about Jesus. This objective demands one cluster of approaches or methods for the study of the Gospels. The other aim has been to discover the theology of the evangelists. This quest of the theology of the Gospel authors has treated the Gospels as themselves the gold to be cherished and appreciated for its inherent value. In the former quest, the Gospels are regarded as a window through which one looks to see something else; in the latter, they are viewed as a mirror which reflects back to the viewer an image of the evangelist's world.

The quest of the historical Jesus was forced upon Christian scholars by the radical treatment of Jesus by H. S. Reimarus and D. F. Strauss. Both Reimarus's eccentricity and Strauss's denial of historicity forced scholars to reassess the Gospel sources. The logic of this history of research may be traced through six stages.

1. Other than the four canonical gospels, what are the sources available for the critical historican's quest for the historical Jesus? There are three possible Greco-Roman sources that are relevant: Pliny the Younger's letter to the Emperor Trajan about 110 C.E.; Tacitus's reference in his *Annals* 15.44 written about 115 C.E.; and Suetonius's *Life of Claudius* 25.4 from about 120 C.E. That there are so few references is not surprising given the fact that such literature comes from the aristocracy who would have had little interest in a despised Jew executed for treason in a remote part of the world. That these references exist, however, is understandable since each involves a disturbance of the public order, a matter of concern to any Roman. Of the three, only Tacitus is of certain value. His statement, "Christus from whom their name was derived was executed at the hands of the procurator Pontius Pilate in the reign of Tiberius," appears to be independent Roman evidence and therefore very valuable. Pliny's information is ultimately derived from the Christians and thus is not independent. Suetonius's sentence about Claudius's expulsion of the Jews from Rome about 49 C.E. is valuable if "Chrestus" really is a garbled reference to Christ ("Christus").

The Jewish evidence concerning Jesus from the early period is limited to JOSEPHUS and the earliest portions of the Talmud. In Josephus's *Antiquities,* there are only two passages with any claim to reliability. The one in 18.3.3, if genuine, must have been interpolated by later Christians for it contains statements that only a Christian could make: "He was the Christ," and "he appeared to them on the third day alive again, the divine prophets having foretold these and ten thousand other wonderful things concerning him." If these Christian assertions are removed, then what remains is a likely statement by Josephus that describes Jesus as a teacher and miracle worker who died on a Roman cross. The other in 20.9.1 is certainly authentic. It mentions Jesus only in passing as it tries to identify the James who was killed at the instigation of the Jewish high priest: "the brother of Jesus who was called Christ, whose name was James." Early evidence from the Talmud is limited. A tradition in *Sanh* 43a speaks of Jesus' crucifixion at Passover time. Another in the same section mentions his having had five disciples. Again, it is not surprising that before Christianity became a power to be reckoned with, the Jewish community would have had little need to refer to its founder. The surprise is the existence of the references that we do have. Taken together with Tacitus, these Jewish texts prove the historicity of Jesus and confirm some key facts about his life found in the Gospels.

The APOCRYPHAL GOSPELS, with the possible exception of the Coptic *Gospel of Thomas,* are of no direct use in the historical reconstruction of Jesus' career. The AGRAPHA likewise are, for the most part, of little use to the critical historian. Paul's letters, the earliest Christian sources, have little to contribute beyond confirming data. The same is true for the rest of the NT outside the canonical Gospels. If one is to know very much about Jesus, it must come from the four canonical Gospels.

2. Once they had recognized that the historians' knowledge about Jesus must come primarily from the four canonical Gospels, scholars found remarkable differences between the first three (Synoptics) and the fourth (John). These differences were of two kinds. First, it was recognized that John and the Synoptics overlapped in only about ten percent of their material. Crucial matter was found in the Synoptics and not in John: e.g., the baptism of Jesus, the temptation of Jesus, Peter's confession at Caesarea Philippi, the transfiguration, the parables, the exorcisms, the last supper viewed as the institution of the Lord's Supper, the agony in the garden, and the cry of dereliction from the cross. Matter crucial to John was missing from the Synoptics: e.g., an early Judean ministry of Jesus, prominent characters like Nicodemus, the Samaritan woman, and Lazarus; certain prominent miracles like the changing of water into wine, the healing of the lame man at the pool of Bethzatha, the imparting of sight to the man born blind, the raising of Lazarus; certain prominent events like the footwashing, the visit of the Greeks to see Jesus, Jesus before Annas at his trial, the beloved disciple, and the appearance to Thomas. This kind of material is complementary and can be explained by the hypothesis that the Synoptics and John each preserve different, but equally accurate, streams of Jesus tradition.

A second kind of difference between John and the Synoptics involves contrast: the Synoptics locate Jesus' public ministry in Galilee except at the end of his career, but John regards Judea as Jesus' homeland and speaks of alternating trips to Galilee; the cleansing of the Temple is first in John and at the end in Synoptics; in the Synoptics Jesus teaches in parables and short pithy sayings, in John his teaching involves long, theological discourses of an argumentative nature; in the Synoptics the theme of Jesus' message is the Kingdom of God, but in John it is eternal life; in the Synoptics Jesus seems to want to keep his messiahship a secret until the very end, in John it is a public claim from the first; the final cause of Jesus' death in the Synoptics is his cleansing of the Temple, in John it is the raising of Lazarus; in the Synoptics Jesus is crucified on the day of Passover, in John it is on the Day of Preparation for the Passover. Moreover, the story of Jesus in the Synoptics is told in terms of exaltation CHRISTOLOGY, whereas in John it is narrated in terms of epiphany Christology. Such differences are not subject to explanation by an hypothesis of different, complementary traditions. Here one is dealing with contrast, and even contradiction.

Prior to D. F. Strauss the differences between John and the Synoptics were explained in such a way that the Fourth Gospel was preferred as an historical source: e.g., Schleiermacher's lectures on Jesus in 1832 were based mainly on John. Strauss's *Life of Jesus* (1835) represented the first attempt to explain the differences between John and the Synoptics in a way that favored the Synoptics in every case. For Strauss the historian's sources for a knowledge of Jesus were not four but three. His influence continues in the work of Rudolf Bultmann and Günther Bornkamm for whom neither the speeches nor the narratives of John are historically reliable because of their theological tendency. C. H. Dodd's *Historical Tradition in the Fourth Gospel* (1963) is a magisterial attempt to maximize the historical dimensions of John. For him both narratives and speeches have a degree of historical reliability because there are parallels with the synoptic tradition in both. The common consensus, however, remains that the Synoptics are better historical sources than John.

3. In trying to explain the similarities among the Synoptics, scholars of the Enlightenment period disagreed on more than they agreed upon; however, all agreed on the rejection of tradition. Augustine's utilization hypothesis which saw the Gospels as written in the order Matthew-Mark-Luke, with each successive author using his predecessor(s) was discarded. With reason as their only resource, they applied a succession of hypotheses to the data: first an original-gospel hypothesis, then a fragment hypothesis, then a tradition hypothesis, and finally another utilization hypothesis. In the first half of the nineteenth century the Griesbach hypothesis was supreme: Matthew was written first, then Luke, and finally Mark as an abridgement of the two earlier Gospels. Not until the death of F. C. Baur was it possible for the two-source theory to gain a hearing in any serious way. H. J. Holtzmann in 1863 popularized the priority of Mark; Karl Weizsäcker in 1864 added a hypothetical sayings source also used by Matthew and Luke (first called Q in 1890 by Johannes Weiss). From this time the two-document hypothesis gained popularity. If Matthew and Luke had used Mark and Q as their primary sources, then it was from these two primary sources that any life of Jesus must be written. B. H. Streeter's *The Four Gospels* (1924) was unsuccessful in trying to add to Mark and Q two other written documents, M and L. Those symbols, however, have remained as designations for tradition peculiar to Matthew and Luke, respectively. It is in the form of two primary sources, Mark and Q, supplemented by oral tradition, M and

L, that the two-source theory has survived to this point as the dominant explanation of the similarity of the synoptic Gospels.

W. R. Farmer's *The Synoptic Problem* (1963) attempted a revival of the Griesbach hypothesis. Although his adherents are vocal, they are few. The main value of his challenge to the two-document hypothesis is the reopening of the question. Its resolution remains in the future. So unclear are the criteria for deciding the matter that some have simply suspended judgment until further light can he had.

4. Form criticism was a child of disappointment. When it became clear that the earliest written sources Mark and Q, were at least a generation removed from the events they claimed to narrate, it was deemed desirable to go behind them to the earliest oral traditions about Jesus. When it became apparent that both Mark (Wrede) and Q (Wellhausen) were theologically colored tradition, then it was a necessity. Form criticism took the insights from prior students of folklore and attempted to penetrate back into the period prior to our earliest written sources. Its pioneers in synoptic studies were Martin Dibelius, K. L. Schmidt, and Rudolf Bultmann, who did their work around the time of the First World War. Their work was popularized for the English speaking world by Vincent Taylor's *The Formation of the Gospel Tradition* (1933).

The form critics' conclusions become clear if seen as answers to three basic questions. First, why was the Jesus tradition preserved by the early church? Given the earliest Christians' belief in an imminent end of the world, they would have had no need to preserve historical material for posterity. They did, however, need some of the Jesus material in their daily activities: preaching (1 Cor 15:3-5); worship (1 Cor 11:23-25); catechesis (1 Cor 7:10-11); and apologetics (Mark 12:13-17). The material was useful so it was repeated; in its repetition it became ingrained in the church's corporate memory and was preserved. Second, how was the tradition preserved until its incorporation in the earliest written sources? The form critics contend that it was preserved as oral tradition in single, self-contained, detached units, each one of which was complete in itself. In the early period, there was no connected outline of Jesus' career. Before long, pre-Gospel collections began to form: e.g., a collection of five conflict stories would circulate by themselves in an order in which the hostility to Jesus rises with each successive conflict (Mark 2:1-3:6); a collection of three parables of the Kingdom each of which contained the key word "seed" (Mark 4:1-34); a collection of five sayings of Jesus held together by key words and link phrases (Mark 9:42-50).

The earliest connected material organized around a chronological principle was the PASSION NARRATIVE. Somewhere in this oral period, in an informal way resembling the formulation of the Jewish Targums, the originally Aramaic tradition was translated into Greek. That this informal process took place in a variety of settings accounts for some of the variety one finds in duplicate traditions in the Gospels. The Gospels represent the gradual coalescing of the traditions over a period of time. Third, what was the motivation for writing the Gospels? From the number of answers that were given two are worthy of mention. The success of the Christian mission beyond the bounds of Palestine created needs greater than the ability of the eyewitnesses to meet. The deaths of the eyewitnesses served as a catalyst for the writing of the Gospels in order to preserve their tradition.

If a source critic operating with the hypothesis of the two-source theory attempted to write a life of Jesus from Mark and Q, the form critic recognized as his primary source materials the individual oral traditions that lay behind the Gospels. Still the question had to be resolved: how does one objectively determine whether or not an individual oral tradition comes from Jesus?

5. Three criteria of historicity have been widely used by scholars to determine which individual traditions go back to Jesus. One such criterion claims that when a tradition is found in multiple sources (e.g., Mark and Q; Mark and M; Mark and L; Mark, Q, and Paul) it may be regarded as going back to Jesus. For example, the saying on marriage and divorce is found in Mark 10:11-12 || Matt 19:9, in Q (Matt 5:32 || Luke 16:18), and in 1 Cor 7:10-11. Not having been created by any one of these three independent sources, the saying in some form must go back very early. The limitation of this criterion is that it can show a tradition is very early, but cannot prove it goes back to Jesus. Another criterion contends that a tradition can be regarded as genuine Jesus material if it shows unmistakable signs of Palestinian origin in language, thought, or topography. Conversely, if a saying shows signs of Hellenistic origins, it obviously cannot go back to Jesus. So, for example, when one notes that the saying on marriage and divorce in 1 Cor 7:10-11 and Mark 10:11-12 allows both the man to divorce the woman and the woman to divorce the man, one knows that this form of the saying comes from a Roman legal context. According to Jewish Law only the man could divorce the woman. The form of the saying that is Palestinian, then, is that which says only the man shall not divorce the woman. The limitation to this criterion also is that it cannot prove that a tradition goes behind the Palestinian church to the Palestinian Jesus. A third criterion, used in conjunction with the other two,is called the negative criterion or the criterion of dissimilarity. It states that if a tradition shows signs of discontinuity with the church that passed it on, then it was not created by the church but goes back to Jesus. For example, in Matt 19:9 and 5:32 the writer added an except clause to the saying about divorce: no divorce except for. . . . In 1 Cor 7:12-15 Paul added an exception to the previously quoted saying about divorce: no divorce except for. . . . The tendency of both Matthew and Paul in Jewish-Christian and gentile-Christian contexts was to make exceptions in the matter of divorce. If the early saying from a Palestinian context absolutely prohibits a man's divorcing his wife, then such a saying shows signs of discontinuity with the church that passed it on. It is, therefore, not likely to have been created by the church but most probably goes back to Jesus.

Once these three criteria have been used together to create a collection of genuine Jesus traditions, if there are other materials that show continuity with them even though they cannot be shown to pass the test of the negative criterion, they may be treated as genuine also. This positive criterion is supplementary to the negative criterion.

From the bricks of oral tradition behind the Gospels that have passed the test of such criteria, the form critic seeks to reconstruct a historian's picture of Jesus. At this point, the question is how the Jesus materials deemed historical are to be fitted together.

6. Lives of Jesus are either arranged chronologically and developmentally or put together topically. The late nineteenth century lives of Jesus operated not only with the two-source theory as a base, but also with two corollaries to the priority of Mark. Mark, they believed, was objective history and yielded developmental information about Jesus. With this view of the sources, they offered a developmental picture of Jesus in which the inner and outer development of Jesus' career were traced. Jesus' outer development was usually described as a movement from initial popularity to ultimate isolation; his inner development was depicted in terms of a messianic consciousness that moved from initial lack of certainty and clarity to ultimate certainty and clarity. The rejection of this type of historical reconstruction of Jesus' career is focused in the work of Rudolf Bultmann. Bultmann, building on the work of W. Wrede and K. L. Schmidt, declared the late nineteenth century quest historically impossible. Wrede had shown that Mark was theologically interpreted tradition, and Schmidt argued that Mark could not provide developmental information about Jesus. There was, then, no way to write a developmental life of Jesus because the sources do not furnish that type of information. Bultmann's *Jesus and the Word* (1926) organized the tradition about Jesus deemed to be authentic in terms of subject matter. Rather than deal with Jesus' life (outer development) and personality (inner development), Bultmann focused on Jesus' message which he arranged in three logical groupings: "The Coming of the Kingdom of God," "The Will of God," and "God the Remote and the Near."

When E. Käsemann called for a new quest of the historical Jesus in 1953, he did not call for a return to developmental lives. Rather he assumed the same view of the sources as had his teacher, Bultmann. The two major contributions of the post-Bultmannians, Bornkamm's *Jesus of Nazareth* (1956) and Conzelmann's "Jesus Christ" (1959), continued Bultmann's logical and topical arrangement of the Jesus material, eschewing all attempts to write developmental lives of Jesus.

The recent quest for the theology of the evangelists began with H. Conzelmann (1954). In his work on Luke he focused his attention on the theology of the author. Two methodological principles were followed. First, he sought to interpret the meaning of the framework, that is, what the arrangement or organization of the Gospel meant. Second, he attempted to interpret the changes which Luke made in his sources, especially Mark. His pioneer work in REDACTION criticism opened the door for other studies on all three synoptic Gospels.

Conzelmann's methodology met with several criticisms. It was objected that not only the changes Luke made in his sources but also the material he included unchanged from his sources offered a clue to his theology. Further, it was argued that an evangelist's tendency or theology may be discovered without reference to his sources and changes made in them. This is true for Mark and ought to be for Matthew and Luke also. Even if one assumed no source theory or did not know a Gospel's sources, it would still be profitable and necessary to compare their differences in a Gospel parallel to see how each developed the common tradition in a unique fashion. Modifications in traditional redaction criticism merged with literary criticism as practiced by non-biblical scholars. The aim became to respect the narrative world of the author and to let it speak on its own terms.

Redaction criticism and LITERARY CRITICISM proved admirably suited to the delineation of the variety of theological motifs in a given Gospel. What eluded either method's grasp was the meaning of a Gospel as a whole. Since all meaning is controlled by context, the question became: what is the context for interpreting a Gospel as a whole? At this point GENRE criticism entered the picture. The meaning of a document as a whole can be discerned in large measure from its participation in and deviation from a larger cluster of similar documents. Especially when genre is understood as a literary category of a particular time, place, and culture is it helpful for interpretation. Then the interpreter has a clue to the social function of such writings.

The claim advanced by K. L. Schmidt and R. Bultmann that the Gospels were literally unique remained critical orthodoxy until the 1970s. Since then, there has been a growing consensus that the Christian Gospels are types of ancient biography. The critical catchword, "The Gospels are not biographies," has been replaced by another: "The Gospels are biographies, albeit ancient ones." This insight has offered the interpreter a preunderstanding with which to approach the Gospel texts as wholes. Genre criticism has become yet another technique to assist in the quest for the theology of the evangelists.

See also FORM/GATTUNG; GENRE, CONCEPT OF; GOSPEL; GENRE, GOSPEL; HERMENEUTICS; INTERPRETATION, HISTORY OF; JOHN, GOSPEL AND LETTERS OF; LITERARY CRITICISM; LUKE, GOSPEL OF; MARK, GOSPEL OF; MATTHEW, GOSPEL OF; RHETORICAL CRITICISM; SOURCE CRITICISM; SYNOPTIC PROBLEM.

Bibliography. G. Bornkamm, *Jesus of Nazareth*; R. Bultmann, *Jesus and the Word* and *The History of the Synoptic Tradition*; H. Conzelmann, *Jesus* and *The Theology of St. Luke*; M. Dibelius, *From Tradition to Gospel*; C. H. Dodd, *Historical Tradition in the Fourth Gospel*; P. C. Hodgson, ed., *The Life of Jesus Critically Examined, by David Friedrich Strauss*; R. N. Longenecker, "Literary Criteria in Life of Jesus Research: An Evaluation and Proposal," in *Current Issues in Biblical and Patristic Interpretation*, ed. G. F. Hawthorne; J. M. Robinson, *A New Quest of the Historical Jesus*; K. L. Schmidt, *Der Rahmen der Geschichte Jesu* and "Die Stellung der Evangelien in der allgemeinen Literaturgeschichte," in *Eucharisterion: Herman Gunkel zum 60. Geburtstag*, ed. H. Schmidt; A. Schweitzer, *The Quest of the Historical Jesus*; B. H. Streeter, *The Four Gospels*; C. H. Talbert, ed., *Reimar-*

us: Fragments and *What Is a Gospel?*; V. Taylor, *The Formation of the Gospel Tradition*; W. O. Walker, "The Quest for the Historical Jesus: A Discussion of Methodology," *ATR* (1969): 38-56; W. Wrede, *The Messianic Secret*.

—CHARLES H. TALBERT

Synoptic Problem [MDB 868b-69a]

•**Synoptic Problem.** The synoptic problem is the problem of explaining the similarities and differences between the first three Gospels. The word "synoptic" means a common view or viewed together, and the Gospels of Matthew, Mark, and Luke are called the synoptic Gospels because in general they use the same approach to the life and ministry of Jesus and contain much very similar material.

One of the first to try to answer the problem was Augustine, whose explanation was that Matthew was the original Gospel with Mark being a condensed version of Matthew and Luke being a composite of both Matthew and Mark.

The dominant view at present is the idea, presented by B. H. Streeter and others, that Mark was written first, and Matthew and Luke depended heavily on Mark's basic framework and content. The evidence is that most of Mark is repeated in Matthew and Luke. However, the similarities between Matthew and Luke that are not found in Mark suggest another source, Q, used by both these writers, but not known by Mark. Even so, there are portions of Matthew and Luke that are not accounted for by borrowing either from Mark or from Q. The solution appears to lie in the assumption that Matthew and Luke each had a private source not available to the others (PLATE 32). Whether these sources were written or oral is not known.

The dominant theory about the synoptic problem has not answered all the questions that have been raised and the subject is still debated by William R. Farmer and others. The debate, while it has not solved the problem to the satisfaction of everyone, has nonetheless called attention to the uniqueness of each of the three Gospels and the theological distinctiveness of each of the three writers. It has also made possible a better understanding of the importance of the difference between interpreting the Gospels as factual history and as confessions of faith. As a result of the debate one is better able to see the Gospels as theological documents and to appreciate their contribution to an understanding of history.

See also GOSPELS, CRITICAL STUDY OF; LUKE, GOSPEL OF; MARK, GOSPEL OF; MATTHEW, GOSPEL OF; Q; REDACTION; SOURCE CRITICISM.

Bibliography. G. W. Buchanan, "Current Synoptic Studies: Orchard, the Griesbach Hypothesis, and Other Alternatives," *RL* 46 (1977): 415-36; W. R. Farmer, ed., *New Synoptic Studies*; B. H. Streeter, *The Four Gospels*. —E. EARL JOINER

[MDB 870]

The Synoptic Problem: Two Proposed Solutions

The Two-Source/Document Hypothesis

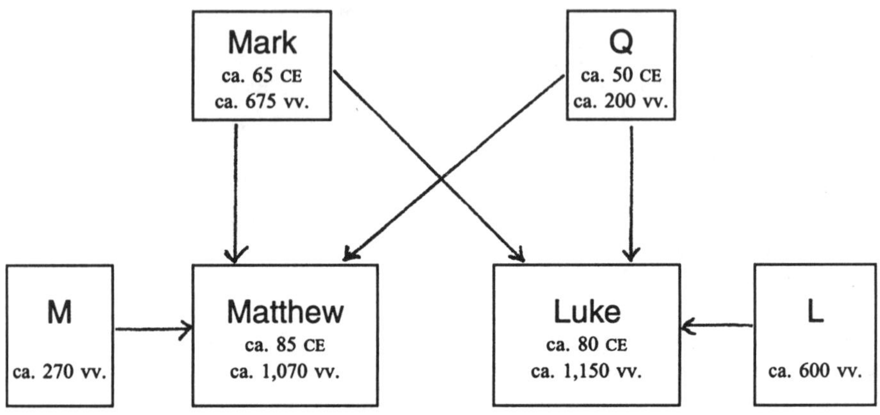

The Two-Source Hypothesis. The so-called "Sayings Source" or Q was a written compilation (no longer extant) of the sayings of Jesus, perhaps in use among the disciples ca. 40 to 50 C.E.

Ca. 65, Mark composed his Gospel from "memoirs" of, or as dictated by, Peter.

Then, perhaps ca. 80, Luke composed his Gospel, using primarily Mark and Q, but adding a substantial amount of his own materials. Luke thus comprises approx. 350 vv. from Mark, 200 vv. from Q. and 600 vv. of materials peculiar to Luke.

Finally, perhaps ca. 85, Matthew prepared his Gospel, using Mark and Q and with some of his own materials. On this hypothesis, Matthew includes approx. 600 vv. from Mark, 200 vv. from Q, and 270 vv. of Matthew's peculiar sources.

The Two-Gospel Hypothesis

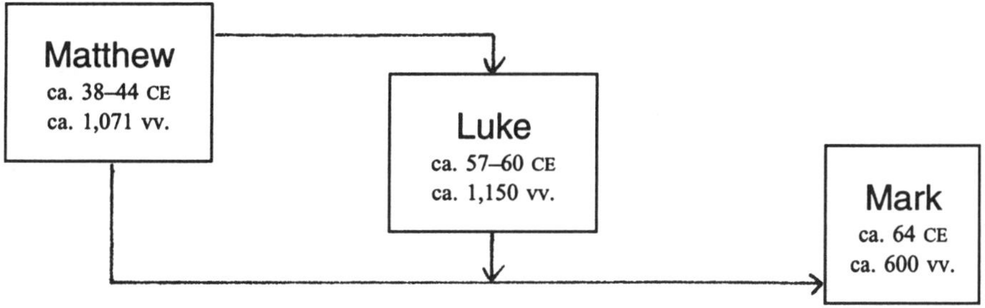

The Two-Gospel Hypothesis. Matthew was composed first, perhaps by 38 to 44 CE, by the apostle, on the basis of his own remembrance and that of his associates, for the Jewish-Christian churches in Palestine.

With Matthew as his primary source, Luke composed his gospel account perhaps ca. 57 to 60, as encouraged by Paul and addressed to the Gentile-Christian churches planted by Paul and his associates.

Finally, Mark, associate of Peter, composed his "confirming account" probably in Rome and perhaps ca. 62 to 64, on the basis of Peter's confirmation of both Matthew and Luke. Mark was addressed to the "church universal" and is a consensus account (not a condensation) that confirms the main features of both Matthew and Luke while adding materials from Peter's eyewitness memoirs.

Other Solutions. Proposed solutions to the so-called Synoptic Problem include the Four-Source, the Fragmentary, the Griesbach (progenitor of various "Two-Gospel" hypotheses), and the Lachmann hypothesis. Also, "Markan-Priority" is variously applied to those hypotheses that presuppose Mark as the first-composed gospel.

See SYNOPTIC PROBLEM. *See also* GOSPELS, CRITICAL STUDY OF; LUKE, GOSPEL OF; MARK, GOSPEL OF; MATTHEW, GOSPEL OF; Q; REDACTION; SOURCE CRITICISM.

—EDD ROWELL

The World of Jesus

Hellenistic World [MDB 368b-72a]

•**Hellenistic World.** *The Political Situation* (PLATES 1, 18). The victorious campaign which the Macedonian King ALEXANDER the Great waged against the vast Persian empire beginning in 334 B.C.E. radically changed the ancient Mediterranean world and the Middle East, both politically and culturally. After Alexander died prematurely in 323 B.C.E., his successors fought among themselves for many years. Several successfully carved out manageable domains from the territories conquered by Alexander and founded rival dynastic kingdoms. The more important founders of Hellenistic kingdoms include Ptolemy (whose dynasty controlled Egypt and, until 200 B.C.E., Palestine), Seleucus (the territories between Syria and India), Antigonus (Macedonia), and Lysimachus (Thrace and Armenia). Meanwhile by 201 B.C.E., Rome had gained complete military control of the western Mediterranean with the conquest of Carthage in North Africa following the First and Second Punic wars (264–241 B.C.E. and 220–201 B.C.E.). Rome continued to expand eastward. In a series of three Macedonian wars (214–205 B.C.E., 200–196 B.C.E., and 148–146 B.C.E.), Rome turned Macedonia and Greece into Roman provinces, and gradually absorbed all of the other major and minor Hellenistic kingdoms. The last to fall was Ptolemaic Egypt which was won by the Romans under Octavian (who later became the Emperor Augustus) in the battle of Actium, on the coast of western Greece, in 31 B.C.E. against Antony and Cleopatra. After the annexation of Egypt, the last of the independent Hellenistic kingdoms, the Mediterranean Sea became, for all practical purposes, a Roman lake. Octavian's victory at Actium and the resultant conquest of Egypt marked the final transitional stage between the Roman republic and the ROMAN EMPIRE, inaugurating a new age of relative peace and prospertiy which lasted for nearly two centuries called the *Pax Romana*. The Roman period, which had begun in 31 B.C.E. lasted until Rome fell in 476 C.E. The eastern half of the empire, with its capital at Constantinople (or Byzantium), survived until it fell to the Turks in 1453. The division of the empire occurred formally in 394 when Valentinian was made emperor of the west, and Valens of the east. The practical Romans absorbed much of Greek civilization and culture, to which they contributed organizational skill, military might and political know-how. The entire period from Alexander to the deposition of the last Roman emperor is called the Hellenistic period, a term first applied in 1836 to the period following Alexander the Great by the German ancient historian J. G. Droysen. Though Droysen erroneously understood the term "Hellenists" in Acts 6:1 to refer to orientalized Greeks, he correctly regarded the blending or syncretism of Greek and Oriental culture as characteristic of this period.

Hellenistic Culture. Though the ancient world was politically and economically controlled by Rome after 31 B.C.E. Hellenistic culture dominated the ancient world from ca. 300 B.C.E. to ca. 300 C.E. (i.e., from the death of Alexander the Great in 323 B.C.E. to the conversion of Constantine in 312 C.E.). The Roman empire encompassed many native cultures, each vitally concerned with the preservation of its own identity and traditions. The dominance and attractiveness of Hellenistic culture throughout the Mediterranean world proved irresistible to many intellectuals who were natives of one or another of the numerous cultures which had become subject first to the Macedonians, then to their successors and finally to the Romans.

Alexander and his successors consciously used Hellenistic culture as a tool for unifying and pacifying subject peoples. Various segments of conquered populations responded in different ways to political and cultural domination by foreigners. Hellenistic culture proved irresistible to some native members of the upper classes, typically including intellectuals, bureaucrats, religious funtionaries, and aristocrats. In contrast to this largely urban minority, resistance to Hellenism was strongest among rural lower classes. Native intellectuals such as Manetho of Egypt, Berossus of Babylon (both early third century B.C.E.) and Flavius JOSEPHUS, the Jewish historian (late first century C.E.), attempted to defend their native traditions in response to the smothering influences of Hellenism by writing propagandistic historical accounts in Greek emphasizing both the priority and superiority of their respective native cultures.

Palestinian JUDAISM came into direct and permanent contact with Hellenistic culture when Alexander subjected Palestine in 332 B.C.E. on his way to liberate Egypt from the Persians. During the entire third century B.C.E. Palestine was under the political control of the benign Ptolemies. The Seleucids, who wrested Palestine from the Ptolemies at the battle of Panion (200 B.C.E.), pursued a more aggressive policy of Hellenization which incited the Maccabean rebellion in 167 B.C.E. Jews, like many other nativistic cultures, had an ambivalent attitude toward Hellenism. They assimilated some aspects of Hellenistic culture more easily than others. The GREEK LANGUAGE, Greek literary and rhetorical forms, Greek styles in art and architecture, and even Greek names were readily adopted. Yet other aspects of Hellenistic culture were more controversial and even repugnant to Jews with a traditional orientation: religious practices, athletic traditions, forms of entertainment and styles of clothing. While accepted by some liberal members of the upper class including the temple priesthood in Jerusalem, these controversial aspects of Hellenistic culture often met with stiff resistance, even to the extent of armed revolt, on the part of the common people. A type of religious protest literature, called apocalypses, flourished in early Judaism as well as in other native cultures dominated by the Greeks and the Romans.

Hellenistic Language. Philip II of Macedon (who ruled from 359–336 B.C.E.) used Attic Greek as the official language of his court and of his diplomatic correspondence. Under his son Alexander (356–323 B.C.E.), Koine ("common") Greek, a populrized form of imperial Attic, became the language of art, science and literature as well as of administration and commerce throughout the Hellenistic world.

The Greek language of the late Hellenistic period can conveniently be divided into two major types, literary and nonliterary Koine. Koine Greek (in contrast to specific dialects like Doric, Aeolic, Ionic or Attic), was a simplified blend of features from Attic and Ionic Greek (dialects of Athens and western Anatolia).

On the basis of the widespread division of Hellenistic Greek into literary and nonliterary Koine, two categories of literature were proposed by late nineteenth century German scholars, *Hochliteratur* ("cultivated literature") produced by and for the educated upper classes of the Greco-Roman world, *Kleinliteratur* ("popular literature"), of which the early Christian literature collectively known as the NT was a prime example. Actually, these categories are ideal types at opposite ends of a complex spectrum of linguistic and literary styles. Recognition of this fact makes it feasible to trace continuities between the patterns and structures of the highest and lowest educational levels. Several scholars have argued for a third kind of Hellenistic Greek between the two extremes of nonliterary and literary Koine. Though there is some disagreement about its exact character, "popular literary Greek" is an appropriate designation of this mediating type of Greek which Lars Ryebeck has labeled *Fachprosa,* "professional" or "technical prose." As the written language of people with some education, it occurs in technical and scientific treatises, in popular philosophical literature, in some of the more literary papyri and in the the NT.

Art and Architecture. The idealism of classical Greek art was gradually transformed during the Hellenistic period into an increasing preference for realism. The emphasis on a more realistic imitation of nature in painting and sculpture determined the subjects selected. Alongside mature men and women, a greater interest is reflected in old age, childhood, and deformity, and to the artistic representation of such emotions as pleasure and pain, and such states as sleep and death. Important developments in sculpture took place during the early Hellenistic period, primarily because of the practice of showing municipal gratitude to benefactors by erecting statues of them in public places. Several artistic styles can be differentiated, each emanating from a major intellectual and cultural center: (1) The Alexandrian style consisted of an impressionistic development of the ideas of Praxiteles of Athens (mid-fourth century B.C.E.), combined with a realistic depiction of the grotesque. (2) The Pergamene style followed the mixed tradition of Scopas (fourth century B.C.E.) and Praxiteles, and is represented by sculptures on the great altar of Zeus from Pergamon depicting the battle between gods and giants. (3) The Rhodian style followed the athletic tradition of Lysippus of Sicyon (late fourth century B.C.E.), and his pupil Chares of Lindos. Rhodes became a major center for bronze casting, while the other centers preferred marble. A typical representative of Rhodian sculpture is the Winged Victory of Samothrace. The creative period of Hellenistic sculpture essentially ended at 146 B.C.E. with the Roman conquest of Greece. Thereafter the Roman demand for enormous quantities of Greek sculpture led to large-scale copying of older works, and Greece became a center for statue manufacturing.

The many new cities founded by Alexander and his successors led to a blossoming of Hellenistic architecture, building and town planning. By the beginning of the fifth century B.C.E. the physical requirements of Greek cities included an acropolis, walls, an agora, a theater, a gymnasium and temples. Some Hellenistic architectural features include the preference for the Corinthian order with its baroque features (rather than the Doric or Ionic orders), the preference for rectilinear rather than curvilinear forms, and the creative use of interior space. There was, in addition, an emphasis on the facade and a tendency to view a building within the setting of other buildings rather than as an isolated work of art (a characteristic of the classical period).

Literature. Both Hellenism and Judaism preserved cultural traditions and ideals of the past through approved collections of classical literature. Works written many centuries before the Christian era (such as Homer and the Hebrew Bible) continued to exert far reaching influences. While Greek literary classics exerted a broad influence on Hellenistic and Roman culture, in Judaism biblical literature was particularly influential. Yet both cultures were traditional in that cultural and religious values of the present were regarded as anchored in the paradigmatic past as mediated by approved literature. Literature produced from the second through the fourth centuries C.E. was also oriented to the past, since the traditional character of both Hellenism and Judaism ensured the preservation of earlier literary genres, forms and styles in later literary activity. Throughout Greek history there was a tendency to single out the most accomplished authors of various literary genres (the most important of which were epic, lyric and dramatic poetry). Much of this scholarly activity centered at the museum of Alexandria (founded by Ptolemy I) which boasted a great library founded by Ptolemy II (when destroyed by fire in 47 B.C.E. it contained about 700,000 books). Aristophanes of Byzantium (ca. 257–180 B.C.E.), a famous grammarian and librarian at the Alexandrian museum, apparently drew up lists of selected or approved authors (cf. Quintillian 1.4.3; 10.154-59). Since the late eighteenth century classical scholars have used the term Alexandrian canon for the catalog of more than eighty classical authors, which included five epic poets, ten orators, nine lyric poets, five tragic poets, and so on. The Alexandrian canon had both positive and negative effects on ancient literature. The works of approved authors were read in schools and by the educated, they were copied, recopied and commented upon, and thus preserved for posterity. The works of unapproved authors, however, were neglected and eventually lost. Hellenistic literary culture regarded the works of approved authors as models worthy of emulation. An orator who wanted to describe a contemporary battle turned to Herodotus, Thucydides and Xenophon for their descriptions.

The *Iliad* and *Odyssey* had an enormous influence on Hellenistic and Roman culture, not only on the art, literature and philosophy of the educated, but also on the common people. Homer has been called "the Bible of the Greeks." This religious analogy is appropriate since both the *Odyssey* and the *Iliad* claimed to be products of the divine inspiration of the Muse, and the author himself was often called "the divine Homer." Homer was central to the educational system, and at the primary level exercises in writing and reading were based on Homeric texts and large portions were memorized. This was reinforced by frequent public recitals of and lectures on the Homeric epics. In religion, Homer provided the Greeks with basic conceptions of the gods of the Olympian pantheon. With regard to private religious practices, oracles were derived from Homeric texts, and Homeric verses were used on magical amulets. Since the purpose of education was character formation, Homer became the primary source for moral and political guidance. Homer was also regarded as a practical guide in the areas of rhetoric, warfare and housekeeping. The Greeks thought that virtually every rhetorical and literary genre was anticipated by Homer. According to Menander Rhetor (third century C.E.), in his discussion of the many subtypes of epideictic oratory, "It is necessary to elaborate on the starting points received from the poet [i.e., Homer], after understanding the basic scheme the poet has transmitted to us."

From the late first century through the third century, there was a widespread nostalgia for the past among both Greeks and Romans. This archaism, which was particularly characteristic of the programmatic rhetorical movement called the Second Sophistic, took several forms. Widespread attempts to imitate the language and literary style of the Attic prose writeres of the classical period (450–330 B.C.E.) is called linguistic Atticism. The preference for literature written in Attic or Atticistic Greek contributed to the neglect and eventual loss of most Hellenistic literature from the late fourth century B.C.E. through the late first century C.E. Thematic archaism was also prevalent. Greek historians focused on the period of Alexander or earlier, and in so doing both neglected and depreciated the events of the more recent past. Orators declaimed on themes from the classical past, such as "Athens the greatest city," and "Alexander the greatest Greek." Archaism was both the cause and result of emphasizing literary models of the classical past. Dissatisfaction with the political and cultural realities of the present was another contributing factor which encouraged both linguistic and thematic archaism.

Native intellectuals in states subject to the Greeks, and then the Romans, used the Greek language and literary genres to explain the history and traditions of their cultures to the Greeks as well as to themselves. The Babylonian priest Berossus wrote a history of Babylon entitled *Babyloniaka* (early third century B.C.E.), dedicated to Antiochus I, in which he interpreted Babylonian history and traditions for the Greek world. Similarly, Manetho, an Egyptian high priest from Heliopolis and a contemporary of Berossus, did the same for Egyptian history in *Egyptiaka,* a history of Egypt written in Greek dedicated to Ptolemy II. In Rome, one of the first historians was Q. Fabius Pictor (late third century B.C.E.) who wrote his *Histories* in Greek to communicate Roman policies and institutions to the Hellenistic world.

Jewish Hellenistic literature, written primarily in Greek using Hellenistic literary forms and traditions, is the best-preserved Hellenized nativistic literature from the

Greco-Roman period. The history of early Jewish literature reflects the increasing domination of Hellenistic literary culture. The penetration of Hellenistic culture into Palestine from the late fourth century B.C.E. on makes it difficult to determine whether particular Jewish writings arose in Palestine or the Diaspora. The SEPTUAGINT, a translation of the Jewish scriptures from Hebrew to Greek during the early third century B.C.E. in Alexandria for Greeks as well as for diaspora Jews, is one important indicator of the impact of Hellenization upon Judaism.

Religion and Philosophy. The political and cultural unity imposed on increasingly larger segments of the ancient Mediterranean world and the Near East, first by the Greeks and then by the Romans, resulted in a period of great creativity in the areas of both religion and philosophy. Previously isolated ethnic traditions came into contact with one other and affected each other in a variety of ways. Religion for the ancients was not an isolatable component of culture but an integral feature which permeated life and thought generally. Cults in the Hellenistic world tended to focus on myth and ritual to the virtual exclusion of theology and ethics. Further, all of the great religious traditions had centers both in their ancestral homeland as well as in a diaspora population of immigrants who worshipped native deities in foreign lands.

Several distinctive forms of religion and religious traditions flourished in the Hellenistic world, including (1) ruler cults, (2) state cults, and (3) MYSTERY RELIGIONS. The ruler cults, which first developed in the Hellenistic kingdoms, provided a religious and political framework for the various national groups united under regional Greek monarchies, and eventually the Roman empire. The Ionian cities of western Anatolia had proclaimed the divinity of Alexander when he liberated them during his campaign against the Persians. Of the mainland Greeks, however, only the league of Corinth voted divine honors to Alexander (324 B.C.E.). Later the Athenians voted divine honors to Antigonus and Demetrius Poliorketes in 307 B.C.E. By 270 B.C.E. Ptolemy Philadelphos had founded a cult celebrating the divinity of both his wife Arsinoe and himself. The deification of rulers was a grateful municipal response to individuals of great merit. Rome adapted features of the Hellenistic ruler cults to the needs of an enormous empire. Julius Caesar was posthumously deified in 42 B.C.E. Thereafter living emperors took the title *divi filius* ("son of god") referring to their imperial dynastic predecessors (thereby legitimating their own rule), and deceased emperors thought worthy of the honor were enrolled with the gods of Rome by an act of the senate. The imperial cult, particularly strong in such eastern provinces as Asia, became a way for provincial expression of loyalty and patriotism.

The traditional state cults of the Greek and Roman cities continued to flourish but were weakened by the subjugation of the *polis* ("city-state"), first to leagues and then to empires. Since the primary function of state cults had been to ensure national prosperity by promoting peace with the gods, the subjugation of cities to larger political units meant that the quest for prosperity had to be pursued at a higher level, such as the ruler cults.

The growing concern of individuals for their own welfare and salvation encourages the proliferation of mystery religions. The Greek terms *mysterion* and *mystes* mean "secret ritual" and "initiant." Mystery cults, then, are essentially voluntary associations of people who have experienced a secret ritual initiation thought to guarantee prosperity in this life and happiness in the life to come. The Eleusinian mysteries, centering in the worship of Demeter and Persephone, is the oldest known Greek mystery religion. Many oriental cults moved westward with native immigrants and were transformed into mystery cults. Among the more prominent of these are the cults of Isis and Osiris, Cybele and Attis and Aphrodite and Adonis.

Numerous philosophical schools and traditions, many of which originally centered in Athens, flourished in major urban centers throughout the ancient Mediterranean world during the Hellenistic period. While Greek philosophy in the classical period tended to focus on three main divisions of logic, physics and ethics, during the Hellenistic period the quest for the *summum bonum* ("the greatest good") resulted in a growing emphasis on ethics. The major philosophical traditions of the Hellenistic world all sought legitimation by tracing their traditions back to Socrates (469–399 B.C.E.). The major competing schools of Hellenistic philosophy include Platonists, Aristotelians, EPICUREANS, CYNICS, STOICS and Sceptics.

See also ALEXANDER; CYNICS; EPICUREANS; GREEK LANGUAGE; MACCABEES; MYSTERY RELIGIONS; ROMAN EMPIRE.

Bibliography. E. L. Bowie, "Greeks and Their Past in the Second Sophistic," *Studies in Ancient Society,* ed. M. I. Finley; J. B. Bury et al., *The Hellenistic Age*; G. Dickens, *Hellenistic Sculpture*; D. R. Dudley, *A History of Cynicism from Diogenes to the 6th Cent. A.D.*; S. K. Eddy, *The King is Dead: Studies in the Near Eastern Resistance to Hellenism (334–31 B.C.)*; J. Ferguson, *The Heritage of Hellenism* and *The Religions of the Roman Empire*; F. C. Grant, *Roman Hellenism and the New Testament*; R. M. Grant, *Gods and the One God*; E. S. Gruen, *The Hellenistic World and the Coming of Rome*; M. Hadas, *Hellenistic Culture*; A. A. Long, *Hellenistic Philosophy: Stoics, Epicureans, Sceptics*; A. J. Malherbe, *Moral Exhortation, a Greco-Roman Sourcebook*; A. Momigliano, *Alien Wisdom: The Limits of Hellenization*; A. D. Nock, *Conversion: The Old and the New in Religion from Alexander the Great to Augustine of Hippo*; F. E. Peters, *The Harvest of Hellenism: A History of the Near East from Alexander the Great to the Triumph of Christianity*; P. Petit, *Pax Romana*; J. H. Randall, Jr., *Hellenistic Ways of Deliverance and the Making of the Christian Synthesis*; J. M. Rist, *Stoic Philosophy*; W. W. Tarn, *Hellenistic Civilisation*; F. W. Walbank et al., eds., "The Hellenistic World," *CAH,* 7/1; F. W. Walbank, *The Helenistic World.* —DAVID E. AUNE

Judaism [MDB 477-78]

•**Judaism.** [*joo*′duh-iz-uhm] The name given to the religion and culture of the Jewish people following the EXILE in 587/6 B.C.E. "Judaism" is derived from Judah, the fourth son of JACOB after whom the Southern Kingdom in ISRAEL was named in the OT. When the Israelites returned to their homeland, which was now the Persian district of Judah, after the Exile, they were called Judahites (hence Jews) and their religion and culture was called Judaism. In the days of the kingdom, the religion of the people is customarily called "Israelite religion"; in the earliest period "Hebrew religion" is used. Yet this should not obscure the fact that in a broader sense all of the OT is part of the history of the Jewish people.

To understand the development of Judaism it is necessary to identify two distinct periods in the history of the Jewish people separated by the destruction of JERUSALEM by the Romans in 70 C.E. The first period begins with the Persians, who conquered the BABYLONIAN EMPIRE and permitted the exiled Jews to return to Palestine, beginning ca. 538 B.C.E. The Persian policy of religious toleration, coupled with the stability of the PERSIAN EMPIRE for 200 years, afforded the Jews ample freedom to reestablish their religion in the wake of the debacle of the Exile. After the defeat of the Persians in 331 B.C.E. by ALEXANDER the Great, Palestine came under the rule of Alexander and his Greek successors. The policies of these kings, first the Ptolemies (301–198 B.C.E.) and then the early Seleucids (198–175 B.C.E.), included religious freedom for the Jews. But things changed with the ascension of Antiochus IV in 175. Antiochus's attempt to suppress Judaism led to the revolt of the MACCABEES (167–142 B.C.E.) which resulted in political independence for the Jews in 142. From the family of Judas Maccabeus, one of the early leaders of the revolt, came the new nation's leaders, the Hasmonean dynasty. Jewish independence lasted until 63 B.C.E. when the Roman general Pompey captured Jerusalem in the name of ROME. Chafing under heavy taxation and incompetent Roman governors, and with the memory of the Maccabean revolt still alive, the Jews rebelled against Rome in 66 C.E. The war ended in disastrous defeat for the Jews in 70 C.E. Judaism would never be the same after 70. The Jews' capital, Jerusalem, was burned; their TEMPLE was destroyed; many of their institutions, such as the SANHEDRIN, were gone; and their hopes were shattered. A new period in the history of Judaism had begun. The equally disastrous rebellion of BAR-KOCHBA in 132–135 C.E. only served to give further impetus to this new direction.

The first period under consideration, sometimes called the Second Temple period or, in its later stages, the late pre-Christian period, is characterized by a number of features. Central is TORAH (the LAW), the divine instruction given by revelation to Israel through MOSES on Mount SINAI. Torah is contained in the five books of Moses—i.e., the Pentateuch—and governs Jewish life and piety. Obedience to Torah was of first importance to Jews. It was upon Torah that the returning Jews were grounded by EZRA. Furthermore, it was because of the necessity of interpreting the Torah for application to everyday life that there arose the professional order of Torah scholars, or scribes, often called RABBIS or sages. These scholars, among whom were the famous Hillel and Shammai, commonly attracted schools of disciples and frequently attained a high degree of public visibility. Their interpretations of Torah were passed along by their disciples from one generation to the next, with the teachings of successive rabbis added to their own. Thus, there developed oral traditions of interpretation alongside the written Torah.

Also important was the Temple. Many of the commandments in Torah involved the offering of sacrifices. This ritual could be performed only in the Jerusalem Temple, which was rebuilt soon after the return from the Exile. The right to offer sacrifices was given exclusively to the PRIENTS, who served as mediators between the people and God in these required acts of obedience and, thus, were viewed by the people as spiritual leaders. The priests were strictly organized, with the high priest at the head. For the HIGH PRIEST were reserved certain acts of the highest cultic significance, such as the offering of the sacrifice on the DAY OF ATONEMENT. In addition to the ongoing private sacrifices, public sacrifices were held twice a day in the Temple, and there were supplementary sacrifices on the SABBATH and during the great festival periods (PASSOVER, Pentecost [WEEKS], TABERNACLES, and DEDICATION), as well as for new moon, NEW YEAR, and the Day of Atonement. The influx into Jerusalem of large numbers of pilgrims coming for the great festivals was common.

Jewish worship was not limited to the Temple. With the renewed emphasis on Torah after the Exile came the rise of a new institution: the SYNAGOGUE. Unlike the Temple, which was limited to a single place, synagogues could be established wherever there were a sufficient number of Jews. Synagogues were primarily houses of religious instruction. Jews in an area would gather on the Sabbath for public prayer, the reading of a passage from Torah (and typically from one of the Prophets), and an exposition or sermon. As ARAMAIC replaced HEBREW as the common language of the Jews in Palestine, the scripture reading came to be followed by an interpretive Aramaic translation, or targum. In addition to offering sacrifices and participating in synagogue worship, typical Jewish piety included such things as observing the Sabbath, fulfilling the regulations concerning cultic purity, and carrying out formal rituals such as the daily recitation of the EIGHTEEN BENEDICTIONS.

During most of this period the Jews were under the control of foreign rulers. Yet the Jews generally had a certain amount of freedom in regulating religious, and often civil, matters. Throughout much of this period authority was concentrated in the hands of the leaders of the clans, or elders, and the priests. The high priesthood, in particular, came to be an office of immense prestige and importance. By the first century B.C.E. the Sanhedrin had become the chief governing body for Jewish internal affairs. Centered in Jerusalem and made up of seventy-one members drawn from the priests, the elders, and the scribes, and with the high priest at its head, the Sanhedrin was the supreme tribunal on matters concerning Jewish law.

For many Jews, matters such as Temple worship and the actions of Sanhedrin were but distant realities. The Exile had scattered Jews outside of Palestine. Those who returned to Palestine were a minority; most remained in their new homes. Eventually those Jews who lived outside of Palestine came to be known as Jews of the dispersion, or the diaspora. Such Jews struggled with maintaining their traditional religion in the context of a foreign culture. Compromises were made at times, but the distinction between diaspora Jews and those in Palestine should not be overdrawn. To be sure, Jews in Egypt or in Rome, for example, took on a particular character. But communication between the Jews of Jerusalem and those of the diaspora served both as a unifying feature within Judaism as a whole and as a check on possible diaspora excesses. Furthermore, foreign influence was not limited to the diaspora; Greek influence in Palestine, which began in the Persian period and intensified after Alexander, had an impact on the development of Judaism in Palestine as well. Thus, Jews of the diaspora studied Torah, gathered together for synagogue worship, and even made pilgrimages to Jerusalem. In addition, since they could no longer read Hebrew, they produced the Greek translation of the scriptures known as the Septuagint (LXX).

The commonality of features in Judaism before 70 C.E. should not overshadow its widespread diversity. All agreed that Torah was central, but disagreements arose over how it should be interpreted. Few denied the importance of the sacrificial cult, but some questioned the legitimacy of how it was being carried out. Further disputes arose over such matters as the proper attitude towards the Roman overlords and who should be the spiritual leaders of the people. Ultimately, the very question of the true identity of Israel was at stake. A host of groups, such as the PHARISEES, the SADDUCESS, the ESSENES, and the various unnamed groups reflected in the Pseudepigrapha arose, competing with one another for the allegiance of the people, and, hence, the right to define Judaism on their terms. This diversity, combined with the lack of a clear victor in this period, suggests that before 70 there was no single "normative" or "official" Judaism; rather, there were many "Judaisms."

The fall of Jerusalem in 70 C.E. marks the beginning of the second period in the development of Judaism. With the Temple destroyed, the sacrificial cult, so important for six centuries, had abruptly ended, along with the authority of the priests. In the wake of such a significant rebellion, the recognized authoritative body in Judaism, the Sanhedrin, could no longer be tolerated by the Romans. All who had participated in the war and survived had seen their hopes dashed. Two questions concerning the future of Judaism now arose. First, who would exert the leadership necessary for confronting the new conditions? Second, given the changed situation, what form would Judaism now take?

The leadership void was filled by the Pharisees. With the permission of the Romans, the Pharisees, who had not generally taken part in the war effort, set up schools for the continued study of Torah and its application to the Jewish people. The pioneer in this movement was Rabbi Yohanan ben Zakkai, who established an academy at Jamnia after the war. Torah scholars such as GAMALIEL II gathered together to formulate a Judaism which could exist without the Temple cult. Thus, they found counterparts to the various elements of the sacrificial system: the Temple would be replaced by the holy people; the priesthood by the holy man; the sacrifices by the holy way of life of the people. The holy way of life included religious duties, acts of kindness and grace beyond those commanded, and, especially, studying Torah. All Jews, therefore, would become like the sages. Torah was now understood to include not only the written Torah given to Moses but also the oral Torah—i.e., the interpretations of the written Torah which had been passed along in the scribal schools. This oral Torah was codified around 200 C.E. by Rabbi Judah the Holy into the Mishnah. After 70, therefore, a normative Judaism took shape. To be sure, in the early part of this period there remained some diversity, to which pseudepigrapic books such as the APOCALYPSE OF ABRAHAM and FOURTH EZRA attest. Similarly, nationalistic sentiment led to a second revolt under Bar Kochba in 132. But with the failure of the revolt, Rabbinic Judaism emerged victorious over all of its competitors. The rabbinic tradition, with its vast literary production of which the Mishnah was only the beginning, has served as the foundation of Judaism ever since.

As a product of the return from the Exile, Judaism therefore forms the religious and cultural contexts within which the later books of the OT must be read. Narratives such as Ezra and NEHEMIAH, as well as the prophets HAGGAI, ZECHARIAH, and MALACHI, illuminate the beginnings of Judaism. But an understanding of Judaism, especially in its two periods, is perhaps even more important for the study of the origins of Christianity. Jesus was a Jew, and his disciples were Jews as well. In fact, for a while early Christianity was little more than one more Jewish group striving to define Judaism on its own terms. Given the diversity within Judaism during this period, Jews, for the most part, seem to have tolerated the Christian movement as yet another sect. After 70, however, the Pharisaic attempts to define and standardize the religion resulted in the Jews taking a firmer stand against Christianity. Even with the gentile mission well established, certain Christian communities, such as those of MATTHEW and JOHN, seem to have been still strongly Jewish after 70. But now the clashes with the Jews, who viewed Christians as heretics, were sharper, and Jewish Christians were forced to face the possiblity that their new faith was indeed a new religion.

See also APOCRYPHAL LITERATURE; RABBINIC LITERATURE.

Bibliography. J. H. Charlesworth, *The Old Testament Pseudepigrapha and the New Testament* and *Jesus Within Judaism*; D. Daube, *The New Testament and Rabbinic Judaism*; W. D. Davies, *Paul and Rabbinic Judaism* and *The Setting of the Sermon on the Mount*; W. D. Davies and L. Finkelstein (eds.), *The Cambridge History of Judaism*, 4 vols.; M. Hengel, *Jews, Greeks, and Barbarians* and *Judaism and Hellenism*; M. McNamara, *Palestinian Judaism and the New Testament*; G. F. Moore, *Judaism in the First Centuries of the Christian Era*; M. J. Mulder, M. E. Stone and S. Safrai, eds., *The Literature of the Jewish People in the Period of the*

Second Temple and the Talmud; J. Neusner, *From Testament to Torah: An Introduction to Judaism in Its Formative Age, Judaism: The Evidence of the Mishnah* and *Judaism in the Matrix of Christianity*; E. P. Sanders, *Paul and Palestinian Judaism*; S. Sandmel, *Judaism and Christian Beginnings*; S. Safrai and M. Stern, eds., *The Jewish People in the First Century*; E. Sch;auurer, *The History of the Jewish People in the Age of Jesus Christ,* rev. and ed. G. Vermes, F. Millar, and M. Goodman; M. E. Stone, *Scriptures, Sects, and Visions: A Profile of Judaism from Ezra to the Jewish Revolts*; V. Tcherikover, *Hellenistic Civilization and the Jews.*

—JOSEPH L. TRAFTON

Jesus [MDB 444b-49b]

•**Jesus**. [jee´zuhs] The evidence for the life and teaching of Jesus of Nazareth comes almost entirely from Christian sources: the four canonical Gospels, a few scattered references in the Letters of Paul and the other NT books, and the apocryphal gospels (especially those which preserve sayings of Jesus unknown in the canonical Gospel tradition). Contemporary pagan and Jewish sources have very little to say about him. What they do say focuses not on the name "Jesus" but on the designation "Christ" (misunderstood in Roman sources as a proper name). The Roman historian Tacitus, in referring to the Christians, mentions that "they got their name from Christ, who was executed by sentence of the procurator Pontius PILATE in the reign of Tiberius. That checked the pernicious superstition for a short time, but it broke out afresh—not only in Judea, where the plague first arose, but in Rome itself" (*Ann* 15.44). A more problematic notice is that of Suetonius, to the effect that the emperor Claudius "expelled the Jews from Rome, on account of the riots in which they were constantly indulging at the instigation of Chrestus" (*Claudius* 25.4). Confusion exists not only over the spelling of the name but over the fact that Suetonius is referring to events in Rome almost two decades after the date of Jesus' death as determined from the canonical Gospels.

The Jewish historian Josephus knew that "Christ" was a title (meaning "Messiah" or "Anointed One") and not a proper name, yet he has little more to say: James, stoned to death by Jewish authorities about 62 C.E., is identified as "the brother of Jesus the so-called Christ" (*Ant* 20.200). A more extensive reference in Josephus is open to serious question because it seems to have been edited later by Christian scribes (*Ant* 18.63-64), yet there is ample ground for believing that Josephus refers once again in that passage to Jesus as "the Christ," with the additional information that Jesus was a teacher, that he performed "suprising works," that Pilate condemned him to the cross, and that the movement continued after his death.

This is about all the data that "secular history" (i.e., history not written by committed Christians) can provide. There is no historical controversy over the fact that Jesus was known as "Christ," that he was (as the creeds say) "crucified under Pontius Pilate," and that the movement he started spread and flourished despite his death. In Christian theology each of these facts was interpreted in a distinctly Christian way: the designation "Christ" meant that Jesus was not only the Jewish Messiah but the divine SON OF GOD; his death on the cross was understood as a sacrifice or atonement for sins; the continuation of the movement was attributed to his resurrection from the dead and his exaltation to heaven as Lord of all. The first two of these are theological confessions made on the basis of faith; they cannot be argued pro or con historically. The third is also a theological confession, but one based on certain historical claims not accepted by everyone: i.e., that the tomb of Jesus was found empty and that he was seen alive by his disciples after his death. Those claims are of interest to historians as well as theologians, but only after they have investigated a more controversial side of the man Jesus, the teaching and the miracles to which Josephus refers.

If by the "life of Jesus" we mean only a sequence of events, it is hardly surprising that historians must settle for something less than absolute certainty. It would be hard to establish a precise chronology or itinerary for the career of anyone who lived nineteen centuries ago. Even the Gospels are divided in their testimony as to whether Jesus' ministry was conducted mainly in Galilee (Mark, Matthew, Luke) or in Jerusalem (John). When NT scholars speak of great uncertainty in our knowledge about Jesus (by the use of such expressions as "the quest for the historical Jesus" or "the search for the real Jesus"), they are usually referring not to a sequence of events but to Jesus' teaching. Did he say what he is represented as saying in the synoptic Gospels? In John? In both? In the non-canonical collections (e.g., the *Gospel of Thomas* or the *Apocryphon of James*)? What was his attitude toward the Jewish law? Did he accept it, reject it, or reinterpret it? If we assume that he proclaimed the KINGDOM OF GOD, or Kingdom of Heaven, what did he mean by this phrase? If we assume that he taught in parables, why did he adopt this method? What was his attitude toward war and violence? Was he more like a biblical prophet, a Jewish apocalyptic visionary, a rabbi, a wisdom teacher or sage, a political revolutionary, a Gnostic who renounced the world, or what? Most crucial for theologians (at least for many of them) is what did he teach about himself? Did he call himself the Christ? Did he claim to be the Son of God, as he is said in John's Gospel to have done? And beyond the matter of his teaching, did Jesus perform MIRACLES of healing? Did he perform exorcisms on those believed to be demon-possessed? Did he turn water into wine, multiply the loaves, walk on the Sea of Galilee? Is it possible for a twentieth-century person even to consider believing such things? The study of Jesus' life is a veritable minefield in which many individuals and groups, Christian and non-Christian alike, have strong vested interests. The world continues to ask, "What is the truth about Jesus, and where is it to be found?"

Some scholars have tried to distinguish the actual words of Jesus from words attributed to him after the fact by his followers by a so-called criterion of dissimilarity, i.e., sayings attributed to Jesus can be accepted as authentic if they are without parallel either in the Jewish world of his time or in the writings of Christians after his death. Other sayings can then be accepted if they agree or if they are natural extensions of these core pronouncements. Still other sayings may be authentic, but cannot be so proven. Such an approach effectively places Jesus of Nazareth outside the chain of cause-and-effect that is the essence of human history and of the history of thought. Consequently, though many scholars claim to be using this method in reaching their conclusions about Jesus, few if any actually do. A better method is to take our sources at face value, with emphasis on features about which several sources are in agreement and with some caution about features where the special interests of one particular source or Gospel seem to have been at work in shaping the tradition. Yet there is no ground a priori for bias against any of our sources, whether one of the Synoptics, or John, or even a noncanonical source such as the *Gospel of Thomas*.

Who Was "Jesus of Nazareth"? A good starting point is the account of Jesus' baptism in the Jordan river by the desert prophet JOHN THE BAPTIST (Mark 1:9-11) (PLATE 54). It is unlikely that Jesus' followers after his death would have made up a story in which he submits to another's authority and receives a rite of washing that was "for the forgiveness of sins" (Mark 1:4). That this incident was a problem for some Christians can be seen not only from Matt 3:14-15 (where John says, "I need to be baptized by you"), but from the careful avoidance in Luke and John of any explicit statement that John baptized Jesus (cf. e.g., Luke 3:19; John 1:32-34; the Baptist's role in Luke-Acts and John is rather that of a witness to who Jesus is). Because of such tendencies, the evidence of Mark's Gospel that Jesus came to receive John's baptism is to be accepted as historical. Jesus must have found something appealing in the proclamation of John the Baptist that the last judgment was very near and that everyone, religious and irreligious alike, must repent of their sins and submit to a new cleansing in preparation for that great day.

All that is said about Jesus' origin in the story of his baptism is that he came to the river "from Nazareth" (Mark 1:9). Nothing is known of Nazareth from the OT or later Jewish sources, even though "Jesus of Nazareth" was a designation that followed him to the day of his death (cf. John 19:19). More information was needed about Jesus' origins. Both Matthew and Luke place alongside the link with Nazareth another tradition, to the effect that Jesus was born in Bethlehem, the "city of David," as a descendant of David's royal line. Matthew devotes a whole chapter to showing how this child born in Bethlehem ended up as an adult in Nazareth, described sarcastically by his enemies as a "Nazarene" (lit., "Nazirite," Matt 2:23). The play on words calls attention simultaneously to Jesus' obscure origins and to the stark contrast (in the eyes of many) between his supposed holiness (like the Nazirites of the OT) and his practice of keeping company with sinners, prostitutes, and tax collectors (cf. Mark 2:17). Luke, while confirming Matthew's testimony that the family was of the royal line of David (Luke 1:32-33; 2:4), admits that Nazareth was the family home of Jesus' parents all along (1:26-27). He reconciles the Nazareth and Bethlehem traditions on the grounds that a Roman census brought the holy family back to their ancestral city just before Jesus' birth (Luke 2:1-7).

Despite the birth stories in Matthew and Luke, Jesus in his own time was known to his contemporaries not as a native of Bethlehem and a messianic claimant from the line of King David, but as a humble Nazarene. Whatever their merit as history, the birth stories were not public knowledge during Jesus' lifetime, perhaps because (as Luke puts it) "Mary kept all these things, pondering them in her heart" (Luke 2:19; cf. v. 51). Even in the Gospel of John, Jesus' first disciples introduced him as "Jesus of Nazareth, the son of Joseph" (John 1:45), and were answered with words that early Christian preachers would hear many times from skeptical Jewish audiences: "Can any good thing come out of Nazareth?" (1:46). In Nazareth itself, the people among whom he had grown up said of him incredulously, "Is not this the carpenter, the son of Mary and brother of James and Joses and Judas and Simon, and are not his sisters here with us?" (Mark 6:3; cf. Luke 4:22). And in neighboring Capernaum they asked, "Is not this Jesus, the son of Joseph, whose father and mother we know? How does he now say, 'I have come down from heaven'?" (John 6:42). The marvelous accounts of Jesus' birth, whatever their value as genuine history, cannot be presupposed in attempting to make sense of the Gospel records of his life and teaching.

The same is true of the spectacular events associated with Jesus' baptism in the Jordan River, the descent of God's Spirit on him like a dove and the voice from heaven announcing "You are my beloved Son; with you I am well pleased" (Mark 1:10-11 || Matt 3:16-17 || Luke 3:21-22). There is no evidence that anyone except Jesus—and possibly John the Baptist—either heard the voice or saw the dove. Consequently those around him did not assume that he was the "Son of God"—whatever they might have understood by that designation. Ironically, the first intimation that he was more than simply "Jesus of Nazareth" comes neither from his family, nor from his disciples, nor from the religious leaders of Israel. It comes from the devil, in the story of Jesus' temptation as recorded in Matthew and Luke, and from the demons and the demon-possessed, in a number of remarkable stories in the Gospels. Just as the devil challenged Jesus twice in the desert as "Son of God," so in the course of his ministry the demons repeatedly confronted him with such words as "What have you to do with us, Jesus of Nazareth? . . . I know who you are, the Holy One of God" (Mark 1:24), or "What have you to do with me, Jesus, Son of the Most High God?" (Mark 5:7). Though the programmatic accounts of Jesus' birth and baptism establish his identity once and for all for the benefit of the Christian reader of the Gospels, the issue is raised first in his ministry by the powers of evil!

The temptation narrative affords yet another clue to the ministry of Jesus as a whole (PLATE 41). His answers to the devil's challenges, drawn from scripture, are centered not on himself but on "the Lord your God" (e.g., Matt 4:4, 7, 10). The God-centered character of his message continues as he begins his ministry in Galilee: "The time is fulfilled, and the kingdom of God is at hand; repent, and believe in the GOSPEL" (Mark 1:15; cf. Matt 4:17). The Kingdom of God, or Kingdom of heaven, becomes the dominant theme of Jesus' proclamation and teaching from this point on, at least in the first three Gospels. Though much attention has been given to what Jesus meant by the "Kingdom," the controlling word in the announcement is not "Kingdom" but "God" (or "heaven," which was for the Jews as indirect way of referring to God). Mark even refers to this proclamation as "the gospel of God" (Mark 1:14; cf. also Paul in 1 Thess 2:8, 9; Rom 1:1). Even in John's Gospel, Jesus is represented as reminding his hearers again and again that he has come not to glorify or proclaim himself, but solely to make known "the Father," or "the One who sent me" (e.g., John 4:34; 5:19, 30; 6:38; 7:16-18, 28; 8:28, 42, 50; 14:10, 28).

As to his own identity, Jesus seems not to have wanted that question raised prematurely. He silenced the demons (e.g., Mark 1:25, 34; 3:12) and told the people he healed not to tell anyone (e.g., Mark 1:43-44; 7:36a). But the more he urged silence, the faster his reputation spread (e.g., Mark 1:45; 7:36b). Some wondered if Jesus might be the Messiah who would deliver his people from Roman rule—just as some had wondered about John the Baptist (Luke 3:15; John 1:19-21). But according to all the Gospels, Jesus was as reluctant as John had been to play out that role. Once in Galilee, when the crowds tried to "take him by force to make him king," Jesus fled to the hills (John 6:15). Instead of claiming the titles of either "Messiah" or "Son of God," Jesus had a way of using the emphatic "I" in pronouncements in which it was not grammatically necessary (as, e.g., Matt 12:28), and a habit of referring to himself mysteriously in the third person as SON OF MAN. The latter expression (*bar enasha* in the Aramaic language that Jesus spoke) meant simply "a certain man," or "someone," yet in some Jewish sectarian circles it had been used to designate a heavenly figure who would represent the people of God and gain their deliverance (cf., e.g., Dan 7:13; *1 Enoch* 46.3). Moreover, Jesus often seemed to speak and act with the authority of God himself. In his teaching he boldly stated, "You have heard that it was said . . . but I say to you" (Matt 5:21, 27, 31, 33, 38, 43). And so radical was his reinterpretation of the Jewish Law that he is represented as prefacing the first of his sermons with the disclaimer, "Do not think that I have come to abolish the law or the prophets; I have not come to abolish them but to fulfill them" (Matt 5:27). Because of such speech and such behavior, the crowds who heard him "were astonished at his teaching, for he taught them as one having authority, and not as their scribes" (Matt 7:29) (PLATE 23).

The Teaching of Jesus. The two reference points for the teaching of Jesus were, first, the Jewish scriptures and, second, his own vision of God and of God's Kingdom. The former interest he shared with all Jewish teachers of his time; the latter he had in common with such biblical prophets as Ezekiel and Daniel, and with the later Jewish visionaries who produced such apocalyptic works as *1-2 Enoch, Testament of Moses, 4 Ezra*, and *2 Baruch*. For the Jesus of the Gospels, the two interests cannot be separated. His appeal to scripture can be seen in the temptation narratives of Matthew and Luke, and in a variety of controversy stories in which he is seen taking issue with current biblical interpretations on many subjects (e.g., sacrifice, the laws of purity, divorce, or the Sabbath). His vision of God and of the Kingdom is seen both in his PARABLES about life in this world (e.g., Mark 4; Matt 15; Luke 8), and in his vivid descriptions of the glory and judgment of God in heaven at the last day (e.g., Matt 8:11-12; 25:31-46; Mark 14:62; Luke 10:18). In either case, ordinary perceptions of reality are radically transformed.

This transformation is evident early in Jesus' ministry in the BEATITUDES with which he begins the SERMON ON THE MOUNT in Matthew's Gospel. Speaking of the crowds from all over Palestine crying out to him in their confusion and pain (Matt 4:24; 5:1), Jesus reveals that he saw them not as they were then, but with the eyes of love, as God saw them. They were the "poor" for whom God's Kingdom was intended, "mourners" to be comforted, and the "meek" who would inherit a new earth. They were a people hungry and thirsty for justice whose hunger would be more than satisfied by God's grace. For the present they were "harassed and helpless, like sheep without a shepherd" (Matt 9:36); it was to them that Jesus believed himself sent (Matt 15:24), and to them in turn that he sent his disciples. They were the "lost sheep of the house of Israel" (Matt 10:6), the nucleus of a restored Israel, and Jesus is said to have appointed twelve of his followers to rule over Israel's twelve tribes (Matt 19:28 || Luke 22:29-30; cf. Acts 1:15-26).

These "lost sheep" were not all the Jews of Palestine, but specifically those not normally expected to benefit from the coming of the Messiah. For their carelessness about the law, many of them were regarded by their fellow Jews as enemies of God, but it was Jesus' conviction that God loved his enemies, and that consequently he and his disciples must love them too (Matt 5:38-48). When he was challenged for enjoying table fellowship with social outcasts (known to religious Jews as "sinners"), Jesus replied, "Those who are well have no need of a physician, but those who are sick; I came not to call the righteous, but sinners" (Mark 2:17). When the religious authorities murmured, "This man receives sinners and eats with them" (Luke 15:1-2), he told three parables to demonstrate that God's joy at the recovery of all such "sinners"—tax collectors, prostitutes, shepherds, soldiers, and all others despised by the pious in Israel—was greater than any joy "over ninety-nine righteous persons who need no repentance" (Luke 15:7; cf. vv. 25-32).

Such an unrestrained celebration of God's mercy on sinners must have seemed to the religious leaders of Jesus' day a lowering of ethical standards and a compromise of the holiness of God. Though there is little evidence that Jesus included non-Jews among the "sinners" to whom he was sent, the principle, "not to the righteous, but to sinners," made the proclamation of the good news of the Kingdom of God to the gentiles after his death a natural extension of his own practice. And in Jesus' own vision of the future, "many will come from east and west and sit at table with Abraham, Isaac, and Jacob in the kingdom of heaven, while the sons of the kingdom will be thrown into the outer darkness" (Matt 8:11-12). In that day twelve uneducated Galileans would "sit on twelve thrones, judging the twelve tribes of

Israel" (Matt 19:28; cf. Luke 22:30). Such is the magnitude of the reversal of present circumstances that comes to expression in the sayings and parables attributed in the Gospel tradition to Jesus of Nazareth.

The kingdom that Jesus proclaimed, like the kingdom his hearers were expecting, was a future kingdom, but Jesus saw it impinging on the present in the repentance and transformation of "sinners" and in the healings and exorcisms God was performing through him (cf., e.g., Matt 12:28 || Luke 11:20). Jesus' teaching as recorded in the Gospels is alive with metaphors and parables of this kind. Depending on our own presuppositions we can regard them as the product of his ingenuity, creativity, or imagination. Or we can attribute them to his prophetic vision of God and of God's future for Israel and the world. Intimations of Jesus the visionary can be found not only in the accounts of his baptism, where he sees a dove descending and hears a voice saying "You are my beloved Son," and in the temptation, where he converses with SATAN, but in a brief passing reminder to his disciples that "I saw Satan falling like lightning from heaven" (Luke 10:18; for other possible examples, cf. Luke 11:49; 12:49-50). At any rate, the parables of Jesus continue to illumine Christian believers and fascinate scholars like wheels within wheels, or wells without bottoms, for they embody the insight of someone who saw things differently and continually turned human expectations and human values upside down. When this is understood, it is not so strange after all that Jesus was crucified.

Conflict in Jesus' Ministry. Opposition to Jesus and his teaching began rather early, according to Mark, at Capernaum (PLATE 52), where the Pharisees and Herodians began to plot ways of getting rid of him (Mark 3:6; cf., in a Jerusalem setting, John 5:16-18). The stated issue was Jesus' willingness to perform healings on the Sabbath (Mark 3:2; cf. 2:24; John 5:16), but it is possible that the healings themselves provoked opposition even apart from the Sabbath question. According to Luke, Jesus looked for hostility—and found it—in his home synagogue at Nazareth when he announced good news to the poor (Luke 4:16-30). Again, Jesus' healings were the issue: "Physician, heal yourself! Do here in your home town what we have heard you did in Capernaum" (Luke 4:23).

Opposition to Jesus came to a head in connection with his practice of exorcism. Religious leaders from Jerusalem came to Galilee to investigate him, and concluded that he was himself "possessed by Beelzebub, and by the prince of demons he casts out the demons" (Mark 3:22; cf. Matt 12:24 || Luke 11:15). Jesus replied that his healings of the demon-possessed were a sign rather that Satan's power was broken and the Kingdom of God was decisively at work in him: " . . . no one can enter a strong man's house and plunder his goods, unless he first binds the strong man; then indeed he may plunder his house" (Mark 3:27; cf. Matt 12:29; Luke 11:21). As Jesus saw it, the "strong man" (Beelzebub or Satan) was now bound, his "house" was being robbed and his captives set free.

In one way this crisis in Jesus' ministry simply confirmed his victory over Satan in the desert after his baptism. Yet it also demonstrated that the "temptation" was by no means over. The Beelzebub controversy, triggered by his healing and saving activity, set a grim precedent for Jesus' relationship with the Jerusalem authorities, and made his eventual arrest and execution almost inevitable. According to Mark, it was from that time on that Jesus began to speak "in parables" (Mark 3:23). There is no doubt that Mark emphasizes (perhaps overemphasizes) the dark side of Jesus' use of this remarkable teaching method (Mark 4:10-12), yet it is likely that parables served as Jesus' way of distinguishing those who were ready to see reality in a new way from those who were not. Parables unfolded his vision of the Kingdom of God to his followers while effectively hiding it from his enemies.

John's Gospel suggests that Jesus may even have used the imagery of his kingdom parables (e.g., the image of planting and growth) to hint at his own eventual arrest and execution on the CROSS (John 12:24, 32). In all the Gospels, in a variety of other images and metaphors (e.g., "drinking the cup," Mark 10:38; a shepherd risking his life for a flock of sheep, John 10:15; spreading fire over the earth, Luke 12:49), and sometimes in quite explicit language (e.g., Mark 8:31; 9:31; 10:33-34), Jesus is said to have announced to his disciples that he would be arrested and tried by the religious leadership in Jerusalem, die on the cross, and rise again from the dead. Even though the Gospel writers may have sharpened these predictions after the fact in light of the fulfillment, there is good reason to believe that Jesus defined his mission from the start, at least in certain respects, as that of the "servant of the Lord" described in Isa 40–66 (e.g., the citation of Isa 61:1-2 in Luke 4:18-19). As his ministry moved toward its completion, the vicarious suffering of the servant (cf. Isa 51:13–53:12) came into ever sharper focus for Jesus (cf., e.g., Mark 10:45; 14:24). He is represented also as comparing himself to the stricken shepherd of Zech 13:7 (Mark 14:27), and, at the end, to the righteous sufferer of the biblical psalms (e.g., Mark 15:34; Luke 23:46; John 19:28). In the drama of his last meal with his disciples, he told them that only his death could guarantee the coming of the kingdom he had proclaimed (Mark 14:22-25 || Matt 26:26-29 || Luke 22:14-20; cf. 1 Cor 11:23-26).

Jesus' anticipation of his own death is of course debated among scholars. The belief of the early church that Jesus was the Son of God could have led the Gospel writers to assume that he knew the end of his life almost from the beginning, and to avoid at all costs the notion that he was taken by surprise at any point (cf. e.g., John 10:17-18). And the belief of the church that Jesus' death was a sacrifice for human sin could have led them to assume that already during his lifetime Jesus interpreted it as such. But the bitterness of the Beelzebub controversy early in Jesus' ministry suggests that an early death at the hands of the religious authorities was a reasonable and realistic expectation. And there is no disputing Jesus' fondness for striking metaphors of conflict (e.g., Mark 3:27), and for surprise violent endings to rather conventional stories (e.g., the death of a bridegroom at his own wedding,

Mark 2:20; the murder of a landlord's son by his tenant farmers, Mark 12:8; an unfaithful servant being "cut in half" by his angry master, Matt 24:51). Is it so strange that someone who saw the world in such "large and startling figures" (Flannery O'Connor's term for an artist's or writer's vision) might have included himself and his own fate in his image-making? The church's contribution to the tradition was probably not to create Jesus' anticipation of his death and resurrection, but to make explicit after the fact what was already implicit in some of his own metaphors and parables. Justice must be done, however, to the fact that when Jesus was arrested and executed, and especially when he appeared alive to his disciples afterward, they were by no means prepared for what happened. The predictions Jesus made are therefore best understood as indirect rather than direct, couched in metaphor rather than literal common speech (cf., e.g., John 16:19-22, 25).

The Death and Resurrection of Jesus. The immediate provocation for Jesus' arrest seems to have been his act of driving the money changers out of the Jerusalem Temple (e.g., Mark 11:15-17; cf. John 2:13-22). This, combined with certain pronouncements he is supposed to have made against the Temple, aroused the Jewish authorities to act decisively against him. During his last week in Jerusalem, Jesus had predicted the Temple's destruction (Mark 13:1-2 || Matt 24:1-2 || Luke 21:5-6) and according to some witnesses had claimed that "I will destroy this temple that is made with hands, and in three days I will build another, not made with hands" (Mark 14:58; cf. Matt 26:61). Distorted as these charges may have been, there was a grain of truth in them, for even the Christians attributed to him the statement, "Destroy this temple, and in three days I will raise it up" (John 2:19), as well as a promise to Peter that "on this rock I will build my church, and the gates of hell will not stand against it" (Matt 16:18). Jesus' intention to establish a new community as a "temple," or dwelling place of God (cf. 1 Cor 3:16-17) was perceived by some as a very real threat to the existing community of Judaism and to the Temple that stood as its embodiment, even though Jesus himself probably had in mind a restoration, not a replacement, of Israel (cf. Matt 19:28 || Luke 22:30). On this basis Jesus was arrested and charged as a deceiver of the people.

A preliminary hearing before the Jewish Sanhedrin, or ruling Council, seems to have ended inconclusively, despite Jesus' reference to himself before the high priest as "Son of man sitting at the right hand of power, and coming with the clouds of heaven" (Mark 14:62; cf. Dan 7:13). The high priest called his pronouncement blasphemy and the Council agreed that such words deserved death, yet there is no evidence that Jesus was formally tried and convicted of anything. If he had been, he would have been stoned to death like Stephen in Acts 7, or as the woman caught in adultery was about to be stoned according to some manuscripts of John 7:53-8:11. If Jesus had been stoned to death without a formal conviction it would have been murder, and murder was forbidden by the Decalogue (cf. John 18:31b, "we are not allowed to kill anyone," probably a reference to the Jews' own law, not to something prohibited by the Romans).

Lacking a conviction by their council, a small group of Jewish priests decided to send Jesus to Pontius Pilate, the Roman governor, with charges against him that would be taken seriously by the Romans: "We found this man perverting our nation, and forbidding us to give tribute to Caesar, and saying that he himself is Christ, a king" (Luke 23:2). Jesus' execution is therefore attributable neither to the Jewish people as a whole nor to the Sanhedrin. The blame rests instead with an unspecified group of priests (presumably including the high priest) who manipulated the Romans into doing what their own law would not allow them to do, and with the Romans, who allowed themselves to be so manipulated. Consequently Jesus died by CRUCIFIXION, a distinctly Roman rather than Jewish method of execution, and his own metaphorical words about being "lifted up" (poorly understood at the time he uttered them) came ironically to realization (cf. John 3:14; 8:28; 12:32; 18:31).

The story of Jesus does not end with his death. His body is said to have been placed in a new tomb belonging to a secret disciple named Joseph (Luke 23:50-56; John 19:38-42) (PLATE 39). There are several accounts of what happened after that. All four Gospels agree that two days later some women who had remained faithful to Jesus discovered the stone over the tomb's entrance rolled away and Jesus' body gone. According to Mark a young man then told the women to tell the rest of Jesus' disciples to go and meet Jesus in Galilee, just as he had promised them (Mark 16:7; cf. 14:28). The most reliable manuscripts of Mark's Gospel end the story there, leaving the rest to the reader's imagination. In Matthew the women carried the news to the disciples, who went accordingly to a mountain in Galilee. There the risen Jesus appeared to them as a group and commanded them to make more disciples, teaching and baptizing among the gentiles (Matt 28:16-20). In Luke the risen Jesus appeared to his disciples not in Galilee but in the vicinity of Jerusalem on the same day he was raised (Luke 24:13-51). Luke adds in the Book of Acts the surprising information that the appearances of the risen Jesus went on over a period of forty days in which he continued to instruct them about the Kingdom of God. John has an appearance of Jesus on EASTER day in Jerusalem to one of the women, Mary Magdalene, another on the same day to ten gathered disciples, another a week later (still in Jerusalem) to the same group plus Thomas (John 20:10-31), and a fourth appearance, at an unstated time, by the Lake of Galilee (John 21:1-14).

These varied accounts cannot be convincingly integrated into one coherent account. Whatever the facts, and whatever their precise order, the disciples' experience of what they took to be the resurrected Jesus transformed them from a scattered and fearful band of refugees into the nucleus of a powerful movement able to challenge and change forever the Roman empire within a few decades. Many theories have been proposed as to exactly what happened. Theologians—and some historians—are often more comfortable with the resurrection as a matter of faith than of fact. But because the historical impact of the resurrection experience is undeniable, it is hard to avoid asking about the historical causes of that experience. Is it conceivable, for example, that Jesus' disciples could have stolen his body, lied about what they had seen, and risked their lives for a lie? If Jesus' enemies stole the body, would they not have produced it when the disciples began to preach that Jesus was alive? These are the kinds of questions that Christian apologists have asked for a long time, and they have not been convincingly answered. Some have replied that the reports of the empty tomb are not essential to the story, and that Christian faith rests not on those reports but on the appearances. Yet Matthew already in the first century emphasized the importance of the empty tomb by recording an attempt by the priestly authorities to bribe Roman soldiers into saying that Jesus' disciples came secretly and stole his body (Matt 28:11-15). And Luke has Peter arguing in the first Christian sermon that "the patriarch David . . . both died and was buried, and his tomb is with us to this day" (Acts 2:29). The force of the argument depends on the assumption that the tomb of Jesus was also known and publicly acknowledged to be empty. Clearly the resurrection faith of the early Christians rested on reports both of an empty tomb and of resurrection appearances. Paul places great emphasis on listing those to whom the risen Jesus "appeared" (1 Cor 15:5-8), but only after he has clearly stated that Jesus "died," "was buried," and "was raised the third day" (1 Cor 15:3-4)—the "third day," presumably, because that was when the tomb of Jesus was found empty. Though it would be an exaggeration to claim that the physical resurrection of Jesus is a proven fact, yet the historical evidence in its favor is extremely strong.

In one respect at least, the resurrection of Jesus is a barrier to understanding the Jesus of history, because of the uncertainty over whether some sayings in the Gospels are to be attributed to Jesus during his lifetime or to the "Risen One" (i.e., to Christian prophets after the resurrection speaking in Jesus' name). Yet in the last analysis, Jesus' resurrection pointed his followers toward, not away from, his career as a real figure in history. The resurrection impelled his disciples to remember, preserve, and keep alive the record of his deeds and words. Several of the accounts of Jesus' resurrection emphasize the need to verify that this divine stranger was "the same Jesus" the disciples had known as a friend and companion on earth (e.g., Luke 24:30-31, 36-42; John 20:27). In all the early Christian sources, the meaning of the resurrection is that the story of Jesus of Nazareth goes on. Mark makes the point with the promise that Jesus will reunite his scattered followers and lead them into Galilee (Mark 16:7). Matthew does it with the risen Jesus' concluding words, "I will be with you always, even to the end of the age" (Matt 28:20). Luke does it with the entire Book of Acts, tracing the spread of the message of Jesus and the Kingdom of God all the way to Rome. John does it with his promise that the Holy Spirit will continue the work of Jesus, and with his picture of the Spirit coming on the disciples from the mouth of Jesus himself (John 20:21-22). The methods are different, but the point is always the same: Jesus' story is not over, for his ministry goes on wherever his name is confessed and his teaching obeyed.

See also BEATITUDES; CROSS; CRUCIFIXION; DIVINITY OF JESUS; EASTER; GOSPEL; GOSPELS, CRITICAL STUDY OF; JOHN THE BAPTIST; KINGDOM OF GOD; LORD

IN THE NT; MESSIAH/CHRIST; MIRACLE STORY; MIRACLES; PARABLES; PILATE; RESURRECTION IN THE NT; SERMON ON THE MOUNT; SON OF GOD; SON OF MAN; TOMB OF JESUS.

Bibliography. G. Bornkamm, *Jesus of Nazareth*; H. Conzelmann, *Jesus*; C. H. Dodd, *The Parables of the Kingdom*; D. Flusser, *Jesus*; J. Jeremias, *New Testament Theology: The Proclamation of Jesus*; M. Kähler, *The So-called Historical Jesus and the Historic Biblical Christ*; G. E. Ladd, *The Presence of the Future*; T. W. Manson, *The Teaching of Jesus*; B. F. Meyer, *The Aims of Jesus*; J. R. Michaels, *Servant and Son*; C. L. Mitton, *Jesus: The Fact Behind the Faith*; G. O'Collins, *The Resurrection of Jesus*; J. Pelikan, *Jesus Through the Centuries*; J. Riches, *Jesus and the Transformation of Judaism*; E. Schillebeeckx, *Jesus: An Experiment in Christology*; A. Schweitzer, *The Quest of the Historical Jesus*; E. Stauffer, *Jesus and His Story*; W. B. Tatum, *In Quest of Jesus*; V. Taylor, *The Life and Ministry of Jesus*; G. Vermes, *Jesus the Jew*.

—J. RAMSEY MICHAELS

—MDB 011296

Matthew [MCB 939-74]

Stephenson Humphries-Brooks

Introduction

Christians approach Matthew as a catechetical manual, as a sourcebook for homily, and as a guide to faith and practice within contemporary Christian communities. Scholars use Matthew as a historical text that informs us about Jesus of Nazareth, the structure of faith of an early Christian author, and/or the faith and practice of an early Christian community of the Mediterranean world in the first century C.E. Moreover, the Matthean depiction of Jesus influences the development of ethical and legal systems in Western culture.

In the following commentary the process of investigation and interpretation begins and ends with the text. Matthew prompts significant questions for a contemporary critical audience broadly conceived.

The Text of the Gospel of Matthew

The Plot of Matthew. We tend to read Matthew as containing an organized series of episodes about Jesus. We find a "plot" of his life complete with complication, climax, and denouement. The series of episodes implies some causal relationship from one event to the next. For example the information that Jesus is adopted into the Davidic royal line by Joseph (1:1-21) helps us to make sense of the visit of the MAGI and the attempt by HEROD to destroy the one born *king of the Jews* (2:1-18).

The plot of Matthew does not directly violate normal historical expectations. In general the sequence of the plot of Matthew conforms to causal and temporal sequence, that is, no events occur out of their normal order. We can easily summarize the plot of Matthew: Jesus is born and adopted into the royal line of Israel. He escapes a murderous plot by a rival king. He is baptized and immediately tempted by Satan. He begins a career of preaching the arrival of the kingdom of heaven. He teaches, performs miracles, recruits disciples. The religious leaders become his enemies. He arrives in the capital city and one of his own disciples betrays him. He is tried and put to death by crucifixion for blasphemy and political sedition. He is buried and resurrected.

Characters and Characterization in Matthew. The episodes that form the plot of Matthew focus on the actions of JESUS, who is the main character. The text depicts Jesus by commentary from the narrator, by Jesus' actions, by commentary from other characters, and finally and most importantly by what Jesus says. The picture that emerges of Jesus is that he is the SON OF GOD, the SON OF MAN. During the process of his story he also becomes invested with all authority and power, a claim the narrator makes for him implicitly by calling him *Emmanuel, . . . God-with-us* (1:23). Jesus himself explicitly claims such power after the resurrection (28:18).

The development of the divine power and authority of Jesus throughout his life occurs in conjunction with a downward trend in Jesus' mundane fortunes. Initially, Jesus appears as a claimant to the throne of David. He is a legitimate threat to Herod and the rulers of Jerusalem. As an adult he takes up residence as a free householder of an urban area, CAPERNAUM (4:13; 9:1). His disciples, also, are depicted as free householders. Contrary to this depiction, Jesus identifies himself as homeless (8:20). At the CRUCIFIXION the text avoids referring to MARY as his mother and names instead only his brothers as her sons, thereby emphasizing his homelessness (27:56; cf. 13:55). At the same time Jesus becomes not only the preacher and teacher of the kingdom of heaven, but also its chief citizen. Ironically, he is crucified as *King of the Jews* (27:37) the same title under which Herod seeks his death. Jesus, therefore, is not depicted as Christ or Messiah in historical terms.

We are led by the Gospel to evaluate other characters according to Jesus' actions and words. With regard to social status as understood in the ancient Mediterranean world three major types of characters appear: powerful urban elites; the free of the cities; women, children, and other supplicants. Repeatedly characters of different status interact in specific episodes. Matthew contains episodes interwoven into the plot to show how characters with lower status displace those with higher status as more dependable witnesses to the kingdom of heaven. Those characters associated with the urban elite oppose Jesus. They are not part of the kingdom of heaven. The disciples remain ambiguous as to their future faithfulness to Jesus. Only women, children, and other supplicants, those of the lowest status according to mundane social-historical perception, appear as faithful witnesses to Jesus (Humphries-Brooks 1991).

The treatment of other characters and character groups is consistent with the treatment of Jesus in the plot of the Gospel. Only as a homeless and marginal person does Jesus become fully empowered; only homeless and marginal people fully perceive and act on the faith that arrives with the kingdom of heaven.

The Speeches of Jesus. The text begins with a carefully plotted series of episodes associated with the birth and early career of Jesus (1:1–5:1). Similarly the conclusion to the Gospel (26:1b–28:20) contains a carefully recounted series of episodes concerning the PASSION, death, and resurrection of Jesus.

In the midsection of Matthew, however, narrative plot becomes less significant as attention shifts to speeches and PARABLES (5:1–26:1a). These serve several functions in the context of the plot of Matthew: 1. They focus attention on the character and person of Jesus; 2. They make the "once-upon-a-time" ministry of Jesus contemporary with every new performance of the text; 3. They describe the kingdom of heaven; 4. Therefore, they provide the vantage point from which all characters and episodes in Matthew are to be judged. We cannot fully understand Matthew by merely understanding the causal sequence of Jesus' life. Rather, we must perceive Matthew as a whole and use information provided in the speeches of Jesus to interpret the activity of those characters described by the plot.

The author asks us by this arrangement of the narrative to pay less attention to the continuous unrolling of the life of Jesus, and more attention to associations in the narrative that reveal the kingdom of heaven. The work must be read as layers, or perceived like a building, "architectonically" (Davies 1964, 14). We become, therefore, actively involved with the text as we construct meaning from it. This perception makes it impossible to read or interpret according to one-dimensional thematic- or plot-oriented outlines. In this commentary, we follow the text as it shifts from plot to speech. The divisions proposed by the outline and commentary are governed by a concern to describe the reading experience for us as a critical contemporary audience. Such divisions do not necessarily reconstruct the experience of the text for the original ancient audience, nor do they attempt to recover the conscious intent of the author who probably did not compose according to an outline.

By disrupting our attention from plot, the speeches and parables of Jesus present a view of the kingdom of heaven as disruptive to perception of the historical world. They invite us, as they invited the ancient audience of the Matthean community, to see the presence of the kingdom of heaven in the world.

Major Themes in Matthew

Based on this analysis the single underlying and organizing theme of the Gospel of Matthew is the arrival of the kingdom of heaven in history and its effect on normal experience. Matthew makes apparent that the mystery of the kingdom of heaven is not limited to or encapsulated by the person of Jesus, but requires a discernment of God's will from the perspective of the kingdom proclaimed by Jesus. In the final analysis, Matthew is not a christological or ecclesiological document, but a *theological* one; its focus is on God.

The kingdom of heaven becomes the major term used to describe the power of God on earth in Matthew. It possesses its own justice, a justice that is unique in terms of politics, ethics, economics, and status orientation. The kingdom of heaven comes into conflict with the historical world familiar to us and represented in the plot of the Gospel as well.

The totality of Matthew exposes a world fractured and restructured by conflict and struggle between the kingdom of heaven and the kingdoms of the world. Clearly those kingdoms are claimed by the power of EVIL represented by a variety of titles including "Satan," "the Devil," "Beelzebul," and "the Evil One." Matthew assumes that the world possessed by evil powers can only be overcome by the intervention of God independent of normal human individuals, institutions, and political structures. God's intervention takes on real political form in the life and teaching of Jesus, which bears witness to and invites discernment of the kingdom of heaven and the battle currently engaged. The conclusion to that conflict will be one of judgment and the removal of evil from the world by God.

Therefore, the kingdom of heaven always takes its bearings from God's end to time rather than from the discernment of God's purposes through past events. The value of persons in its justice is based upon God's righteousness that includes a balance between GRACE and judgment. Matthew depicts God's righteousness at odds with normal political existence because such human justice is in the control of evil.

The worldview of Matthew accords with views expressed in early Christian and Jewish APOCALYPTIC LITERATURE. It has its roots in the prophetic tradition of JUDAISM and in modes of thought that come from a combination of traditional Hebrew culture with Hellenistic thought. Unlike the Jewish and Christian apocalyptic tradition out of which it arises, however, Matthew abandons the view of God as divine warrior who opposes the institutionalized violence of oppressive regimes with invasions of heavenly death-dealing hosts. Consistently, Jesus in Matthew resists the use of violence to combat violence. Rather, the antidote to death in Matthew comes in the resurrection of Jesus by God.

The Composition of the Author

The Gospel of Matthew recounts the significant events of Jesus' life in such a way that those who read it know that these events are not regarded by the author as fictions or fabrications. One of the most popular genres of the ancient world is biography. Ancient biographers seek to reveal to their audiences the essential truth about a person through actions and speech (Talbert 1988). But further, by encountering the truth about a particular person, the audience becomes educated into the universal truths that inform action in the world. An ancient audience, therefore, anticipates that Matthew will educate them not only about the person, Jesus, but through him about their own appropriate action in the world.

The accurate depiction of historical event remains of paramount importance for most modern biographers. For the ancient biographer, including the author of Matthew, the unveiling of truth that cannot be contained in the merely historical is of paramount importance. After all history is mere appearance: biography lays bare essence not otherwise apparent. Therefore, Matthew contains only a selection of the events of Jesus' life told in such a way as to effect a change in the audience. The following commentary is guided by the thesis that the author of Matthew constructs a biography because it most effectively educates the church community into the way of life that characterizes the kingdom of heaven. As such, Matthew, even though it may not prove to be historical in the modern sense, may not be regarded as fiction. For the author and for the original audience, witness to the kingdom of heaven in the life of Jesus is not entertainment, but a matter of life and death.

The author uses both direct quotations from and allusions to the scriptures of Judaism (after about 150 C.E. Christians refer to these as the "Old Testament"), particularly the divisions known as the Law and the Prophets. On at least twenty-two occasions Matthew contains direct quotations from the Prophets. In seventeen of these instances the quotation is introduced by a formula, for example, *All this took place to fulfill.* Additional quotations from and allusions especially to the Law may be found throughout Matthew (see Brown 1977, Gundry 1967, and Stendahl 1968).

While citations from the Jewish scriptures appear in Matthew, at no point does the text explicitly cite or give evidence of other early Christian writings. This may mean that at the time Matthew was composed, no other Gospels were regarded as "scripture" by the author or the Matthean community. Most scholars think, however, that the author knew at least two early Christian writings. One, the Gospel of Mark, provided the majority of the episodes and their arrangement for the author. The second, a collection of sayings of Jesus at least partially in written form provided the sayings and parables found both in Matthew and Luke. Scholars refer to this source as Q.

In addition to these two sources of information the author has access to a broad assortment of traditions handed on within the community for which Matthew was written. These may have included narratives about Jesus, such as the birth account, sayings of Jesus, and parables not otherwise attested in the Gospels. Generally, such material is referred to as "M" by scholars and may have been in both oral and written form (see Brooks 1987).

The familiarity with the Jewish scriptures demonstrated from the text of Matthew allows us to suppose that those writings, particularly the Law and the Prophets, had a significant literary influence on the author and the Matthean community. Furthermore, the adoption of a popular genre, biography, known to all Greek-speaking audiences of the Mediterranean world indicates that the author and community live and work within the broader culture of their day. The Gospel of Matthew is a hybrid of diverse cultural traditions focused through the inspired creative genius of an individual.

The author carefully and subtly arranges and uses the sources and traditions available from the history of the church community for which Matthew was written. In that sense, to the extent that we read Matthew as a self-contained textual world, we are subject to the intent of the author. We also, because we bring to the text our own preconceptions and perceptions, may see implications in the text that the author did not consciously intend. To that extent we participate in the revelatory superfluity of the text. The commentary will be guided by both aspects of the text. We shall, however, remain within the confines of the text by seeking to interpret only that which may be found in Matthew. To offer a critical interpretation means to offer an interpretation that accounts for the text as written, not as we wish it.

From about the middle of the second century onward, major churches thought that the Gospel of Matthew was written by MATTHEW, a disciple of Jesus. The sources that report this opinion, however, are suspect and we do not know the identity of the author of the Gospel. Since we do not know who the author is, in our commentary we will simply speak of "the author" and of the book by its shortened traditional title "Matthew." The story of the call of the tax collector in 9:9 refers to the man by the name *Matthew*. Since the parallel passage in Mark 2:13-14 calls the tax collector "Levi" this passage may indicate a conscious change on the part of the author that shows that the disciple Matthew played an important role in the founding of the community.

Speculation on the personal history of the author depends exclusively on the interpretation of implicit and perhaps tenuous evidence in the text itself. It has been suggested that the author was a converted Jewish RABBI or scribe, or that the author was a non-Jewish convert to a Jewish-Christian community, or that the author was a member of a "school" of scribes within a Jewish-Christian community.

While almost all recent scholarship refers to the author as "he," we can be no more sure of the gender of the author than of the author's name. Many women in the Mediterranean basin of the first century possessed the education necessary to write the Greek found in Matthew. We know from other early Christian writings that women occupied high places in early Christian communities. The Gospel itself indicates the consistent and faithful witness of key women to Jesus. Such a motif in the Gospel leads us to suspect that women played important roles in the formation and transmission of the Matthean tradition. There is no secure historical means to determine the gender of the anonymous or pseudonymous author of a NT book from its content.

Internal evidence makes it probable that Matthew was written after the destruction of the Temple of Jerusalem in 70 C.E. Matt 22:7 apparently contains an allusion to this event. IGNATIUS, writing between 110 and 115 C.E. is the first writer to quote Matthew. Other less-clear indications may help us to further limit the date of composition. Matthew's use of Mark may be helpful. Mark (according to most scholars) was composed no earlier than 67 C.E. Some time must have elapsed during which Mark was used by and commented on in the community of Matthew. The modifications to Mark noticeable by a comparison with Matthew would indicate some significant duration of use and commentary within the community, perhaps by a scribal school. Further, as we shall see below, the history of the community implied by the text would indicate a separation of the community from the synagogues of its city that would best fit in the decade between 90 and 100. These considerations would suggest that Matthew was composed sometime between 90 and 105 C.E.

The Matthean Community

Perhaps no other question has exercised recent interpreters so much as the question of the social, historical, and religious configuration of the community of Matthew. We shall summarize here the view that emerges from and informs the following commentary (see Kingsbury 1988, 147–60).

The Greek of Matthew indicates that the community was most likely urban. While at times the Greek of the text is semitic in flavor or style, there is little indication that the audience was bilingual, knowing both Greek, the *lingua franca* of the Mediterranean world, and Aramaic, the language of rural Syria and Palestine. The semitic nature of the Greek would fit well, however, with the Greek spoken and written by residents of a major city of the eastern Mediterranean, such as Antioch in Syria. When we add to the linguistic observations the evidence from Ignatius of Antioch who first quotes the Gospel, then a good working hypothesis is that the community of Matthew was to be found in Antioch of Syria (modern Antakya, Turkey) in the last decade of the first century.

The community was relatively well-off and enjoyed material prosperity. Jesus and the disciples are characterized as ministering to cities and being resident householders in cities. The word "city" is used no fewer than twenty-six times in Matthew. The text also refers to a wider variety and larger amounts of money than those that occur in Mark or Luke (Kingsbury 1988, 152-3).

The religious configuration of the community remains problematic, probably not least because our understanding of ethnic relationships, of which religion is a part, remains fragmentary for the ancient Mediterranean world. We may venture the following suggestions.

The community for which the author writes is Jewish with regard to its authoritative scripture. We know from Jewish documents of the third to sixth centuries that early the Law or Torah: (Genesis–Deuteronomy) and the Prophets (Joshua–Kings [excluding Ruth]) were recognized as canonical.

Matthew also shows high regard for the Temple in Jerusalem (5:23-24; 23:16-21). Further, we detect no animosity toward the Temple cultus per se, although appropriate Temple worship and use is advocated. Therefore, with regard to the religious institution of the Temple, Matthew seems to represent some segment of Judaism in the first century.

The author portrays the PHARISEES as a powerful religious elite in control of the synagogues. The text of Matthew constantly refers to "their" synagogues in a pejorative sense. The corresponding institution ordained by Jesus is not "our" SYNAGOGUE but rather the *ekklēsia* (gathering, community). Further, the community may not use synagogue titles of respect for each other (23:8-12). Finally, 10:16-23 and 23:34-36 indicate the strong possibility that the some members of the community or their predecessors have suffered persecution at the hands of synagogue authorities. Such considerations indicate that the community of Matthew does not associate with the Jewish synagogues of its city.

Furthermore, the community recruits members who are not originally from Judaism, that is, "gentiles." The resurrected Lord sends the disciples out to all of humanity or the *nations* (28:16-20). There may be other references in the text to non-Jewish proselytes within the community as well (e.g., 6:7-8; 23:15). We may conclude that the community of Matthew was composed of Jewish-Christians and their gentile converts who had a positive regard for the Jewish scriptures and Temple, while constituting themselves outside of the local synagogue(s) of their city (see Brown 1983). The community had its own means of internal organization including provisions for the reception of new members.

From the perspective of the study of religions, a community that both identifies with a dominant established tradition and separates itself from other institutions representative of that tradition may be considered a sect. As the commentary explores, this sect holds to specific beliefs about its founder, Jesus. With regard to its adherence to the person of Jesus Christ, then, this Jewish sect may also be called CHRISTIAN.

The text contains few indications about the terms used within the community for community members. The term "Christian" does not occur. Nor does the text ever refer to the community as the "New" or "True" Israel. Terms of equality dominate, however. Jesus speaks of "brothers," "children," and "little ones" when referring to members of the community. We may suspect, however, that two groups are recognized as given special gifts by God: prophets and teachers (scribes [Kingsbury, 1988, 158]). While these two groups probably possess specific gifts appreciated by the community, they are not associated with special church office or privilege.

There are indications that some from these groups are trying to assert hierarchical preeminence at the time of the publication of the Gospel. They do this by invoking traditions about the preeminence of PETER and THE TWELVE. Matthew was written in part as a corrective to these tendencies. It reasserts the egalitarian tradition of the community and denies the sanction of Jesus to those who would assert authoritative doctrinal or interpretative power over the community members. The commentary explores the religious perspective of the author and the sect from which the author and text emerge and to which it speaks.

The author sought to bear witness to the events of Jesus Christ and by the composition of the Gospel to give the audience a perspective that would inform the faith and practice of their religious community. The text, therefore, gives evidence of both perceptions the author had of the intended original audience and conventions operating at an unconscious level. These perceptions and conventions interest us because we wish to understand and be informed by the beliefs and practices of our ancient forebears.

Having begun with the text of the Gospel of Matthew, however, we consider also the appropriation of this faith into our own historical moment. This happens first and foremost because we take seriously the claim of the Gospel to bear witness to Jesus Christ and his revelatory value for the real world. We undertake, therefore, to understand the faith to which the Gospel of Matthew bears witness and to ask how we might responsibly receive and understand the meaning of the Gospel text for our own lives.

Theologically, therefore, we will accept as our interpretative starting point the claim of Matthew that God has manifested God's self in the life of Jesus of Nazareth and ask what that might say to our own historical moment.

For Further Study

In the *Mercer Dictionary of the Bible*: DEMON IN THE NT; GOSPEL; GOSPELS, CRITICAL STUDY OF; JOHN THE BAPTIST; KINGDOM OF GOD; MATTHEW; MATTHEW, BOOK OF; MIRACLE STORY; PASSION NARRATIVE; Q; REDACTION; RESURRECTION IN THE NT; RHETORICAL CRITICISM; SCRIBE IN THE NT; SLAUGHTER OF THE INNOCENTS; SON OF GOD; SON OF MAN; SYNOPTIC PROBLEM; TEMPTATION OF JESUS; TRANSFIGURATION.

In other sources: J. C. Anderson, "Matthew: Gender and Reading," *Semeia* 28 (1983): 3-27; H. D. Betz, *Essays on the Sermon on the Mount*; R. E. Brown and J. P. Meier, *Antioch and Rome*; W. D. Davies and D. Allison, *A Critical and Exegetical Commentary on the Gospel according to Saint Matthew*, ICC; D. Garland, *Reading Matthew: A Literary and Theological Commentary on the First Gospel*, Reading in the New Testament Series; D. R. A. Hare, *Matthew*, Interp; D. Harrington, *The Gospel of Matthew*, SacPag 1; J. D. Kingsbury, *Matthew As Story*, 2d ed; A.-J. Levine, *The Social and Ethnic Dimensions of Matthean Salvation History: "Go nowhere among the Gentiles . . . " (Matt. 10:5b)*, Studies in the Bible and Early Christianity 14; U. Luz, *Matthew 1–7: A Commentary*; J. P. Meier, *The Vision of Matthew. Christ, Church, and Morality in the First Gospel*; D. Patte, *The Gospel According to Matthew: A Structural Commentary on Matthew's Faith*; D. Senior, *The Passion of Jesus in the Gospel of Matthew* and *What Are They Saying about Matthew?*; F. Stagg, *Matthew*, BBC.

Commentary

The following outline indicates shifts between plot and speech and provides a guide to the dominant strategies for reading the text. The heading of each section comes directly from the text itself. The outline may be read, therefore, as a summary of and guide for the reading of the Gospel. Within the major divisions of plot and speech, the outline and commentary try to emulate the structure and language of Matthew as closely as practical and possible. Such an organization will allow for easy reference to the text of Matthew as we proceed. An outline, however, may be used only as a constructive entry point into the text for our generation of readers. The commentary seeks to open up new interpretations, not offer the final word or closure on previous ones.

The commentary presumes that our discussion will proceed with the Gospel of Matthew open before us so that we may hear the voice of the author constantly correcting and informing us as part of the interpretative enterprise.

An Outline

I. Plot: The Book of the Birth of Jesus Christ, 1:1–5:1
- A. An Account of the Genealogy of Jesus the Messiah, 1:1-17
- B. The Birth of Jesus the Messiah Took Place, 1:18-25
- C. In the Time of King Herod, Wise Men Came, 2:1-25
- D. John the Baptist Appeared, 3:1-17
- E. Jesus Was Led Up by the Spirit to Be Tempted by the Devil, 4:1-11
- F. Now When Jesus Heard That John Had Been Arrested, 4:12–5:1

II. Speech: Jesus Began to Speak, and Taught Them, 5:2–7:27
- A. Then He Began to Speak 5:2-16
- B. Do Not Think That I Have Come to Abolish, 5:17-48
- C. Beware of Practicing Your Righteousness, 6:1-34
- D. Do Not Judge, 7:1-23
- E. Everyone then Who Hears, 7:24-27

III. Plot: When Jesus Had Finished Saying These Things, 7:28–10:4
- A. The Crowds Were Astounded, 7:28-29
- B. When Jesus Had Come Down from the Mountain, 8:1-17
- C. Now When Jesus Saw Great Crowds, 8:18-22
- D. And When He Got into the Boat, 8:23–9:8
- E. As Jesus Was Walking Along, He Saw Matthew, 9:9-17
- F. While He Was Saying These Things, 9:18-34
- G. Then Jesus Went about All the Cities and Villages, 9:35–10:4

IV. Speech: These Twelve Jesus Sent Out, 10:5-42.
- A. Go Nowhere among the Gentiles, 10:5-15
- B. See I Am Sending You out like Sheep, 10:16-23
- C. A Disciple Is Not above the Teacher, 10:24-42

V. Plot and Speech: Now When Jesus Had Finished, 11:1–12:50
- A. He Went on to Teach, 11:1-30
- B. Jesus Went through the Grainfields on the Sabbath, 12:1-50

VI. Speech: He Told Them Many Things in Parables, 13:1-52
- A. A Sower Went out to Sow, 13:1-9
- B. Why Do You Speak to Them in Parables?, 13:10-23
- C. He Put before Them Another Parable, 13:24-34
- D. This Was to Fulfill, 13:35
- E. Then He Left the Crowds, 13:36-52

VII. Plot and Speech: When Jesus Had Finished These Parables, 13:53–17:27
- A. He Came to His Hometown, 13:53-58
- B. Herod the Ruler Heard about Jesus, 14:1-12
- C. Jesus Withdrew to a Deserted Place, 14:13-21
- D. Jesus Made the Disciples Get into the Boat, 14:22-36

E. The Pharisees and Scribes Came from Jerusalem, 15:1-20
F. Jesus Left That Place and Went Away to Tyre and Sidon, 15:21-39
G. The Pharisees and Sadducees Test Jesus, 16:1-12
H. Jesus Asked His Disciples about the Son of Man, 16:13–17:23
I. The Children Are Free, 17:24-27

VIII. Speech: Who Is the Greatest in the Kingdom of Heaven? 18:1-35
A. He Called a Child, 18:1-5
B. If You Put a Stumbling Block before One of These, 18:6-35

IX. Plot and Speech: When Jesus Had Finished Saying These Things, 19:1-29
A. Some Pharisees Came to Test Him, 19:1-12
B. Then Little Children Were Being Brought to Him, 19:13-15
C. What Good Deed Must I Do to Have Eternal Life?, 19:16-29

X. Speech: But Many Who Are First Will Be Last, 19:30–20:16

XI. Plot: While Jesus Was Going Up to Jerusalem, 20:17–21:27
A. The Son of Man Will Be Handed Over, 20:17-28
B. As They Were Leaving Jericho, 20:29-34
C. When They Had Come near Jerusalem, 21:1-17

XII. Speech: What Do You Think?, 21:28–22:14

XIII. Plot and Speech: Then the Pharisees Went and Plotted to Entrap Him, 22:15-46
A. Is It Lawful to Pay Taxes to the Emperor, or Not?, 22:15-22
B. Some Sadducees Came to Him, Saying There Is No Resurrection, 22:23-33
C. When the Pharisees Heard That He Had Silenced the Sadducees, 22:34-46

XIV. Speech: Then Jesus Said to the Crowds and to His Disciples, 23:1–26:1
A. The Scribes and the Pharisees Sit on Moses' Seat, 23:1-36
B. Jerusalem, Jerusalem, the City That Kills the Prophets, 23:37–24:26
C. After the Suffering, 24:27-35
D. But about That Day and Hour No One Knows, 24:36–25:30
E. When the Son of Man Comes, 25:31-46
F. When Jesus Had Finished Saying All These Things, 26:1

XV. Plot: The Son of Man Will Be Handed Over to Be Crucified, 26:2–28:20
A. The Passover Is Coming, 26:2-16.
B. On the First Day of Unleavened Bread, 26:17-75
C. When Morning Came, 27:1-56
D. When It Was Evening, 27:57-66
E. After the Sabbath, 28:1-15
F. Now the Eleven Disciples Went to Galilee, 28:16-20

Plot: The Book of the Birth of Jesus Christ, 1:1–5:1

The first sentence of Matthew is ambiguous as to the intention of the book and immediately gives us clues to the multidimensionality of meanings in the Gospel (see Brown 1977, 45-232 for a thorough treatment of the Matthean infancy narrative). The translation, "A book of the birth of Jesus Christ," presents a literal rendering of the Greek into English. Does the phrase refer to the entire Gospel, or only to the first section ending at 2:23, or should we understand the phrase to refer only to 1:1-18 and accept the more restrictive interpretation offered by the NRSV? The translation offered by the NRSV also raises the question of how to understand the use of the term *christos* in Matthew. Should we understand this title to be a general surname for Jesus or does it bear the specific political implications associated with the Davidic monarchy? As we read this section, we become aware of the multilayered conflict between the kingdoms of the world and the kingdom of heaven. It establishes the major themes that will be further developed as the Gospel proceeds.

An Account of the Genealogy of Jesus the Messiah, 1:1-17

The genealogy introduces Jesus as the Messiah who comes from the line of DAVID and ABRAHAM. The Greek *christos* rendered by the NRSV according to its Hebrew/Aramaic equivalent as *Messiah* means "anointed" in reference to the king of Israel. While "Christ" becomes the surname of Jesus in Christianity quite early, it retains its reference to political power. The narrator uses the term as a proper name for Jesus only here and in 1:18 (see also 1:17). The genealogy establishes that Jesus is the legitimate, albeit adopted, heir to David's throne (v. 16). The genealogy points out the historical claim that Jesus is a royal, messianic figure who, like David, might establish rule over Israel.

The genealogy also establishes a tie between Jesus and non-Israelite proselytes. It begins with Abraham. He is the ancestor of all of Israel and therefore of David. He also is the first convert to the God of Israel and may be seen as the patron of all proselytes.

Furthermore, the genealogy refers specifically to four ancestral women. *Tamar* (v. 3) is regarded as an Aramean in some traditions (Jub 41:1). *Rahab* and *Ruth* (v. 5) are non-Israelites who marry into Israel. And in v. 6, *Uriah*, a Hittite, is named to identify *Bathsheba*, the mother of *Solomon*, thereby emphasizing her relationship to non-Israel.

In addition to the concern with non-Israelites the presence of these particular women in a patrilineal genealogy points to the faithfulness of God to justice for the marginal. TAMAR must seduce her father-in-law Judah in the disguise of a prostitute as a means of gaining justice under the rule of levirate marriage (Gen 38:26). RAHAB, a prostitute, hides the spies of Israel from the king of Jericho. She expresses faith in the God of Israel (Josh 2:12; see 6:17-25). RUTH and NAOMI gain social justice from the patriarchy of Bethlehem by deftly reminding the next-of-kin of the obligations to justice that go along with property possession in Israel (Ruth 3:1–4:6). They gain security over against the greed of a patriarchally organized society that would condemn them to penury. Finally, BATHSHEBA is taken by David in an adulterous union (1 Sam 11:1– 12:25). The story shows her as powerless in the face of the king's lust. David, God's anointed, is alone responsible for the adultery and murder that results. Later, she presses for Solomon's inheritance of the throne.

Each of these women either explicitly or tacitly express their faith in God. In the cases of Tamar and Bathsheba the direct injustice of patriarch and king comes to the fore. These common elements coupled with the absence of the more well-known royal mothers, for example, Sarah, Rebecca, or Rachel, indicate that the genealogy is designed to persuade the reader that sexual relations as preferred by patriarchal society frequently do not serve the purposes of the God of justice. We may look for faithfulness and righteousness to emerge not from the political and ethical center that stands for correct order but from the chaotic and questionable fringes.

The Birth of Jesus the Messiah Took Place, 1:18-25

1:18-19. His mother Mary had been engaged. These verses provide a narrative transition to a carefully written scene of a dream annunciation to JOSEPH. Joseph is a *righteous man* (v. 19). These words may refer to his piety in legal observance. They also align Joseph with the characterization of Jesus (3:15) and children of the kingdom of heaven elsewhere in the Gospel (see especially 5:20 and 6:33). Furthermore, such terms and Joseph's characterization accord with the appropriate behavior of a member of the messianic lineage as depicted in Isa 9:6-7.

1:20-21. An angel of the Lord appeared. In the dream annunciation Joseph is clearly instructed about the circumstances of Jesus' conception and as to Joseph's future action in adopting Jesus as his legal heir. Jewish law, similar to both Greek and Roman law, provided that by naming the child the father claimed all the rights and duties of legal paternity. Joseph does as he is instructed and thereby becomes the first character in the Gospel to be shown to fulfill the will of God.

1:22-23. All this took place to fulfill. The text introduces a quotation from a prophet with the phrase *All this took place to fulfill.* The following quotation comes from Isa 7:14. A Greek form of the text is quoted which has the term VIRGIN rather than the Hebrew form which has a word meaning any young woman who has reached puberty. The Hebrew text makes no comment on the previous sexual activity of the woman. By introducing this reading, the author directs attention to the unusual nature of the conception of Jesus.

By the placement of this scene after the genealogy, the author provides a new perspective that distances Jesus from the royal lineage of Messiah. At the end of the genealogy the author sets the stage by referring to Joseph as *the husband of Mary,* rather than as Jesus' father. The author also suggestively refers to the one *called the Messiah* (1:16). This designation proves inadequate for Jesus. In 1:23 the citation designates Jesus not as Messiah, but as *Emmanuel.* At least a portion of the original audience must not have understood Hebrew, since the author explains the meaning of the name as *God with us.*

The presentation of the genealogy and adoption of Jesus in Matthew serves several functions. It shows the unusual relationship of Jesus to the royal household of David. It links Jesus with the tradition of incorporation of non-Israelites into Israel. God works in unusual ways in order to extend the message of Israel's God to non-Israelites. It reminds us of stories about God's dealing with Israel for the sake of God's justice in behalf of the marginal outside of the social and political structures controlled by the patriarchy.

The genealogy also focuses attention on women as bearers of faith. The virginal conception along with the presence of the four women in the genealogy emphasizes God's power manifested through faith for the sake of God's justice and righteousness. Women of abused status bear in their bodies the signs of faith that come into the world from God. The virginal conception disjoins Jesus from the normal royal patrilineage.

In the Time of King Herod, Wise Men Came, 2:1-25

2:1-12, 16-18. He was frightened. The interaction of characters in these episodes constitutes a major means by which the text forms the audience's judgment about Jesus and the world into which he is born. The text depicts Herod along with the entire city of Jerusalem as frightened at the announcement of the birth of Jesus, who is the only character identified as *King of the Jews* in Matthew. The *chief priests and scribes of the people* (v. 4) are the male religious and political leaders who reside in Jerusalem and who have power to advise Herod. They use their education to deduce, by scriptural interpretation, that the Messiah comes from BETHLEHEM. Finally, this information is used by Herod as the basis for his attempt to murder Jesus which results in the murder of all children in and around Bethlehem (v. 16). The combination of political power and scriptural interpretation results in the annihilation of innocent children who have no power in this world of the urban political elite. There are no records of Herod's murder of the children in Bethlehem outside of this text.

The wise men remind us that Jesus even as a child draws foreigners, non-Israel, to himself. The idea of wise men, magi, or astrologers from the East, perhaps priests of Zoroastrianism or Mithraism, has particular appeal to the Greek-speaking Mediterranean audience of the first century, who tend to regard things Eastern with both fascination and fear. Abraham was also from the East (Gen 12:4).

2:13-15. An angel of the Lord appeared to Joseph. The dream of Joseph and the departure to Egypt align Joseph with the patriarch Joseph who also descended into Egypt and was noted for his dreams and interpretations (Gen 37:1–47:28). Jesus escapes the plot of a murderous king, reminiscent of the plot by PHARAOH to kill the male children of the Israelites (Exod 1:22). Clearly the story of the descent into Egypt and return is shaped by a desire to align the story of Jesus with Jewish tradition of the EXODUS from Egypt.

2:19-23. When Herod died. The concluding verses provide the motivation for the removal to Nazareth and also provide yet another scene of the opposition of the political rulers of Jerusalem to Jesus. By the conclusion of this section, those associated with the powerful elites of Jerusalem are characters not to be trusted; indeed, they are intent on the destruction of Jesus.

Furthermore, the author aligns Jesus in important ways with the common history of Israel both in terms of explicit commentary by the prophets and in terms of story reminiscent of important events in Israelite history. The action of Archelaus is perfectly understandable as the response of earthly kings to an earthly threat to their throne from David's heir. The virginal conception and angelic appearances indicate that the point at issue is to understand Jesus from the perspective of God and not in normal political and social terms. Joseph adopts God's perspective and becomes the father who protects and nurtures rather than owning his family.

John the Baptist Appeared, 3:1-17

3:1-12. Repent for the kingdom of heaven has come near. John the Baptist looks and acts like ELIJAH or ELISHA. Both prophets are noteworthy for their opposition to the royal household of AHAB. Both function as warriors in behalf of the God of Israel (1 Kings 17–21; 2 Kings 1–13). John announces judgment not based on ethnic identity, as the PHARISEES and SADDUCEES suppose, but according to action by those who follow God's will. Admission into the kingdom of heaven does not depend on ethnic identity or religious status. The kingdom of heaven as judgment arrives in the ministry of John and will continue into Jesus' ministry. The kingdom of heaven invades the world for the purpose of judgment.

3:13-17. Jesus came from Galilee to be baptized by John. John preaches the arrival of the kingdom of heaven. The term *kingdom of heaven* indicates the actualizing of the foreshadowing in birth and dreams in the previous sections. Jesus by his baptism associates with a kingdom configured differently from the kingdom of Herod.

Verse 15 epitomizes the content of the previous verses: the kingdom of heaven contains righteousness or justice. Here, Jesus shows himself as servant of the righteousness that belongs to the kingdom of heaven. His character arises out of the will of God. His behavior provides the antinomic and determinative opposite to that of the Pharisees and Sadducees. In the same way that the events of Jesus' birth have been shown to fulfill the will of God expressed in the prophets, the action of Jesus as an adult also fulfills God's will.

The text may imply that Jesus' baptism is one of repentance (v. 6). God approves of his action by announcing Jesus' sonship. Jesus correctly perceives the kingdom of heaven and its justice. Here the text introduces for the first time Jesus' own awareness of his divine sonship by virtue of a visionary experience from the heavens and direct communication by a voice.

Jesus Was Led Up by the Spirit to Be Tempted by the Devil, 4:1-11

The scene bears similarities to the wanderings of Israel in the DESERT recounted in Exodus, Numbers, and Deuteronomy. Unlike Israel, however, Jesus successfully resists temptation to sin and indicates clearly the nature of his ministry and proclamation (Meier 1979, 59–62).

The temptation occurs in three scenes culminating dramatically in the temptation to possess universal political power (4:3-4, 5-7, 8-11). In each scene *the devil* speaks first followed by a quotation of Jesus from the Law (Deut 8:3; 6:16; 6:13 at vv. 4, 7, 10). The devil is shown to be a powerful and intelligent individual learned in techniques of scriptural argumentation.

In the final scene, vv. 8-10, Satan asserts that he owns the kingdoms of the world. Jesus does not dispute the point, but rather responds with a quotation from the Law that places the issue on the theological grounds of the lordship of God. Two points emerge from this scene. First, evil powers possess and control the mundane political process. Second, the coming of the kingdom of heaven means that a new politics arrives, one overseen by God. We meet here a view derived from Jewish apocalyptic perspectives as found for example in Isaiah 56–66, Zechariah, Daniel, and 1 Enoch (Hanson 1979). The underlying view is one of a world in antinomic conflict (see Martyn 1985).

The scene opens up a multi-dimensional drama being worked out in the life of Jesus. What appeared to be a political power play between the urban elite of Herod's household and the adopted son of David is the universal struggle between the kingdoms of the world ruled by Satan and the kingdom of heaven. The two dimensions mutually inform and interact with each other throughout Matthew.

Now When Jesus Heard That John Had Been Arrested, 4:12–5:1

4:12-17. He made his home in Capernaum. Jesus resettles to CAPERNAUM as a householder. The citation in vv. 15-16 refers to the same prophetic context as the citation in 1:23 (Isa 9:1-2) and reconfirms Jesus' status as God-with-us. It also emphasizes that Jesus' ministry begins both in traditional Israelite tribal territory (Zebulun, Naphtali) and among non-Israelite peoples (*Galilee of the Gentiles*, v. 15). The ministry is set amidst ethnic diversity. Within this context, Jesus begins the same proclamation as John (3:2). This episode is framed by the notation of John's arrest and the repetition of his preaching. Such framing suggests that the ministry and destiny of John serves as a model for the ministry and destiny of Jesus.

4:18-22. He saw two brothers. The following episode illustrates the immediate fulfillment of the citation of v. 15. Jesus recruits his first followers. They are depicted as male Israelite householders like himself. The Greek names PETER, ANDREW, JAMES, and JOHN show by comparison with the name ZEBEDEE, the father of James and John, the cultural diversity of the generation who will constitute the disciples.

4:23–5:1. Jesus went throughout Galilee. The third episode illustrates the PROPHECY of 4:16. Jesus' actions define him not as a mundane political revolutionary, but as witness to and embodiment of a kingdomwhose concern is healing and *good news of the kingdom* (v. 23). For the first time in Matthew we encounter the term "gospel" (NRSV mg.). In 9:35 and 24:14, as here, it is the *good news of the kingdom*. Good news, the preaching of Jesus (and John?) therefore belongs to the kingdom of heaven. According to the prophecy of v. 16, this gospel means the elimination of death. The place names imply that Jesus' activity attracts not only Israelites but also non-Israelites as well. Both *Syria* (v. 24) and the *Decapolis* (v. 25) are composed of non-Israelite territory and non-Jewish populations. From the beginning of his ministry Jesus heals and preaches to both Jewish and gentile crowds.

Matthew 5:1 may be read either as the first verse of the next literary section or as the conclusion to the previous plot section. Since we are organizing our commentary according to shifts in reading strategy, 5:1 is the last plot notation until 7:28-29. These two inclusive sentences establish for the reader that Jesus speaks both to the disciples and the crowds. Hence the content of the following speech is directed at a universal and multicultural audience. The teaching may be read as representative of Jesus' proclamation. Unlike the preaching of 4:23, the following teaching takes place outside of the confines of the synagogue.

Speech: Jesus Began to Speak, and Taught Them, 5:2–7:27

Explicitly, the SERMON ON THE MOUNT focuses attention on the content of the kingdom of heaven with emphasis on the righteousness that belongs to that kingdom (5:20; 6:1; 6:34). Implicitly, the speech also reveals more to us about the character of Jesus and his relationship to the kingdom of heaven.

The sermon on the mount introduces a new literary technique that is used throughout the Matthean speeches and parables. The narrated story that frames the sermon consistently occurs in the past tense, while the speech itself is stated in the present tense as direct discourse. Because the speech takes up considerable space, our temporal orientation becomes dehistoricized. We experience the sermon as the direct address of Jesus to us. By this technique the text of Matthew invites the reader to take up Jesus' perspective as definitive.

Then He Began to Speak, 5:2-16

5:2-12. Blessed are the poor in spirit. The form of these verses corresponds closely with blessings found in the wisdom writings of JUDAISM (cf. Pss 1:1; 32:1; 41:1; 119:1-2; 128:1; Sir 25:7-11). They have distinct characteristics that mark them, however, as peculiar to the tradition about Jesus. First, vv. 4, 5, 6, 7, 8, and 9 contain a statement of reward in the future in their result clause. By comparison, vv. 3, 10, and 11, which refer to the kingdom of heaven as reward, are present tense. It becomes apparent that these blessings are set in a time that is different from and yet impinges upon the current historical moment. The kingdom of heaven is a present possession and a future reward for God's children. These blessings then, are eschatological and apocalyptic in nature.

Each of the BEATITUDES represents the reality of the kingdom of heaven as opposed to the normal experience of historical reality. The first clause of each beatitude mentions a group of people who, in the ancient world, are not considered at the center of political, religious, or social power. By completing the list with two beatitudes concerning persecution, Jesus makes it clear that these blessings describe the destiny of God's children within the kingdoms of the world. Their comfort is and will be in the kingdom of heaven (v. 12). The beatitudes define the kingdom of heaven from the perspective of God's future.

The time and content of the kingdom flows backwards from an assured future into the oppressive kingdoms of the present. This backward flow may be seen as the epistemological crux of interpretation for understanding the kingdom of heaven in Matthew.

5:13-16. You are the salt of the earth. The concluding verses to this section summarize the current status of God's children and imply a subtle warning about the results of failure to fulfill that status by the negative comparisons involved.

Verse 16 also identifies the work of the children of God with that described for Jesus by 4:16.

Do Not Think That I Have Come to Abolish, 5:17-48

5:17-20. I have come not to abolish but to fulfill. Jesus in v. 17 adopts self-consciously the perspective given by the narrator of the Gospel when citing prophetic passages and when constructing scenes alluding to the Law or Prophets. The following commandments are to be read as expressing the apocalyptic-eschatological filling up of canonical tradition. Verse 17 implies a polemic against a group of opponents that holds that Jesus is guilty of the abolition of God's will as expressed in the Law. Based on v. 20 we may suspect that the group is the scribes and Pharisees. In response to this position, Jesus does not argue, he asserts. He at no point in the subsequent commandments submits his judgment to the structures of scriptural exegesis.

Verse 18 suggests that the Law has a temporal limit at the juncture of the ending of heaven and earth. Jesus later confirms that this temporal limit will be reached (24:35). What transcends the temporal limits of history, however, are the words of Jesus. In this sense they displace the Law, regarded by significant portions of first-century Judaism as eternal. In Matthew the Law may be conceived as limited and bounded by history and therefore subject to the evil powers that are brought to light by the arrival of the kingdom of heaven.

Verse 19 poses the most perplexing problem for interpretation in this paragraph. The reference of *these* is not absolutely clear. It may refer backward to the commandments of the Law indicated by the phrase *not one letter, not one stroke* (v. 18), but that reading is grammatically difficult since no plural noun occurs in the phrase. Or, alternatively, it may refer forward to the subsequent commands of 5:21–7:27. This second reference, while not a common construction, is grammatically possible and may make the best sense of the composition of the speech as a whole.

Jesus uses a form that suggests a curse and a blessing for those who break or keep these commands. The blessing is enhanced status in the kingdom of heaven. The curse is not exclusion from the kingdom, as we might expect, but simply a lower status in the kingdom. If this verse refers to the commands of Jesus, then v. 19 makes clear that the following commands are not entrance requirements but the characteristics of children of God already in the kingdom.

Verse 20 provides a polemical summation and perhaps an indication of the opponent group envisioned by the statement of v. 17. The verse calls to mind 3:7 where the Pharisees were first introduced as those who appeal to their ethnic identity as a means of ensuring their acceptability to God as children of Abraham. Here they are apparently a group who possess some form of recognizable "righteousness" or "justice" that is insufficient for entry into the kingdom of heaven. Verses 17-20 establish a clear division between the presentation of the commands of Jesus and the interpretation of the Law by the Pharisees. The character of this excessive righteousness becomes the focus of the remainder of the speech.

5:21-48. You have heard that it was said. In this section five statements use an antithetical formula on the pattern of 5:21 (Brooks 1987, 74–7). In addition, 5:31 contains a shortened form of the formula that functions to relate the saying on DIVORCE to the previous antithesis on ADULTERY. The saying on divorce occurs as a subpoint to the broader structure of this section. Each of these antitheses is composed of three elements: (1) the thesis, *You have heard that it was said*; (2) a scriptural citation or paraphrase; (3) the antithesis, *But I say to you.* The phrase *to those of ancient times* in the theses of vv. 21 and 33 refers to those who received the written Law on Sinai. The citation of scripture from the Law that follows each thesis in (2), supports this identification.

Since the formula refers to the scene of the giving of the Law on Sinai, then we should recall that scene. In Exodus Moses acts as the spokesperson between God and the people. Exodus 20:1 makes clear that the DECALOGUE is spoken by God.

The implication of Jesus' claim is contained in the third part of each saying. *But, I say to you* shows that he is the originator of what follows. By referring to written Law, rather than ORAL TRADITION or a rabbi's opinion, Jesus emphasizes his identification with God and his independence from the confines of the institutions of normal religion. Official teachers teach with the support of group authority, sanctioned by official and historical institutions, and seek to interpret canonical texts harmoniously. Jesus, on the other hand, appeals to no group authority, has the support of the tradition of no official historical institutions, and interprets the Mosaic Law antithetically.

In three of the sayings that follow this pattern, the antitheses on MURDER, adultery, and love of neighbor, Jesus extends and radicalizes existing interpretation of the Law. In the remaining three, on divorce, oaths, and talion, he utters new commands that may be seen by those outside the kingdom to revoke the plain meaning of canonical Law (Meier 1976, 131–61). Jesus as God-with-us takes his bearings not from Sinai but from the future of the kingdom that is now present. He further commands fellow members of the kingdom to do likewise. Fulfillment for the Gospel of Matthew means perception of the righteousness of God from the perspective of God's future, not the historical past.

Beware of Practicing Your Righteousness, 6:1-34

6:1. For you have no reward. Jesus continues the theme of righteousness begun in 5:20. Unfortunately, this connection is blurred in the NRSV translation *practicing your piety.* The Greek word is the same word translated as *righteousness* in 3:15, 5:20, and 6:34. The Gospel makes no distinction between what we might call acts of piety and other ethical acts.

6:2-18. So whenever you give alms. Jesus discusses almsgiving, PRAYER, and FASTING. Jesus' teaching alters significantly but does not preclude public worship. He offers specific restrictions and a theological principle: that which can be understood as rewardable by public acclaim should be avoided. Matthew 6:2-18 is unique to Jewish and Christian documents of the first century in its designation of God as *your Father who sees in secret.* The inclusion of these teachings here may be motivated out of a polemic against what the author regards as inappropriate worship forms within the community. The attempt seems to be to separate the community's worship from synagogual practice and from non-Jewish types of worship habits being brought into the community by gentiles (vv. 7-8). Jesus' injunctions prohibit the assignment of status to members of the community by virtue of their financial donations, laudatory prayers, or works of pious observance. Thereby, this teaching on righteousness implies social equality between all children of God. Any judgments on individual righteousness are left only to God.

6:19-21. Do not store up treasure on earth. Jesus completes the description of God's righteousness begun antithetically in vv. 1-18. This saying describes the dualism between heaven and earth that determines the allegiance of the heart based upon the storing of treasure.

6:22-23. The eye is the lamp of the body. Jesus describes an interaction between LIGHT and DARKNESS that can result in failure to see. These verses also unify physical and moral perception (Betz 1985, 85). Hence we cannot talk about a physical and spiritual dualism because the kingdom of heaven as indicated by Jesus' speech in Matthew regards the material, physical cosmos as coextensive with the spiritual cosmos. Division occurs not along spiritual/physical lines but along the lines demarcated by light-darkness, good-evil.

6:24. No one can serve two masters. Jesus contrasts two figures as competing lords: God and Mammon (Gk.). Mammon, that is, *wealth*, is depicted as a lord who rules over the things of the earth and (by parallel relation with v. 23) associates with evil and darkness. A person's place within the realm of one lord determines allegiance and the truth of perception.

6:25-34. Do not worry about your life. Jesus concludes with a more precise discussion of this interactive dualism. Verse 25 centers attention on the authority of Jesus, who describes the world as it is to true sight.

Verses 26-32 describe first the created order as apparent to usual mundane perception. By the use of the terminology *his righteousness,* v. 33 makes explicit the connection between the kingdom of God and the righteousness of God. In order for God's righteousness and God's kingdom to be realities that are sought, they must not only be possessions of God but also available for possession by others. Therefore, *his righteousness* indicates that one is to seek both the kingdom and the righteousness that belong to God and comes as a gift from God, the Lord who grants true sight.

The guarantee that follows in v. 34 is not based on the theological idea of the continuity of God with creation, but rather on the radical discontinuity between God and the world, which is in the possession of evil powers. Verse 34 presupposes that the outcome of the confrontation has already occurred in God's future, or kingdom of heaven. It presumes that this confrontation issues in the final victory of God. Once again is visible the remarkable truth that time flows from future to present in the text of Matthew. The righteousness of God is thus both the presupposition and end for the disciple.

The apocalyptic instruction given through Jesus becomes a powerful education. It does not provide the terms of admission into God's rule. Rather it draws the disciple more deeply into the mystery of the kingdom which is a new creation by God and in which the disciple is found. Jesus describes the boundary line between God's kingdom and the kingdom of evil that rules the world. The world thinks possessions and the reduction of anxieties about material security are prime issues in life. The children of the kingdom of God know what lord they serve and recognize that the righteousness that comes from God is their only pursuit. They are guaranteed on the basis of the power-infused authority of Jesus as God-with-us that they will find this righteousness. They are free from the anxieties of this world (see further Humphries-Brooks 1989).

Do Not Judge, 7:1-23

7:1-6. For with the judgment you make you will be judged. Jesus warns against judgment of another within the community. "Brother" is used regularly in Matthew to indicate other members of the community. The Greek word need not refer only to males and the NRSV uses the word *neighbor*. Jesus advises self inspection for HYPOCRISY.

Verse 6 indicates that as readily as Jesus prohibits judging for the sake of exclusion or hierarchy, he also enjoins care over the dispensation of those things that belong to God's kingdom to those incapable of appropriating them. There seems to be an ideological distinction here that may refer to problems of mission. Verses 1-5 refer to intracommunity relationships while v. 6 refers to relationships with those of the outside. It may also refer to those within the community who in the past have proven unworthy or unteachable from the perspective established by Jesus in the Gospel.

7:7-14. Ask and it will be given you. By comparing the positive behavior of broken humanity with God's infinite grace, the saying promises the resolution of judgment between good and evil in the future of God out of which and to which the kingdom of heaven moves. The community must wait in anticipation of that final fulfillment guided by the rule of mutual care embodied in v. 12.

Taken alone, the statement *in everything do to others as you would have them do to you; for this is the law and the prophets,* would miss the reference in the text of the sermon to the inbreaking of the kingdom of heaven, which Jesus claims is the fulfillment of the Law and the Prophets (5:17). The fulfillment is not salvation built out of the ethical systems of the past somehow summarized in a wise saying like v. 12, but rather it is grace that comes from the future into the present as apocalyptic-eschatological event.

7:13-14. Enter through the narrow gate. Verse 12 is situated between the grace of God artfully referred to by a short narrative in vv. 7-11 and the judgment of God clearly demarcated by the saying on the narrow gate in vv. 13-14. This tension reflects a fundamental theological insight in Matthew. The Gospel of Matthew represents throughout its text the problems of life as a child of the kingdom between the CRUCIFIXION and the PAROUSIA. At stake is the child's education to the insight that privilege and status come not from human will or action but only from God.

7:15-23. Beware of false prophets. Jesus warns against false prophets who appeal to his name as a means of validating their mighty words and works. These warnings indicate the probability that the Matthean community experienced divisions created by some type of early preachers and miracle workers. Verse 20 reminds the audience of the charge of John the Baptist in 3:8 to the Pharisees and Sadducees. Apparently, these false prophets are to be understood as a phenomenon parallel to the religious leaders of Jesus' day. They are hypocrites when tested against the content of the commands of Jesus that provide the greater righteousness referred to by 5:20. Jesus, however, remains consistent in his advice. Warning is given, the audience is to recognize them when they come (v. 20). They are to be known by tests of orthopraxy, not orthodoxy, but no action against such individuals is to be taken.

Everyone Then Who Hears, 7:24-27

The concluding simile emphasizes the urgency of the sermon. The speech takes on the significance of life and death. The idea of foundation upon rock will be later exploited by Jesus in 16:13-23 in response to the confession of Simon Peter.

The sermon on the mount becomes the perspective by which all subsequent and previous narrative should be judged. Further, the text is so structured here and throughout the sermon as to press upon the audience the urgency to interpret their own personal and corporate histories from the same perspective. In short, the text presumes that its readers are children of God, members of the kingdom of heaven.

Plot: When Jesus Had Finished Saying These Things, 7:28–10:4

Both Israelites and non-Israelites emerge from the crowds as the supplicants of Jesus. By the end of the section, however, the crowds are narrowly conceived of as Israelite. This careful description of the narrowing of Jesus' ministry exclusively to Israel provides the setting for the speech of 10:5-42 and the plot of chaps. 11–12.

The arrangement of episodes in this section also follows a careful pattern of three sets of three miracle stories divided by three sections that describe Jesus' disciples (Meier 1979, 67–73). The content of each episode shows unnamed supplicants as better examples of faith than the disciples. Careful attention to the details of these miracles demonstrates that the speech or behavior of the supplicant frequently reveals to Jesus the faith of the individual and provides the opportunity for the exercise of Jesus' power.

The Crowds Were Astounded, 7:28-29

Jesus has *authority*. The underlying Greek concept more closely relates to what we might call directed, intelligent power. It is power appropriate to God-with-us (cf. 1:23). The word will be repeated again at the conclusion of the Gospel (28:16).

The crowds have been present all along to hear the sermon. The description of the kingdom provided by Jesus is presented not only to the disciples but to all. Verse 29 compares the speech of Jesus to that of normal human traditioners. The term *their scribes* implies that the crowds are part of Israel's institutions. Nevertheless, the following miracle stories include non-Israelite supplicants who emerge from the crowds.

When Jesus Had Come Down from the Mountain, 8:1-17

This section is composed of three healings: the leper, the centurion's slave, and the mother-in-law of Peter. The stories highlight the faith of the supplicants. The clearest pattern occurs in the healing of the centurion's slave. In vv. 9-13 the text depicts in detail the faith of the centurion by direct speech. The status of the centurion as non-Israel and the status of the ill slave give precise detail to the text and evoke Jesus' amazement. The plot shows Jesus as being educated into the will of God with regard to non-Israelites and slaves. The character, Jesus, perceives the faith of the centurion by his speech.

The centurion, like the leper before him, addresses Jesus as "Lord." Based upon what we have learned from the discussion of lordship in 6:19-34 as well as the use of this term of Jesus only in a confessional sense throughout the whole of the Gospel, we may understand that the use of the term is a sign of faith. The scene shows Jesus applying the perception of the kingdom of heaven to actual events within his ministry.

While the account of the healing of Peter's mother-in-law is not as detailed as the accounts of the two other healings, we may infer that Jesus perceives faith in her, or (on the pattern of the slave) in her behalf.

Now When Jesus Saw Great Crowds, 8:18-22

The kingdom overturns obligations of property and paternity, two of the most revered institutions of the ancient Jewish and non-Jewish world. Jesus addresses the scribe in v. 19, thereby tying the verse to the scribes in 7:29. Further, a disciple, which one we are not told, is given the even more severe injunction in v. 22. We are left not knowing the reaction of either character. We may presume that the disciple is also involved in the following episode.

Jesus himself denies his own status and identifies here for the first time with the homeless and fatherless, that is, those unprotected by the normal social and religious structures of the day. He implies that his disciples must do the same.

And When He Got into the Boat, 8:23–9:8

8:23-27. A windstorm arose on the sea. The miracle of the stilling of the storm provides important contrasts with the previous set of miracles. Unlike the supplicants, the disciples do not emerge from the crowd. Since we do not know the decision reached by the disciple in the previous episode, we cannot yet judge whether Jesus' disciples, like himself, will renounce their status as free householders. Identical to the leper and the centurion, they address Jesus as "Lord." But their address is interpreted by Jesus to mean that they are of *little faith*. Surprisingly Jesus finds faith in great measure among the nameless with little or no status, while the faith of his disciples by comparison is untrustworthy and meager. By asking about the nature of the humanity of Jesus in v. 27, the disciples provide the question which will be answered by the two subsequent miracles. Each depicts more fully the nature of faith and the person of Jesus and his authority.

8:28-34. Two demoniacs met him. The element of faith seems missing altogether in the story of the Gadarene demoniacs. But the demoniacs place this story on a different footing from the others by addressing Jesus as SON OF GOD, the first humans to do so in the Gospel. This story boldly depicts a direct exorcistic battle between the Son of God and the demonic realm. It is therefore an appropriate story here because it prepares for the claim to power by Jesus in the subsequent story.

Unlike the parallel story in Mark, two demoniacs rather than one are mentioned. The text may be constructed in this way under the influence of the Jewish legal provision that requires two witnesses to any act (Deut 19:15). The witness to the Son of God recognizes him by non-human power. In this case, those enslaved to evil recognize their liberator, but fear him as conqueror.

In the ancient understanding, different sorts of demons lived in different places. Some lived in water, others in the air, or on land. All were regarded as striving for power over some host creature. The demons, by asking to be allowed to go into the SWINE, seek to trick Jesus into allowing them to continue their lives. They do not fool Jesus, however. The story might well have elicited humor from the Matthean community if a significant portion were ethnically Jewish and therefore regarded the swine as unclean animals.

The text leaves it to the reader to surmise the townspeople's motivation for asking Jesus to leave. One possible motive that is consistent with the Matthean view of material possession would be that they feared further property destruction. The sanity of two demoniacs is less important than a herd of swine to these people. They do not recognize the presence of God and God's righteousness and do not seek it. The fact that this event occurs in the DECAPOLIS, a collection of non-Jewish cities, also may serve to emphasize that not all mission to the gentiles was necessarily successful. It may constitute part of Jesus' motivation for limiting the mission to Israel in 10:5.

9:1-8. Some people were carrying a paralyzed man. The contrast between the supplicants and the disciples continues in the last miracle of this trio, the healing of the paralytic (9:2-8). The supplicants form the model for faith as opposed to the antimodel provided by the disciples.

Jesus recognizes the faith of the paralytic's friends and heals him. The faith of a group of unknowns becomes the positive model to which we may compare the faith of the disciples. The story also becomes the occasion for Jesus to initiate a dispute with the scribes. Verse 5 makes clear that Jesus has provoked his opponents into an error of theological judgment by forgiving the man's sins. God in the healings of Jesus makes whole a created order broken and diseased by sin, an instrument of evil. Healing is the grace of God expressed through the SON OF MAN as a sign that the power of evil is coming to an end.

As Jesus Was Walking Along, He Saw Matthew, 9:9-17

9:9-13. He got up and followed him. By singling out the tax gatherer by name, the Gospel directs attention to the fact that the kingdom is composed of sinners. Sinners, or the unrighteous are, therefore, those who exceed the righteousness of the PHARISEES (5:20). The author repeatedly ironizes the religious self-consciousness of this group thereby exposing the claim to religious status as part of condemnable hypocrisy.

9:14-17. The disciples of John came to him. The disciples of John concur with the Pharisees in the religious observance of FASTING. Jesus interprets fasting as mourning the unrighteous state of the world prior to the coming of the day of the Lord. The conclusion of Matthew promises Jesus' presence to the end of the age (28:20). Verse 15 indicates, therefore, that the children of the kingdom continually experience the presence of the bridegroom so that signs of mourning such as fasting are inappropriate. This verse adds to the understanding of religious observance begun in 6:1-18 and may suggest that even the type of fasting envisioned by 6:16-18 is unnecessary. The apocalyptic-eschatological context of the audience is the time after the crucifixion and before the coming of the Son of Man to judge, but the wedding feast continues in its celebration because Jesus remains with his community (see also 18:20).

Viewed from the perspective indicated by v. 15, the *both* of v. 17 refers to the *new wine* and *fresh wineskins*. Jesus indicates the radical disjuncture of the kingdom with religious forms that precede it or oppose it historically.

While He Was Saying These Things, 9:18-34

9:18-26. A leader came in and knelt before him. The placement of the story of the woman with hemorrhages within the story of the leader's daughter highlights the contrast of the faith of the woman with the unfaith of the crowds (vv. 22, 25). Matthew lets us infer that Jesus *seeing her* recognizes her faith and comments on it. The Greek text of Matthew does not contain *of the synagogue* (v. 18). The author probably did not intend for this civic leader to be understood as part of that institution. This accords with the overall characterization of Jesus' ministry as moving outside of the confines of traditional synagogue authority and with a general antipathy to the synagogue. The reading of the NRSV in v. 18 seems to be an unfortunate confusion of the Matthean story with the similar story in Mark 5:36.

9:27-31. Two blind men followed him. The idea of seeing as an essential metaphor for faith continues in the story of *the two blind men*. Here Jesus perceives their faith by direct question (v. 28).

9:32-34. A demoniac was brought to him. The following miracle indicates the division that Jesus creates within Israel. It fulfills to some degree the apocalyptic statement of 9:17. The crowds are amazed, while the Pharisees explicitly assign his power to the realm of evil.

Then Jesus Went about All the Cities and Villages, 9:35–10:4

The division described narratively in 9:32-34 now receives direct comment by Jesus in vv. 35-38 and is followed by his own reaction to the situation of a divided Israel in 10:1-4. The two scenes are written in such a way as to relate closely to each other, therefore, we have chosen to include 10:1-4 as the conclusion to the previous plot narrative.

Matthew 9:35 restates 4:23 and acts as an inclusionary summation but unlike 4:23 focusses exclusively on Israel. The text adds the observation that the crowds have no leadership (v. 36). The gathering opposition of the synagogue authorities summarized by their indictment of Jesus in the previous episode shows that they have an unsound eye and cannot discern the kingdom. Therefore, Jesus directly addresses this problem discovered within Israel by summoning THE TWELVE for the first time (10:1-4).

Speech: These Twelve Jesus Sent Out, 10:5-42

Go Nowhere among the Gentiles, 10:5-15

Jesus' ministry as depicted from 4:23 has included both Israel and non-Israel. The sending of the disciples exclusively to Israel is in response to Jesus' discovery of the blindness of its leaders not to a preordained plan of salvation first to Israel and then to non-Israel.

The specific nature of the mission spelled out in vv. 7-8 corresponds precisely to the ministry of Jesus depicted in 4:23–9:35. The disciple reproduces what has been learned observing the master. The prohibition of accepting payment (vv. 8b-10) demands ministry in identification with the homeless SON OF MAN (8:20). Finally, this ministry carries with it both grace and judgment as indicated by vv. 13-15.

See, I Am Sending You out like Sheep, 10:16-23

From v. 16 onward the speech takes on significance beyond the events narrated in the text of the Gospel. Jesus foretells judicial action at the synagogue level and trial by non-Israelite leaders (vv. 17-20). Within the text, however, the disciples are never so treated. Therefore, we may suspect that this prediction applies to some time after the crucifixion and prior to the PAROUSIA. The Matthean community either knows of those who have undergone persecution or anticipates it. Such a mission results in the direct dissolution of family ties.

The limitation of the time frame of the mission to Israelite cities in v. 23 to the time prior to the coming of the Son of Man may indicate that the mission to Israel continues even in the time of the Matthean community. The coming of the Son of

Man is clearly described in Matt 24 and that arrival is different from the beginning of the end time that arrives with the CRUCIFIXION and resurrection of Jesus.

A Disciple Is Not above the Teacher, 10:24-42

10:24-25. If they have called the master Beelzebul. These verses continue the shift of focus for the audience begun by the mention of the Son of Man in v. 23. The reference to *Beelzebul* shows that the conflict with the Pharisees in history is nothing other than a portion of the world-encompassing conflict between the kingdom of heaven and the kingdoms of the world (see 9:34; 12:24). Therefore, the trials depicted in 10:17-23 should be reread not only in reference to the particular politics of sectarianism in the ancient world, but also as a sign of the apocalyptic conflict initiated by the preaching of Jesus and the ministry of his disciples.

10:26-31. Have no fear of them. The following verses depict from various angles the reality of this apocalyptic conflict. An alternative translation of the beginning of this verse reads, "Do not fear them, for there is nothing hidden that will not be *apocalypsed*." The following verses direct attention to appropriate allegiance during the apocalyptic hour. Hope is grounded in the justice and mercy of God as the juxtaposition of judgment and grace makes clear in vv. 28-31; Jesus provides images of God as both righteous judge and caring parent.

10:32-38. Everyone who acknowledges me. Jesus relates the problem of the disintegration of households in normal historical existence to the creation of a new family in the kingdom of heaven. The conflict initiated by the arrival of the kingdom results in both death to normal patriarchal structures and death for the individual. The series begins in v. 35 with relationship to the father and concludes in a manner consistent with the teaching in 9:21-22. The image of cross-bearing in v. 38 results in the conundrum of v. 39. The problem of this paradoxical teaching can be solved only by applying what we learn from the whole of Matthew. Jesus shows that the disciple must identify with Jesus' own destiny in terms of crucifixion and resurrection. The antinomic opposition to death is life given from God.

10:40-42. Whoever welcomes you. Jesus discusses reward as a paradoxical concept. It refers both to the reward of God within God's kingdom as well as the destiny of the prophets and the righteous placed at the mercy of the kingdoms of the world (see 23:29-39). Children of the kingdom cannot avoid the conflict. The conclusion in v. 42 introduces the idea that the emissaries of Jesus have in their OBEDIENCE the sanction of the judgment of the kingdom. It also directs attention to *these little ones*. The reference must be to those supplicants seeking healing from the disciples with the same faith as the supplicants in Matt 8-9. Hence, the rule of justice employed by Jesus as God-with-us (cf. 1:23) in the apocalyptic moment is one of service to those who are at the margins and have no advocate, save God.

Plot and Speech: Now When Jesus Had Finished, 11:1–12:50

With this section the text fully manifests the ambiguity between plot and speech narration in the Gospel of Matthew. Two major movements of plot can be discerned: (1) Jesus teaches and preaches *in their cities* (11:1-30); (2) Jesus disputes with the Pharisees (12:1-50). The activity of Jesus combined with dialogue and brief speeches indicates that the gospel comes to the nation Israel and that both its people and its leaders reject it. The urban mission of Jesus within Israel fails.

The text directs us to perceive within these historical events the confrontation with the kingdom of evil brought about by Jesus. The confrontation becomes apparent through Jesus' interpretation of event. With this section, the strategy of speeches enters into the middle of the strategy of plot in the same way as the kingdom moves into the world. Literary pattern represents world palingenesis (Wilder 1982, 34).

He Went on to Teach, 11:1-30.

11:1-6. He went on to proclaim in their cities. John sends disciples to Jesus to determine if he is the Messiah. Jesus does not affirm the title but answers by a recapitulation of his ministry (vv. 4-6). The language of Jesus echoes Isa 61:1-2, a passage that refers to a prophetic, not messianic, anointing and ministry. The conclusion in v. 6 establishes the basis for reproach and judgment against the cities and against the Pharisees in the following episodes. We are not told of John's reaction to Jesus' reply, rather this episode provides the opportunity for the speech of Jesus that follows.

11:7-30. Jesus began to speak to the crowds. These verses comprise one extended speech by Jesus addressed to the urban Israelite crowds (vv. 7, 20). The first section (vv. 7-19) serves to differentiate the ministry of Jesus from that of John. Verse 11 appears to consign John to the mundane historical plane and to separate him to some degree from those in the kingdom of heaven. Notwithstanding this indication, however, vv. 12-14 show that he is the initiator of the presence of the kingdom of heaven in the historical world and the recipient of the first attacks of violence by those who serve the kingdoms of the world. We should read v. 12 in the context of the arrest, imprisonment, and eventual beheading of John by Herod, who belongs to the urban power elite reckoned throughout Matthew as servants of evil (3:12; 11:2; 14:1-12). Verse 12 interprets the two-level battle observable in the realm of mundane historical existence interpenetrated by the powers of evil aligned against the power of God. In this context, v. 14 indicates that John is a new type of emissary not to be confused with the *prophets and the law* (v. 13).

Verses 16-19 conclude this first section by interpreting the crowds as like children whose whims cannot be satisfied. In the illustration religious and cultural practices related to weddings and funerals are invoked (Jeremias 1972, 160–62). Even though John adopts the perspective that the arrival of the kingdom is a time of repentance and mourning, while Jesus adopts the perspective of the wedding feast, neither the judgment nor the grace of God is acceptable to the crowds.

Therefore, Jesus condemns the cities for their lack of repentance in vv. 20-24. Following this general condemnation Jesus makes clear that only the least powerful of status groups receive the apocalypsis of God. The word translated by the NRSV as *infants* should better be understood from context as the direct antonym to the *wise and intelligent* (v. 25), that is, uneducated and naive. Along with v. 27 this passage makes clear what has been implicit throughout the ministry of Jesus: those who manifest faith to Jesus do so by the gift of God's gracious will and Jesus responds by revealing God to the faith that comes from God.

The idea of education links vv. 28-30 with the preceding section. Jesus addresses the uneducated and naive and offers them a particular education that results in rest. Jesus does not characterize the apocalyptic-eschatological message of the kingdom as difficult or impossible.

Jesus Went through the Grainfields on the Sabbath, 12:1-50

12:1-14. His disciples began to pluck heads of grain. After the aside to those chosen from among the least, we view the unfaith and condemnation of the greatest, the leadership represented by the Pharisees. In two scenes they initiate disputes over proper SABBATH observance (12:1-8; 9-14). In each case Jesus invokes an emergency situation to claim the overturning of mundane sabbath observance as the will of God. The emergency alluded to in these stories is the arrival of the kingdom of heaven. The Pharisees, on the other hand, remain on the side of historical perception with the result that they make plans to kill Jesus.

12:15-21. Many crowds followed him. The narra-tor interrupts the disputes with the Pharisees with a citation of Isa 42:1-4. The quotation shows that the future of the kingdom of heaven lies with the gentiles. The interruption recalls earlier sections of Matthew that imply that non-Israel is included in the mission of Jesus. In this regard it may well be that v. 15 refers to "many" who follow him (instead of *many crowds*) and that we are to understand this as a reference to predominantly non-Israelite groups. Reliable ancient manuscripts do not contain the word "crowds," which in this section of Matthew has been used to refer to Israelites. Verse 16, therefore, indicates that during this special period of Jesus' ministry, the mission to non-Israel should remain secret.

12:22-45. By Beelzebul this fellow casts out demons. The concluding episode in this series of disputes with the Pharisees exposes once and for all their allegiance to and determination by the powers of evil. Jesus responds to their accusation by an extended speech (vv. 25-45). Jesus is in the business of destroying the kingdom of Satan (vv. 25-28). Underlying the story of the strong man bound (v. 29) is an apocalyptic perspective of the world possessed by evil powers. Jesus interprets his role as miracle worker as robbing those powers of their control over human beings. The Pharisees oppose such activity as impious because it violates the sabbath. By refusing to recognize the power of God in the action of Jesus, religious leaders judge themselves. By accusing Jesus, the Pharisees reveal their true origin. Such misnaming of powers is unforgivable (vv. 32; 33-37).

Verses 38-45 pronounce the eschatological judgment of the Son of Man against the Pharisees. The sign of Jonah indicates the time between the death and resurrection of Jesus. It also links Jesus in his death to the Son of Man, who will judge.

The references to Nineveh and the queen of the South enhance the theme of the discovery of faith among non-Israel and women begun in the genealogy.

The story of the unclean spirit indicates that those whose origin is in the power of evil rather than in God, condemn themselves to a descending cycle of absorption into the realm of Satan (vv. 43-45). What begins as religious propriety may end in acts of evil. The religious leaders are this type of person. They oppose Jesus on the historical and religious plane and in doing so dwell more and more radically and enslave themselves more and more surely to the kingdom of Satan until there is no escape. Their plot to kill Jesus referred to in 12:14 is only the historical manifestation of the power that controls their lives and destiny.

The speech concludes with positive instructions about Jesus' own household (vv. 46-50). By the use of terminology derived from family relationships, Jesus throughout Matthew develops a model of the community of the kingdom of heaven that is both similar to and distinct from patriarchal families. The will of God determines the reality of family relationships rather than allegiances based on blood or ethnic ties. Consistently in Matthew all status markers normal in human society are transcended or negated by participation in the kingdom of heaven.

Speech: He Told Them Many Things in Parables, 13:1-52

Two small movements of plot divide this speech into four episodes in which Jesus' speech is directly addressed to two different character groups (Bauer 1988, 131). In addition, the four episodes are interrupted by a citation of scripture by the narrator. The integration of plot with speech represents the permeation of the current historical process by the kingdom of heaven. Matthew 13:52 states the purpose of the speech: to train scribes for the kingdom of heaven. As we explore this speech, therefore, we need to be aware that here we have evidence of the process of training for the kingdom as well as its content.

A Sower Went out to Sow, 13:1-9

The scene of the first parable by Jesus in Matthew links it closely with the preceding narrative. Jesus addresses the parable to the crowds. Given the previous section of narrative, the setting implies that these crowds are predominantly Israelite. The emphasis of the parable seems to fall on the miraculous production of the seed (v. 8).

Why Do You Speak to Them in Parables?, 13:10-23

13:10-17. To you it has been given. The PARABLES divide the disciples from the crowds. Israel has been judged first by the miracle-working activity of Jesus and now is being judged by the parables. The judgment of parable-telling comes in revealing the fact of nonperception of the kingdom of heaven (v. 13). Further, Jesus himself interprets this judgment as a fulfillment of the prophetic judgment of Isa 6:9-10, a prophecy that specifically indicts the rulers and people of Jerusalem for their refusal to repent. The parables act as an eschatological sealing of the consciousness of the people for judgment by God.

13:18-23. Hear the parable of the sower. While the parable appears to emphasize the miraculous gift of an excessive harvest, Jesus provides to the disciples a specific key to interpret the parable at a deeper level: the different types of soils represent different types of people and their response to the word. In each case the opposition to the word is connected to the kingdom of Satan. Verse 19 connects it to the *evil one* himself. Verse 20 connects it to persecution; the source of persecution is not only human institutions but also the lord served by those institutions. Verse 22, which identifies the cares and wealth of the world as the seduction away from the word, may be read with reference to 6:24 and understood to indicate that wealth is under the control of Mammon (cf. 6:24), a servant of the *evil one* as well.

According to Jesus, the key to understanding the parable is the ability to see a two-level conflict in the present moment. The conflict on the surface may appear to be a historical one: normal worldly cares, greed, and persecution destroy one's attention to the word of salvation to humans. But more, all of these are weapons in the struggle of the kingdom of the evil one against the incoming kingdom of heaven. This understanding cannot be deduced from the parable itself, which emphasizes the miraculous growth of the kingdom, but only from the proper perspective provided by Jesus to those to whom the secrets of the kingdom have already been given. The trained scribe adopts the apocalyptic perspective of Jesus in order to properly interpret the parables at all levels.

He Put before Them Another Parable, 13:24-34

Jesus addresses the three parables that follow the interpretation to the crowds once more (v. 34). Since they are addressed to the crowds composed of urban Israel who are being judged by the parables, no interpretation of these parables is provided. We shall wait to offer an interpretation of these parables from Jesus' perspective when the text returns to these parables at v. 36.

This Was to Fulfill, 13:35

The narrator interrupts the development of the parable speech of Jesus with an interpretative citation of prophetic scripture. The citation comes from Ps 78:2 and is traditionally attributed to ASAPH who according to 2 Chr 29:30 was a seer or prophet. According to Ps 78:2-4 the parable reveals what previously has been hidden. In Matthew, Jesus uses parables on the one side to judge the crowds and on the other to instruct the disciples and through them all members of the kingdom of heaven.

Then He Left the Crowds, 13:36-52

13:36-43. Explain to us the parable. Jesus explains in allegorical fashion the parable of 13:24-30. The key to interpretation remains an apocalyptic-eschatological perspective. Judgment is reserved for the Son of Man who is both the sower of good seed and the judge at the end of the age. The interpretation of Jesus makes clear that his ministry to Israel as the Son of Man forms the basis for justice in the final time. The justice of God assigns proper place to those found as children of the kingdom or children of the evil one at the end time.

13:31-32. The kingdom of heaven is like a mustard seed. At this point we return to the earlier parables (13:24-34), since we now have a pattern of interpretation established by the presentation of the text. While Jesus himself does not provide an interpretation, the text presumes that we can provide one based upon the method of Jesus. The parable of the mustard seed, therefore, may be interpreted as referring to the planting of the kingdom of heaven through the ministry of Jesus. The result is an unexpected home for the homeless (v. 32).

13:33. The kingdom of heaven is like yeast. The parable of the leaven breaks the pattern of its group of parables since planting is not involved. Jesus is compared to a woman, or perhaps the female character is God. The emphasis falls on the miracle of leavening. The image indicates the active nature of God's kingdom through Jesus. As the depiction of the miracles of Jesus in Matthew makes clear, the kingdom of heaven is not simply beset and beleaguered by the Evil One and its children, it also is in the business of claiming territory for itself.

13:44-45. The kingdom of heaven is like treasure. This pair of parables emphasizes the inherent and almost irrational value of the kingdom; the emphasis in both falls on the activity of the individual in selling all that he has for the sake of the treasure of the kingdom. Jesus provides a parabolic expression of the activity he advocated in 6:19-34. The theme will be further developed in 19:16-29.

13:47-50. The kingdom of heaven is like a net. The final parable of the speech returns to the theme of eschatological judgment already emphasized by the parables of the sower and the weeds among wheat. Here, presumably since Jesus is speaking only to the disciples and through them to the audience, parable and apocalyptic-eschatological interpretation occur together.

13:51-52. Have you understood all this? The parable discourse concludes with a dialogue between Jesus and the disciples. Verse 52 marks the purpose of the discourse as the training of scribes for the kingdom of heaven. The simile invites an apocalyptic-eschatological reading, first, because of its place within the parable chapter. The reversal of normal historical sequence in the phrase *what is new and what is old* points in the same direction. The perspective induced by the speeches of Matt 13 begins with the new: the inbreaking of the kingdom of God into the world. God's arrival creates a division within humanity through the parables of Jesus. Humans are being judged by the ministry of Jesus who is already the coming Son of Man. From the Matthean perspective, the division of humanity occurs for the first time in the life of Jesus. The final process of judgment will not be complete until some point in the historical future.

Plot and Speech: When Jesus Had Finished These Parables, 13:53–17:27

The plot focuses on the reaction to Jesus' person and message on the part of three groups of characters: crowds, Pharisees, and disciples.

He Came to His Hometown, 13:53-58

NAZARETH rejects Jesus and on the basis of this lack of faith he performs no miracle (v. 58). The story implies that the rejection comes out of the towns-people's association with the synagogue. They seek to understand Jesus as part of a human household, composed of his mother and brothers (v. 55). By depending on a social perspective, the people of Jesus' hometown become offended at him. According to Jesus, national identity, ethnicity, and association with family prohibits the perception generated by God's kingdom (v. 57). After this episode, Jesus moves outside of normal social and religious institutions for the proclamation of his message.

Herod the Ruler Heard about Jesus, 14:1-12

HEROD the ruler along with his wife Herodias brings about the death of JOHN THE BAPTIST. Herodias's daughter, unnamed by the narrator, has no real power vis-à-vis her mother. She is both an object of her stepfather's lust and the means to accomplish Herodias's murderous intent. The story does not portray the daughter as culpable for her actions. She extends the Matthean theme of the victimization of children begun in the infancy narrative. The text exposes the stupidity of male pride and the false valuing of personal status by showing Herod's adherence to a frivolous oath (see 5:37) and acquiescence to her unjust request so as to preserve his personal power in the eyes of those assembled. Among the kings of the world, children, especially female children, become tools instead of persons.

Jesus Withdrew to a Deserted Place, 14:13-21

The miracle of the feeding of the five thousand and the walking on the water occur together in all four Gospels. The association probably was influenced by the similar stories about MOSES, ELIJAH, and ELISHA found in the Jewish scriptures. Matthew, however, contains its own peculiar emphases. The focus in each story becomes the disciples and their faith.

Whereas previous miracles have emphasized the marginality of the supplicants, this miracle by its setting depicts the advent of the kingdom as outside of the cities, synagogues, and households of Israel. The enactment of the feeding miracle before the crowds reflects compassion. The crowds' eagerness to follow Jesus and the presence among them of the sick implies that Jesus recognizes faith from their action.

The disciples and their response become the focus by virtue of their request of Jesus. The disciples reflect a lack of faith since they judge according to mundane historical needs and satisfaction of those needs (cf. Patte, 209–11). Jesus' blessing directed toward the heavens draws attention to the power of God expressed through the miracle.

Jesus Made the Disciples Get into the Boat, 14:22-36

The first scene depicts Jesus walking on the water to the disciples who as a group fail to recognize him and take him to be a ghost. The motif of their lack of discernment implicit in the previous story becomes explicit.

Peter acts both as an individual and as a representative of the Twelve. Jesus recognizes and emphasizes his lack of faith (v. 31). His behavior remains consistent with the previous behavior of the disciples in a similar situation at 8:26. The author depicts Peter throughout the Gospel as undependable and doubting.

The Pharisees and Scribes Came from Jerusalem, 15:1-20

Jesus condemns the PHARISEES for substituting their will for God's will. Jesus regards their interpretation as opposed to God's commandments. Verses 6-9 indicate that such a tradition is a human, not divine, institution and imply that their tradition antithetically opposes the word of God. For Jesus the word of God means the will of God revealed to be righteous and just in the eschatological time of Jesus' ministry. The function of the parable like those of Matt 13 must be to judge the crowd.

Beginning with v. 12, Jesus interprets the parable of 15:11. The scene shows that the disciples have not understood the speech of Matt 13, nor have they understood the actions of Jesus. They as yet lack faith that comes from the perspective of the kingdom. In Matthew faith and understanding appear to be two aspects of the same gift from God.

Jesus Left That Place and Went Away to Tyre and Sidon, 15:21-39

15:21-28. A Canaanite woman started shouting. The use of *Canaanite* rather than SYROPHONECIAN as in Mark 7:26 emphasizes that the woman comes from an ethnicity traditionally an enemy of Israel worthy of extermination (see Josh 12:20). The story of the Canaanite woman shows that Jesus himself can initially fail to perceive faith and thereby refuse access to the kingdom to those to whom he was sent. Jesus, an Israelite man, allows himself to be duped by the appearance of this supplicant as a woman and a non-Israelite.

Jesus refuses to hear her petition and strives to silence her by ignoring her (v. 23a). But the woman demands a hearing for her daughter's need. The disciples become upset at her noisy importunity and plead for Jesus to *send her away* (v. 23b). The male householders strive to silence the supplicating woman and assign her to the margins.

At v. 24 Jesus finally engages in conversation with her after reiterating his statement of mission in the same words as 10:5. Matthew depicts Jesus' earlier mission up to that point as universal. During that mission Jesus recognizes and heals women supplicants from Israel as well as men of both Israel and non-Israel (Matt 8–9). Here, for the first time, Jesus confronts a non-Israelite woman.

Jesus' journey to TYRE AND SIDON indicates an intention to transcend the borders of the Israelite homeland with his mission. Therefore, on the basis of the previous behavior of Jesus and the development of plot in this section, we might anticipate that here Jesus himself will move beyond the ethnic and national boundaries imposed since 10:5. Such a return would confirm the earlier indications in Matthew of a universal mission.

The speech and action of Jesus do not accord with either his own actions or speeches elsewhere and therefore disconfirms our expectations. The woman, however, proves to be a better theologian than Jesus. She willingly identifies her utter abasement as a crumb-lapping dog and refers to the "Lords' table" from which she begs scraps. This phrase is usually translated as *masters' table* thereby referring to the people of Israel who are also understood as the *children* in Jesus' response of v. 26. Such a reading is difficult within the larger context of Matthew since the narrative previously condemned the people and leadership of Israel as unrepentant.

The woman appears, at one level, to argue a truism—dogs eat crumbs from their masters' table. At a second level, however, the woman's statement implies a confession of faith. In Matthew the singular *Lord* occurs as a confessional title used by supplicants of Jesus. Jesus recognizes in this title the presence of faith. The woman uses this form of supplication in vv. 22, 25, 27. By using the plural the woman shows that she recognizes not only Jesus but also God as her lord. She understands the table as the table of the final banquet presided over by God and the SON OF MAN, that includes all despite accidents of ethnicity. Her interpretation accords with Jesus' own interpretation of the faith of the centurion in 8:10-13. Her understanding can come only from God.

Jesus pronounces her faith and heals her daughter. The author does not shrink from showing Jesus as learning from a woman of an inappropriate ethnicity. Both status as woman and as non-Israel are highlighted in order to show the apocalyptic faith that comes from the kingdom of heaven and that destroys all historical claims to prerogatives within the kingdom. Even Jesus in this Gospel can be educated by such faith.

15:29-39. He passed along the Sea of Galilee. The following episodes show Jesus re-initiating a self-conscious ministry to gentiles after the education by the woman (cf. Gundry 1982, 317–22). Galilee has already been associated with the gentiles in 4:13-18. The healing ministry and the feeding miracle apparently take place on the eastern shore of the Sea of Galilee in the general area of the DECAPOLIS. *Magadan* (v. 39) is on the western shore. The sentence *And they praised the God of Israel* (v. 31) indicates clearly that the crowds are non-Israel. Jesus fulfills the prophecy of Isa 61:1-2 specifically for a non-Israelite crowd. The miracle of the feeding of the four thousand contrasts with the earlier feeding of the five thousand performed for a predominantly Israelite crowd.

The Pharisees and Sadducees Test Jesus, 16:1-12

Within the plot of Matthew this episode repeats in an abbreviated form the episode found in 12:38-42. Therefore, the episode offers another opportunity for Jesus to condemn the religious leadership. He does so as the Son of Man who will die. Implied is the eschatological perception that the crucifixion and resurrection of Jesus function not only to include children in the kingdom of heaven, but also to judge. Matthew presents Jesus as Son of Man who judges: first, during his historical ministry to the cities of Israel; second, by his death and resurrection; and third, in his PAROUSIA. Such a rich conceptualization of the Son of Man indicates the fluidity with which the author discerns the movement of time and event along spatial axes. The future of God erupts in Matthean narrative where God wills it regardless of the clocks of historical causality. Such thought here and elsewhere proves disorienting to those of us accustomed to narratives that express a worldview that privileges historical sequence and causality. The disciples represent the historical viewpoint as well. They lack faith (v. 8) and perception (v. 11). They finally gain some understanding (v. 12).

Jesus Asked His Disciples about the Son of Man, 16:13–17:23

The previous episodes introduce an extended section composed of three episodes in which Jesus directly teaches the disciples about his person and destiny. Jesus connects the titles, Son of God and Son of Man. Peter and the other disciples with him fail to understand Jesus. Ultimately, they are pronounced faithless. Ironically as Jesus reveals himself fully to them the disciples' own lack of faith becomes apparent.

16:13-27. You are the Messiah. To Peter, first, and then later to all of his disciples, Jesus gives power of interpretation and adjudication (16:19 and 18:18). This development is surprising, since PETER and THE TWELVE have yet to be shown to be trustworthy.

Peter—whom Jesus calls *rock* (for the foundation of the community in the eschatological moment)—is given power to *bind* and *loose*, which is understood to be the power to interpret the kingdom of heaven on earth. He is the chief scribe in a school of scribes.

In what sense Peter or Peter's confession constitutes the *rock* on which the community is built remains ambiguous in the text. The ambiguity may be due to the fact that the following scene de-centers and uproots Peter and his tradition from any claim to authoritative hegemony over the Matthean community.

The bestowal of authority is followed immediately by the condemnation of Peter (vv. 21-23). The juxtaposition creates ironic tension. In v. 23 Jesus places Peter in the same relationship to the kingdom of heaven as the powerful urban elites. He is to be found with Satan aligned against God. As elsewhere in Matthew, Jesus knows this not by superhuman insight but by what Peter says. Peter expresses misperception—the wrong epistemology—in v. 22. The condemnation of Peter indicates that the confession of v. 16 is only partial and inadequate from the viewpoint of Jesus and the author. Indeed it is dangerous. Jesus is not the Messiah that Peter would like, the David who will restore Israel to its national independence, but rather he is the Son of God and Son of Man who judges and who dies for the entire world. Peter seeks the kingdom of humans dominated by the evil one and opposed to the kingdom of heaven whose agent is God-with-us. Peter is christologically, theologically, and politically in error.

17:1-21. Jesus took with him Peter and James and his brother John. The section demonstrates who Jesus is and the disciples' failure to understand his identity as the Son of God who is also the Son of Man who will suffer. This failure of perception results in their condemnation as *faithless and perverse* (v. 17).

The implicit comparison between Jesus and MOSES and ELIJAH established in the miracles of the feeding and the walking on the water becomes explicit here. In addition the themes of the lack of faith and understanding of Peter and the other disciples continue. Peter wants to engage in a building program (v. 4) rather than listen and must be silenced from heaven by the same words heard at Jesus' baptism. Jesus supersedes the authority of Moses and Elijah. Their appearances here may represent the impending end of time. Both were regarded by some segments of Judaism as returning from heaven in the final days prior to the DAY OF THE LORD (cf. Mal 4).

As in the previous section, a warning about the earthly destiny of the Son of Man follows direct revelation from God about who Jesus is as the Son of God (v. 9). The disciples again indicate their lack of insight because they ask about Elijah, rather than addressing the more apparent issue of the identity and destiny of Jesus (vv. 10-12).

Verses 14-21 conclude this section and focus attention on the disciples' lack of faith. Jesus condemns them as a group in terms almost identical to the condemnation of the Pharisees and Sadducees in 16:4. Supplicants, however, have faith. The disciples cannot heal because of their little faith (v. 21).

17:22-23. As they were gathering in Galilee, Jesus said. These verses contain a concluding teaching about the Son of Man in Galilee. They provide an inclusion with 16:13 in which Jesus answers his own question of his identity and destiny. Furthermore, the episode is written so that when we come to the gathering of the eleven disciples in Galilee after the resurrection (28:16-20) we will be immediately reminded of the disciples and their distress at Jesus' prophecy. As is shown in the teaching about the Son of Man who must suffer and die, the disciples lack the faith to understand Jesus and his destiny. The faithless disciples gathered in Galilee are greatly distressed. Later in Galilee some will doubt (28:17).

The Children Are Free, 17:24-27

The episode singles out Peter. Jesus frees the children of the kingdom from religious obligation and sees the Temple tax as imposed by the kings of the earth. A historical problem is addressed, as well as the true origin and allegiance within the kingdom. The miracle places the provision in the hands of God and conforms to the teaching on Mammon in 6:19-34. Hence the plot of Matthew provides concrete examples of the principles articulated in the speeches of Jesus that describe the constitution and politics of the kingdom.

Verse 27 makes clear that violent resistance must not be the course of action for the child. To refuse to pay would align Jesus with political seditionists that might use the power of Mammon withheld from the Temple officials for the purpose of bringing down the kings of the world. Implicit here is the theological and political principle that the means can never justify ends. The use of worldly power necessarily brings enslavement to the powers of the world.

Speech: Who Is the Greatest in the Kingdom of Heaven? 18:1-35

Matthew 13:52–17:27 contains little or no plot advancement. Therefore, the movement to the fourth extended speech by Jesus fuses without disruption into the preceding section. The immediately preceding episode provides an excellent introduction to the speech since it highlights children as free within the kingdom and the world. Literarily, the speech represents an artistic use of both dialogue and parable. It is organized into two parts. The first answers, *Who is the greatest in the kingdom of heaven?* (vv. 1-5). The second explores the question of how the *little ones* are to be treated (vv. 6-35). The weight of the speech rests on the last point. Thereby, Jesus shifts the attention of the audience from rank in the kingdom to service and relationship within the community or *ekklēsia*.

Matthew infuses ecclesiology with theology. Unlike the narrative section that precedes it, direct reflection on the person of Jesus, christology, is absent or at best only implied in the fact that he is the speaker. Rather, the entire focus is on the kingdom of heaven, the master who deploys it, and the relationship of the children of that kingdom in their historical gathering to one another. In this speech Jesus teaches about living in mundane human community as children of God. Politics becomes focussed through ethics.

He Called a Child, 18:1-5

Jesus presents for the first time an expanded teaching on the understanding of status within the kingdom. While Jesus has used diminutive terms such as "children," "little ones," and "naive ones" in prior contexts, he here presents a coherent view.

In Matthew children are characters of the lowest and most vulnerable status. They never speak in Matthew. Herod murders them. Those who are healed are healed at the request of adults of higher status. If we understand the daughter of Herodias to be still a child, then we must also recognize sexual abuse implied as an aspect of children's status in Matthew. No children, except Jesus himself, receive names in Matthew.

This representation accords well with the place of children in the ancient world. While there is some evidence for the romanticization of children in the art and literature of Hellenistic culture, such ideas appear to have had little effect on the treatment of children. Infanticide, for example, was advocated by many moral philosophers as a means of eliminating unwanted or handicapped children. How common the practice was, we have no way of knowing. Similar to our society, children in the ancient world have minimal civil rights and remain completely under the domination of their fathers. Children are regarded as naive, uneducated, and foolish. No philosopher or wise man would seek to emulate them. Jesus appears to be unique in the ancient world in his valuation of children as exemplars for the life of a community.

These points should help reveal to us the uncomfortable irony that the ancient audience would likely feel at this episode. The disciples are free male householders who receive the instruction of Jesus. They should be the wise and pious models of the kingdom. Jesus instructs them to become like the child. The aspiration to humility runs opposite to the desire for knowledge and maturity. The kingdom of heaven requires the direct reversal of status aspirations.

If You Put a Stumbling Block before One of These, 18:6-35

Jesus constructs an answer to a question not asked by the disciples. By this rhetorical device he shifts attention to the question of relationships within the kingdom of heaven and its specific historical manifestation, the community. These verses fall into three sections: vv. 6-9; 10-14; 15-35. The extensive discussion of the last section indicates the emphasis of the speech that moves from the general conceptuality of the kingdom to the specifics of individual religious communities. As we interpret these verses we should remember that the teaching of vv. 2-5 shows that we should presuppose a community in which all members have the status of children and therefore no hierarchical roles may be assigned.

18:6-9. Woe to the world. Jesus warns against being the cause of temptation to other members of the kingdom in graphic terms of eschatological judgment.

18:10-14. Take care. Jesus offers the positive alternative to this negative behavior. The shepherd's behavior in the parable beginning in v. 12 constitutes foolishness. By leaving the ninety-nine on the mountain he endangers his entire livelihood. Seen from the perspective of the kingdom, however, the shepherd represents God's care for the lost.

18:15-35. If another sins against you. The third section follows logically and forcefully on these first two principles. Verses 15-20 apply in a practical case the principle enunciated by the parable. The reader of the English text has the disadvantage of a language that makes no formal distinction between you (pl.) and you (sing.). In Greek, however, there is a clear distinction. Verses 15-17 in Greek use you (sing.). Hence, they should be read as referring to the behavior of the one wronged toward the one doing the wrong. The conclusion of the process in v. 17 allows for the entire community to be brought together to settle the dispute. The outcome of the process, should it not result in reconciliation, is that the sinner be regarded as a gentile *tax collector*. Given the depiction of these groups in Matthew as those most likely to hear the message of the gospel then the offended party is being instructed to consider the sinning community member as a mission field for the gospel. Matthew provides no basis for the practice of excommunication or exclusion from the community by a hierarchical collegium, group of elders, or those who appeal to the traditional lineage of the apostles (cf. Thompson 1970).

Verses 19-20 support this interpretation. They return to the use of the you (pl.) in reference to the disciples and/or the community envisioned as the audience of the speech. This "you" group is the group described earlier in v. 4 as having the status of children. Hence, claim to status privilege would remove one from the presence of either the Father or Jesus and withhold divine sanction for the decision of the community. Verse 20 indicates the presence of Jesus as God-with-us (cf. 1:23) to guarantee the status-free structure of the community. In this context, Jesus bestows anew the privilege of judgment and interpretation earlier granted to Peter. This time, however, the unity of the speech makes it clear that such privilege depends upon the perception by the disciple of her/his own dependence on God and equal status before God with all other members of the community. The view of the historical church that emerges from Matt 18 therefore is a congregation of equals whose access to God and Jesus depends upon their continued affirmation of their nonhierarchical, noncentric status.

Peter presses the teaching further. Does he genuinely desire a mathematics of GRACE? If so, then he adopts a casuistic stance already condemned by Jesus in the Pharisees. He displays a behavior appropriate only to the leadership of their synagogues, not to the leadership of the community. The parable that Jesus tells to conclude this speech indicates the theological basis of equality among all children in the kingdom. It should be read according to the apocalyptic-eschatological method taught in Matt 13. From the perspective of God's judgment, the child of the kingdom should extend to those sinning against itself the same mercy extended by God to the child, otherwise it condemns itself to the judgment of God. The child of the kingdom must be merciful, as God is merciful, must be perfect as God is perfect, or it transgresses the delicate balance between grace and justice advocated so eloquently by Jesus. Such a balance can be seen only from the eschatological perspective of God's future coming in the Son of Man, whose apocalypse is now in Jesus.

Plot and Speech: When Jesus Had Finished Saying These Things, 19:1-29

In the following episodes Jesus eliminates claims to special religious and social privileges claimed through Israelite custom and law by the male heads of households.

Some Pharisees Came to Test Him, 19:1-12.

19:1-9. Is it lawful for a man to divorce? Jesus protects women from invidious impoverishment by males and conforms to the overall concern of the text for the marginal. The scene applies the apocalyptic-eschatological perspective to the problem of DIVORCE. Jesus concerns himself only with the practice of men unilaterally divorcing their wives as provided by Mosaic Law. He does not discuss the relatively modern phenomenon of a mutual decision to dissolve a household.

By combining quotations from Gen 1:27 and 2:24, Jesus reveals the intention of God at creation to be for males to leave their family and property for their wives. This matrilocality constitutes the opposite of property relationships of the first century. The law that allows for divorce was given by Moses, not God, because of the formation of patriarchal marriages after the advent of SIN. Even within the current patrilocal practice, a man who has undertaken responsibility for a household may not abandon it, according to Jesus. Male householder property rights that include possession of their wives come not from God, but from humans.

Only in the case of *unchastity* (v. 9) may men unilaterally dissolve their marriages. The exception is obscure since the Greek word used refers to almost any sort of undesirable sexual activity. It may refer to marriages discovered to be incestuous by first-century Judaism but allowable in the non-Jewish world (see 5:31; Meier 1976, 147–50; Baltensweiler 1967, 88–100). Therefore, the exception might refer particularly to problems among non-Jewish proselytes within the Matthean community.

19:10-12. It is better not to marry. The disciples apparently find the elimination of their privileges in marriage so harsh as to be almost unbearable. Jesus, having eliminated the preeminent place of the Israelite male as disposer of household property including women, further indicates that maleness is not essential for inclusion within God's kingdom. Infertile, phallically disempowered males may be as blessed by God as others. Such a teaching contradicts directly the prescriptions of the Law that refuse a EUNUCH access to the congregation of Israel (Deut 23:1). Such prescriptions reserve full righteousness before God only for "normal" phallically capable males. Jesus aligns himself, rather, with the prophetic tradition of Isaiah that foresees the eschatological time as a time when eunuchs will enter the congregation of Israel (Isa 56:3-5). Jesus sees that time as now. Therefore, women and nonmales hold as high a position of privilege in the kingdom as males.

Then Little Children Were Being Brought to Him, 19:13-15

The immediately preceding episode shows the disciples to be fixed on their own privilege as male householders so as to exclude the marginal. In this episode, in spite of the instruction of Matt 18, they still are unable to accept and act upon the kingdom as proclaimed by Jesus. Therefore, he must instruct them again in speech that eloquently testifies to God's concern for the powerless. "Suffer the little children to come unto me and forbid them not for of such is the Kingdom of heaven" (KJV). By its forceful simplicity the theological and social radicality of this verse eludes its appropriation by the original readers and by all subsequent readers of Matthew.

What Good Deed Must I Do to Have Eternal Life?, 19:16-29

The third episode concludes a consideration of the situation of the male householder in the kingdom of heaven. Two conversations occur: one, between Jesus and a young man (vv. 16-22); the second, between Jesus and the disciples led by Peter (vv. 23-29).

19:16-22. Why do you ask? In the first conversation, the dispersal of material wealth for the poor is placed at the end of a discussion of righteousness according to the Law. Jesus' statement in v. 21 epitomizes the demand of God given through Moses in Deut 15:4-5. This scripture describes the sabbatical year of the remission of debts in Israel. God guarantees that there will be no poor "if only you will obey the Lord your God by diligently observing this entire commandment that I command you today" (see also Lev 25). In the historical field, the keeping of the Law, as indicated by the claim of vv. 18-20, must include the elimination of the poor in Israel. The continued presence of the poor should be regarded as a sign of the unrighteousness of those who have possessions. The young man cannot go this far (v. 22).

19:23-29. It will be hard for a rich man. More than the historical field emerges here. The teaching of 6:19-34 illuminates the underlying cause of the young man's failure as being in the lordship of Mammon. Only the powerful lordship of God can overcome economic investiture. The disciples recognize that the problem exists not only for the extremely wealthy but for householders such as themselves (v. 25). Their reply to the teaching parallels their response in 19:10. They resist applying the perspective of the kingdom to their own status.

Peter seeks to identify himself and his brother disciples with the homelessness of Jesus (v. 27). Nevertheless he remains fixated on hierarchical privilege ensured by eschatological reward. Jesus' answer deftly avoids promising material hierarchy by leaving unspecified the nature of the hundredfold reward (v. 29; cf. Mark 10:30).

Verse 28 seems to promise the power of judgment to the apostles at the PAROUSIA. The immediate context strongly circumscribes understanding this verse as guaranteeing privilege. The parable that follows (20:1-16) further arrests the plot and opens a window into the organization of the kingdom as a uniform field infused by God's justice and grace. Should we not also read irony here, since the disciples are given power over only the judgment of Israel patriarchally arranged in tribes. This patriarchy is no longer valid in the kingdom in which only the Son of Man exercises universal judgment (Matt 24–25).

Speech: But Many Who Are First Will Be Last, 19:30–20:16

The parable compares the kingdom of heaven to a *householder who*. According to the interpretative perspective taught in Matt 13, we should understand the householder either to be God or Jesus as the Son of Man/Son of God. Jesus draws on prophetic teaching tradition by reference to the figure of the *vineyard* as a figure of Israel's relationship to God (Isa 5).

The householder promises those hired at nine o'clock to pay *whatever is just* (v. 4). The question of righteousness thereby becomes the focus of the parable. Verse 8 provides the setting for the conflict with which the parable ends. It provides those hired first with the opportunity to see the act of payment. This act of payment defines within the plot of the parable what is just.

No hierarchy of merit exists among the workers at the conclusion of the parable. Jesus depicts economic relationships within the kingdom of heaven as a uniform field of power whose nature is utterly nonhierarchical. The choice implied in v. 13 is whether or not to remain in the harvest field.

Verse 15, "Am I not allowed to do what I want with what is mine? Or is your eye evil because I am good?" (author trans.) refers to teaching by Jesus found in 6:23 where the same phrase *your eye is evil* denotes a connection between physical sight and moral judgment. The author ends the parable with a question about the appropriate judgment to be made.

In v. 16 Jesus echoes 19:30. In what way did the last become first and the first last? Clearly, it was not in the reward granted: all are equal. Rather, v. 16 forces us to reread v. 8, to stand with those hired first, and to decide about the justice of the kingdom of heaven.

The last receive their wages for the day. A *denarias* constitutes the amount necessary to sustain a worker and family for one day. According to the theological economy of the Gospel of Matthew, physical sustenance is guaranteed by God in the kingdom of heaven. Matthew 6:19-33 indicates that more than this causes anxiety that emanates not from God, but from the kingdom of Satan. The first hired, along with the disciples and the audience of the Gospel, are invited to see the justice of God, and choose.

Plot: While Jesus Was Going Up to Jerusalem, 20:17–21:27

The Son of Man Will Be Handed Over, 20:17-28

20:17-19. They will condemn him to death. The episode begins with Jesus' prediction of his death and resurrection as the Son of Man and concludes with his interpretation of his death as a servant, the Son of Man, who gives his life for many. Jesus emphasizes the complicity of both the chief priests and scribes along with the Roman ruler in v. 19. The elite of Jerusalem who sought to kill Jesus as a child will accomplish their intention shortly. The prediction of the resurrection completes the prediction theologically and in parallel with v. 28 shows the result of the service of the Son of Man. In Matthew, the crucifixion and resurrection are always held together as one event of salvific significance.

20:20-23. The mother of the sons of Zebedee came. The reference to the rulers in v. 25 reminds us of the historical plane infused by evil powers. The action of the mother of the Zebedee brothers coincides with this historical emphasis by presuming that there will remain a hierarchical organization in the kingdom. Her presence here indicates perhaps the presence of those other than the male disciple band during the ministry of Jesus. She will reappear in the narrative at the foot of the cross. She, unlike her sons who abandon Jesus prior to his death, learns the meaning of kingdom and service.

20:24-28. When the ten heard it they were angry. The disciples also are in grave danger of hoping for a hierarchy in the kingdom of heaven that mirrors the hierarchy in the kingdoms of the world. Jesus predicts a nonhierarchical, noncentered system with no special privileges afforded to the disciples except service and death. Here the historical destiny of the Son of Man becomes the epistemological key for the disciples to understand the destiny of the children of the kingdom.

As They Were Leaving Jericho, 20:29-34

Two blind supplicants emerge from the crowds and form an ironic counterpoint to the blindness of the disciples in the previous scene. The last healing before entering Jerusalem emphasizes that these two supplicants, unlike the inhabitants and rulers of Jerusalem, see and follow Jesus. They not only form a counterpoint to the blindness of the disciples, but they also function as witnesses against the city of Jerusalem.

When They Had Come near Jerusalem, 21:1-27

21:1-17. You will find a donkey tied and a colt. The quotation from Zech 9:9 has shaped the emphasis in vv. 2 and 7 that *two* animals are brought and ridden. The image evoked by the text makes Jesus into a sort of circus rider. We may doubt whether an ancient author intended to propose a difficult if not impossible physical act. Rather, concern to show the precise fulfillment of prophecy may override more mundane considerations.

The literal fulfillment of the prophecy results in the perception of Jesus as the Davidic Messiah by the crowds (v. 9). Zechariah's prophecy, however, refers not to the triumphal entry of the Davidic monarch but rather to the arrival of the Lord God at the endtime (Zech 9:14-17). Using ZECHARIAH, the narrator makes clear that the crowds misunderstand Jesus' entry as a messianic act. The crowds also misunderstand him to be a PROPHET (v. 11). Rather, the entry into Jerusalem constitutes the final arrival of God in power to usher in the endtime.

Verses 12-17 continue to characterize Jesus as the arrival of God in the Temple. He claims rulership over his Temple both by his words and action (vv. 12-13). He heals in the Temple as a sign of the presence of God. Verses 15-16 emphasize the objection of the Temple leadership to the cries of *children*. Jesus' response taken from Ps 8:2 identifies himself as God. The entry into Jerusalem and cleansing of the Temple constitute the episodes in which Jesus' status as God-with-us in the eschatological time becomes fully apparent. Jesus by action and scriptural reference proclaims who he is.

21:18-22. He was hungry. The withering of the FIG TREE functions within the plot of this section as a sign of the impending judgment against Jerusalem. It also provides another opportunity for the disciples to perceive faith. The disciples are challenged to faith by the sight of the tree.

21:23-27. By what authority? Jesus forces the urban elites to choose between the sources of John's authority. They refuse because of political considerations. Jesus' argument implies that since John is the lesser of the two, if they do not understand John, they cannot understand him.

Speech: What Do You Think?, 21:28–22:14

The previous episodes have made clear that Jesus is God. The continued BLINDNESS of the rulers of Jerusalem results, therefore, in the following three parables of judgment. Not since the parables of Matt 13 has Jesus developed an extended speech composed of parables and interpretation. Three parables occur: two sons (21:28-31a); vineyard (21:33-41); and wedding banquet (22:1-14).

The first two parables receive immediate interpretations. The parable of the two sons receives a direct interpretation by Jesus that judges the chief priests and elders of the people for their failure to respond to the way of righteousness proclaimed by John (21:31b-32; 3:7-10). Jesus provides an interpretation to the second parable by scriptural citation. This parable of the vineyard understood from an allegorical eschatological-apocalyptic perspective refers prolepticly to Jesus' own death. The reaction of the chief priests and Pharisees in vv. 45-46 makes this interpretation apparent.

The final parable of the wedding feast contains within it elements that specify it as an ALLEGORY of apocalyptic judgment. Therefore, it is not followed by an interpretation. In v. 7 the rage of the king involves a destruction of the city of the murderers and probably refers to the actual destruction of Jerusalem in 70 C.E. Verses 11-14 recount the judgment against those within the banquet indicating that those within the kingdom are also liable to judgment.

The section builds to a forceful conclusion. The parables refer allegorically to the judgment of God that has already arrived. The author expects the audience to see the judgment of God against the urban ruling elite of Jerusalem for the rejection of John the Baptist and for the death of Jesus in the destruction of Jerusalem in 70. At some future date the judgment of God will be completed, including judgment of members of the kingdom. The same understanding of God's justice in the final days will be restated in the final speech of Jesus in Matt 23-26.

Plot and Speech: Then the Pharisees Went and Plotted to Entrap Him, 22:15-46

The return to plot in this section shows three arguments in which Jesus silences the PHARISEES and SADDUCEES.

Is It Lawful to Pay Taxes to the Emperor, or Not?, 22:15-22

In the first episode the Pharisees seek to entrap Jesus as a political seditionist. His reply operates at two levels. First, it affirms that economic systems rely on the political authority for their daily functioning. Therefore, taxes belong to that authority. On a second level, however, the response relativizes such political authority. The coin bears the emperor's image. The unspoken question of theological importance therefore would be, what bears the image of God? According to Gen 1:27, humans, male and female, bear God's image. Jesus' response implicitly lays the claim of God to humanity as God's own. The answer fits with the Matthean view that the kingdoms of the world are under the sway of the evil one who controls Mammon. Political claims over human beings are contrary to the will of God who by creation confirms God's Lordship over humanity. In a real sense, Jesus' answer is seditious. Governments regularly claim power over human lives and bodies.

Some Sadducees Came to Him, Saying There Is No Resurrection, 22:23-33

The episode of the Sadducees' challenge to the idea of resurrection accords with the depiction of JOSEPHUS, a Jewish historian of the first century, of the Sadducean sect (*BJ* 2.164–66). They deny the resurrection from the dead based on the fact that it is not recorded in the Pentateuch, the only scripture that they hold as authoritative. Jesus interprets Exod 3:6, a central confessional passage in the Pentateuch, from within his power as God to refer to the resurrection. The Sadducees are silenced.

When the Pharisees Heard That He Had Silenced the Sadducees, 22:34-46

The final episode of silencing of Jesus' opponents occurs in two parts: vv. 34-39 and vv. 41-46. In the first the Pharisees receive an answer directly from the Law (Deut 6:5; Lev 19:18). Jesus' interpretation remains clearly within the traditions of Judaism.

Jesus then turns the tables on the Pharisees and asks for their own interpretation. The quotation comes from a psalm attributed to David (Ps 110:1). Jesus regards David as the speaker, therefore, the implication is that David refers both to God (the first Lord) and also to the Messiah (the second Lord). Therefore, David adopts the same theological position as we noted of the Canaanite woman in Matt 14. The Messiah must be regarded as prior to, not descended from, David. From the perspective of Matthean christology, the conundrum presented by Jesus can be resolved only by seeing Jesus as God-with-us.

Speech:
Then Jesus Said to the Crowds and to His Disciples, 23:1–26:1

The speech blends almost without seam into the preceding narrative and emphasizes in discourse form what has already been portrayed through emplotment. The Matthean literary technique shows the full leavening of the historical with the mythopoeic. The kingdom of heaven interprets and alters the causality of history through the action and speech of God-with-us.

We should avoid the tendency to fragment this speech into discreet components. Rather, its literary organization functions within the world of the text to describe the judgment of various political-religious groups and institutions. Like the parables found in 21:28–22:14, the speech also refers to events known to the Matthean community. That referentiality serves to guide possible interpretations of the text.

The Scribes and the Pharisees Sit on Moses' Seat, 23:1-36

Jesus condemns the leaders of the SYNAGOGUE who interpret Mosaic Law. He accuses them both of improper action and improper interpretation of the Law (vv. 2-28). The community should avoid titles of respect and hierarchy adopted from the synagogue (vv. 8-12). Such hypocrisy, Jesus implies, results in unbelief that leads to murder of the righteous emissaries of God, both in the past and in the future (vv. 29-36). The future emissaries include prophets, sages, and scribes sent by Jesus who will be persecuted and killed by the religious institutions led by the Pharisees (34). Such behavior results in bloodguilt that will be judged within a generation (36).

Jerusalem, Jerusalem, the City That Kills the Prophets, 23:37–24:26

Jesus associates the Pharisees and scribes of the synagogues with the guilt of the city of Jerusalem. The condemnation of Jerusalem provides a transition to the prophecy of the judgment of the Temple (24:1-28). Jesus dwells on the details of some form of military campaign against the city emphasizing that this aspect of judgment (while necessary) is not the coming of the Son of Man or Messiah (vv. 5-8; 15-26). Jesus' viewpoint conforms closely to the view of the Hebrew prophets who understand the judgment of God to come upon the unrighteousness of Israel/Judah particularly by foreign military action against Jerusalem. God uses mundane historical power to God's own purposes of justice.

The destruction of the Temple and Jerusalem will be accompanied by persecution and by false prophets (vv. 9-14). Jesus counsels endurance to the end including active continuation of his own ministry beyond the confines of Israel to the whole world. Only upon the completion of this universal mission will the end come.

After the Suffering, 24:27-35

Jesus briefly describes the coming of the Son of Man to gather the children of the kingdom. Here the theological perspective moves beyond prophetic conceptualities like those of the previous section to apocalyptic-eschatological modes of thought. The endtime is not conceived in a messianic fashion as the reconstruction of mundane political structures through the power of a righteous king supported by God. Rather, the entire cosmos is involved (v. 29) in an event that obliterates historical reality and continuity (v. 35). Jesus provides no details except the enigmatic statement that all will take place before *this generation* passes away (v. 34). The reference may be to those who read the Gospel, rather than to the disciples per se.

But about That Day and Hour No One Knows, 24:36–25:30

The section of sayings that follows continues the emphasis on avoiding idle speculation and begins a call to watchful attentiveness. Jesus warns against counting days and hours implying that such preoccupation distracts from watchful, faithful attentiveness (vv. 36-44). The issue is so important that Jesus tells three parables illustrating the principle. Each parable addresses the community of believers. Each grows in length and intensity. Failure results in expulsion from the kingdom (25:30).

When the Son of Man Comes, 25:31-46

Jesus depicts the final universal judgment by the Son of Man. The metaphor of the sheep and the goats is used; nevertheless, this section is not a parable but a direct vision of the final judgment. The principle of judgment invoked by the Son of Man is to identify the presence of Jesus with supplicants, the marginal, indicated by the *least of these*. The Gospel shows this group to be the women, children, and other supplicants among whom faith is consistently found in the Gospel. The idea of the Son of Man hidden among these is consistent with the idea of God as one who sees in secret (6:1-18). The result of failure to perceive the presence of God in the marginal, silent ones including the homeless, imprisoned, and sick is eternal punishment (v. 46).

When Jesus Had Finished Saying All These Things, 26:1

Only with the concluding transitional sentence do we recognize the full importance of this section. It concludes the sayings of Jesus in Matthew. It announces the arrival of the judgment of God through the Son of Man in the world.

The concluding formula asks the reader to reconsider the entirety of the preceding section in the terms of the total context of Matthew. We must not read this text as a bifurcation of salvation-history into an "us-them" perspective on God's actions with Israel first and then Christianity. Rather, the text makes the radical claim that holds institutions accountable for their historical refusal of the gospel of the kingdom. It portrays a universal people of God composed of both Jews and non-Jews whose response to the kingdom determines, individually and not ethnically, their destiny in the judgment of God's day.

Matthew identifies the enemies of Jesus as the leadership and people specifically and historically aligned with the kingdoms of the world. The text portrays their judgment already to have been accomplished by the destruction of their city and shrine of ethnic, political, and religious identity. Such a portrayal arises as a prophetic vision from within the traditions of Judaism, not as an externally imposed historical analysis. For Matthew the judgment falls not on Jews as a family (Gk. *genos)* or race (Gk. *ethnos)*, but upon the leaders of national religious institutions. This leadership has opposed the arrival of the kingdom from the birth of its proclaimer and Lord. For the Matthean community this judgment begins with the crucifixion of the Son of Man and ends with the destruction of Jerusalem by the Romans in 70.

Matthew also portrays a universal judgment of the world at some indefinite and incalculable time. This judgment will separate evildoers from the children of the kingdom based upon their faithful action toward the marginalized among whom Jesus dwells. The insistence that faith comes first and foremost from the least is raised to the principle of eschatological justice. Both the mercy of God and the righteousness of God cohere in the scene of final judgment.

Matthew reserves for the community the strongest warning to watchfulness in three parables. Failure in preparation may lead even the most well-intentioned into outer darkness. If we ask what the members of the community are to engage themselves in while watchfully waiting, these parables integrate with the prediction that the proclamation of the gospel must go first to the world. The community in word and deed bears witness to the kingdom of which they are a part. Members cannot smugly await final salvation while the world tears itself asunder.

Therefore, the final speech of Jesus locates its anticipated audience between the destruction of Jerusalem in 70 and the manifestation of the Son of Man at the final judgment. We should not make the mistake of associating the apocalyptic-eschatological viewpoint of the text as indicating an expectation of the chronologically imminent return of the Son of Man. Matthew ties the judgment directly to the witness-bearing mission of the community. Historically seen the chronological duration of that witness is of no consequence to the urgency of an apocalyptic-eschatological expectation of the kairotic imminence of the kingdom of heaven. The mercy and righteousness of God are always and everywhere imminent. The vision of God's grace and justice cannot be limited by historical causation.

Plot: The Son of Man Will Be Handed Over to Be Crucified, 26:2–28:20

Each section of the PASSION NARRATIVE contains episodes that allow the audience to view the actions of various characters or character groups in relationship to Jesus. Their faithfulness, doubt, or opposition becomes apparent as they respond to the unfolding of Jesus' faithfulness to the will of God as he suffers, dies, and is resurrected.

The Passover Is Coming, 26:2-16

26:2. The Son of Man will be handed over. The Gospel of Matthew portrays Jesus, especially in his passion, to be aligned with the events that befall him. These are the last things and they are overseen by the will of God. The disciples are reminded once again of the impending death by crucifixion of the Son of Man.

26:3-5. They conspired to arrest Jesus. *The chief priests and elders of the people* previously in collusion with Herod were unsuccessful in destroying the child Jesus (2:4). Now they will be successful in collusion with PILATE, but not before Jesus has completed his mission. Their plot is left incomplete for the moment since they require stealth.

26:6-13. A woman came to him. The episode returns to the disciple band and provides a contrast between the faith of the marginal and the little faith of the inner circle. *Simon the leper* (v. 6) does not appear elsewhere in the Gospel of Matthew, but he recalls the leper healed by Jesus at the beginning of his ministry (8:1-4). An unnamed woman shows that she has understanding superior to the disciples concerning the person and destiny of Jesus. They should apply the understanding given by Jesus previously that he is about to die (most recently at 26:2 and also at 16:21; 17:22-23; 20:17-19). No prediction to the woman occurs in Matthew. The text allows the inference that she has this knowledge by divine will. In addition Jesus links her act inextricably with the proclamation of *this good news* (v. 13).

26:14-16. One of the twelve went to the chief priests. With the action of Judas, the plot to arrest and kill Jesus is completed. By inserting the anointing at Bethany between the two episodes of plotting, Matthew allows reflection on the disciples' lack of faith in perceiving the divine will and on the collusion of one of their band with the opposition. Among the Gospels, only Matthew develops the story of JUDAS and does so as one of a pair of negative examples of discipleship. The other is PETER. Money motivates Judas.

On the First Day of Unleavened Bread, 26:17-75.

26:17-19. My time is near. Jesus shows his alignment with God's will and control over his destiny by directing the preparations for his last Passover with his disciples. In identifying *my time* Jesus in Matthew uses the Greek word *kairos* rather than *chronos* indicating thereby a time of fulfillment and new beginning (Senior 1985, 60).

26:20-30. One of you will betray me. Jesus shows for the first time that he knows that he will be betrayed. Judas reveals himself to Jesus as the betrayer. In a typical Passover meal of the first century, all of the disciples are likely to have dipped their hand into the same bowl. The notation in v. 23, therefore, only indicates that Jesus knew that one of the Twelve would betray him, not which one.

Even in the face of this knowledge and with Judas presumably still present Jesus interprets his own death for his disciples using the bread and cup as parabolic symbol. In Matthew no specific interpretation of the bread as body is given, rather the interpretation of the cup as *blood of the covenant, which is poured out for many for the forgiveness of sins* (v. 28) stands as interpretation of the entire symbolic act. By declaring this act an interpretation of his impending death, Jesus combines the ideas of the covenant-making sacrifice with the image of the sin offering also found in Jewish ritual and tradition. The combined force of the religious symbol contextualized into the life of Jesus, God-with-us (cf. 1:23), remains a mystery that transcends sacrificial or covenantal religious symbolization and interpretation.

Jesus adds to this complex religious experience by making the celebration of his death a promise of the final banquet within the coming kingdom of heaven. The performance of this parable in the midst of the twelve disciples in spite of their unfaith and even betrayal holds open the promise of forgiveness. Set within the action of Peter and Judas, the words of Jesus take on particular poignancy. The use of the plural *you* in v. 29 may well imply that even the betrayer will be found in the kingdom.

26:30-35. You will all become deserters. In the face of the promise of v. 29, Jesus predicts the desertion of all of the disciples (v. 31). This is followed by a denial by Peter and all of the disciples who emphasize their willingness to die with Jesus. While Peter is depicted as an individual disciple, the text makes us aware that his behavior characterizes the disciples as a group.

26:36-56. Sit here while I pray. Such characterization continues into the next episode in GETHSEMANE (vv. 36-46). The disciples, Peter and the sons of Zebedee are especially mentioned, are unable to watch and pray with Jesus. Jesus' admonition to *stay awake and pray* (v. 41) associates this episode with his previous instruction on the coming of the Son of Man (24:36-25:30) and further develops the implication that his death means the eschatological coming of the Son of Man. Verse 46 directly links the fate of Jesus with the fate of the Son of Man.

The narrator reminds us that Judas is *one of the twelve* yet again at his arrival in v. 47. In this episode, Judas aligns himself not only with the power of money but also with the power of violence to which Jesus has been opposed throughout Matthew. This alignment even afflicts the disciple band, presumably one of which (v. 51) initiates armed resistance against the arresting officials. Jesus repudiates the use of violence to protect his life and mission (Senior 1985, 86). He remains consistent with his own teaching throughout the Gospel. Additionally, he repudiates the traditional Jewish and Christian anticipation of the intervention of Yahweh God as a warrior in behalf of the righteous. Such an understanding is deeply embedded in the Hebrew traditions of the EXODUS (e.g., Exod 14-15) and is heightened in the apocalyptic traditions of Isaiah, Zechariah, and Daniel. While 26:52-54 closely parallels Rev 13:10, the overarching apocalyptic vision expressed in Matthew clearly refuses the solution of divine warfare advocated by the apocalyptic tradition of the Book of Revelation. Jesus, while recognizing the warrior aspect of God, declares such a solution to be aside from the will of the Father (vv. 52-56). The Matthean depiction of the crucifixion remains consistent with such a vision. For the Matthean apocalyptic view, directly informed as it is by the suffering of the Son of Man who is God-with-us, the antidote to the structured and legal power of political violence is not retributive violence. Both are rooted in evil. The antinomic opposition to death is resurrection, not death and blood, however justified, in return.

26:57-75. Those took him to Caiaphas. The final episode of the section recounts an interrogation at the house of the high priest, CAIAPHAS. The procedure was not a normal judiciary procedure of the SANHEDRIN according to what we know of such procedures in the first century. Caiaphas swears an oath in order to get Jesus to speak, contrary to the teaching of Jesus (5:33-37). Jesus answers by declaring the immediate arrival of the Son of Man. The scene shows that the end of the age and the PASSION of Jesus are considered as one event by Matthew. Matthew does not locate the coming of the Son of Man purely at the end of history, but sees the end of history as already present in the historical moment of Jesus' passion. Such a view strains narration, dependent as it is on sequential reading.

The actions of Peter invite comparison with those of the HIGH PRIEST since they follow immediately and conclude the scene. Peter, questioned three times, denies knowledge of Jesus concluding with an OATH in v. 74. By this action Peter aligns himself against Jesus and with the same power that informs the oath-taking actions of Jesus' opponents. He is portrayed in the narrative as in grave danger of joining them in their opposition. His weeping at the remembrance of Jesus' prediction is left ambiguous by the narrator. It should not be taken as showing more than an emotional response to his own failure (cf. Senior 1985, 95–102).

When Morning Came, 27:1-56

27:1-10. Judas repented. While Peter's weeping remains opaque, the conclusion to the story of Judas reveals more about Judas' inner motivations. The episode of Judas interrupts the movement from the high priest's house to the trial by Pilate. The scene stresses the guilt of the religious leadership and the innocence of Jesus, as well as Jesus' obedience to God's will indicated by a citation of prophecy (cf. Kingsbury 1988, 88).

Judas sees his error in the condemnation of Jesus and declares that Jesus is innocent. Judas declares his sin (v. 4). The narrator states that Judas, *repented.* By returning the money he acts on that new perception. The word translated *repented* (v. 3) also occurs in the parable of the two sons in 21:29, 32 to indicate the change of mind of the first son who later is judged to do the will of the father. Typically the author uses a different Greek word to mean "repent" (3:2, 8, 11; 4:17; 11:20, 21; 12:41). Judas indicates his frame of mind both by what he says and what he does.

The suicide of Judas constitutes an antitype to the innocent death of Jesus who also is "hung" in crucifixion. Both may be seen as condemned to a death under the curse of the Law according to Deut 21:23. The portrayal remains ambiguous, however, since Judas is the only disciple to "change his mind." While he is not present to witness the resurrection, we are only left to wonder whether his doubt was removed by what he saw (v. 3). No other disciple is portrayed as recognizing the innocence of Jesus and acting to ameliorate his own denial.

27:11-26. Jesus stood before the governor. The charge before Pilate shifts to political sedition. Pilate completes the work begun by Herod and eliminates the adopted Davidic heir. While the opponents of Jesus believe him to be *King of the Jews*, Jesus himself will not confirm their viewpoint. The ascent of Jesus to messianic kingship in Matthew is a result of his opponents' charges. His descent to identity with marginal and homeless people comes through his own fulfillment of the roles of SON OF MAN and SON OF GOD according to the righteousness of the kingdom. Only Jesus of all the male characters in the Gospel succeeds in this self-emptying (cf. Phil 2:5-11). Such emptying earns him the condemnation of the leaders.

Counterpoint to Pilate's behavior is that of his wife (v. 19). She affirms the innocence of Jesus at his trial. She knows his innocence from a dream. In Matthew the only other dreams mentioned occur to Joseph and the magi in the infancy narrative. Her dream is a revelation of divine will to which Pilate will not listen. The unnamed woman knows the truth.

The action of the crowds in vv. 24-25 has been used in the history of Christian interpretation to condemn Jews as "Christ killers." Such a view exceeds the text and misses the viewpoint of Matthew, rooted as it is in Israelite prophetic tradition. In this climactic scene, the Gospel makes clear that Jerusalem, its leaders and people, reject Jesus. The author crafts this scene in accord with what we have already observed in Matt 23–25. The destruction of Jerusalem by the Romans in 70 constitutes for the author the judgment of God against Jerusalem, its rulers and people, in retribution for the crucifixion of Jesus as the Son of Man, Son of God, the unrecognized God-with-us (cf. 1:23). The event coincides rather precisely with a "generation" if we accept ca. 30 C.E. as the death date of Jesus. In Jewish tradition forty years usually is regarded as a generation (see Senior 1985, 116–22).

The Gospel indicates a continuing mission to all in 28:16-20 as well as perhaps to any cities of Israel remaining post-70 (see 10:23); it does not depict a salvation-historical rejection of Israel or of the Jews by God. It does not even depict condemnation for all of Israel for the crucifixion of Jesus. Rather the condemnation remains specific.

27:27-30. The soldiers took Jesus. Matthew depicts with great care and circumspection the brutal torture of Jesus by the Praetorian guards. The episode shows the control Pilate has over the crucifixion and emphasizes the political nature of Jesus' condemnation. The title *King of the Jews* is emphasized; other titles are excluded. Herod's fear of political sedition by a messiah culminates in Rome's derision of the same pretender.

27:32-44. This is Jesus, King of the Jews. The text shows Jesus as the legal heir to David's throne, therefore, the ruling elite correctly see him as a historical threat. We know, however, that the threat to the mundane order runs deeper because Jesus is not the Davidic Messiah of historical anticipation, but rather is the Son of Man, Son of God, God-with-us who undercuts and robs the kingdoms of the world of their power rooted in violence, death, and injustice. Jesus is a threat because in his person and proclamation he embodies the lordship of God and God's kingdom. The ruling center rightly seeks to kill him in order to preserve their power undergirded by the evil whose face takes shape in hypocrisy and violence. These perceptions come to the fore in the taunts of the bandits, religious leaders, and bystanders. They combine traditional titles of the Davidic monarch and deride Jesus as Son of God and King of Israel.

27:45-54. Darkness came over the whole land. Five responses to Jesus' death occur. First, the earth responds with darkness. Second, Jesus responds with the theological question of abandonment to the power of death. Third, the bystanders respond by seeking to drug him and provide more time for their jeers. Fourth, God responds by initiating the turn of the ages, opening the tombs. Fifth, the CENTURION responds by the affirmation of Jesus' divine sonship.

The climax of the plot of Matthew occurs in this scene. Jesus' own cry and death raise the question of God's response and dependability. Jesus' statement of mind in his final moment reveals the pernicious evil of death. God's resurrection prolepticly indicated in vv. 52-53 is the cause for recognizing Jesus' emptying on the CROSS transformed into life for all by God's will. Death is not further education for Jesus, but rather is regarded in the text as annihilating even his perception of relationship to the God to whom his life bears witness. In Jesus' death the kingdom of God arrives in power to liberate from death those who have fallen asleep. The answer to Jesus' question is the resurrection from God.

27:55-56. Many women were also there. The women followers of Jesus receive introduction. They, parallel to THE TWELVE, have followed him from Galilee. They also witnessed the events narrated previously in Jesus' life. Two are named. Mary Magdalene does not appear previously in Matthew. The second Mary almost certainly is the mother of Jesus (see 13:55; Gundry 1982, 579). She is not named as his mother in order to preserve the emphasis in the text on Jesus as a homeless and householdless person. These two women provide consistent witness to the life, death, burial, and resurrection of Jesus. Mary, the mother, can bear witness to his identity from birth.

When It Was Evening, 27:57-66

Two episodes contrast faithful followers with the opponents. Missing are the eleven disciples. In v. 57 JOSEPH of Arimathea, *a rich man* and *a disciple*, is said to have provided for Jesus' burial. He apparently was drawn through the eye of the needle by God (19:23-26). Unlike the Twelve who had left everything (19:27) Joseph aligns himself as a marginal follower of Jesus, as do the two Marys who watch the tomb.

In opposition to the faithfulness of Joseph and the Marys, the political and religious opponents post their own guard. The text by this juxtaposition emphasizes the difference between centralized violent guarded authority and marginal faithful watchfulness.

After the Sabbath, 28:1-15

Two episodes emphasize the resurrection of Jesus as part of the eschatological turn of the ages and the proper response to the event. The Marys are consistent witnesses to the biography of Jesus on the historical plane. Also to them comes the revelation of God's resurrection of Jesus (vv. 2-3). The angelic messenger sends the women to re-include the eleven who have denied Jesus (vv. 5-7). The eleven will see him in Galilee. The Marys see him immediately: *Suddenly Jesus met them and said, 'Greetings!' And they came to him, took hold of his feet, and worshipped him*

(v. 9). Their response to the resurrection provides a model with which we may compare subsequent responses.

The response of the chief priests to the account of the guards provides a negative foil to the Marys. They use the power of money to silence the news of the resurrection. Their disinformation continues to deceive the Jews to the author's own day. This deception may be emphasized here because it has a negative impact on a continuation of a mission to JUDAISM by the Matthean community.

Now the Eleven Disciples Went to Galilee, 28:16-20

The final scene of Matthew opens the story of Jesus as God-with-us (cf. 1:23) into an all-powerful future. It also leaves open the future of the eleven and with them the orientation of the audience of the Gospel.

The appearance to the eleven completes the episode begun with the appearance to the women and should be read as a third response to the resurrection. We understand that the women faithfully fulfilled their mission. The response of the eleven also directly parallels that of the women, *when they saw him, they worshipped him, but some doubted* (v. 17; emphasis added). This verse is constructed so as to continue the irony that has attended the characterization of the disciples throughout the narrative. The only character said to doubt previously in the plot is Peter (14:31). The verse also reminds us of the pattern of each episode of *little faith* on the part of the disciples (8:26; 14:31; 16:8; 17:20) and each episode of faith and worship on the part of the marginalized. The disciples have never been shown to be effective interpreters, teachers, or missionaries within the text. The text, therefore, will not allow for the conclusion that in 28:19 the authority of Jesus is transferred to the disciples. Nor does it clearly rehabilitate them as faithful apostles after their abandonment of Jesus.

The scene as written subverts and destroys any claim by the disciples and/or their institutional heirs to patriarchal or hierarchical authority over gentiles, women, children, or other supplicants within the community. The text remains true in its emplotment and characterization to a vision of the kingdom of heaven that decenters, de-marginalizes, and in short abandons all -archic, -centric structures with their attendant systems of status.

The audience and not the disciples becomes *scribes trained for the kingdom* (13:52). The work involved in the commission of 28:19-20 is left to those who accept the role and education provided them by Matthew. They behave not like the disciples, but like the faithful of the margins.

Nevertheless, the eleven are not assimilated to the character of the Pharisees . They are left as ironic example. The commission does not transfer Jesus' authority to them. Rather, Jesus remains with them (v. 20), while reserving his own complete power to himself to the end of the age. His story may not be closed by any but God's power expressed through Emmanuel, God-with-us (cf. 1:23).

Works Cited

Baltensweiler, H. 1967. *Die Ehe im Neue Testament.*

Bauer, David R. 1988. *The Structure of Matthew's Gospel: A Study in Literary Design.* Bible and Literature series 15.

Betz, Hans Dieter. 1985. "Matthew 6.22-23 and Ancient Theories of Vision," in *Essays on the Sermon on the Mount*, 71–87.

Brooks, Stephenson H. 1987. *Matthew's Community: The Evidence of His Special Sayings Material.* JSNTSup 16. (*See also* Humphries-Brooks, Stephenson.)

Brown, Raymond E. 1977. *The Birth of the Messiah.* 1983. "Not Jewish Christianity and Gentile Christianity but Types of Jewish/Gentile Christianity," *CBQ* 45:74–79.

Davies, W. D. 1964. *The Setting of the Sermon on the Mount.*

Gundry, Robert H. 1967. *The Use of the Old Testament in St. Matthew's Gospel, with Special Reference to the Messianic Hope.* 1982. *Matthew: A Commentary on His Literary and Theological Art.*

Hanson, Paul D. 1979. *The Dawn of Apocalyptic.* Rev. ed.

Humphries-Brooks, Stephenson. 1989. "Apocalyptic Paraenesis in Matthew 6:19-34," in *Apocalyptic and the New Testament. Essays in Honor of J. Louis Martyn*, ed. Joel Marcus and Marion L. Soards, 95–112. JSNTSupp 24. 1991. "Indicators of Social Organization and Status in Matthew's Gospel," SBLSP 30:31–49.

Jeremias, Joachim. 1972. *The Parables of Jesus.* Second ed.

Kingsbury, Jack Dean. 1988. *Matthew as Story.* Second ed.

Martyn, J. Louis. 1985. "Apocalyptic Antinomies in Paul's Letter to the Galatians," *NTS* 31:410–24.

Meier, John P. 1976. *Law and History in Matthew's Gospel. A Redactional Study of Matt 5:17-48.* AnBib 71. 1979. *The Vision of Matthew: Christ, Church and Morality in the First Gospel.*

Patte, Daniel. 1987. *The Gospel according to Matthew: A Structural Commentary on Matthew's Faith.*

Senior, Donald. 1985. *The Passion of Jesus in the Gospel of Matthew.*

Stendahl, Krister. 1968. *The School of St. Matthew and Its Use of the Old Testament.* Second ed.

Talbert, Charles H. 1988. "Once Again: Gospel Genre," *Semeia* 43:53–73.

Thompson, William G. 1970. *Matthew's Advice to a Divided Community. Matt 17:22–18:35.* AnBib 44.

Wilder, Amos Niven. 1982. *Jesus' Parables and the War of Myths: Essays on Imagination in Scripture*, ed. James Breech.

Mark [MCB 975-1006]

Sharyn E. Dowd

Introduction

Of the more than twenty extant gospels, Mark is one of the four that was finally included in the CANON of the early church. Its traditional title "The Gospel according to Mark" did not come from the hand of the author, but was added to a copy of the manuscript during the second century C.E. The name and gender of the author, the date and place of composition, and the intended audience are all unknown.

Mark in Context

Before Mark there was no genre of literature known as "gospel," a term that means "good news." The author of Mark (another term for the author in this commentary is "the evangelist") was not inventing a new genre, but writing a biography of Jesus. Like many ancient biographies, Mark was written not to provide a list of facts about Jesus of Nazareth, but to interpret the significance of the life, death, and resurrection of *Jesus Christ, the Son of God* (1:1). Thus, this biography is a kind of narrative theology. It proclaims Christian faith in the form of a story.

Mark is a popular ancient biography. That is, it was not stuffy elite literature written in elevated language, but a lively story written in a popular style that was easy to read, much like paperback novels today. Of course, the author did not invent the stories; they had been handed down through preaching and teaching in the early Christian communities. What the evangelist did was to arrange the material in its present order and retell the story of Jesus so those who heard the story read aloud would understand how committing themselves to Jesus and his way would affect their lives.

Books were expensive in the ancient world, and not everyone could read, even if books had been easily accessible. It is likely that the Gospel of Mark was intended to be read aloud and heard by an audience of gathered Christians, rather than read privately by one person.

The structure of Mark is distinguished by various kinds of repetition. Repetition is useful in helping the listening audience keep track of the story. For example, in 3:10 the audience hears that people could be healed by touching Jesus. In 5:24b-34 an example is given of a woman who actually was healed by touching Jesus' clothes. Then in 6:56 the audience is reminded again that even touching Jesus' clothes was enough to bring healing to people. Repetition reinforces the point.

Other kinds of repetition found in Mark are the INCLUSIO and the CHIASM. The inclusio is simply a frame. The same information or phrase that begins a unit of material is repeated at the end. This A-B-A form is familiar to us because of its use in many musical compositions.

The chiasm is similar except that the repetition is more extensive. Not only do the first and last parts match each other, but the second and next-to-last also match, and so on. Chiastic structures can be as short as a sentence (*The sabbath was made for humankind, and not humankind for the sabbath*, 2:27), or as long as several pages. These patterns of repetition and other literary devices were used by ancient authors to indicate where thought units began and ended. The chapter divisions now found in the NT were added in the thirteenth century C.E. and often do not reflect the actual literary shape of the text.

Some ancient authors did not like for the sections of a work to be joined end to end like blocks in a row. They preferred that the sections overlap, like links in a chain. The author of Mark was one such author. That is why the outline that begins this commentary may look strange to modern eyes. The reader will notice that one section begins at a point before the end of the previous section. These "hinges" or "hooks" in the structure of the Gospel will be pointed out in the outline and in the commentary.

Mark is a popular biography written from the presuppositions of the apocalyptic worldview, so although it is not an apocalypse like the Book of Revelation, it is in a sense apocalyptic literature. The evangelist believed that in the ministry of Jesus, God's kingdom or reign was breaking into history. The resurrection of Jesus was the beginning of the end. Soon the forces of Satan would be defeated for good and Jesus would return for his *elect*, or "chosen ones" (13:27). The apocalyptic presuppositions of the Gospel of Mark are the reason for the prevalence of conflict and even the language of warfare in the story. Jesus is the divine warrior who does battle with the enemies of God who afflict God's creation with illness, demonic possession, and temptation.

Mark is a popular biography written from within an apocalyptic worldview with a feeling of urgency. Therefore, the author uses every means available to persuade the Christians who hear the story to remain faithful. Two of these means are Jewish scriptural interpretation techniques and Hellenistic rhetorical techniques.

Even though God has done something radically new in Jesus, the evangelist is certain that everything about Jesus is in perfect continuity with the way that God has dealt with people in the past. Everything in the Gospel of Mark is interpreted in terms of the way it fits in with the OT. The author's favorite OT books seem to be Isaiah, Daniel, and the Psalms, although others are used as well to help explain the meaning of Jesus' story.

In ancient Greek schools pupils like the author of Mark learned rhetorical techniques, that is, appropriate ways of proving a point or persuading an audience. Studying how the NT writers used these techniques and adapted them to suit their material is called RHETORICAL CRITICISM. Some of these techniques will be discussed in the commentary.

The Gospel of Mark can be very helpful to the church today not only because of *what* it tells us about the theological significance of what God has done in Christ, but also because of *how* it combines a variety of cultural and literary traditions into an intricate and interesting whole in the service of that good news.

This commentary is intended as a reading guide to the Gospel of Mark. It has been deliberately written in such a way that it will make no sense to the reader who does not have a Bible open alongside the commentary. No commentary can be a substitute for the Bible itself.

For Further Study

In the *Mercer Dictionary of the Bible*: APOCALYPTIC LITERATURE; APOCRYPHAL GOSPELS; DISCIPLE/DISCIPLESHIP; ESCHATOLOGY IN THE NT; GENRE, CONCEPT OF; GENRE, GOSPEL; GOSPEL; GOSPELS, CRITICAL STUDY OF; INCLUSIO; KINGDOM OF GOD; MARK, GOSPEL OF; MARK, LONG ENDING OF; RHETORICAL CRITICISM; SON OF GOD; SON OF MAN; SYNOPTIC PROBLEM; TWELVE, THE; WOMEN IN THE NT; WORSHIP IN THE NT.

In other sources: W. Harrington, *Mark*; E. S. Malbon, "Narrative Criticism: How Does the Story Mean?" *Mark and Method*, ed. Anderson and Moore, 23–49; E. Schweizer, *Good News according to Mark*; L. Williamson, *Mark*, Interp.

Commentary

An Outline

I. Prologue, 1:1-15
   Frame: Good news, 1:1-3
   A. John Announces the One Who Will Baptize in the Spirit, 1:4-8
   B. Jesus Is Baptized in the Spirit, 1:9-11
   C. The Spirit Thrusts Jesus into Battle with Satan, 1:12-13
   Frame: Good News, 1:14-15
II. Ministry in Galilee and in Gentile Territory, 1:14–8:30
   A. Paradigmatic Beginning of Jesus' Ministry, 1:14–3:12
   B. Extension of Jesus' Ministry and Intensification of Conflict, 3:7–6:30
   C. Jesus' Ministry Removes Barriers between Jews and Gentiles, 6:14–8:30
III. On the Way, 8:22–10:52
   Frame:Healing of Blind Man in Two Stages, 8:22-26
   Introductory Narrative, 8:27-30
   A. First Passion Prediction Unit, 8:31–9:29
   B. Second Passion Prediction Unit, 9:30–10:31
   C. Third Passion Prediction Unit, 10:32-52
   Frame: Healing of Blind Man Immediately, 10:46-52
IV. Ministry and Passion in Jerusalem, 11:1–16:8
   A. Jesus and the Temple, 11:1–13:37
   B. Passion and Resurrection Narratives, 14:1–16:8

Prologue, 1:1-15

The prologue is held together by a frame or INCLUSIO in 1:1-3 and 1:14-15. Both ends of the inclusio contain the word *good news* (εὐαγγέλιον) followed by an ambiguous prepositional phrase (good news of/about Jesus Christ, v. 1; good news of/about God, v. 14). Although there are a number of scriptural allusions in the prologue, the author of Mark names only Isaiah (v. 2). This makes it clear that the evangelist is interpreting the story of Jesus in terms of the theology of Isaiah, particularly the portion often called Deutero-Isaiah (chaps. 40–55).

Jesus' announcement in v. 15 echoes the prophetic promise that the time of slavery and bondage is filled up and the time of God's favor is on the way (Isa 40:1; 49:8). The good news is that God reigns (Isa 52:7). This message is first announced by a voice crying in the wilderness, *Prepare the way of the Lord*! (v. 3; Isa 40:3 LXX). Thus, the ministry of Jesus is interpreted as a new exodus from bondage into freedom, like the new exodus from exile announced by Isaiah. But the audience of Mark will soon learn that like Isaiah, Jesus speaks to people who have deaf ears and hardened hearts. He enacts God's liberating power in the presence of people whose eyes see only dimly or not at all (4:12; 8:17-18; Isa 6:9).

Within the frame provided by vv. 1-3 and vv. 14-15, there are three smaller units, each of which emphasizes the activity of the Spirit in connection with the ministry of Jesus: vv. 4-8, 9-11, 12-13. The frame and the inner sections are knit together by repeated words and phrases: *messenger(s)* (1:2, 13); *in the wilderness* (1:3, 4, 12); *baptize/baptizer/baptism* (1:4, 5, 8, 9); *Jordan* (1:5, 9); *son* (1:1, 11); *proclaim* (1:7, 14); *repent/repentance* (1:4, 15).

John Announces the One Who Will Baptize in the Spirit, 1:4-8

In this unit John the baptizer announces that although he immerses in water, the coming stronger one will immerse in the Holy Spirit. This will be necessary, the audience may surmise, because John's water baptism does not effect the reversal of mindset (μετάνοια, usually translated "repentance") to which he calls the inhabitants of Judea. Although they confess their sins, the narrative is silent about any change of mind and heart. That there is none is made evident by the blindness, deafness, and hardness of heart with which Jesus' message is greeted in the subsequent narrative. Only the transforming baptism in the Holy Spirit, promised but not narrated in the Gospel of Mark, will effect a change to God's way of thinking (8:33) and result in bold witness (13:11).

In this first appearance in the story, John wears the costume of ELIJAH (v. 6; 2 Kgs 1:8). This identifies him as the forerunner promised in Mal 3:1; 4:5 (v. 2; 9:11-12) and prepares for his persecution by a scheming queen (6:17-29; 9:13).

Jesus Is Baptized in the Spirit, 1:9-11

The baptism scene establishes Jesus' God-given identity for the information of the audience of the Gospel. In Mark, John does not share Jesus' vision of the descending Spirit (v. 10; cf. John 1:32), nor does the voice from heaven make a public announcement (cf. Matt 3:17). Thus, only Jesus and the audience understand that Jesus' baptism legitimates him as PROPHET, servant, and anointed royal SON OF GOD. The bystanders at the story level see only a country boy from Galilee joining in the mass confession and baptism in the Jordan River.

It does not occur to the author of Mark, as it does to the author of Matthew, that Jesus' baptism as one of the crowd requires the explanation that Jesus had no sins to confess (cf. Matt 3:14-15). On the contrary, the Markan Jesus identifies with the sin of his people even as he accepts his call to the prophetic vocation (Isa 6:5). In this way, the baptism prefigures the passion: "He was counted among the lawless" (Isa 53:12 LXX).

Sight (v. 10) is reinforced by hearing (v. 11). The voice from heaven, like the narrator (vv. 2-3), quotes scripture; again the evangelist emphasizes the continuity between the good news and the old, old story of God's self-revelation in the past. The heavenly voice quotes a combination of Ps 2:7 ("You are my son"— God's word to the Davidic ruler) and Isa 42:1b ("my chosen, in whom my soul delights"—God's word to the servant).

But there is another, more disturbing element: the word *beloved* (v. 11) which comes not from the psalmist nor from the prophet but from Gen 22:2. This is the story about a brush with death of another "beloved son"—Isaac. For Jesus there will be no ram in the thicket; he will give his life to redeem others (10:45).

The Spirit Thrusts Jesus into Battle with Satan, 1:12-13

Here the narrator introduces the conflict that will drive the plot of the Gospel: the cosmic conflict between Jesus, God's agent, and Satan, leader of the resistance to God's reign. Later in the Gospel, Satan will be identified with Beelzebul, the chief of the demons (3:22-27). The exorcisms, which will begin in 1:21-27, will demonstrate that Jesus was the victor in this desert encounter.

In ancient thought, human beings who could remain unharmed in the presence of wild animals were believed to be the recipients of divine favor and protection; Romulus, the founder of Rome, was believed to have been saved from starvation by a wolf. In the Israelite wisdom traditions, it was the righteous sage who was protected against wild animals (Ps 91:11-13). According to Isa 11:6-9, all humanity will be at peace with the animals in the reign of God, when "a shoot shall come out from the stump of Jesse" upon whom "the spirit of the Lord shall rest" (11:1-2). Thus, the narrative logic is complete when, immediately after the wilderness testing scene, the Markan Jesus announces that God's reign is imminent (1:14-15).

Ministry in Galilee and in Gentile Territory, 1:14–8:30

The first major section of the Gospel is an interpretation of the in-breaking reign of God in Jesus' ministry of teaching, exorcism, healing, and forgiveness. The section begins with Jesus' initial proclamation of God's reign in 1:14-15 and concludes with Peter's identification of Jesus as the one anointed to bring in God's reign (8:27-30).

The portrait of Jesus presented by the evangelist combines elements of the OT prophetic traditions, Davidic kingship motifs, and Hellenistic understandings of the wandering teacher/philosopher and his band of followers. This enabled both gentiles and Jews in the audience to grasp the significance of Jesus and his revelation of God.

Paradigmatic Beginning of Jesus' Ministry, 1:14–3:12

The section 1:14–8:30 is made up of three overlapping subsections: 1:14–3:12, 3:7–6:30, and 6:14–8:30. These develop the audience's understanding of Jesus progressively, beginning with a paradigmatic depiction of the various aspects of his ministry in 1:14–3:12. This subsection may be outlined as follows: Introductory summary of Jesus' message (1:14-15); Calling the first disciples (1:16-20); Jesus' power over illness and demonic oppression (1:21-45); Jesus' authority to forgive sins and interpret scripture (2:1–3:6); Concluding summary of Jesus' healings and exorcisms (3:7-12).

1:14-15. Introductory summary of Jesus' message. Returning to Galilee after his baptism and encounter with Satan in the Judean desert, Jesus begins to proclaim "the good message of God" (τὸ εὐαγγέλιον τοῦ θεοῦ, v. 14). The deliberate ambiguity informs the audience that God's message, proclaimed by Jesus, originates with God and is a message about God. Specifically, it is a message about the kingdom of God, that is, God's reign or sovereignty, which has come near (ἤγγικεν).

This is an eschatological message, because, although God is the rightful sovereign over all creation, God's sovereignty is presently contested by evil and its human agents. In Jesus' ministry the reign of God that will soon be fully present is experienced in a preliminary way by those who encounter Jesus. His teaching and ministry of power prefigure the final defeat of all opposition to God's sovereignty and show what life will be like when God reigns unopposed (Boring 1987, 131).

The appropriate response to this proclamation is repentance and trust (v. 15). The two are related; only the one who trusts that God, and not evil, is ultimately in control is prepared to undergo the change of mindset and attitude signified by the imperative *Repent!* Those who persist in holding a human outlook rather than adopting God's view of reality (8:33b) are not ready to trust the good news that God reigns.

1:16-20. Calling the first disciples. The author of Mark does not narrate the call of each individual named in the list of disciples (3:16-19). The call story at the beginning of the Galilean ministry is meant to characterize the summons to all disciples: they are to follow Jesus, who will cause them to fish for people (v. 17).

In this story the Markan Jesus does not behave in the way that was most typical of rabbis or philosophers in antiquity. Jewish rabbis and most pagan philosophers did not recruit followers. Rather, those who wanted to learn sought out a teacher and requested permission to become a disciple. However, the Greek writer Diogenes Laertius repeats two call stories that are similar to the story in Mark 1:16-20.

In one story the philosopher Socrates encounters Xenophon in an alley and asks him where various kinds of food can be bought. Xenophon answers correctly. Socrates then asks where people can become good and honorable. When Xenophon does not know the answer, Socrates says to him, "Then follow me and learn."

The second story concerns Zeno, the founder of Stoicism. He is portrayed as sitting in a book shop reading Xenophon's biography of Socrates. Impressed with the life of the great philosopher, Zeno asks where men like Socrates might be found. At that moment Crates, a disciple of Socrates was passing by, so the bookseller pointed to him and said to Zeno, "Follow that man." Zeno then became Crates' disciple.

The similarities with the Markan call story are: (1) people are engaged in the daily activities of life with no thought of seeking a teacher; (2) a teacher suddenly attracts their attention; (3) there is an imperative summons to "follow"; and (4) they respond by becoming disciples.

It is likely that the author of Mark chose this model over the more common one in which the student seeks a teacher because this summons/response pattern conforms more closely with the theology of the OT. In the OT God takes the initiative, calling into a covenant relationship people who are going about their business with no thought of being called by God. This is true of Abraham (Gen 12:1-4), Jacob (Gen 28:10-17), Moses (Exod 3:1-6), and Israel as a people (Deut 6:21-25).

The initiative of God is also an important feature of prophetic call stories (Amos 7:14-15; Jer 1:5). Isaiah speaks of Israel as "called" by God (42:6; 49:1). The Markan Jesus calls disciples in a way that conforms to the biblical understanding of the way God relates to the chosen people.

The specific promise of the Markan Jesus is that those who had been catching fish would now catch human beings (v. 17). Again the evangelist is drawing upon a metaphor that would have been familiar to both the Jewish and the gentile members of his audience. The analogy of fishing was used in the Israelite wisdom tradition as well as in Greek educational philosophy to speak about the way in which people were lured by the bait of the teacher's ideas and thus were prevented from wasting their lives in meaningless pursuits.

Greeks hoped to be caught in the nets of the gods rather than being snared by the evil spirits that were also out fishing for people. The Hebrew prophets spoke of Israel's enemies as God's fishers, gathering in the people of Israel for judgment—a judgment designed to lead to their repentance and return to covenant faithfulness (Ezek 17:19-21; Jer 16:16). So when Jesus' disciples go out to heal and to preach that people should repent (6:12) they are fulfilling Jesus' promise that they will become fishers for people.

1:21-45. Healings and exorcisms. This section and the one that follows it are both organized in the literary form of the chiasm, sometimes called a "concentric" or "ring" composition:

A Jesus makes a demon "go out from" a man.
Jesus contrasted with the scribes, 21-27
B Jesus' reputation goes from a synagogue into "all Galilee," 28
C Simon's mother-in-law is healed by Jesus, 29-31
D Summary: healings and exorcisms, Jesus' identity, 32-34
C' Simon interrupts Jesus' prayer, 35-38
B' Jesus goes into synagogues in "all Galilee," 39
A' Jesus makes leprosy "go off of" a man.
Jesus contrasted with the priests, 40-45.

The parallel elements will be considered together.

In A (vv. 21-27) Jesus casts a demon out of a man in the Capernaum synagogue. The response of the people is noteworthy. They exclaim, *What is this? A new teaching—with authority! He commands even the unclean spirits, and they obey him*. In this way the evangelist makes the point that Jesus' teaching includes not only what he says, but also what he does. His teaching and his healings and exorcisms form a unified whole. One is not more normative than the other.

In A' (vv. 40-45) the disease the Bible calls LEPROSY seems to have been thought of as demonic in character, at least in an early stage of the transmission of this story. Three elements in the story are more characteristic of exorcism stories than of healing stories: (1) Jesus' anger in v. 41 (see note *n* in the NRSV) and in v. 43; (2) the verb "cast out" (ἐξέβαλεν) in v. 43; (3) the report of the result of Jesus' action in v. 42 (*Immediately the leprosy left him*; cf. v. 26: "it [the demon] went out of him").

In both stories Jesus' authority and power are contrasted with those of the religious establishment. He has authority that they do not have and he can make a leper clean, whereas they can only give official recognition to the cure that has already taken place.

The hostility toward Jesus that becomes explicit in 2:1–3:6 is prepared for by these two stories. Jesus' behavior disrupts the established lines of teaching authority and the traditional ways of dealing with uncleanness. He should have become ritually unclean when he touched the leper; instead, the leper became clean. Because healing leprosy was understood as something that only God could do (2 Kgs 5:7) this story makes it clear that Jesus' power and authority are not his but God's. As *the Holy One of God* he has indeed *come to destroy* the demons and illnesses that afflict humankind (1:24). But he will be persecuted because his authority comes from God and not from the religious establishment.

In B (v. 28) Jesus' reputation goes out *throughout the surrounding region of Galilee.* This notice prepares for B' (v. 39), when Jesus himself goes into synagogues *throughout Galilee.*

Simon, the first disciple Jesus called (v. 16), plays a role in both C (vv. 29-31) and C' (vv. 35-38). In vv. 29-31 the Markan Jesus heals Simon's mother-in-law. She responds by "serving" (v. 31). It is customary in a healing story for the last element in the story to constitute some kind of proof that the person has indeed been restored to health. But in this story, the nameless woman's service has another point; it is the mark of a true follower of Jesus, as James and John will be reminded in 10:45.

Simon appears again in C' (vv. 35-38), where he and his companions seek Jesus, who has slipped out of CAPERNAUM before dawn to pray. Like so many sincere activists in today's churches, Simon sees no point in wasting time in prayer when there are hurting people back in Capernaum to be helped. The contrast in the story is between Simon's human-centered concerns and Jesus' focus on God as the source of his direction and his power to heal. Jesus is not lacking in compassion, but he demonstrates the importance of putting priority on the discovery and the doing of God's will. In this case, his assignment is not to continue healing people in Capernaum, but to move out into other areas.

The central part of the chiasm (vv. 32-34) sums up the healing and exorcistic activity of Jesus, which the individual stories are intended to illustrate. Jesus attracts large numbers of the sick and demon-possessed and restores them to wholeness. Here for the first time the evangelist introduces a theme that will become increasingly problematic as the story progresses: the issue of Jesus' identity: *He would not permit the demons to speak, because they knew him* (v. 34).

Indeed the demons do know him; the one in v. 24 knows that he is *the Holy One of God* and that he has *come to destroy* the demons. The disciples, however, do not do as well as the demons; they puzzle over Jesus' identity and fail to understand him despite their close association and private instruction. Indeed, the last words on the lips of any disciple in the Gospel are "I don't know the person of whom you are speaking" (14:71, author trans.).

Since the audience of the Gospel has been fully informed about Jesus' identity since 1:1, the disciples' confusion and Jesus' puzzling commands to silence create a tension and expectation that contribute to the movement of the narrative.

By the end of the section Jesus' fame has spread so widely that he *could no longer go into a town openly* (v. 45) without being overwhelmed by the numbers of people coming to him.

2:1–3:6. Controversies. The previous section demonstrated Jesus' authority and power over demons and illness—an authority that was superior to that of the religious establishment. In this section, which is also arranged chiastically, the author of Mark tells five controversy stories which demonstrate Jesus' authority to forgive sins and to interpret scripture in nontraditional ways.

Jesus' authority to forgive sins is linked by the evangelist with his specific concern for sinners, rather than for righteous people who seek no forgiveness. According to Mark, protecting and enforcing religious law is not the focus of Jesus' ministry. Jesus and his followers, past and present, serve a God who is interested in reconciling sinners, feeding the hungry, and healing the sick.

This focus puts Jesus in conflict with religious people whose power depends upon identifying and ostracizing sinners. At first their opposition is limited to private criticism (2:6), but by the end of the section they are plotting to destroy Jesus (3:6).

It is important to note that the author of Mark does not criticize Jews or Jewish leaders as such. That is to say, Mark does not sanction anti-Semitism. Rather, like the OT prophets, the evangelist points out that God's reign runs counter to the claims of all who attempt to preempt God's sovereign authority, even those who claim to represent God. The section may be outlined as follows (Dewey 1980):

A Healing of paralytic. Controversy plus healing [call of Levi (2:13-16) echoes 1:16-20 and prepares for 2:15-17], 2:1-12
  B Controversy over eating. Jesus and his disciples eat with the wrong people, 2:15-17
    C Controversy over fasting (not eating), 2:18-22
  B' Controversy over eating. Jesus' disciples acquire food in the wrong way, 2:23-28
A' Healing of withered hand. Controversy plus healing, 3:1-6

The parallel passages will be discussed together.

A (2:1-12) and A' (3:1-6) lay the groundwork for the two trials of Jesus and establish his innocence ahead of time. In 2:7 the scribes accuse Jesus of blasphemy (cf. 14:64) because he exercises God's prerogative to forgive sins. They are correct that only God can do this, but they miss the point. The audience realizes that Jesus is not blaspheming because his authority comes from God.

It is not illegal on the SABBATH to command a person to stand up in the SYNAGOGUE and stretch out his hand (3:1-5). Jesus has done nothing wrong (cf. 15:14). His opponents are the guilty ones because they plot to commit murder, which is not legal on any day of the week. Jesus saves life (3:4); for this he will die.

B (2:15-17) and B' (2:23-28) emphasize God's initiative toward human beings. The community whose life is centered on fellowship with Jesus is a community of sinners and their religious practice represents God's provision for their benefit, not their attempt to please God.

The call of Levi (2:13-16) is important preparation for the controversy over eating with sinners because tax collectors (publicans) were not only regarded as dishonest, but were also despised as collaborators with the Roman overlords. Revolutionary groups who might have applauded Jesus' association with the poor peasants would have been appalled by his association with the running dogs of Roman imperialism.

But the Markan Jesus is not captive to ideological categories. The only requirement for his company is to understand oneself as a sinner—no better than the lowest form of human being one can imagine. "If you don't consider yourself to be in that category," the Gospel writer says, "then don't count yourself among the associates of Jesus."

If the point of Christian community is *not* to avoid sinners, then the point of sabbath observance is *not* to be religious, but rather to meet human need. *The sabbath was made for humankind, not humankind for the sabbath* (2:27). Furthermore, Jesus, the Son of Man, is lord even over the sabbath and over the scriptures, which he interprets to prove his point: David broke religious laws to feed his hungry troops (1 Sam 21:1-6). The Gospel writer cites David's act during the days of ABIATHAR, which poses a problem for careful readers of the Bible.

Right in the center of the chiastic structure is the controversy over fasting (2:18-22). In an oblique reference to the CRUCIFIXION, the Markan Jesus speaks of a time when he (the bridegroom) will be *taken away* (v. 20). That will be the time for fasting.

The discussion about fasting leads into a pair of sayings on the relationship between the old and the new. The good news that Jesus brings is by its very nature disruptive of old patterns. New and flexible structures are necessary, because the fermentation of the gospel will soon destroy containers that are rigid and fragile.

Taken together, 1:21-45 and 2:1–3:6 present a complete overview of Jesus' ministry, which the evangelist regards as normative for the church in his own day. The church is about the business of teaching, healing, casting out demons, building a community of sinners, and meeting human needs. Jesus' authority to interpret scripture overrides that of the old establishment and creates new wineskins flexible enough to allow for the gospel's disruptive bubbling.

But it is not a cheap victory. It will cost Jesus his life and it will cost his followers every shred of security and self-righteousness.

3:7-12. Conclusion. The large section 1:14–3:12, which establishes the basic pattern of Jesus' ministry, concludes with a summary in 3:7-12. The return to the sea with the disciples (3:7) forms an INCLUSIO with the original calling of the disciples by the sea (1:16).

There Jesus had promised to make the former fishermen into fishers for people. Here the audience learns that Jesus himself is a successful people-fisher; not only has he attracted crowds from Galilee, but people have come from long distances after hearing about him.

The summary reemphasizes Jesus' ministry of healing and exorcism and reminds the audience that although the demons knew Jesus' true identity as Son of God, Jesus did not permit them to make him known to others.

Extension of Jesus' Ministry and Intensification of Conflict, 3:7–6:30

3:7-12. Introduction. This summary serves not only to conclude the previous section, but also to introduce places and ideas that will be important in the second and third major sections of the ministry in Galilee and gentile territory.

The crowd that follows Jesus includes people from Galilee, Judea, Jerusalem (which is in Judea), Idumea (home territory of the Herodians), the territory east of the Jordan River, and the region around TYRE AND SIDON (Phoenicia). Information that sick people were pressing around Jesus attempting to touch him prepares for the story of the hemorrhaging woman (5:25-34).

The mention of Tyre and Sidon prepares for Jesus' visit there in 7:24-30 and explains to the audience why the SYROPHOENICIAN woman expected Jesus to be able to exorcise her daughter. According to Mark, gentile followers of Jesus had spread the word in their home territory about the miracles they had seen in Galilee.

The boat that will become the platform for Jesus' teaching in 4:1 and the means by which he himself ventures into gentile territory in 5:1 is introduced in 3:9. The material in 3:13–6:30 may be outlined as follows:

A Disciples appointed ("sent out ones," *sent out,* 3:14), 3:13-19
  B Misinterpretation by family and religious leaders, 3:20-35
    C Jesus' words and deeds heard and seen but not always understood, 4:1–5:43
      1. Jesus' words (collection of parables), 4:1-34
      2. Jesus' deeds (collection of miracle stories), 4:35–5:43
  B' Misinterpretation by associates in home town, 6:1-6
A' Disciples *sent out* ("sent out ones," 6:30), 6:7-13

3:13-19. Disciples appointed. As Baptist translator Helen Barrett Montgomery points out, the word translated "apostle" in most English Bibles actually means "missionary" or "one sent out" (1924, Mark 3:14, n. 1). Thus the material in 3:13–6:30 is framed by an emphasis on Christian mission (3:13-19 and 6:7-13, 30).

But the author of Mark is careful to make clear that mission *follows* a period of developing a relationship with Jesus:

And he appointed twelve (whom he also named missionaries) in order that
(1) they might be with him and in order that
(2) he might commission them
(a) to proclaim and
(b) to have authority to cast out the demons
and he appointed the twelve. (author trans.)

In the ancient world it was thought that a disciple could not properly carry out the instructions of the teacher without first spending a great deal of time in the teacher's presence. The Gospel of Mark applies this insight to Christian formation.

The active ministry of the disciples is patterned after that of Jesus himself: proclamation (cf. 1:14) and spiritual warfare (cf. 1:21-27, 34, 39; 3:11-12), speech and action. Neither is optional and one may not be substituted for the other. It is worth noting that the authority of the disciples extends only to demons. They are given no authority over other followers of Jesus.

In Mark, THE TWELVE named in chap. 3 do not constitute an inside group of disciples who have special privileges. The size of the group called "disciples" or "followers" of Jesus varies from scene to scene in Mark, and includes, besides the twelve named here, Levi (2:14), *many* tax collectors and sinners (2:15), Mary Magdalene, Mary the mother of James and Joses, Salome (15:40), Bartimaeus (10:52), and the Gethsemane "streaker" (14:51). The greatest privilege bestowed in the Gospel seems to be the gift of "the mystery of the reign of God" (4:11 author trans.), and that gift is said to have been given to a group larger than the twelve. Thus, "twelve" should be understood as symbolic of the new people of God; the number corresponds to the twelve tribes of Israel in the OT. It does not delineate an exclusive group.

3:20-35. Misinterpretation by family and religious leaders. In this unit, a controversy with the scribes is framed by the misunderstanding of Jesus by his family of origin and their replacement by "those who do the will of God" (author trans.). Since the controversy involves two charges by opponents, to which Jesus responds in reverse order, the result is a chiastic structure (Robbins 1989, 172, n. 27):

A Jesus' family comes to seize him, 20-21
B Accusation 1: He has Beelzebul, 22a
C Accusation 2: By the prince of demons he casts out demons, 22b
C' Refutation 2: Satan would not cast out demons, 23-27
B' Refutation 1: Saying Jesus has an unclean spirit is blasphemy, 28-30
A' Jesus' true family consists of those who do the will of God, 31-35

In 3:21, members of Jesus' family respond to the crowds that he is attracting by coming out to seize him because in their opinion Jesus is out of his mind (ἐξέστη, lit. "standing outside [himself]"). In 3:31, however, the evangelist turns the tables; now the family is standing outside (ἔξω στήκοντες) by contrast with those who are seated around Jesus on the inside.

The Markan Jesus explains that his kin are not those who are related to him by blood, but those who are related to him by sharing his purpose: doing the will of God. The message to the audience is twofold: (1) Sometimes even one's own relatives will think one crazy for doing the will of God; (2) Those whose relatives misunderstand their Christian commitment find a new family in the Christian community, just as Jesus did (cf. 10:29-30).

When the scribes accuse Jesus of having Beelzebul and of using that demon's power to perform exorcisms, the audience would have understood that they were accusing Jesus of practicing magic. Magicians were believed to have gained control of spirits that they could call upon to do their bidding. Spells and incantations were used to force the gods and spirits to do the will of the magician or witch who was casting the spell.

When an ancient miracle worker was accused of practicing magic, his defense often was to claim that he had not used incantations, but had prayed. He was not, after all, a magician trying to force the gods to do his will, but a pious person who did only the will of the gods. So when the author of Mark portrays Jesus and his followers as those who "do the will of God" he is relying upon a commonly accepted line of argument to make his point.

Further, the Markan Jesus responds to his opponents by pointing out that it would be inconsistent for Satan, the ruler of demons, to allow his power to be used to cast out demons. Finally, the audience is reminded of the real source of Jesus' power—the Holy Spirit that came into him at his baptism (1:8, 10). The scribes' false attribution of the work of the Holy Spirit to Satan is not an innocent mistake. It is an unpardonable sin.

As the scene closes Jesus and his associates are inside and those who misunderstand and oppose him are standing outside. This contrast between insiders and outsiders, which seems so clear-cut in this passage, will become increasingly problematic as the story progresses.

4:1-34. Jesus' words (parables). The parable chapter is the first of only two long speeches by the Markan Jesus. The other is the apocalyptic discourse in chap. 13. In fact, both speeches are primarily about eschatology. In chap. 4 the author of Mark combines PARABLES and sayings from the Jesus tradition to explain why the proclamation of God's reign is meeting with resistance and to assure the audience that despite the present apparent lack of progress, God's reign will eventually burst forth in amazing fruitfulness.

A secondary and related concern of chaps. 4 and 13 is a warning against apostasy. This is regarded by the evangelist as a danger even for those who have experienced God's grace mediated through Jesus.

The author of Mark has arranged the material into a carefully constructed chiastic arrangement (Marcus 1986, 221):

A Narrative introduction, 1-2
B Seed parable (public teaching), 3-9
C Statement about hiddenness (private teaching), 10-12
D Allegorical explanation of parable (private teaching), 13-20
C' Statements about revelation (private teaching), 21-25
B' Seed parables (public teaching), 26-29, 30-32
A' Narrative conclusion, 33-34

According to this arrangement, all three seed parables are addressed to the crowd that assembles in 4:1 and is left behind in 4:36. This public teaching frames the private teaching to "those around him with the twelve" (v. 10, author trans.). The private teaching, while it picks up the agricultural images of the parable in the allegorical explanation (vv. 13-20), also introduces images drawn from domestic life: lamp, basket, bed, lampstand, house, and measure (vv. 21-25).

Agricultural images were commonly used by Hellenistic writers to teach lessons about education and improvement of character. They were used in the OT and in apocalyptic Judaism to teach about God's will and God's coming reign. The Markan Jesus combines these emphases, but alters the images to suit his purposes.

The seed parables (vv. 3-9, 26-29, 30-32) make three points:

(1) The ultimate success of God's reign is inevitable, despite present appearances to the contrary. Although much seed falls on unproductive soil, the good soil will yield a harvest abundant beyond all imagination.

(2) God's reign is the result of what God does, not the result of what human beings do. All the farmer has to do is sow the seed. Everything else is outside his control. This is a marked contrast with Hellenistic emphases upon the importance of human effort in producing a good "harvest," but it coincides with the apocalyptic idea that in the drama of history God is the primary actor and human beings merely respond to God's initiative.

(3) God's reign is inclusive, but not imperialistic. The parable of the mustard seed speaks of God's reign as a plant with large branches that shelter the birds of the air. In Dan 4:10-17 the BABYLONIAN EMPIRE is portrayed as a large tree; in Ezek 31:3-14 the same image is used for ASSYRIA. The author of Ezek 17:22-24 regards that image as appropriate for the glorious Messianic kingdom that was expected after the humiliation of the exile. But the Markan story deflates all this grandiosity by comparing God's reign, not to a mighty cedar, but to a humble mustard bush. It doesn't look like much, but it provides shelter for all who flock to it (Waetjen 1989, 108–109).

The sayings on hiddenness and revelation (vv. 10-12, 21-25) have presented a challenge to interpreters over the centuries. In the Markan context, three points are being made:

(1) Just as Isaiah's words were meant to prevent understanding and repentance, so Jesus' parables prevent understanding and repentance by those "outside" who oppose God's reign (vv. 10-12).

(2) Concealment is not the last word. *There is nothing hidden, except to be disclosed; nor is anything secret, except to come to light* (v. 22).

(3) Those who have been "given the secret of God's reign" (v. 11, author trans.) had better not be complacent. They need to pay attention to the insight they have (v. 24). This includes not only the disciples in the story, but the audience of the Gospel as well.

The central emphasis of the passage falls on the allegorical interpretation of the first seed parable. The Markan Jesus says that understanding this parable is critically important for understanding all the parables (v. 13).

The parable itself pointed to the ultimate success of God's reign. The interpretation explains why the present circumstances are so difficult and why so much seed fails to bear fruit. The explanation is a typically apocalyptic one: God's reign is temporarily opposed by Satan and his forces.

In the first case, Satan snatches away the word before it takes root. This is a reference to people who, although they hear the message, do not even begin as followers of Jesus.

The second and third cases are about people who begin as followers of Jesus, but fail to follow through in discipleship. Some are unable to withstand *when trouble or persecution arises on account of the word* (v. 17) and some are distracted by the concerns of the present age (an apocalyptic term), the seductive power of wealth, and the desire for "things" other than the "things of God" (8:33, author trans.). APOSTASY, according to Mark, can be a response either to difficulties or to comfortable circumstances.

When Christians encounter opposition and persecution, or when they see converts lost to the seductive addictions of increased ease and affluence, they are not to be discouraged. This is all part of the ministry to which they are called. Their part is to keep sowing. The rest is up to God.

4:35–5:43. Jesus' deeds (miracle stories). The unit of parables is followed by a unit of miracle stories. Like the parables, the miracles proclaim the reign of God and are a source of misunderstanding for some. Jesus' words are heard, but not understood; his deeds are seen, but not perceived (cf. 4:12).

The miracle stories are grouped in two pairs:

A Conquest of demonic storm, 4:35-41
Setting: on the sea, on the way to gentile territory
Beneficiaries: male disciples
Level of threat: the disciples fear that they are about to die

A' Conquest of demons in GERASA, 5:1-20
Setting: near the sea, in gentile territory
Beneficiary: male gentile
Level of threat: the demoniac lives among the dead

B Healing of hemorrhaging woman, 5:24b-34
Setting: Jewish territory

Beneficiary: female; ritually unclean; ill for 12 years
Level of threat: she is in the process of dying (life is draining away)

B' Raising of Jairus' daughter, 5:21-24a, 35-43
Setting: Jewish territory
Beneficiary: female; ritually unclean corpse; twelve years old
Level of threat: she is already dead when Jesus arrives

The confidence that God's unlimited power is at work in Jesus is called "faith" in these miracle stories (5:34). The evangelist puts them here not merely to record Jesus' past activity, but to encourage those who hear the stories to resist paralyzing fear (4:40; 5:36) and to maintain confidence in God's power to overcome evil, sickness, and death.

In the first pair of stories Jesus' role as divine warrior against evil is emphasized. The storm that Jesus and his disciples encounter on the Sea of Galilee is interpreted in the narrative as an attempt by demonic forces to keep Jesus from invading gentile territory (5:1-20). In order to make sense of the Markan Jesus' movements back and forth across the sea, the reader should consult a map of the area (MBD, plate 23). Jesus "rebukes" the storm (4:39) in the same way that he addresses the demons (1:25, 3:12). Like the demons, *the wind and the sea obey him* (4:41). The sea represents the forces of chaos and death, over which Jesus, the life-bringer, exercises control.

But the disciples are still in the dark, asking, "Who then is this?" The demons know, the audience knows, but even those who have been given the mystery of the reign of God fail to perceive the meaning in what they see.

Having resisted the onslaught of the sea demons, Jesus lands in gentile territory and immediately encounters more demons in a militant mood. A whole legion of them are tormenting a man whose days of living death are passed *among the tombs and on the mountains* (5:5). Like Pharoah's army, however, these enemy troops rush into the sea and are drowned (5:13). Again the victory goes to the divine warrior. Chaos becomes order and wholeness (5:15).

But again Jesus' saving power is seen by blind eyes. The Gerasenes see the loss of the pigs and send Jesus away. Before he goes, he commissions the former demoniac to tell *how much the Lord has done* for him (5:19). The man's response has two effects: (1) By preaching (κηρύσσειν, cf. 1:14, 3:14), he does what disciples are supposed to do. He becomes one who makes the deeds of the Lord "known . . . among the nations" (Isa 12:4); (2) His proclamation equates the merciful activity of the Lord with the ministry of Jesus (5:20). The answer to the disciples' question, "Who then is this?" is "Jesus is the Lord."

In the second pair of stories the setting shifts from gentile to Jewish territory and the emphasis shifts from cosmic combat to healing, but the boundary-crossing character of Jesus' ministry is still apparent. Having crossed geographical boundaries to release a gentile from bondage, Jesus now crosses traditional purity boundaries to restore life to two suffering women.

Neither woman is ritually "clean" when Jesus encounters her. According to Torah, vaginal bleeding renders a woman unclean (Lev 5:19-30) and all corpses are unclean (Num 19:11-21). In these stories the theme first sounded in the cleansing of the leper (1:40-45) is repeated. Although Jesus should have become unclean by touching the bleeding woman and the dead girl, exactly the opposite happens. His touch restores both women to health and to states of ritual purity.

Both Jairus and the bleeding woman are portrayed positively as having faith in Jesus' healing power. Jairus is called upon to "keep on believing" (5:36, author trans.) for an even greater miracle than healing after his daughter is pronounced dead before Jesus' arrival.

Jairus is a leader of the synagogue—a religious and social insider. He has a right to ask for help and he does so directly, but not arrogantly. Rather than flaunting his social and religious status, he humbles himself (5:22-23), an attitude that Jesus will praise in 9:35, 10:41-45.

The anonymous woman, by contrast, has been a religious and social outsider for twelve years, experiencing neither the worship of God nor human embrace. She has no right to jeopardize Jesus' ritual status by touching him. However, she refuses to be defined by her situation and takes bold action on the basis of what she has heard about Jesus (5:27; cf. 3:10).

Whereas the parables emphasize assurance of the *final* victory of God's reign, this unit of MIRACLE STORIES promises *present* help for those who call on Jesus with confidence in his power.

6:1-6. Misinterpretation by associates in hometown. This second instance of misinterpretation of Jesus' miracle-working activity by intimate associates corresponds to 3:20-35 in Mark's chiastic outline of 3:13–6:30. Like the scribes (3:22), the people of Nazareth raise questions about the source of Jesus' power and wisdom. They recognize that Jesus is doing miraculous things and that he has been given extraordinary wisdom (v. 3), but they do not see in these phenomena the inbreaking of the reign of God. They do not admit that God is the source of Jesus' power.

They point to Jesus' ordinary occupation; he is a carpenter, not a scribe or a rabbi. He does not come from a traditional family; they call him *son of Mary* (v. 3) rather than the traditional "son of Joseph" (cf. Luke 4:22; John 6:42). The hometown boy is getting something from somewhere, but where? No one suggests God.

The evangelist comments, *they took offense at him* (ἐσκανδαλίζοντο ἐν αὐτῷ). This phrase can mean two things in Mark. In 4:17; 9:42-47; and 14:27 it means to be caused to abandon allegiance to Jesus after beginning as a disciple. Here, however, it is used of nonfollowers and means that the people of Nazareth were prevented from becoming Jesus' disciples.

The people of Nazareth are like the seed that fell beside the path: they never take root at all. Their opinions of who Jesus is prevent their seeing God at work in his miracles. Jesus is amazed by their unbelief.

In the miracle stories (4:35–5:43), to "have faith" means to have confidence in Jesus' power. Here the evangelist expands the definition beyond that. To recognize that Jesus has power is not enough; it is necessary to recognize that Jesus' power and wisdom come from God, and from no other source.

The conclusion of this scene is strangely paradoxical. The evangelist says that *[Jesus] could do no deed of power there* and then says *he laid his hands on a few sick people and cured them* (v. 5). The reason for this odd sentence is that the author of Mark wants to summarize his complex view of the relationship between faith and miracles.

On the one hand, confidence in Jesus' power (faith) is basic if the Christian community expects to experience that power in its life and ministry (5:34, 36; 9:23; 10:52). On the other hand, there are no absolute conditions that can limit God's freedom to act in sovereign power. Even when faith is inadequate, grace may extend miraculous help (4:35-41; 6:5; 9:24-27).

The Markan Jesus summarizes the misunderstanding of Nazareth with a traditional proverb: *Prophets are not without honor, except in their hometown, and among their own kin, and in their own house* (v. 4). Many Christians have found it so.

6:7-13, 30. Disciples sent out. The large section 3:13–6:30 concludes with Jesus' sending out of the disciples to do the ministry to which he had appointed them at the beginning of the section (3:13-19). Having now been with Jesus (3:14b) and observed his ministry of word (4:1-34) and deed (4:35–5:43), the disciples are ready to be sent out in pairs to proclaim repentance and to exercise Jesus' authority over the demonic spirits. They also bring God's healing to the sick.

There is no hint here of the kind of dispensationalist understanding of miracle that came to characterize the church in later generations. The author of Mark believes that Jesus' followers are to replicate his ministry. They do not do this alone, but with others. There are no superstars or lone rangers.

Finally the evangelist stresses accountability. Mark 6:30 is not merely a narrative conclusion. It suggests that disciples will give an account of their faithfulness to the one who sent them out.

In Mark 6:8-11 the Gospel writer sets out instructions for missionaries. They are allowed to have a walking stick and a pair of sandals, which are all they need to get from one place to another. They are not allowed to carry bread, money, a begging bag, or an extra tunic. For the necessities of life they will have to depend on God and God's people. Like the Israelites who lived from one day's supply of manna to the next, they are radically dependent on God's providential care.

The rejection that missionaries encounter is not regarded as a surprising development, but as an expected outcome. The response is to be neither discouragement nor vindictive reprisal, but continued ministry elsewhere. The result is not the problem of the sowers. All they have to do is sow.

Jesus' Ministry Removes Barriers between Jews and Gentiles, 6:14–8:30

This third and final subsection of 1:14–8:30 picks up and expands the theme of the inclusion of the gentiles that was introduced in 5:1-20. The section is framed by identical speculations about Jesus' identity: Is he John the baptizer reincarnated? Is he Elijah, the forerunner of the Messiah? Is he some other prophet? (6:14-16; 8:27-30).

In chap. 6 the question of Jesus' identity is left hanging, but the question of whether his opponents will succeed in destroying him (3:6, 3:19) is clarified in a chilling flashback. The execution of John the baptizer suggests that the prospects are grim for those who run afoul of Herod and his partisans.

Beginning at 6:31, Jesus feeds and heals first Jews (6:31-56) and then gentiles (7:24–8:10). Between the ministry to Jews and the ministry to gentiles, a discussion with Pharisees over the proper understanding of religious defilement (7:1-23) prepares for the move to the gentiles in 7:24.

The section closes with summaries illustrating the failure by Jesus' opponents (8:11-13) and by his disciples (8:14-21) to perceive the significance of his ministry. The arrival at Bethsaida in 8:22 marks the end of the sea crossings that began in 4:35; the story of the blind man healed in two stages (8:22-26) prepares for the discipleship section 8:22–10:52, which ends with the only other healing of blindness in Mark (10:46-52).

<u>6:14-29. Death of John the baptizer.</u> The execution of John the baptizer by Herod Antipas is confirmed by Josephus (*Ant* 18.5.2), who understood it as an attempt to prevent John's organizing a political revolution. Mark's macabre interpretation of the episode is designed to foreshadow the passion of Jesus and perhaps also to suggest future suffering for his followers, who have just been sent out on their first assignment.

It is important to notice the artistry of this story, which is one of the more obvious of the Markan "sandwiched" narratives. The story is told between the sending of the disciples in vv. 7-13 and their return in v. 30. After the disciples have been sent out, the narrator informs the audience that "King Herod heard of it, for Jesus' name had become known."

Herod's participation in the speculation about Jesus' identity prepares for the narrative flashback of vv. 17-29. Herod's own conclusion is that Jesus' power is due to the fact that he is a reincarnation of the executed prophet. This failure to identify God as the source of Jesus' power has already been labeled "unbelief" by the evangelist (6:1-6).

The Markan account of the circumstances leading to John's death is the longest and most melodramatic that has been preserved. It is also replete with OT allusions. By calling Herod the tetrarch a "king" and by making John's criticism of Herod's immoral marriage (Lev 18:16, 20:21) the reason for his imprisonment, the evangelist identifies John with the long line of prophets who rebuked kings (1 Sam 15:17-29;

2 Sam 12:1-15; 2 Kgs 20:16-18; Jer 38:14-23) and of martyrs who upheld the law in the face of royal opposition (2 Macc 6:18–7:42; 4 Macc 5–18).

The primary prophet that the author of Mark has in mind, however, is Elijah, with whom he identifies John elsewhere in the Gospel (1:6-7; 9:11-13). In this story Herodias plays Jezebel to John's Elijah. But whereas Jezebel was unsuccessful in eliminating Elijah, Herodias succeeds in destroying John.

The involvement of the young daughter is a particularly chilling detail. Textual variants make it uncertain whether the evangelist regards her as the daughter of Herodias only, or also of Herod (see NRSV v. 22, mrg). Commentators usually assume that the dance was erotic, although this is likewise uncertain. What is plain, however, is that she is put by the evangelist into the same age group as Jairus's twelve-year-old daughter. The same word (κοράσιον) is used for both. One little daughter is restored to life; one participates in a grisly murder. It is the child who adds the detail of the platter. John's head is the final course in this macabre banquet (Anderson 1992).

John's headless body is claimed by his disciples and laid in a tomb. When Jesus' time for burial comes, however, his disciples will be nowhere to be found.

6:30-56. Ministry to Jews. This section has three parts: the feeding miracle (vv. 31-44), the sea-walking story (vv. 45-52), and a series of healings (vv. 53-56). The first and third take place on the western side of the Sea of Galilee, that is, in Jewish territory. The three-part series opens and closes with references to the crowds that surround Jesus and the disciples (v. 31 [cf. 3:19]; vv. 54-56).

In the first of two feeding miracles in the Gospel, Jesus is portrayed as the faithful shepherd promised to Israel in the prophetic and APOCALYPTIC LITERATURE (Ezek 34:23; Jer 23:4; PssSol 17:40). Because both Moses (Exod 3:1) and David (1 Sam 16:11) had been shepherds, the shepherd became a metaphor for the religious and political leaders of Israel and also for Yahweh, Israel's ultimately faithful shepherd.

The prophets criticized Israel's leaders for being irresponsible shepherds (Isa 56:11-12; Jer 23:1-2; Ezek 34:1-10), or for leaving the people unprotected, without a shepherd (Ezek 34:5; cf. Num 27:17; 1 Kgs 22:17; cf. Isa 53:6). Through the prophets, Yahweh promised to replace the unworthy shepherds, either by shepherding the people himself, or by raising up a faithful shepherd, usually a Davidic leader (Ezek 34:11-16; Jer 23:3-6; Isa 40:11; 49:9b-10).

By invoking these images in v. 34, the author of Mark proclaims the good news that the eschatological shepherd has arrived to provide for the needs of God's people. As their shepherd, Jesus teaches the crowds (v. 34b), provides them with food (v. 42; cf. Ezek 34:2, 8; Isa 40:11; Ps 23:2), and heals their sick and injured (vv. 53-56; cf. Ezek 34:4). There is also an implicit criticism of the religious leaders who oppose Jesus; they are the irresponsible shepherds condemned by the prophets.

The desert setting of the feeding miracle (vv. 34-35) reminds the audience of the Isaian theme of the New Exodus (Mark 1:3) and of God's miraculous provision of manna during the original Exodus. Both this story and its gentile counterpart (8:1-10) foreshadow the last meal Jesus will share with his disciples. There, as in the feeding stories, Jesus takes bread, pronounces a thanksgiving or a blessing, breaks the bread, and gives it to his disciples (14:22). Not only is the hunger of the crowd satisfied, but the leftovers fill twelve large baskets typically used by Jews for carrying loads. The number twelve further reinforces the Jewish cultural setting. Interestingly enough, the disciples, who have just returned from a mission on which they were forbidden to take bread (v. 8), manage, when pressed, to produce five loaves and two fish (v. 38).

After the feeding the Markan Jesus sends the disciples across the sea toward Bethsaida on the *other side* (v. 45), that is, in gentile territory. Jesus dismisses the crowd and, like Moses and Elijah before him, retires to the mountain to meet with God.

It soon becomes apparent, however, that without Jesus' leadership the disciples are not going to make it to gentile territory; again they are meeting with opposition, as in 4:35-41. Seeing this, the Markan Jesus again demonstrates his superiority over the hostile sea power by striding across the sea (vv. 47-52), an activity attributed to God in Job 9:8 and Isa 43:16. His intent was to walk ahead of them—to guide them, like a good shepherd, to their destination. However, the disciples do not recognize him and cry out in fear.

Continuing the imagery of the New Exodus, the narrator has Jesus identify himself with the self-designation of Yahweh, "I am" (Exod 3:14, Isa 41:4, 43:10-11). Thus the author of Mark provides the audience with a defintive answer to the question raised by the disciples in the previous sea-rescue story: *Who then is this?* (4:41). The promise of deliverance is reinforced by an echo of Deutero-Isaiah's *Do not be afraid* (v. 50; cf. Isa 43:10, 43; 45:18; 51:2). Sadly, none of this clarifies things for the disciples, who remain "utterly astounded."

Their astonishment reveals that they have missed the exodus allusions completely. They *did not understand about the loaves* (v. 52—the renewal of provision in the wilderness), or about Jesus' being the eschatological shepherd who takes care of his own, or about the way being made for God's people through the sea and the desert, or about Jesus' revelation of the character of God and God's reign in his person and ministry.

Worse yet, the narrator informs the audience that, like Jesus' opponents (3:5) and *those outside* (4:10-12, alluding to Isa 6:9-10) their hearts have been hardened. Despite their having been chosen and sent out on a successful mission, despite their having just participated in Jesus' own miraculous ministry, the disciples seem to be in danger of becoming outsiders. The narrator leaves the audience no room for complacency.

The trip to gentile territory aborted, Jesus and the disciples disembark at Gennesaret on the Jewish shore and are immediately surrounded by people seeking healing (vv. 53-55). As their shepherd, it is Jesus' responsibility to heal them (Ezek

34:4) and he does so. Echoing 3:10 and 5:24b-34, the narrator reports that people were healed merely by touching Jesus' clothes (v. 56).

This series of three episodes repeats the pattern seen throughout the Gospel in which Jesus' ministry has three components: teaching, healing, and domination of the demonic powers. The pervasive image throughout this series is the Jewish expectation of the eschatological shepherd who will feed, heal, and lead his flock to safety through watery chaos and threatening wilderness. The next section of the Gospel redefines membership in this eschatological flock.

7:1-23. Redefinition of clean/unclean. Coming immediately after the teaching, feeding, and healing of the Jewish crowds, this section prepares for the mission to the gentiles by challenging the understanding of defilement represented as that of the religious establishment and by asserting Jesus' authority to replace ritual boundaries with ethical ones. The Markan Jesus does not eliminate the notion of impurity; rather, he redefines it.

The literary structure follows the pattern set in 3:20–4:34: a controversy with authorities from Jerusalem is followed by a parable and its private interpretation to the inquiring disciples. The controversy (7:1-13) appears to be over the validity of the oral law. At a deeper level, it is about the way in which human sinfulness uses religion as a way of avoiding confrontation with God.

The parable (vv. 14-15) and its interpretation (vv. 17-23) deny the polluting character of nonkosher foods and insist that impurity is caused by behaviors that destroy human community. That this material was understood by some early readers as a literary parallel to the parables in chap. 4 is indicated by the addition of v. 16: "Let anyone with ears to hear listen," which is a scribal attempt to achieve conformity with 4:9, 23.

Whether or not one must perform ritual hand rinsing before eating (vv. 1-5) must not have been a burning issue for Christians at the time the gospel was written, since the evangelist finds it necessary to explain the practice in a long parenthesis (vv. 3-4). The religious leaders want to know why Jesus' disciples do not observe the oral traditions *of the elders* prescribing such cleansing rituals (v. 5). Jesus' answer is given in chiastic form (Gundry 1993, 349):

A Biblical citation from the prophets (Isa 29:13, LXX) with application, 7:6-7
B Accusation: *You abandon the commandment of God and hold to human tradition*, 7:8
B' Accusation: *You have a fine way of rejecting the commandment of God in order to keep your tradition*, 7:9
A' Biblical citation from the law of Moses (Exod 20:12; 21:17) with application, 7:10-13

The Markan Jesus asserts that the oral tradition was not, as its proponents thought, a way of guaranteeing faithfulness to God's will by building a fence around Torah. Instead, people had found a way to put religion to their own use; a veneer of religion covered a complete reversal of God's explicit commandment. Instead of honoring mother and father by providing for them, the subject of Jesus' illustration uses a religious vow to put the resources the parents need out of their reach.

Since the evangelist has to explain the meaning of *corban* (v. 11) and the hand-washing issue to the audience, it is unlikely that he is attacking Jewish practices familiar to and controversial among Christians or defending Christians against Jewish opponents. Rather, the author may be critiquing the tendency within the Christian community itself to prefer the practice of religion over obedience to God. Human traditions and lip service substitute for wholehearted self-surrender, as Isaiah said so well.

The parable about inside and outside (vv. 14-15) and its interpretation (vv. 17-23) complete the unit. The Markan Jesus begins as he did in 4:3 by addressing the crowd with the command, *Listen!* What follows is a change of subject from the previous discussion. There the issue was *how* one might eat; here it is *what* one may eat. The parable demands an explanation since the *word of God* so important to Jesus in v. 13 explicitly forbids the ingestion of foods that *defile* a person. Furthermore, the second claim of the parable seems to contradict Torah, which teaches that defecation does not defile the defecator (Gundry 1993, 354-55). Again, as in chap. 4, the disciples' question provides the opportunity for the evangelist to explain to the audience.

Everything turns upon an assumption that is not stated directly until v. 21, but ultimately derives from the Isaiah quotation: it is the human heart that is the locus of purity and defilement. What goes in through one's lips and down into one's stomach cannot defile because (as Torah teaches) its evacuation into the latrine does not cause impurity in the person. That which does not involve the heart does not pollute. But although what comes out of the intestines does not pollute, what comes out of the heart certainly does.

Lists of vices like the one in v. 21 are common in Hellenistic discussions of ethics (cf. Epictetus, *Diss* 2.16.45) and appear frequently in the NT (Rom 1:29-31; 1 Cor 6:9-10; Gal 5:19-21; Eph 5:5; Rev 21:8; 22:15). Everything on Mark's list is destructive of human relationships and is condemned by the OT. The Markan Jesus thus does not deny the authority of scripture, but he does revoke the food laws in favor of Isaiah's emphasis on the importance of the attitude of the heart toward God. In the evangelist's view, devotion to God results in right relationships with other human beings.

To make sure the audience does not miss the point, the author points out parenthetically that in this statement, Jesus "made all foods clean" (author trans.). Again Jesus is seen to speak *as one having authority* by contrast with the scribes (1:22). Having made all foods clean in this section, the Markan Jesus proceeds in 7:24-30 to make all persons clean as well.

7:24–8:9. Ministry to gentiles. Like 6:31-56, which described Jesus' ministry to Jews, this section consists of three stories: exorcism of a Syrophoenician woman's daughter (vv. 24-30), restoration of hearing and speech to a man (vv. 31-37), and the feeding of 4,000 in the DECAPOLIS (8:1-9). Whereas the first panel *began* with a feeding miracle, this panel *ends* with one. Both sections witness to Jesus' power to heal disease and to defeat demonic powers.

The transition from the previous material in 7:1-23 is marked by a change of setting. Jesus goes alone into Phoenicia, not to preach or to heal, but to escape (v. 24). His vacation is cut short, however, by an "uppity" woman who invades his private space with a request for help (Wahlberg 1975, 13). The narrator has prepared the audience for this story by making certain that there were people from Tyre and Sidon present in 3:7-12 to benefit from Jesus' healings and exorcisms; the audience is to understand that the woman has "heard about him" from other gentiles who have encountered the power of Jesus.

The evangelist's description of the woman specifies the three ways in which she is unworthy to make demands on Jesus: She is female, a Greek (probably meaning "pagan" by religion), and a Syrophoenician by race. Like the Jewish father Jairus, this pagan mother bows at Jesus' feet and makes her request. She wants her daughter whole.

The Markan Jesus responds with the mission strategy that everyone knew was the right one: Jew first, then gentile (Isaiah; Luke–Acts; Rom 1:16; 2:9-10). It isn't right, he says, to take the bread from the table of the descendants (τέκνων, v. 27) and toss it out (βαλεῖν) to the dogs. Like any Palestinian Jew, the Markan Jesus is portrayed as thinking that all urban dogs are scavengers who run wild in the streets; Jews did not have house dogs. It would be unthinkable to deprive the descendants of Abraham of their due in order to minister to gentile dogs.

The woman responds out of a different cultural context. For her it is not a matter of sequence but of simultaneity. "In our culture," she explains, "the children (παιδίων, v. 28) and the house dogs eat at the same time" (Dufton 1989, 417). By changing the cultural context, the woman appeals to the experience of her people; they were receiving the benefits of Jesus' ministry before he ever left Galilee. They went to him before he came to them. There is enough healing for everyone all at the same time. No one need be deprived or made to wait.

By replacing the word for descendants (implying those entitled to an inheritance, 12:19) with the word Jesus will later use to describe those who are included *despite* their lack of status (9:37, 10:14), the woman completes her rhetorical coup and wins the argument (Grimes 1991). The woman's effective sermon (λόγος, cf. 2:2, 4:33) achieves its goal; the unclean spirit leaves her daughter. Having made clean all foods in the previous section, the Markan Jesus now makes clean all races and peoples. It is worth noting that according to Mark, this anonymous woman won a place at the table not merely for her daughter, but for every gentile Christian who reads these words.

Mark next displays his lack of interest in geography by having Jesus travel north to Sidon in order to arrive in the region of the Decapolis, southeast of Phoenicia on the eastern (gentile) side of the Sea of Galilee. Here Jesus heals a deaf man, one who, although he has ears, cannot hear (8:18, cf. 4:9, 12, 23). This suggests that the spiritual deafness Jesus continues to encounter may ultimately be overcome as well.

Having made it possible for the man to hear and also to speak, Jesus promptly commands him and the witnesses to the miracle to keep silent, but to no avail. Like the Jewish leper, these gentiles ignore Jesus' instructions and proclaim (κηρύσσειν, 1:45, 7:36) his mighty works. Their words echo Gen 1:31 LXX and Isa 35:5-6. In the Gospel of Mark, even the gentiles quote the Law and the Prophets to announce the good news of God's eschatological reign.

There is no change of scene at the beginning of the story of the feeding of the 4,000; the gentile setting of 7:31-37 remains the same. What has changed is the cast of characters; the disciples have rejoined Jesus after missing every previous encounter with gentiles. Sadly, they have learned nothing from their earlier experience and repeat their despairing question, *How can one feed these people with bread here in the desert?* (8:4). Although the audience might have forgiven them for not expecting a miracle the first time, this time their dismay is inexcusable.

Jesus, however, is unperturbed by the disciples' anxiety about scarcity and again lays claim to their meager supplies. The Syrophoenician woman turns out to be right after all. When everything the disciples have is given to Jesus, he transforms it into enough to feed the whole crowd of undeserving gentiles without depriving the disciples at all. They collect enough leftovers to fill seven baskets large enough to hold a man (σπυρίς, 8:8, Acts 9:25).

This story brings the third subsection of 6:31–8:9 around to where it began—with the feeding of the 5,000 in 6:31-44. By this time everyone must surely have eyes to see and ears to hear the truth about Jesus and the inauguration of God's reign. The summaries with which the section concludes indicate that the this is *not* the case.

<u>8:10-30. Conclusion of the Galilean ministry.</u> The ministry of Jesus in Galilee and in gentile territory closes with three scenes that summarize the major themes of 1:14–8:9: words and deeds, controversy and opposition, blindness and deafness, scarcity and bread. The failure to hear, see, and understand that the audience has come to expect from the "outsiders" who oppose Jesus has by this time clearly become a problem for the "insiders" as well.

The last Galilean encounter with opponents (vv. 10-13) is bracketed by trips across the sea. In v. 10 Jesus and his disciples leave gentile territory and cross over to Dalmanutha. The place is unknown, but the encounter with Pharisees suggests a Jewish setting. Besides, the concluding boat trip, which begins in v. 13, is a crossing *to the other side* and the boat lands at Bethsaida on the eastern (gentile) side of the sea. Thus the setting of 8:11-12 is a Jewish one.

There are few surprises here. The audience already knows that the Pharisees and the Herodians are plotting to kill Jesus (3:6). The Pharisees are often associated with the scribes (7:1) who have been Jesus' opponents from the beginning (2:6, 16, 24).

The Pharisees' request for a sign is not equivalent to the requests for healing and exorcism that have been made to Jesus so far in the narrative. The evangelist makes this clear in two ways.

(1) They ask for a *sign* (v. 11), rather than making a specific request for a specific need. Mark's word for miracles that are portrayed in a positive light is δύναμις, "powerful act" (6:2, 5, 14; 9:39); σημεῖα, "signs," on the other hand, are understood negatively as acts done to establish one's identity or status (13:22). That is what the Pharisees request here: a sign *from heaven* as proof that Jesus is someone they should take seriously.

(2) Their motive is revealed to the audience by the omniscient narrator who knows everyone's motives in the story: they ask in order to put Jesus to the test (v. 11). Since the activity of "testing" Jesus has already been identified as the program of Satan (1:13), it is clear that the Pharisees remain opposed to Jesus' mission.

Jesus' refusal to give a sign makes two points that are theologically important to the evangelist:

(1) The miracles in the Gospel are not to be understood as "signs." They prove nothing about Jesus' identity or status. This will become even more clear when the audience learns that *false* messiahs perform signs in order to prove who they are (13:22).

(2) The opponents' request for a sign from heaven shows that they have not understood that every aspect of Jesus' life is "from heaven." They do not recognize that God is the ground and source of Jesus' ministry (cf. 3:20-35; 6:1-6).

The last of the three boat scenes in the Gospel (vv. 14-21) brings to a climax the disciples' incomprehension. In 4:35-41 they had asked, *Who then is this?* and Jesus had asked, *Have you still no faith?* In 6:45-52 the disciples had failed to recognize Jesus and he had answered their previous question with the divine self-definition, "I am." The narrator had remarked that *they did not understand about the loaves, but their hearts were hardened* (6:52).

In this final scene it becomes clear that the disciples still do not understand about the loaves. Even after two miraculous feedings they are worried about their scarcity of bread. This is more than the Markan Jesus can tolerate, and he fires questions at them faster than they can answer: *Why are you talking about having no bread? Do you still not perceive or understand? Are your hearts hardened? Do you have eyes, and fail to see? Do you have ears, and fail to hear? And do you not remember?* (vv. 17-18). Even his review quiz on the number of baskets of leftovers after each feeding leaves them baffled.

The audience comes to the chilling realization that indeed the disciples are deaf and blind, indeed their hearts are hardened. Worse yet, these are the characteristics of *those outside* (4:10-12; Isa 6:9-10). If the disciples are to be counted among the outsiders, who is left on the inside? And how can one be sure of remaining inside, when the boundaries seem so fluid?

Finally in v. 22 Jesus and the disciples arrive in gentile Bethsaida, their destination ever since 6:45. There, Jesus heals a man of a particularly stubborn case of blindness. The story is narrated in such a way as to provide a parallel to 7:31-37 (the healing of a deaf man): Jesus arrives (7:31; 8:22a); people bring to him an afflicted person and beg Jesus to touch him (7:32; 8:22b); Jesus takes the person aside and performs some healing action (7:33; 8:23); the healing is confirmed (7:35; 8:25b); and Jesus attempts to conceal the healing from public notice (7:36; 8:26). After the devastation of vv. 14-21 these two stories hold out hope that Jesus may yet be able to heal the disciples' spiritual blindness and deafness as well.

The issue of Jesus' identity closes the large section 6:14–8:30. Is Jesus John the baptizer come back to life? Is he Elijah? Is he some other prophet? Just when it appears that the disciples have found the right answer (*You are the Messiah, v. 29*), the audience learns that there is more to messiahship than anyone bargained for. With that unsettling revelation, the evangelist begins the third major section of the Gospel.

On the Way, 8:22–10:52

The healing of the blind man at Bethsaida (8:22-26) and the story of Peter's confession at Caesarea Philippi (8:27-30) both have dual functions in the structural plan of the Gospel. Their functions in the narrative of the Galilean ministry have already been discussed, and we now turn to a study of the third major section of the Gospel in which the Markan Jesus teaches his disciples about the community implied by God's reign and about the role of suffering in Jesus' life and in the lives of his followers. Of course, the teachings of Jesus in this section have become the vehicle by which the evangelist teaches *his* audience on these topics.

We have already seen how Mark takes over Isaiah's imagery of sight and hearing, blindness and deafness. The material in 8:27–10:45 is framed by two stories about the healing of blindness—the only two such stories in this Gospel. Within this frame there is a narrative introduction (8:27-30) that sets the stage for the section. The subsequent material is arranged in three units of similar structure but differing length: 8:31–9:29; 9:30–10:31; and 10:32-45.

Each of these units begins with a prediction of Jesus' suffering and death (PASSION prediction). The prediction is followed by a response by disciples indicating that they do not understand the significance of what Jesus is telling them. This provides the Markan Jesus with an opportunity to engage in further teaching about the nature of discipleship.

The author of Mark has already indicated that although the disciples have eyes, they cannot see (8:18). Even though they have been given the secret of the reign of God, they have not perceived or understood it because their hearts are hardened (4:11; 6:52; 8:17). The teaching on the way to Jerusalem is Jesus' attempt to penetrate their blindness with the light of understanding. To indicate that purpose the evangelist begins the teaching section with the story of the healing of a blind man.

This is the only healing story in any Gospel that suggests difficulty or partiality in achieving the result. Jesus puts saliva on the man's eyes and lays his hands on him, then checks to see how the healing is going: *Can you see anything?* (v. 23). The man reports partial sight (8:24). Jesus lays his hands on his eyes again and this time the man *looked intently and his sight was restored, and he saw everything clearly* (v. 25). This two-stage healing prepares for the encounter with the disciples that follows it.

That encounter takes place *on the way* to the villages of Caesarea Philippi. Of the sixteen references to "the way" (ὁδός) in Mark, half are concentrated between 8:27 and 11:8. In this section "the way" is the way to the cross, which becomes clear for the first time in the passion predictions. It is also *the way of the Lord* about which Isaiah wrote in the citation that began the Gospel (1:2-3). This way out of bondage into freedom, this second Exodus is a way the disciples are going to find especially distasteful. But then Isaiah also wrote, "My plans are not like your plans nor are your ways like my ways (ὁδοί, LXX), says the Lord."

Introductory Narrative, 8:27-30

This is the moment the audience of Mark has been waiting for. In 4:41 the disciples had asked, *Who then is this, that even the wind and the sea obey him?* In 6:50 Jesus had answered their question: *I am* (cf. Exod 3:14; Isa 43:10, 25; 45:18; 51:12). But their concern over bread in the last boat scene (8:14-21) showed that they were still blind to what they had seen.

Now the Markan Jesus asks them directly about his identity, beginning with what others are saying (v. 27). The speculations are those heard in Herod's court back in 6:13-15. Then comes the question that has challenged would-be disciples in the centuries since Mark first wrote it: *But who do you say that I am?* (v. 29).

Peter, speaking for the other disciples as he so often does in Mark, replies, *You are the Messiah* (v. 29; "Christ" is the Greek word for the messianic role or office). The audience breathes a sigh of relief. At last the disciples have seen the light. But Jesus interrupts the applause with a command to silence: *He sternly ordered them not to tell anyone about him* (v. 30). The audience knows that Peter is right (1:1), but apparently there is more to learn about who Jesus is before the news can be spread.

First Passion Prediction Unit, 8:31–9:29

The evangelist places the first passion prediction immediately after Peter's confession and Jesus' command to silence in order to show that before Jesus can be proclaimed as the Messiah, the component of suffering must be integrated into the messianic role.

Jesus' suffering is interpreted as a necessary part of the coming of God's eschatological reign by the use of the word translated *must* (δεῖ) in the NRSV (v.

31). The inbreak of God's reign can be seen in Jesus' miracles and exorcisms, but before its final consummation Jesus will have to be killed and to rise from death. By contrast with his usual mode of speech *in parables*, the passion prediction is crystal clear (v. 32).

Peter, as the representative of all the disciples, rejects the necessity of the passion. Jesus' retort means that to reject the necessity of suffering is to identify with Satan, Jesus' cosmic opponent (1:13; 3:22-27). The critique of Jesus' opponents in 7:6-13 here becomes the critique of the disciples: they are substituting human values and attitudes for the values and attitudes characteristic of God. From God's point of view there is no contradiction in a suffering healer, a victimized rescuer, a dying life-bringer. That the disciples see a contradiction indicates that they are looking with human half-sight. Like the blind man at Bethsaida, they need a second touch before they can see clearly.

Having added the component of suffering to the definition of messiahship, the Markan Jesus proceeds to add it to the definition of discipleship in 8:34–9:1. To follow behind the miracle worker is not enough; followers will deny themselves and accept the instruments of their own execution. Real life is found in losing one's life for the sake of Jesus and his good news. The desire for self-protection is the surest way to lose everything.

The concept of self-denial here must be interpreted in the context of the Gospel of Mark. It does not mean giving up certain pleasures or desires. It does not mean adopting the posture of a doormat by abandoning all sense of self. It means, rather, abandoning all claims to self-definition and accepting God's program for and God's claim upon one's life.

This is what the Markan Jesus does in 14:36. He has a will of his own, but he chooses God's will instead. In 14:62 Jesus denies himself publicly by the paradoxical act of boldly *claiming* his God-given identity and role. As a result, he takes up his cross and saves his life by losing it. Peter, by contrast, becomes the example of one who tries to save his life by denying *his* God-given identity and role as a follower of Jesus. For a Christian to deny herself, then, is to have the courage to be who she truly is. A Christian who tries to protect himself from persecution as a follower of Jesus denies Jesus and loses the ground and center of his life.

Denying Jesus, or *being ashamed* of him and his teaching, has serious consequences. Of such a person Jesus will *be ashamed* when he comes as eschatological judge (8:38), and that judgment will be very soon (8:39). It is clear that the evangelist finds it necessary to issue a strong warning about the consequences of apostasy during persecution.

The next scene in this unit is the transfiguration. Exodus symbolism is again prominent: Moses, a high mountain, a cloud, the shining appearance of God's messenger, the building of tabernacles (9:5, NRSV *dwellings*). Along with Moses the lawgiver appears the prophet Elijah, with whom the evangelist has linked John the baptizer (1:2-8; 6:17-29).

John (Elijah) was present at Jesus' baptism, the first time the voice from heaven spoke (1:9-11). On that occasion Jesus received the Holy Spirit's presence and power for his ministry of teaching, healing and exorcism. Now the voice from heaven speaks again in the presence of Elijah and Moses to confirm the necessity of Jesus' humiliation and suffering just announced in 8:31. The *beloved son* will die (cf. Gen 22:2). At the baptism the voice was addressed only to Jesus; now the voice addresses the disciples: *Listen to him!* But this is not a message they are able to hear.

On the way down the mountain Jesus again enjoins silence *until after the Son of Man had risen from the dead* (9:9). The disciples raise the question about Elijah's coming as the forerunner (Mal 4:5). Indeed he has come, says Jesus, and you see what happened to him! (6:17-29).

The final story in the first passion prediction unit is the healing of the demon-possessed boy (9:14-29). Here the author of Mark has two points to make: (1) God's miraculous power and human confidence in that power are inextricably linked, and (2) God's power is not an impersonal force to be manipulated, but a gift to be prayed for. In order to make these two points, the evangelist uses this story of a botched exorcism to criticize the father and the crowd for their lack of faith and to criticize the disciples for their prayerlessness.

Having been disappointed once, the father is understandably skeptical and desperate: *If you are able to do anything, have pity on us and help us* (9:22). But in Mark, Jesus' *ability* to help is never at issue; the leper was right when he said, *If you choose, you can . . .* (1:40). So Jesus answers, *If you are able!—All things can be done for the one who believes* (9:23). Still desperate and still honest, the father cries out, *I believe; help my unbelief* [by healing my son]! (9:24). To this request Jesus immediately responds.

Faith is needed for miracles in Mark, but sometimes miracles are needed to awaken faith in Jesus' power (Dowd 1988, 107-14).

But the father's lack of faith is not the whole story. When the disciples get Jesus alone *in the house*, where all private teaching takes place, they ask the reason for their failure (9:28). Jesus' answer is that *this kind* of demon comes out only for those who cultivate the habit of prayer (as Jesus himself does 1:35; 6:46). Disciples do not give orders to God as magicians in the ancient world were known to do; rather, they make requests out of the quality of their relationship with God.

Second Passion Prediction Unit, 9:30–10:31

This unit is carefully organized, with a number of overlapping structures. After the passion prediction and the disciples' failure to understand (9:30-32), the teaching material that follows is held together by an inclusio: *Whoever wants to be first must be last* (9:35) and *Many who are first will be last, and the last will be first* (10:31).

Within this frame, two major subjects are dealt with. First the Markan Jesus holds out hope for the powerless in 9:33–10:16. This material has its own frame: receive children (9:33-37) and receive God's reign as a child (10:13-16). The second topic is hope for the powerful (10:17-27); their salvation is impossible for humans but possible for God (10:27).

The last item in the unit is a conversation between Jesus and his disciples on the rewards awaiting those who give up everything to follow Jesus (10:28-31). This conversation concludes with the saying on last/ first that closes the frame on the entire unit.

The material in 9:30-50 is set in Galilee. The movement from the mountain of transfiguration south toward Jerusalem has begun. The second passion prediction introduces for the first time in the disciples' hearing the notion that Jesus will be betrayed. The audience, of course, has known of the betrayal and the identity of the betrayer since 3:19. The disciples do not understand and are afraid to ask questions (9:32).

All the teaching in chap. 9 takes place *in the house* in Capernaum. It begins with Jesus' awareness of an argument among the disciples (9:33) and ends with his admonition that they have peace among themselves (9:50). According to the narrator, the argument was about who was the greatest; this gives the Markan Jesus the opportunity to emphasize that the values of God's reign are the reverse of those of this age. The one who serves everyone else is the greatest.

Jesus follows up by identifying with one of the "last" of society—a child. To welcome a powerless child is to welcome Jesus himself. The high infant mortality rate in antiquity contributed to the marginalization of children. Perhaps fewer than half lived to their fifth year (Wiedemann 1989, 16). They had only recently come from the divine realm and were likely to leave this life at any time; thus, they were not fully human beings.

On the other hand, this marginal status conferred on children a certain mystery. They were thought to be closer to the gods than adults and sometimes even their casual utterances were regarded as omens. (The best-known instance of this belief occurs in Augustine's account of his conversion, *Conf.* 8.12.) This context enables the evangelist to portray Jesus as designating children as the bearers of his presence when they are welcomed in his name.

The phrase "in your/my name" links this story with the one that follows. Although the disciples want to limit exorcism in Jesus' name to their own group, the Markan Jesus insists that all who minister wholeness in his name are to be recognized as *for us* (v. 40). The use of *the name* makes it clear that the issue here is not the ultimate status of non-Christians who do good works; rather, the issue is openness toward the ministry of Christian groups other than one's own. But anyone (even a non-Christian) who shows mercy toward the Christian community will be rewarded (9:41; cf. Matt 25:31-46).

Calling attention back to the child in his arms, the Markan Jesus pronounces an ominous warning against influencing a believing child (or any new Christian?) to commit apostasy (v. 42). On the topic of apostasy in general, the sayings in vv. 43-48 make it clear that "it is better to enter life having renounced certain cherished acts than to go into hell having done it all without restraint" (Via 1985, 18). Self-fulfillment is not to be equated with "entering into life," and self-indulgence may lead to self-destruction.

In 10:1 the scene shifts even further south. The mention of Judea anticipates the setting of chaps. 11–16. At this point the Pharisees reenter the picture and raise the question about divorce. The Markan Jesus explains that the Mosaic permission of divorce was not an expression of God's intent, but reflected the situation of fallenness and human *hardness of heart*.

The appeal to creation serves Mark's eschatology; God's reign, which is breaking through in Jesus' ministry, restores the possibility of relationships as they were intended in the beginning. The conversation with the disciples (vv. 10-12) changes the status of women from victims to responsible moral agents. No longer merely passive in marriage and divorce, they too must take responsibility for their decisions and actions. It should be noted that the evangelist believes divorce and adultery can be forgiven. The only unpardonable sin is blasphemy against the Holy Spirit (3:29).

The second reference to children portrays the disciples as still unable to get the point. Just as in the second feeding story, they have learned nothing from their previous experience. Despite 9:37 they try to prevent children from having access to Jesus (Tannehill 1977, 401). Jesus now says that the childlike are the primary citizens of God's realm (v. 14) and that everyone who enters God's realm must enter *as a little child* (v. 15).

This is "not an invitation to childlike innocence and naivete but a challenge to relinquish all claims of power and domination over others" (Fiorenza 1983, 148). God's reign cannot be achieved or earned; it must be received in the way that children in antiquity received what they needed for life. According to the Markan Jesus, people enter the reign of God, not in a proud triumphal procession, but in complete vulnerability, with no claim to any rights or status. It was not what the disciples had in mind.

Their amazement that it is humanly impossible for a rich person to enter God's reign (v. 26) reflects the relationship between wealth and religion in which prosperity was regarded as a blessing from God and therefore a sign of righteousness (Deut 28:1-14; Prov 13:25; 15:6; 37:25-26). In the world of Greco-Roman polytheism, wealth made it possible to persuade the gods with fine sacrifices and to be initiated into a variety of mystery religions (Apuleius, *The Golden Ass*).

The fact that Jesus expects a rich and religious person to renounce all the possessions and righteousness that he has acquired (v. 21) shocks the rich man and the disciples. They want to know who *can* be saved, if not this one. Jesus' answer is consistent with his earlier sayings about the advantage of the powerless. Humans cannot achieve salvation; God gives it away for free. Those who are accustomed to living on handouts will find it easier to enter God's reign than those who are accustomed to paying their own way. But God can do anything—even save a rich person (v. 27).

Peter misses the point about having no claim and attempts to convert his abandonment of possessions into an asset (v. 28). This gives the Markan Jesus an opportunity to recapitulate the theme of 3:31-35. The family that has been lost as a result of Christian conversion is replaced by the Christian community in the present and eternal life in the future (vv. 29-30).

This new family is radically different from the old, however, because it includes no fathers. In antiquity, the father had almost absolute control over the other members of the family. Control from above by a person who has power over others is repudiated by the vision of Christian community articulated by the Markan Jesus. God is the only father (8:38; 14:36; 11:25). The fatherhood of God in the context of Markan theology has the same function as the kingship of God: it guarantees a church made up of equals. God rules precisely in order to make sure that no one else does.

The evangelist cannot resist one wry addition to the list of blessings Christians receive *in this age*. Along with the new family, houses, and fields come persecutions (v. 30). Besides, *many who are first will be last, and the last first* (v. 31). For Peter, the disciple who was called first, this could be construed as a warning.

Third Passion Prediction Unit, 10:32-52

Much shorter than the previous two units, this one nevertheless begins with the longest and most detailed of the three passion predictions; it is virtually an outline for Mark 14:43–16:8. "The way" has taken Jesus and his disciples almost to Jerusalem and all of the instruction Jesus has given his followers so far has not made a dent in their amazement and fear (v. 32).

The placement of vv. 35-40 immediately after the passion prediction results in dramatic irony. The story about the request of James and John is narrated in such a way that the audience sees them stepping up briskly, as though they had been waiting impatiently for Jesus to stop talking. Their request is a boorish *non sequitur* after Jesus' solemn recitation of the tortures about to be inflicted on him.

In the first passion prediction unit the Markan Jesus had spoken about his coming in glory as eschatological deliverer (8:31, 38; 9:12). Peter's acclamation of him as the Messiah (8:29) was qualified, but not rejected, and the heavenly voice at the transfiguration alluded to one of the royal psalms (9:7; Ps 2:7). The narrative suggests that although James and John had no understanding about the passion (9:32) or the resurrection (9:10), they had understood the part about glory and royalty and were determined to participate in it. They ask to be seated next to Jesus *in your glory* (v. 37).

Jesus begins his response with a warning: *You do not know what you are asking* (v. 38). Indeed they do not, for the positions they request on Jesus' right and left will be the positions of two crucified criminals (15:27). Taking up their vision of royalty, Jesus then reminds them that those closest to the king have to drink from his cup; if the wine is poisoned, they share the death intended for the ruler (v. 38; cf. Gen 40:1-13; 41:9-13; Neh 1:11b–2:1; Xenophon, *Cyropaedia* 1.3.9, Suetonius, *Claudius* 44.2).

There may be a pun on the word "baptize" in v. 38, since one of the meanings of the verb was "to destroy (e.g., a person by drowning, or a ship by sinking)" (Beasley-Murray 1990, 85). James and John apparently understand the question in the sense of ritual washing and answer brashly, *We are able* (v. 39). The gospel song based on their reply perpetuates their naivete.

As it turns out, their quest is frustrated. Jesus can guarantee martyrdom for James and John, but not glory (v. 40). The prediction of their martyrdoms here suggests that their blindness and self-seeking will finally be replaced by faithfulness.

The anger of the other disciples upon learning that the two brothers were seeking special privileges gives the Markan Jesus an opportunity to teach about the upside-down values of Christian leadership (vv. 41-45). The community is not to be modeled on secular Roman ("gentile") structures. The teachings of 9:35 and 10:31 are recapitulated for emphasis: The one who wants to be great must be a servant; the one who wants to be first must be the slave of all.

In v. 45 the evangelist provides the christological rationale for this role reversal. Christian leaders must be servants because *the Son of Man came not to be served but to serve, and to give his life a ransom for many.* The first half of this saying interprets the ministry of Jesus up to this point as "service." All of his miracles and exorcisms, his teaching with authority, his winning arguments with the religious leaders, were done not to call attention to his status or power, but to serve. This is the point most often missed by interpretations of Mark that attempt to set miracle working and service in opposition to each other. They are synonyms, not opposites.

The second half of the saying points forward to the passion narrative. The word usually translated "ransom" here has the general meaning of a price paid for the release of a slave or prisoner of war. It is one of at least three understandings of the efficacy of Jesus' death that the author of Mark has incorporated into his Gospel. As we will see, the PASSION NARRATIVE is based primarily on the theme of the suffering righteous man, derived from the thought of ancient Israel and developed in the Hellenistic Jewish wisdom literature. To this general picture the author of Mark adds the metaphors of (1) covenant sacrifice (14:24) and (2) liberation from bondage (10:45).

The related verb, meaning "redeem," "ransom," or "set free," is important in the theology of Deutero-Isaiah, although the noun used in Mark 10:45 appears only once (45:13). Isaiah connects the concept of ransom/redemption/liberation with the interpretation of the return from exile as a second Exodus (41:14; 43:1, 14; 44:22-24; 51:11; 52:3; 62:12; 63:4, 9). Since this Isaian theme is central to Mark's theology, it is possible that the evangelist intends the saying to be understood as a metaphor for the freedom from bondage that will be effected by Jesus' death. This would be an understanding of the cross that would correspond with the freedom experienced by the human beneficiaries of Jesus' ministry of exorcism. The powerful one who has served by healing the broken bodies and psyches of humanity will also effect their ultimate freedom by giving his life.

The "way" section of Mark ends with the story of Bartimaeus, which closes the frame on the entire section, but is also linked explicitly with the previous request of James and John. Like the brothers, Bartimaeus brings a request. Jesus asks him exactly the same question he asked James and John: *What do you want me to do for you?* (10:36, 51). The repetition signals the audience that the misguided ambition expressed in the previous story is about to be corrected. Bartimaeus asks for the one thing that all the characters in Mark need most—sight. Jesus heals him with a word; the contrast with the two-stage healing of the blind man at Bethsaida is dramatic.

Bartimaeus's response to his healing is the response Jesus has been calling for throughout this section of the Gospel. As soon as he can see, he begins to follow Jesus *on the way* to Jerusalem, the place of crucifixion. To see aright is to walk the way of the cross unflinchingly. This vision and faithful response however, is not a human achievement. It is a divine miracle.

Ministry and Passion in Jerusalem, 11:1–16:8

The healing of Bartimaeus on the way out of Jericho marks the end of the "way" section. The rest of the narrative is set in Jerusalem and its environs. This final division of the Gospel falls into two parts. The passion and resurrection narrative (14:1–16:8) is preceded by a literary unit focused on Jesus' actions and sayings in and about the Temple (11:1–13:37).

Jesus and the Temple, 11:1–13:37

This unit of deeds and words is bracketed by references to the Mount of Olives. In 11:1-11 Jesus leaves the Mount of Olives and enters Jerusalem and the Temple; in 13:1-37 Jesus leaves the Temple, predicting its destruction, and goes to the Mount of Olives, where he delivers an apocalyptic discourse on the coming of the Son of Man.

The material between Jesus' entry into and exit from the Temple begins with two stories about Jesus' actions (the fig tree incident and the expulsion of the merchants and moneychangers, 11:12-25). This is followed by a series of teachings and controversies (11:27–12:44).

11:1-25. Deeds. This section is marked by a continual shift in location between Bethany and the Jerusalem Temple, whereas the setting for all the controversy and teaching material in 11:27–12:44 is the Temple itself. Of course, even this action material is not devoid of teaching, as the Markan Jesus interprets his actions to his opponents and to his disciples.

Jesus' power and authority are the primary emphases of the narrative of his initial actions in Jerusalem. The finding of the colt for the ride into Jerusalem (vv. 1-6) and the similar story of the finding of the room for the final meal (14:12-16) demonstrate Jesus' powers of prediction and his authority to requisition what he needs. Now that he has three times redefined his messiahship by combining access to divine power with vulnerability to rejection and death, the Markan Jesus has no need to conceal his identity as the one who inaugurates the reign of God.

The acclamation of the disciples in chiastic form (vv. 9b-10: hosanna, blessed, blessed, hosanna) is based partly on Ps 118:26. This psalm portrays a procession of thanksgiving to the Temple and emphasizes national sovereignty and defeat of Israel's enemies. Here translated into an apocalyptic mode, the psalm fragment is incorporated into a shout of welcome for the eschatological savior promised by Isaiah (33:22). Both Jewish and gentile members of Mark's audience would have recognized this as a procession to celebrate a victory, but unlike the group of disciples pictured in the narrative, the audience would have appreciated the irony of the scene. Whereas Roman triumphal processions ended with the execution of the prisoners of war, this one will end with the execution of the victor.

Only in Mark is Jesus' provocative action in the Temple sandwiched between the beginning and the end of the strange story of the withered fig tree. Unlike his modern interpreters, the author of Mark was completely unconcerned about the propriety of Jesus' destroying a helpless tree. The evangelist is interested in the way in which the destruction of the fruitless tree foreshadows the destruction of the Jerusalem Temple which, in his view, had also failed to bear the expected fruit.

Although Isaiah had written that the Temple was to be "a house of prayer for all the gentile nations" (56:7, author trans.), the Temple hierarchy had made it into a "robbers' hideout" (v. 17, author trans.) where they huddled together, claiming the protection of the holy place. This had been Jeremiah's complaint in his famous Temple sermon (7:11), from which the Markan Jesus quotes. The objection is not that dishonest merchants are cheating the public. The word λῃστῶν means not cheats, but muggers or pirates, who use their "hideouts" not for robbing people but for evading detection and punishment.

The author of Mark interprets Jesus' actions not as a cleansing or reform of the Temple, but as a cancellation of Temple worship altogether. The Markan Jesus makes it impossible, not only for proper sacrificial animals to be procured and money changed for the Temple taxes, but also for the priests to carry through the Temple the vessels necessary to perform the rituals. Because the gentiles had been excluded from prayer in God's house, God's authoritative representative signals the end of all prayer in the Temple.

This, however, requires a reinterpretation of the conditions for effective prayer. Like all ancient religions, JUDAISM had a tradition of understanding the temple of the deity as the place where petitions were sure to be granted (1 Sam 1:1-29; 2 Kgs 19:14-37; 2 Macc 3:24-40). If the Temple, the holy place where God is especially present, is rejected, how can the followers of Jesus expect their prayers to be effective?

The answer comes with the reassurances about prayer in vv. 22-25. There are two conditions for effective prayer: faith (vv. 22-24) and forgiveness (v. 25). To *have faith* means to maintain the confidence that God is able to do what is otherwise impossible (9:23; 10:29). This faith is not "saving faith" but certainty about a worldview that early Christians shared with Hellenistic Jews and adherents of Neopythagorean philosophy. By contrast, the Platonists held that some things were impossible for the gods and the Epicureans argued that the gods did not intervene to perform miracles in response to human prayer.

But confidence in God's power must be combined with the clean slate provided only by God's forgiving disciples' sins. The catch is that in order to be forgiven, they will have to forgive each other (v. 25).

The evangelist replaces the holy place with the holy people who forgive and are forgiven and who stubbornly maintain their Christian worldview in the face of the philosophical alternatives. This is the ideal. But the Markan Jesus has already shown that God reserves the option of providing miraculous assistance to those who have inadequate faith (4:40; 8:4; 9:24). In Mark, the power of God overcomes even human unbelief.

11:27–12:44. Words in the Temple. In this teaching section, set in the Temple, the evangelist places a three-part discussion of theology and ethics between two three-part discussions which focus on christology (A—11:27-33; 12:1-9, 10-12; B—12:13-17, 18-27, 28-34, A'—12:35-37, 38-40, 41-44). The section begins with Jesus walking around in the Temple like a peripatetic philosopher (11:27) and ends with Jesus sitting to teach his disciples like a Jewish rabbi (12:41). These two postures correspond to the types of argumentation used throughout the section. Thoroughly Jewish modes of scriptural exegesis are combined with thoroughly Hellenistic rhetorical ploys, and all are set into an apocalyptic frame of reference.

The first christological subsection (11:27–12:12) makes the point that like the Davidic king who celebrates victory over his enemies (Ps 118), Jesus will be vindicated by God. His rejection and death are not the last word. The stone the builders rejected has become the cornerstone of the new temple, replacing the fruitless Jerusalem Temple. This new temple, the Christian community, is the house of prayer for all the gentiles that the previous Temple had failed to become. Thus, Isaiah's apocalyptic vision of the inclusion of the gentiles in the people of God is fulfilled in the Christian community (Isa 2:2-3; 56:6-7; Marcus 1992, 111-29).

Subsection A begins with a conversation with Jesus' opponents that links the teaching section with the series of actions that preceded it. The religious leaders confront Jesus over the issue of his authority to suspend the Temple cult. The audience, of course, knows the right answer to the leaders' question and Jesus' counterquestion: both John's and Jesus' authority came not from human beings, but from God (1:11; 9:7). Jesus' opponents are caught in the trap of their own cowardice, but their answer, *We do not know* (11:33), is ironically true. Indeed, their ignorance and blindness mark them as *those outside* (4:10-12).

The confrontation with the opponents continues as Jesus takes the initiative in the parable of the vineyard (12:1-9). Developing the imagery of Isa 5:2, the Markan

Jesus takes an accusation that Isaiah directed against the whole people of Israel and focuses it specifically on the religious leaders. As interpreted by the Psalm quotation in 12:10-12, the parable becomes another prediction of Jesus' rejection, death, and vindication.

Subsection B consists of three encounters arranged in a chiastic structure with a central focus on the reality of the resurrection (Donahue 1982). This issue is dealt with in the conversation with the Sadducees (12:18-27). The form of Jesus' response is the rhetorical device known as an enthymeme (a syllogism in which one of the members is implied rather than stated):

Major premise (implied): God speaks accurately in scripture.
Minor premise: In scripture God speaks of the dead in the present tense (Exod 3:6).
Conclusion: The dead live in the presence of God. Resurrection is true.

The centrality of the resurrection is bracketed by conversations dealing with the ethical implications of theological claims. In 12:13-17 the Markan Jesus uses another enthymeme to escape a rhetorical trap designed to get him in trouble either with the people, who disliked paying Roman taxes, or with the Romans who demanded the payment. The implied major premise is: Ownership is established by the seal imprinted on something. Since the denarius bears Caesar's image, it is to be given to Caesar. What then is to be given to God? Obviously, that which bears God's image, that is, human beings (Gen 1:26-28). They are preeminently the "things of God," which must be surrendered completely to God. It is this self-giving to God that characterizes the Markan Jesus, as 14:32-42 will make strikingly clear.

The question about the great commandment (12:28-34) completes the theological discussion. The stress is on monotheism and its implications. God was contrasted with Caesar in 12:13-17; here the obligation to love God with the entire self is combined with the obligation to love one's neighbor as oneself. The scribe who recognizes that Jesus' emphasis accords with the theology of Deutero-Isaiah (45:21, "There is no other god besides me") is not far from the eschatological reign of God foreseen by the prophet and inaugurated in Jesus' ministry.

By having the scribe cite the prophetic critique of sacrifice without obedience (1 Sam 15:22; Hos 6:6; Mic 6:6-8) the evangelist delivers a final blow to the Temple system. Its fruitlessness is conceded by one of its own scholarly elite. After this coup, no one puts any more questions to the Markan Jesus (12:34b).

In subsection A', the initiative shifts. Now it is Jesus' turn to ask the questions. He turns the conversation back to christology by making the point that the expectation of a royal Davidic messiah is inadequate. Although the evangelist clearly makes Davidic claims for Jesus with his use of Pss 2, 118, and 110, Jesus' messiahship is both more and less than the title *Son of David* suggests. Whereas the Davidic messiah was merely a human ruler who would defeat human enemies, Jesus is the divine warrior who defeats the demonic powers and ushers in God's reign. Unlike the expected Davidic messiah Jesus' victory is won by losing—by humiliation and death (Marcus 1992, 130-50).

The theme of judgment on the religious leaders is sounded again in 12:38-40. The scribes who *devour* widows' houses (Isa 1:17, 23; 10:2; Ezek 22:25) clearly do not live by the standard advocated by one of their own number in 12:32-33 (Beavis 1989, 102). By contrast, the widow in 12:40-44 performs the exemplary action. Like Jesus, she gives God everything she has, even "her whole life" (12:44, author trans; cf. 12:17, 30). This giving of one's life recalls 10:45. The widow gives all she has to live on; Jesus will give his life to set God's people free.

13:1-2. Transition. Having been in the Temple since 11:27, the Markan Jesus now leaves the Temple and predicts its destruction: *Not one stone will be left here upon another*. What was implicit in 11:15-17 here becomes explicit. This closes the section of teaching in the Temple and prepares for the following teaching *opposite the temple* (13:3).

13:3-37. Words opposite the Temple (the apocalyptic discourse). This second long speech by the Markan Jesus has a number of common features with the parable discourse in chap. 4. Both assume the cosmic conflict myth so fundamental to apocalyptic thought. Both contain repeated admonitions to pay attention (4:3, 9, 23, 24; 13:5, 9, 23, 33, 35, 37). Both use parables from nature (4:3-9, 26-32; 13:28-29), and both contain allegorical applications of parabolic material to discipleship (4:13-20; 13:34-37, Donahue 1988, 61).

It is characteristic of both speeches that an extended discourse punctuated by second-person-plural imperatives tends to blur the distinction between the addressees at the story level and the audience of the Gospel as a whole. The "you" of the teaching material reaches out to include the listeners in any subsequent time (Tannehill 1980, 141).

The scene in chap. 13 is the Mount of Olives. The cast of characters is exactly the same as that of the first scene of the Galilean ministry (11:16-20): Jesus, Peter, James, John, and Andrew. The only function of the disciples in this scene is to ask two questions. They are not mentioned again.

The disciples' questions are: (1) When will these things happen? and (2) What will be the sign? They are portrayed as regarding the destruction of the Temple, which Jesus has just predicted, as a catastrophic event that would surely be preceded by a significant omen. They understand themselves as insiders who are entitled to be let in on the secret (cf. 4:11).

Jesus, however, has more important information to impart. He never mentions the Temple again; rather, he begins to talk about false and true signs of the eschatological consummation of God's reign. Although he is answering a question the disciples have not asked, he takes up the two issues they have raised in reverse order, beginning with how to recognize the sign of the end (vv. 5-27) and moving to the issue of the time of the end (vv. 28-37).

The Markan Jesus first explains that no historical event can be read as a sign of the eschaton (vv. 5-23). This material is arranged chiastically:

A Danger of deception, 5-6
B Prediction of future events, 7-8
C Persecution and mission, 9-13
B' Appropriate response to future events, 14-20
A' Danger of deception, 21-23

The section begins and ends with warnings that there will be deceivers who will make messianic claims for themselves and others and perform miracles in order to lead Christians astray (vv. 5-6, 21-23). Their apocalyptic interpretations of events are to be ignored (vv. 21, 23).

B and B' describe historical and natural events that might be misinterpreted as signs of the end (vv. 7-8) and prescribe the proper way to respond to such difficult times (vv. 14-20). Christians must always be ready to move quickly in times of crisis. Attachment to possessions will have to be put aside and even the most natural relationships will pose a problem (vv. 15-17). But although the suffering will be terrible, God is in control and will provide for God's chosen people. The right response is prayer and trust (vv. 18-20).

The center of the chiasm focuses on the persecution of the church (vv. 9-13). Like Jesus, Christians will be handed over, betrayed, brought to trial, and put to death. They are not to be afraid, because the Holy Spirit will enable them to bear witness. In the midst of their persecutions, they must continue to preach the gospel to the gentiles, because this is part of the divinely ordained prelude to the end (v. 10). *The one who endures to the end will be saved* (v. 13).

Scholars usually assume that the events described in vv. 5-23 were already taking place at the time of the writing of the Gospel. Jesus is portrayed as speaking in the past about events in the future, which is the evangelist's present. It is likely that the audience of the Gospel is facing some of the things described in this section. Some may already be in the past. But there is no way of knowing that all the events in this description are past or present. The evangelist may anticipate that some of these difficulties lie ahead for the church and may wish to prepare them to respond appropriately.

After an extensive discussion of events that are *not* signs of the end, the Markan Jesus turns to the real sign of the end: the coming of the Son of Man on the clouds, amid cosmic upheaval, to gather the elect from all over the earth (vv. 24-27). When they see Jesus coming for them again, they will know that the end is about to take place; no natural or political disasters that take place before that are to distract them from their mission.

As for the question of "When?" the Markan Jesus takes care of that in short order. This brief section (vv. 28-37) begins and ends with a parable. The parable of the fig tree makes the point that when the disciples see "these things" (i.e., the coming of the Son of Man, vv. 24-27), they will know that he is *at the very gates*

(v. 29). In other words, when you see it happening, you will know that it is happening, and not before!

This is reinforced by repeated reminders that *you do not know when* (vv. 33, 35). In fact, no one knows except the Father. The futility of calculation based on "signs of the times" could not be more dramatically portrayed. But if "biblical prophecy" workshops are not appropriate, neither is complacency. The parable of the returning landlord (vv. 34-36) emphasizes the suddenness of the arrival of the eschaton. Since you do not know, be ready and alert at all times. The final exhortation is addressed explicitly to the audience: *What I say to you I say to all: Keep awake* (v. 37).

Passion and Resurrection Narratives, 14:1–16:8

Jesus' death in Mark. In their struggle to interpret the humiliation and crucifixion of Jesus, early Christians made use of a variety of biblical and cultural resources. Ancient people, both Jews and pagans, knew that life was often unfair. The individual psalms of lament preserved the complaints of the righteous person who suffered unjustly at the hands of enemies. In Plato's *Republic* (361e-362a), Socrates is challenged by dialogue partners who suggest that the truly righteous person will "hold his course unchangeable, even unto death," having "to endure the lash, the rack, chains," and "finally, after every extremity of suffering, he will be crucified." That the execution of just persons was not merely a theoretical possibility is made clear by the interpretations of Socrates' own death at the hands of the state (Plato, *Apology*, *Phaedo*; Xenophon, *Memorabilia*).

But human beings recoil from the notion that the death of the upright is meaningless. The psalmist cries out for vindication. The Isaian Servant Songs interpret the death of the servant as vicarious suffering for the sins of others. The author of the Wisdom of Solomon transforms the victims into the judges of their persecutors (4:16–5:2). The Greeks made heroes of kings and soldiers who died to save the lives of others. The Maccabean martyrs are portrayed as giving their lives to atone for the sins of their compatriots (2 Macc 7:38; 4 Macc 6:28-29).

The Gospel of Mark draws upon a number of these biblical and extrabiblical patterns to interpret the death of Jesus as a necessary part of God's eschatological victory over all that enslaves and distorts human life. Although blameless, Jesus is unjustly condemned and crucified. His death redeems enslaved humanity (10:45) and seals a covenant (14:25) that brings even gentiles into the people of God. Vindicated in the resurrection, he leaves the tomb empty as he leads his followers on the way of mission and martyrdom.

The overall organization of the Markan passion narrative is controlled by chronology; within that framework the individual episodes are carefully crafted for rhetorical and theological effect. The sense of speed and energy so characteristic of the Galilean ministry is replaced by a series of solemn notices of the passing of time (14:1, 12, 17; 15:1, 26, 33, 34, 42) as the evangelist tolls the agonizing final hours of Jesus' life.

The story of the anointing woman (14:3-9) has two literary functions in the outline of the Gospel. With the story of the widow's offering (12:41-44), it forms a frame (INCLUSIO) around the apocalyptic discourse in chap. 13. In both cases, women are praised for their actions, which point forward to Jesus' giving of his life and to his burial. The women are contrasted with the religious leaders, who exploit them (12:40) and oppose Jesus (14:1-2).

With the story of the three women who go in search of Jesus' corpse to anoint it for burial (16:1-8), the story of the anointing woman in 14:3-9 forms a frame around the passion narrative. Her act makes theirs unnecessary. Jesus has already left the tomb and is on the way to Galilee.

14:1-11. Plot and anointing. The story of the anointing woman is sandwiched into the narrative about the plot to kill Jesus (vv. 1-2, 10-11; cf. Ps 10:7-8; Wis 2:12). Judas provides the missing link that will enable the religious leaders to "arrest Jesus by stealth" away from the crowds.

Having redefined the concepts of clean and unclean verbally in 7:1-23, Jesus now acts on that redefinition by having dinner in the house of an "unclean" leper. In an act reminiscent of the OT prophets, a woman comes in and anoints Jesus' head, signifying his royal authority (2 Kgs 19:1-3; 1 Sam 10:1; 1 Kgs 1:38-49; Ps 133:2). Like many of Jesus' own words and actions, the woman's deed is misunderstood by those present; they criticize her extravagance.

But Jesus defends the woman and reinterprets her action as an anointing for burial. Just as Peter's confession of Jesus as the Messiah had to be reinterpreted in terms of the passion, so the woman prophet's confession of Jesus as the Messiah by her action requires reinterpretation. The royal anointing becomes a burial rite. It is the only anointing that the Markan Jesus will receive, since by the time his women disciples arrive at the tomb with their spices, Jesus will be gone.

14:12-31. The Last Supper. The preparation for the Passover meal again confirms Jesus' foreknowledge of events (cf. 11:1-6). The two sent ahead to prepare are joined in v. 17 by Jesus and THE TWELVE, suggesting that the evangelist wanted to make clear that attendance at this important meal was not limited to the group named in chap. 3.

Jesus predicts his betrayal by one of those at table with him (Ps 41:9). The disciples are portrayed as claiming innocence in the form of a question that implies a negative answer: *Surely, not I?* (v. 19). Jesus' response reflects the apocalyptic viewpoint that all is happening in accordance with God's plan (v. 21a) and human beings are nevertheless culpable for their opposition to God's elect (v. 21b).

Ignoring the symbolic actions usually associated with Passover meals, the narrator introduces new symbols. The broken bread is Jesus' body; the cup of wine is his blood. The reference to covenant sacrifice (v. 24; cf. Exod 24:8; Zech 9:11) points backward to God's faithfulness in the past. The reference to the messianic banquet in "the reign of God" (v. 25, author trans.) points forward to eschatological vindication and celebration in communion with God (Isa 25:6).

On the way to the Mount of Olives, Jesus predicts the apostasy of all his disciples and their reunion with him in Galilee (vv. 27-28; cf. Zech 13:7-9; 14:4). Their tentative *Surely, not I?* of moments before now becomes a bold assertion of loyalty even to the point of death (v. 31b). But by this time the audience is more inclined to believe Jesus. If he says that the disciples will flee and Peter will deny him three times, that is what the audience expects.

14:32-42. Gethsemane. This scene is carefully constructed. The prayer of Jesus is at the center. Leading up to the prayer, three verbs of motion (vv. 32a, 33, 35a) are followed by three requests by the Markan Jesus: to the larger group of disciples (v. 32b), to Peter, James, and John (v. 34), and finally to God (v. 35b).

The prayer itself expresses confidence in God's power (*for you all things are possible*) and makes a direct request (*remove this cup from me*). Thus the evangelist shows that Jesus follows his own instructions; he has faith and he asks for a miracle every bit as stupendous as tossing a mountain into the sea (11:22-24). He asks to be spared the cross, after having repeatedly acknowledged its necessity in the preceding narrative. But now in his practice of prayer the Markan Jesus adds something that was not in his earlier teaching about prayer: submission to the will of God. This is what distinguishes the Markan Jesus from the numerous other miracle workers and magicians of antiquity; he does God's will, not his own.

After the prayer, Jesus returns to find his disciples sleeping. They have fallen into the trap about which he warned them in the parable of the absent landlord (13:34-36). Again, as at the transfiguration, they do not know how to respond (v. 40; cf. 9:6).

It is important to notice that the Markan theology of prayer does not *substitute* submission to God's will for petitionary prayer. The two are combined as the Markan Jesus wrestles with God three times *saying the same words* (v. 39). Finally he wakes the sleeping disciples in time to confront Judas and his lynch mob.

14:43-52. Arrest. With the arrival of the arresting party, Jesus' predictions begin to be fulfilled in rapid-fire succession. He is betrayed by Judas (cf. 14:18) into the hands of the religious leaders (cf. 10:33). Despite their boasting of a few hours before (14:27), all his disciples desert Jesus to save themselves (8:34-38). Mark emphasizes the complete abandonment of Jesus by repeating the *all* of 14:31b in v. 50. The story of the terrified youth who flees naked has two functions: it reminds the audience that the group that attended the supper and followed Jesus to Gethsemane was larger than "the twelve" and it makes a graphic comment on the cowardice and shame of the flight of the disciples. Nowhere in Mark is there any suggestion that the young man is to be identified with the author of the Gospel.

14:53-72. Sanhedrin trial/denial of Peter. The evangelist weaves together the story of the Sanhedrin TRIAL OF JESUS, which takes place inside the residence of the high priest, and the story of Peter's denial, which is set outside in the courtyard. He narrates the introduction to the trial scene (15:53), then the introduction to the denial (15:54), proceeds with the trial narrative (15:55-65), and then completes the denial story (15:66-72). This emphasizes the point that these events are to be understood as occurring simultaneously, even though they must be narrated sequentially.

From this point forward the passion narrative is riddled with dramatic irony. Jesus' enemies bungle their plot against him because their false witnesses (Pss 27:12; 35:11) cannot get their stories straight. Ironically, though, their *false* testimony is true; although the Markan Jesus has not said that he will destroy the Temple and replace it with one *not made with hands* (v. 58), that is in fact exactly what will happen. The Christian community will replace the Temple as the *house of prayer for all the nations* (11:17).

Since the opponents fail in their attempt to condemn him, Jesus has to condemn himself. In order for his commission from God to be fulfilled, Jesus has to give true testimony about himself, which the Sanhedrin then misinterprets as blasphemy. Here the evangelist brings together all the aspects of Jesus' identity. In response to the high priest's question, *Are you the Messiah, the Son of the Blessed One?* (v. 61, a reverent Jewish circumlocation for "God"), Jesus answers with the divine self-designation, *I am* (v. 62; cf. Isa 43:10, 45; 43:25; 45:18; 51:12; cf. Wis 2:13-20a), and adds the Danielic image used already in 8:38–9:1 and 13:26—the Son of Man coming on the clouds (Dan 7:13-14). All this identifies the one who will shortly die the most shameful possible death in the company of criminals.

By thus identifying himself correctly, Jesus "denies himself," doing God's will rather than his own. As a result, he will take up his cross, saving his life by losing it. Meanwhile, out in the courtyard, Peter is denying Jesus, forfeiting everything by attempting to save his own life. And the evangelist arranges for Peter to fulfill Jesus' prophecy of his denial in excruciating detail at the exact moment that Jesus is being mocked by the Sanhedrin as a false prophet (14:65; cf. Isa 50:6).

But in his denial, Peter ironically tells the truth. The fact is that he does not really *know this man* (v. 71). He never has. He breaks down in tears. Having "been ashamed" of Jesus, he has put himself into the category of those of whom the eschatological judge will ultimately *be ashamed* (8:38). Peter "the Rock" is rocky soil indeed (4:16-17).

15:1-15. Trial before Pilate. This section of the passion narrative begins with Jesus' being "handed over" to Pilate (15:1) and ends with his being "handed over" by Pilate to the crucifixion squad (15:15). The unit is held together by the vocabulary of "binding" (15:1, 7) and "releasing" (15:6, 9, 11, 15; Robbins 1992, 1165-67). The title "King of the Jews" is heard first on the lips of Pilate (15:2, 9, 12) then in the taunts of the soldiers (15:18), and finally on the lips of the religious leaders (15:32). Although the evangelist has spoken of God's kingship, and implied Jesus' kingship by the titles "Messiah" (one who is anointed) and "Son of God," he does not allow Jesus to be called "king" openly except by his enemies. They do not know how right they are because they cannot imagine a king who reigns from a gallows and triumphs by dying in public disgrace.

Jesus, the one who calls God "Abba" (father, 14:36) has been falsely arrested as though he were a rebel bandit (14:48). The crowd chooses death for the one who restored life to others, while a genuine rebel bandit who has committed murder (15:7) goes free. "Barabbas," ironically, means "son" (*bar*, cf. Bartimaeus, 10:46) of the "father" (*abba*, cf. 14:36).

15:16-20a. Mocking. This short unit highlights the humiliation of Jesus and the irony of the kingship motif. It is arranged chiastically:

A Jesus is led into the courtyard, 16
 B Jesus is clothed and crowned as a king, 17
  C The soldiers mock Jesus in speech: "Hail, King of the Jews!" 18
  C' The soldiers mock Jesus in actions: knelt down in homage, 19
 B' Jesus is stripped and clothed in his own clothes, 20a
A' Jesus is led out of the courtyard, 20b

15:20b-25. Crucifixion. The repetition of the verb "to crucify" marks the beginning and end of this unit (vv. 20b, 24, 25). Simon, an African from Cyrene with a Jewish name (probably to be understood as having come to Jerusalem for Passover), is conscripted to carry Jesus' cross. He thus becomes the first of those who pick up the cross and follow Jesus (cf. 8:34). His sons Alexander and Rufus (typical gentile names) must have been well known to the original audience of Mark, since Simon is identified for the audience by association with his sons' names.

The soldiers' offer of myrrhed wine is further mockery; this drink was a delicacy (Pliny, *NatHist* 14.15.92-93). It would have served as a numbing agent as well, which is why the Markan Jesus refuses it; he follows his own advice to stay alert (13:37; Gundry 1993, 944, 956). Jesus is then crucified naked while the soldiers gamble for his clothing, the mere touching of which had once conferred healing (5:27-29; 6:56; cf. Ps 22:18).

15:26-32. Ridicule of Jesus on the cross. This section is tied together by repetition. The mocking inscription on the cross, *"The King of the Jews"* (v. 26), is picked up by the religious leaders when they ridicule Jesus as *Messiah, King of Israel* (v. 32a). Those crucified with Jesus are mentioned in v. 27 and v. 32b (cf. Isa 53:12). Jesus is *blasphemed* (NRSV mg.) by passersby, "mocked" by the religious leaders, and *taunted* by the revolutionaries on his regal right hand and left hand (cf. 10:37; Ps 22:7-8; Wis 2:17-20). Twice he is invited to save himself (v. 29, 30).

Again Jesus' enemies say more than they know. They articulate the paradox of the passion with the words, *He saved others; he cannot save himself* (v. 31). Only by not saving himself can Jesus save the *many* for whom his life is given as ransom (10:45) and with whom God initiates a covenant in his blood (14:24). If anyone is ever to see and believe it is essential that Jesus *not* come down from the cross now (v. 32a).

15:33-39. Death of Jesus. The darkness recalls Isa 13:9-10; 50:3. Jesus' first loud cry (and the only word from the cross in Mark) is the beginning of Ps 22. Having begun his references to this psalm in 15:22 with Ps 22:18 and moved backward to Ps 22:6-7 in 15:29-30, the narrator ends at the beginning of the psalm with a cry of desolation rather than with the victorious note on which the psalm ends (Robbins 1992, 1175-80).

These last words of Jesus are a prayer, but they contrast sharply with his prayer of submission in 14:36. The evangelist apparently believes that there is no contradiction between commitment to doing the will of God and the anger and abandonment one feels when God's will leads to unbearable suffering and Godforsakenness. The Markan Jesus models the expression of honest anger in the prayers of the faithful.

But like everything else that he has said, these words of the Markan Jesus meet with misunderstanding. Bystanders think that he is calling on Elijah rather than on God (v. 35). Not only that, but Elijah's role is interpreted in terms of his miracle-working power, whereas the Gospel of Mark understands Elijah/John the baptizer as Jesus' predecessor in rejection and suffering (6:14-29; 9:11-13).

The offer of sour wine recalls Ps 69:21: "for my thirst they gave me vinegar to drink." The irony of the misunderstanding is heightened for those members of the audience who would have been familiar with the next verses of Ps 69: "Let their eyes be darkened so that they cannot see" (23a). The three hours of darkness mirror the spiritual blindness of those who see Jesus without understanding and cannot comprehend his words, his actions, or the significance of his passion (Marcus 1992, 183-84).

Jesus' death is portrayed in such a way as to recall the moment of his baptism. The spirit that went into Jesus then (1:10, τὸ πνεῦμα . . . εἰς αὐτόν) now bursts forth from the dying Jesus (15:37, 39, ἐξέπνευσεν) with a loud cry. At the same time, a portent occurs at the Temple inside the city walls. There was an ornate tapestry hanging in front of the outer doors of the Temple, on which, according to JOSEPHUS, "was portrayed a panorama of the heavens" (*BJ* 5.5.4.212-14). This tapestry is ripped apart (ἐσχίσθη) from above by unseen hands (15:38), just as the heavens had been ripped apart (σχιζομένους) at the baptism (1:10) prior to the descent of the Spirit into Jesus (Ulansey 1991).

The tearing of the Temple tapestry has two functions in Mark: (1) it portends the destruction of the Temple that had been prophetically enacted by the Markan Jesus in 11:15-16 and explicitly predicted by him in 13:2; (2) it minimizes the significance of that destruction by interpreting the death of Jesus as the release of the divine Spirit into the world. No longer is the presence of God to be found in a special way in the Temple; instead, the apocalyptic inbreaking of God's reign, inaugurated by Jesus' victory over the demons, is now marked by the pouring out of that same eschatological Spirit into the world as it struggles to give birth to the new creation. Before his own martyrdom, John had prophesied that Jesus would "baptize in the Holy Spirit." The Markan crucifixion account shows that the baptism in the Holy Spirit that empowers the church for ministry and bold witness (13:11) is made possible by the death of Jesus.

The response of the centurion to Jesus' death is a "confession" only in the ears of Mark's audience. On the level of the story it is a sarcastic comment on the lips of a jaded professional executioner who has just watched one more peasant revolutionary die calling on his God: "Oh sure—*that's* a son of Zeus all right!" (v. 39; Fowler 1991, 205–208). His attitude is the same as that of the others at the foot of the cross: if Jesus had really been anybody special, he would have been translated to heaven before dying such a shameful death (Origen, *CCel* 2.68).

Ironically, however, the centurion represents all the gentiles who will hear the gospel and make a sincere confession as a result of Jesus' death (13:10; cf. Isa 52:15; 2:1-4; 56:6-8). Their inclusion has already been prefigured in the proclamation of the gentile man whom Jesus freed from demonic oppression (5:20) and in the insistence of the gentile woman that Jesus is the "Lord" at whose table even the *dogs* will be satisfied (7:24-30).

15:40-47. Burial. This unit is framed by the description of Jesus' female disciples who watch (from a safe distance) as he is crucified and buried (v. 40, 47). These women are followers of Jesus and participants in the servanthood that he has described as the essence of his mission (v. 41; cf. 1:31; 10:45). They do not come forward to bury him, however.

John's disciples had taken his decapitated corpse and laid it in a tomb (6:29) but there is no one to perform this service for Jesus except one of the enemies who condemned him. Joseph is portrayed as a pious but misguided member of the Sanhedrin (v. 43; not a secret disciple as in Matthew and John) who buries Jesus out of adherence to the requirements of Torah. Deuteronomy 21:22-23 specifies that a criminal who has been impaled must be buried before sundown, lest the land be defiled (Brown 1988, 236). The fact that Joseph is still *waiting expectantly* (v. 43) for God's reign shows that he has missed the whole point; God's reign began to burst into existence before his very eyes, but he condemned the messenger (not dissenting from the verdict as in Luke). Now he tosses Jesus' body into a nearby tomb (not his own tomb or a new tomb as in Matthew, Luke, and John) without even washing it, let alone anointing it for burial.

16:1-8. Empty tomb. After his burial, the Markan Jesus is neither seen nor heard again, although his message is conveyed to the women by the young man at the empty tomb. Mark is the only canonical Gospel that narrates no appearances of the risen Jesus. The spurious later additions to the Gospel show how unsatisfactory this decision was to subsequent readers of the text. Later editors would add stories of appearances, creating the long ending of Mark that continues to puzzle devotional and scholarly readers alike.

It would be a mistake, however, to conclude that since the resurrection is not narrated the evangelist wished to emphasize the absence of Jesus between the resurrection and the eschaton. The Markan miracle stories provide abundant evidence that the author of Mark wanted to encourage beleagured Christians to have confidence in the presence and power of the risen Lord in the midst of their difficulties (e.g., 4:35-41). The abrupt ending is deliberate, but it puts the emphasis on mission rather than on the absence of Jesus.

At the beginning of chap. 16 the women followers of Jesus are seen belatedly making their way to the tomb to anoint Jesus' body. They are not expecting a resurrection, despite Jesus' repeated predictions, but at least they are still on the scene, unlike the men, whose absence is highlighted by the women's conversation about who is going to do the heavy work of rolling away the "very large" stone from the entrance to the tomb (vv. 3-4).

After this conversation, the rest of the narrative is framed by the women's entering the tomb in v. 5 and exiting the tomb in v. 8. In the tomb they encounter a young man in white, whose numinous quality is established by his resemblance to the transfigured Jesus (9:3). The response of these three disciples, like that of the three disciples at the transfiguration, is fear (16:5; cf. 9:6), but the messenger begins with the greeting, "Fear not!" (v. 6, author trans.).

Stating the obvious, he continues: "You are looking for Jesus of Nazareth, the crucified one. He has been raised (cf. Isa 52:13). He is not *here*" (v. 6, author trans.). Seeking for Jesus is never the right response in Mark (cf. 1:37); following Jesus is. So the messenger now shifts into the imperative mood: "Go tell his disciples (even Peter!) that he is leading you into Galilee; *there* you will see him, just as he told you" (v. 7, author trans.).

Several things are significant about this message. First, the message is delivered in indirect discourse and uses the second person plural. This makes it clear that the women are among those who are to go to Galilee; the messenger does not say, "Tell his disciples that he is leading them into Galilee; there they will see him just as he told them."

Second, the encounter with Jesus that is promised in the message is an example of unmerited grace based solely on the earlier promise of Jesus (*just as he told you*, v. 7). Nothing accounts for the inclusion of the apostate disciples in the community of the resurrection except for Jesus' promise to them in 14:28. Persistently blind, deaf, and hard of heart, they proved themselves "ashamed of Jesus" when the chips were down and by every criterion operative in the narrative so far they should be counted among the outsiders who have no part in God's reign. Even Peter is included, his denial forgiven.

The amazing grace according to Mark is that even those who fail all the tests articulated by the Markan Jesus may yet hear the reconciling call of the Risen Lord and be given another opportunity to follow him on his way. And this good news is "just as it is written in the prophet Isaiah," (cf. Mark 1:2), where the author of Mark had read

> Fear not, for I have ransomed you; I have called you by name; you are mine. . . . I will say, "Lead my sons from far away and my daughters from the end of the earth—everyone who is called by my name. For I created [them] for my glory and I formed them and made them. I led out the

people who are blind, yet have eyes, who are deaf, yet have ears . . . I, I am the Lord and besides me there is no savior." (Isa 43:1-11 LXX)

The message is given to the women disciples who flee in fear and silence. That, of course, made no difference, since everyone knew that if the women had told about the resurrection, they would not have been believed (Luke 24:10-11). But somebody must have met Jesus on the way of ministry and martyrdom because the story has just been told again. The abrupt ending of the Gospel of Mark leaves no one else to bear witness to the Risen but unseen Lord except the audience of the story's most recent telling. And that is as it should be.

Works Cited

Anderson, Janice Capel. 1992. "Feminist Criticism: The Dancing Daughter," *Mark and Method*, ed. J. C. Anderson and S. D. Moore, 103–34.

Beasley-Murray, G. R. 1990. "Baptism," MDB.

Beavis, Mary Ann. 1989. *Mark's Audience.*

Boring, M. Eugene. 1987. "The Kingdom of God in Mark," *The Kingdom of God in Twentieth-Century Interpretation*, ed. W. Willis.

Brown, Raymond E. 1988. "The Burial of Jesus (Mark 15:42-47)," *CBQ* 50:233–45.

Dewey, Joanna. 1980. *Markan Public Debate*. SBLDS 48.

Donahue, John R. 1982. "A Neglected Factor in the Theology of Mark," *JBL* 101:563–94. 1988. *The Gospel in Parable.*

Dowd, Sharyn. 1988. *Prayer, Power, and the Problem of Suffering*. SBLDS 105.

Dufton, Francis. 1989. "The Syrophoenician Woman and Her Dogs," *ExpTim* 100:417.

Fiorenza, Elisabeth Schüssler. 1983. *In Memory of Her.*

Fowler, Robert M. 1991. *Let the Reader Understand.*

Grimes, Betty J. 1991. "The Syrophoenician Woman," M.Div. paper, Lexington Theological Seminary.

Gundry, Robert H. 1993. *Mark.*

Marcus, Joel. 1986. *The Mystery of the Kingdom of God*. SBLDS 90. 1992. *The Way of the Lord.*

Montgomery, Helen Barrett. 1924. *The New Testament in Modern English.*

Robbins, Vernon K. 1989. "Rhetorical Composition and the Beelzebul Controversy," *Patterns of Persuasion in the Gospels*, by B. L. Mack and V. K. Robbins, 161–93. 1992. "Psalm 22 in the Markan Crucifixion," *The Four Gospels 1992.* Festschrift Frans Neirynck. BETL 100.

Schüssler-Fiorenza, Elisabeth. *See* Fiorenza, Elisabeth.

Tannehill, Robert C. 1977. "The Disciples in Mark: The Function of a Narrative Role," *JR* 57:386–405. 1980. "Tension in Synoptic Sayings and Stories," *Int* 34:138–59.

Ulansey, David. 1991. "The Heavenly Veil Torn: Mark's Cosmic *Inclusio*," *JBL* 110:123–35.

Via, Dan O, Jr. 1985. *The Ethics of Mark's Gospel.*

Waetjen, Herman C. 1989. *A Reordering of Power.*

Wahlberg, Rachel Conrad. 1975. *Jesus according to a Woman.*

Wiedemann, Thomas. 1989. *Adults and Children in the Roman Empire.*

Luke [MCB 1007-42]

J. Bradley Chance

Introduction

Luke is the third Gospel in the NT. Like the other Gospels it describes the life and teachings of Jesus of Nazareth. Unlike the other Gospels it has a sequel attached to it, the Acts of the Apostles. That both Luke and Acts, commonly referred to simply as Luke-Acts, were written by the same person can be seen by comparing the prologues of each work. The employment of geography to structure the story depicts God's universal offering of salvation. The centrality of JERUSALEM in the narratives serves to remind the reader of God's promises to Israel. The movement of the story in Acts "to the ends of the earth" (Acts 1:8) gives expression to God's salvific concern for everyone, everywhere.

Luke and the Other Gospels

Luke shares much in common with the other two synoptic Gospels, Mark and Matthew, leading interpreters to conclude that some type of direct literary relationship exists between them. Since the nineteenth century, biblical scholars have generally agreed that the Gospel of Mark was employed as a source by the authors of both Luke and Matthew. In addition, interpreters argue that both Luke and Matthew employed a source called Q which consisted primarily of sayings of Jesus. A significant minority of biblical scholars rejects this "two-document hypothesis," arguing that Luke's primary source was the Gospel of Matthew. Luke also shares certain affinities with the Fourth Gospel, such as the somewhat similar story found in Luke 5:4-9 and John 21:5-11 about a miraculous catch of fish. Few scholars have concluded, however, that there existed a direct literary relationship between these two gospels.

Authorship

IRENAEUS (ca. 180 C.E.) expresses the common view of the church fathers concerning the authorship of Luke-Acts: "Luke, too, the companion of Paul, set forth in a book the Gospel as preached by him" (*AdvHaer* 3.1, 1). Colossians 4:14 and Phlm 24 do refer to a certain Luke, implying that he was an occasional associate of PAUL. Irenaeus also viewed the so-called "we sections" of Acts (cf. Acts 16:10) as the author's indication of his close relationship with Paul (*AdvHaer* 3.14, 1). Modern interpreters note that neither the Gospel nor Acts offers any explicit word concerning the author's identity. Furthermore, the author of Luke-Acts seems to offer a very different portrait of Paul than that offered by Paul himself in his letters. In fact, the author of Acts shows no awareness that Paul was even a prolific letter writer. This evidence leads many scholars to reject the conclusion that the author of Acts was a companion of Paul, much less the specific person named Luke. Some current interpreters have reasonably defended the traditional identification of Luke as the author of Luke-Acts (e.g., Fitzmyer 1981, 35-51). The issue cannot be resolved, so it is best not to base one's interpretation of the narrative on any particular hypothesis concerning the actual identity of the real author. "Luke" is a name used primarily for convenience.

Date and Place of Composition

Luke's description of the fall of Jerusalem (19:43-44; 21:20; cf. the much more general reference in Mark 13:14), leads most interpreters to conclude that Luke was composed after the fall of Jerusalem (70 C.E.). The fact that Luke shows no knowledge of Paul's letter writing activity suggests a date of composition 100 C.E., before the approximate time when Paul's letters began to circulate as a collection. Any author as informed as Luke claims to be (Luke 1:1-4) would surely have known of such a collection. Hence, one may suggest a date of composition between 70 and -100 C.E. No one knows the place of composition, although many suggestions have been offered, both by ancient and modern readers of Luke-Acts.

Genre

Knowing the genre of an ancient text can guide the modern reader in reading the text as an ancient might have. Regrettably, modern scholars can reach no consensus concerning the genre of Luke and Acts. Do they represent separate genres, with the Gospel showing affinities with ancient biography (Burridge 1992) and Acts looking something like an ancient historical novel (Pervo 1989)? Does Luke-Acts represent a type of ancient history (Aune 1987)? Ancient biography (Talbert 1988)? Clearly, the subject of the Gospel is Jesus, allowing the conclusion that readers are reading an ancient biography. But Jesus is a character within a larger story describing God's dealings with Israel and the rest of the world; hence, readers should not hesitate to look for a bigger story within this story about Jesus.

For Further Study

In the *Mercer Dictionary of the Bible*: APOSTLE/APOSTLESHIP; APOSTLES, ACTS OF THE; DISCIPLE/DISCIPLESHIP; ESCHATOLOGY IN THE NT; GOSPELS, CRITICAL STUDY OF; HOLY SPIRIT; KINGDOM OF GOD; LORD'S SUPPER; LUKE; LUKE, GOSPEL OF; PASSOVER; REDACTION; SON OF GOD; SON OF MAN; SOURCE CRITICISM; SYNOPTIC PROBLEM; TRAVEL NARRATIVE; TWELVE, THE; WOMEN IN THE NT; WORSHIP IN THE NT.

In other sources: D. E. Aune, *The N.T. in Its Literary Environment*; R. A. Burridge, *What Are the Gospels? A Comparison with Graeco-Roman Biography*; J. A. Fitzmyer, *The Gospel according to Luke I-IX*, AncB; R. Pervo, "Must Luke and Acts Belong to the Same Genre?" *SBLSP* (1989): 309-16; C. H. Talbert, "Once Again: Gospel Genre," *Semeia* 43 (1988): 53-73; R. C. Tannehill, *The Narrative Unity of Luke-Acts*, 2 vols.

Commentary

An Outline

I. Prologue, 1:1-4
II. Preparing the Way, 1:5–4:13
   A. Preparation through Announcement, 1:5-56
   B. Preparation through Wondrous Births and Childhoods, 1:57–2:52
   C. Preparation through John's Preaching, 3:1-20
   D. Preparation through Jesus' Baptism and Temptation, 3:21–4:13
III. The Galilean Ministry of the Spirit-Anointed Prophet, 4:14–9:50
   A. Release to the Captives, 4:14–6:16
   B. Proclaiming the Favorable Year of the Lord, 6:17-49
   C. Release to the Oppressed, 7:1–9:50
IV. The Anointed Prophet's Journey to Jerusalem, 9:51–19:44
   A. Beginning the Journey, 9:51–10:42
   B. Understanding the Present Time, 11:1–13:35
   C. The Leaven of the Pharisees, 14:1–16:31
   D.Persistence for the Journey to Come, 17:1–18:30
   E. Approaching Jerusalem, 18:31–19:44
V. Exodus from Jerusalem, 19:45–24:53
   A. The Temple Ministry, 19:45–21:38
   B. The Hour of Darkness, 22:1–23:56
   C. Entering into Glory, 24:1-53

Prologue, 1:1-4

Luke is the only one of the four Gospels to begin with a formal, literary prologue. This prologue has a number of characteristics found in the formal prologues of other ancient biographies, historical narratives, and even fictional works. First, one finds a statement concerning the author's awareness of earlier, similar works ("many have undertaken to compile a narrative," 1:1 RSV). This may be a reference to Mark and Q, assuming the two-document hypothesis. Luke may have known of other narratives. Second, a statement of the contents of the work (*events that have been fulfilled among us*, v. 1) and a plan of presentation (*to write an orderly account for you*, v. 3). Third, a statement rehearsing the author's qualifications (vv. 2-3). Such statements were often rhetorical attempts to gain the reader's confidence rather than literal records of the author's research techniques. Fourth, a statement of purpose (v. 4). Fifth, identification of the addressee (*Theophilus,* v. 3). Finally, a very good literary style, which is discernable even in English translations. Regrettably, the prologue offers no help in identifying specifically the author of the narrative, since it lacks what was a common feature of prologues: the author's name.

Although readers learn nothing of the author's identity, the text does imply some things about the author. First, he uses a masculine participle in the word translated as *investigating* (v. 3) to describe himself. Second, he makes no claims to having been an eyewitness, but rather describes himself as the recipient of tradition which goes back to *eyewitnesses and servants* (v. 2). Third, the author presents himself as informed and educated. Such an impression is made not only by what he says about how carefully he has investigated everything, but the very style of the prologue itself. It is clear that the author is calling the reader to take the forthcoming narrative seriously.

The prologue also implies certain things about the reader, whom the author identifies as *Theophilus*. If this were an actual person, his identity is unknown. Luke may be addressing the gospel to any "lover of God," which is what the name literally means. Regardless, the text assumes a reader who has had some previous instruction in the Christian tradition. The text also assumes an inquisitive reader who wishes to be better informed and who desires to *know the truth* (v. 4) about these matters. The very use of a formal prologue, inviting readers to compare this narrative to other works of history and biography, implies readers who would appreciate a narrative about Jesus and his followers written from a cultured, even cosmopolitan perspective.

In short, any reader, ancient or modern, who assumes the role of the reader implied by the text will approach the narrative as an informed, inquisitive, and cosmopolitan reader sympathetic with the Christian tradition. That is the perspective that shall be employed in the following commentary.

Preparing the Way, 1:5–4:13

In this first section of the narrative Luke will provide a context in which readers can understand the public ministry of Jesus. Hence, the "way" is not only being prepared for Jesus, but for the reader. This narrative of preparation indicates that Jesus' story finds its roots in the story of the OT, the story of Israel and Israel's God. Jesus' story is the realization of the hopes of Israel and the promises made by God to Israel's ancestors, Abraham, Isaac, and Jacob. Further, this coming salvation will be not only for Israel's glory but will offer revelation to the gentiles also.

John's public preaching announces that the time of the Lord's coming is at hand, placing the people of Israel and the reader at the edge of the time of the actual realization of the promises and hopes. Jesus' BAPTISM and testing by the devil offer some real insight into the profound significance of the work he is about to accomplish.

Preparation through Announcement, 1:5-56

Like the Gospel of Matthew, Luke begins his "narrative concerning the things which have been fulfilled among us" (author trans.) with an account of the birth of Jesus. Each of them likely constructed their infancy narratives on the basis of limited yet common traditions for the purpose of conveying to their readers something of the purpose and significance of Jesus' life—a common function of ancient biographical birth accounts. (See Fitzmyer 1981, 305-309.)

Readers of Luke's birth narrative should note in Gabriel's announcements to ZECHARIAH and MARY similarities with birth announcements of OT worthies (such as ABRAHAM), including the presence of an ANGEL, a message about the child, and sometimes even human questioning (cf. Gen 16:7-13; 17:1-22; Judg 13:3-20). These OT allusions, combined with a literary style reminiscent of the LXX, the Bible of Luke's readers, and the primary setting of Jerusalem and the Temple, places Luke's story and, hence, his readers into the world of the OT.

1:5-25. Announcement to Zechariah. Zechariah and ELIZABETH are introduced as stock, pious characters out of the OT, being described as righteous, blameless, and of priestly descent. Even their childless state puts them in company with OT heroes like Abraham and SARAH. During his priestly service Zechariah receives the vision of Gabriel concerning John's birth. Like heroes who have preceded them, Zechariah and Elizabeth will have a child late in life. This child will also resemble OT heroes, especially Elijah (1:16-17). Comparison with ELIJAH raises a note of expectation: the Lord is coming! Israel must be prepared! (cf. Mal 4:5-6).

Zechariah is struck dumb as an immediate and concrete sign to address his skepticism. It also renders Zechariah unable to offer the priestly blessing to the people waiting outside, perhaps implying that the old way of receiving the blessing of God is about to pass away. The story ends with a clear word that the announcement has come true—Elizabeth has experienced the favor of God.

1:26-38. Announcement to Mary. This angelic announcement also refers to a wondrous birth—but it is even more wondrous than that of John. Mary's child will be conceived by the power of the HOLY SPIRIT. While John was compared to the great prophet Elijah, Jesus is called *the Son of the Most High* and will sit on the throne of DAVID and *reign over the house of Jacob forever* (vv. 32-33). Long awaited hopes for the messianic king are finally going to be realized. Gabriel's talk of the Holy Spirit, denoting the dynamic presence of God, Elizabeth's conception, and his concluding words, *nothing will be impossible with God* (vv. 35-37), serve to indicate the direct intervention of God into the story of the people of Israel. Mary's obedient response (v. 38) offers a model for all who experience God's favor (v. 28) to emulate.

1:39-56. Announcement of the mothers. When the two relatives meet, Elizabeth, being filled with the Holy Spirit, offers Mary a blessing. Mary is blessed because she is an instrument of God, bearing the Lord as *the fruit of [her] womb* (v. 42), and because she has responded to God by believing (having faith in) the word spoken to her (v. 45). The stirring of John in Elizabeth's womb and her filling with the Spirit confirm once again the power and immediate presence of God.

Mary offers up a hymn of praise (the MAGNIFICAT, vv. 46b-55), making explicit what has been intimated in the narrative: God is accomplishing great things. Specific blessings are coming Israel's way in fulfillment of God's promises to Israel's ancestors. Among these blessings is a great reversal of stations (vv. 51-53) commonly associated with the messianic age.

Preparation through Wondrous Births and Childhoods, 1:57–2:52

1:57-66 The circumcision and naming of John. The angelic announcement now finds fulfillment. John's circumcision continues the theme of Jewish piety (v. 59). In obedience to the vision (v. 13), Zechariah confirms Elizabeth's statement that the child shall be named "John" (vv. 60-63). His tongue is then loosed, evoking praise from him and fear from the neighbors and relatives (v. 65). Exciting expectations are raised among the people as they ask *what then will this child become?* (v. 66).

1:67-80. The Benedictus. Zechariah, filled with the Spirit, answers their question through *prophecy* in vv. 68-79. Zechariah repeats an important theme of Mary's Magnificat: God is fulfilling promises made of old to Israel's prophets (v. 70) and ancestors (vv. 72-73). Themes of deliverance abound: *redeemed, mighty savior for us, saved from our enemies, rescued from the hands of our enemies*. John, as *prophet of the Most High*, shall prepare the Lord's ways offering *knowledge of salvation, the forgiveness of their sins* (v. 77), leading to *the dawn from on high* to break in and offer *light to those . . . in darkness*, and *the way of peace* (vv. 78-79). But Israel, and the reader, must wait until the day when John appears *publicly to Israel* (v. 80).

2:1-20. The birth of Jesus. Luke is aware of the tradition that Bethlehem was the place of Jesus' birth. He uses a vague reminiscence of a census around the time of Jesus' birth as a means of explaining how Joseph and Mary came to be in Bethlehem. What confuses interpreters is the fact that the *registration . . . taken while Quirinius was governor of Syria* (v. 2) occurred in 6 C.E., long after "the days of King Herod" (1:5, d. 4 B.C.E.). Luke notes that Joseph, Mary's fiancee, was a descendant of David and Bethlehem was *the city of David* (v. 3) to emphasize the point that Jesus is to be the one to inherit *the throne of his ancestor David* (1:32).

The announcement to and visitation of the shepherds (vv. 8-20) allows for a number of important themes to be reiterated or introduced. The angelic announcement, which includes a *sign* (v. 12), indicates the activity of God. Shepherds as the recipients of this *good news of great joy* denote the lowly whom God is lifting up (1:52). Jesus is specifically identified as *a Savior* and *the Messiah* (v. 11). Just as expectations were raised among the people regarding John, all who hear the shepherds' report are *amazed* (v. 18). The shepherds' *glorifying and praising God* (v. 20) represents appropriate response to the great thing God is accomplishing.

2:21-40. The presentation of Jesus. The piety of Jesus' parents is made evident as they circumcise Jesus, name him in obedience to the angelic vision (v. 21), and do all that is necessary *according to the law of Moses* (v. 22). The favored status of the lowly, the poor, and humble (cf. 1:51-53) is reinforced by notification that Jesus' parents offer the sacrifice of those who are poor (v. 24. cf. Lev 12:8).

SIMEON too embodies pious characteristics, being guided by the Spirit, *righteous and devout, looking forward to the consolation of Israel* (v. 25). His hope is fulfilled as he is permitted to see Jesus. His words of praise introduce a new element into this story: this salvation is for "all of the peoples"—glory for Israel, *revelation to the Gentiles* (v. 32). Even Mary and Joseph *were amazed at what was being said about him* (v. 33), inviting readers to pause and reflect on what was so amazing about what Simeon has just said: even the gentiles will benefit from this savior! But then Simeon offers a final, ominous word: *the falling and rising of many in Israel* is coming. Jesus will be *a sign that will be opposed.* Even Mary will not be spared this dividing sword (v. 35). ANNA, a PROPHET, further shows how the truly pious of Israel recognize the significance of Jesus and what he has to offer those *looking for the redemption of Jerusalem* (v. 38).

2:41-52. Jesus at the Temple. This final story serves to foreshadow Jesus' ultimate obedience to God (v. 49), even over family (cf. Mary's experiencing the sword of division, v. 35), and his authority as an interpreter of God's law. The latter is evidenced by the astonishment of *teachers . . . at his understanding and his answers.* A final note (v. 52) confirms the favored status of Jesus.

Preparation through John's Preaching, 3:1-20

3:1-6. Historical introduction. The historical details offered by Luke serve to root the story of Jesus in world history. *The fifteenth year of the reign of Emperor Tiberius* is most likely 28/29 C.E. Pontius PILATE, who governed Judea 26–36 C.E., will play a role in Jesus' trial (chap. 23), as will HEROD (*ruler of Galilee* 4 B.C.E.–39 C.E.). Philip, Herod's brother, and Lysanias play no role in the story. Verse 2 leaves the impression that Annas and CAIAPHAS jointly held the office of high priest. Annas, the father-in-law of Caiaphas, actually held the office from 6–15 C.E. Caiaphas was the actual ruling high priest during Jesus' ministry (18–36 C.E.). Neither Annas nor Caiaphas appears by name anywhere else in Luke's story, but Luke must have one of these in mind when he refers to Jesus' hearing at the *high priest's house* (Luke 22:54).

This detailed introduction also provides for John the kind of historical introduction that is found in OT prophetic books (cf. Isa 1:1; Jer 1:1-3). This is a most fitting introduction since John has already been referred to as *prophet of the Most High* (1:76). John prepares the way by *proclaiming a baptism of repentance for the forgiveness of sins* (v. 3). Luke does not interpret the connection between baptism, repentance, and forgiveness. Perhaps he understood John's baptism as a kind of foreshadowing of (preparation for) Christian baptism (cf., e.g., Acts 19:1-7). John had already been introduced as one whose work would involve repentance, or turning (1:16-17), and forgiveness of sins (1:77). Now he is carrying out that role. The quotation from Isa 40:3-5 (vv. 4-6) is longer than that offered in either Matthew or Mark and emphasizes the cosmic and universal significance (*all flesh shall see the salvation of God*; cf. 2:32) of what is about to happen.

3:7-17. The preaching of John. John's preaching focuses on three issues. Verses 7-9 make clear the necessity of repentance in the face of the eschatological wrath that is coming. Talk of wrath might seem surprising, but both Mary (1:51-53) and

Zechariah (1:71-73) have already spoken of reversals that are necessary to set the world right. Despite such declarations as 1:55 and 1:73, John makes clear that repentance is needed even from the children of Abraham.

Verses 10-14 offer specific examples of repentance—a radical change of priorities, values, and ethical behavior. The fact that even *tax collectors* and *soldiers* are depicted among *the crowds that came out to be baptized by him* indicates that all are afforded the opportunity to prepare themselves for the coming of the Lord.

Verses 15-18 begin with people wondering whether this one *might be the Messiah*. The crowds clearly recognize the eschatological implications of John's message. Their inquiry leads John to point their attention to another: *one who is more powerful than* he is coming. Readers know that this is Jesus. John proclaims that this mighty one will carry out the baptism of salvation (*Holy Spirit*) or damnation (*fire*), dividing humanity into wheat and chaff. Recall Simeon's prophecy concerning the *falling and rising of many in Israel* (2:34).

3:18-20. The imprisonment of John. Neither Matthew (4:12; cf. 14:3-4) nor Mark (1:14a; cf. 6:17-18) informs the reader of John's arrest until after Jesus had been baptized. In Luke, however, John exits the stage prior to Jesus' baptism when Herod throws John in prison because he openly preached against Herod's marriage to his brother's wife. (JOSEPHUS confirms this fact, although he states that Herod feared the political implications of John's preaching [*Ant* 18.5.2].) The way has now been prepared for the Lord.

Preparation through Jesus' Baptism and Temptation, 3:21–4:13

Although the way has been prepared for Jesus through the proclamation of repentance and forgiveness, Jesus must be prepared through divine commissioning and a period of testing.

3:21-22. The baptism of Jesus. Unlike Matthew (3:13-17) and Mark (1:9-11), Luke does not state that John baptized Jesus; in fact, he leaves exactly the opposite impression. Rather, Luke speaks of Jesus' baptism in an almost parenthetical statement associating Jesus' baptism with that of *all the people*. Luke offers no clues that Jesus was in need of repentance and forgiveness. But such identification prepares for the special ministry of Jesus to outcasts and sinners of Israel.

Luke notes that the Spirit descends upon Jesus while he is praying. The eschatological mission that is about to commence requires prayer and the enabling of the Spirit. No hint is given that any other than Jesus heard the voice confirming the identity of Jesus as God's *Son, the Beloved* with whom God is *well pleased* (contra? Matt 3:17). Informed readers would catch the allusion to Ps 2:7, a psalm of enthronement in which the LORD declares "you are my son," and recall the promise made to Mary (1:32). They would also note the allusion to Isa 42:1, an oracle concerning God's servant who receives God's spirit "to bring forth justice to the nations" (ἔθνη), and recall Simeon's prophecy that Jesus would be *a light for revelation to the Gentiles* (ἔθνη, 2:32).

<u>3:23-38. The genealogy of Jesus.</u> Matthew also offers a genealogy of Jesus (Matt 1:2-16), although it is not the same genealogy. The genealogies of Matthew and Luke, like other ancient genealogies, served to make a statement about the identity of Jesus. From Luke's genealogy one learns that through Joseph, Jesus' legal father (*the son [as was thought] of Joseph*, [v. 23]), Jesus is indeed of the line of David, although, interestingly, not of the royal line (cf. v. 32; Jesus is descended from David's son Nathan, not Solomon). Perhaps Luke was aware of specific prophecies such as those found in Jer 22:24-30; 36:30-31, stating that the Davidic dynasty would end with JEHOIACHIN (Coniah in Jer 22:24), son of JEHOIAKIM (cf. esp. Jer 22:30). Further by tracing Jesus' genealogy back to ADAM and God (v. 38) the genealogy also "serves to explain in still another way the relation of Jesus . . . to God and to the human beings he has come to serve" (Fitzmyer 1981, 498). The genealogy reinforces the impression made by the baptism story: that Jesus identifies with "all the people" and is God's son.

<u>4:1-13. The temptation of Jesus</u>. Luke's narration of the temptation, or testing, of Jesus is most similar to the account found in Matt 4:1-11 (cf. Mark 1:12-13), although the order of temptations is not the same. Luke introduces the temptation narrative by twice noting Jesus' close association with the *Holy Spirit* (v. 1), stating that Jesus was *full of the Holy Spirit*, and that he *was led by the Spirit in the wilderness*. Recall that Luke has closely juxtaposed the descent of the Spirit and the affirmation of Jesus' sonship in 3:22 and has just concluded the genealogy of Jesus with the phrase *son of God* (3:38). This allows the conclusion that it is Jesus, in his role as Son of God, who is being led by the Spirit into the wilderness. Twice Jesus' adversary begins his challenges to Jesus by saying *if you are the Son of God* (vv. 3, 9), confirming that, indeed, this narrative is primarily about Jesus and his work as God's Son.

The reason for Jesus' pilgrimage to the wilderness is clearly stated: Jesus *for forty days . . . was tempted by the devil* (v. 2). By portraying the time of testing as extending throughout the time of the forty days (contra Matt 4:1-3), Luke portrays a most intense and significant struggle.

The reference to *forty days* might be nothing more than a way of indicating an extended duration of time. One would not be reading too much into the text to find some sort of symbolic significance. For example, Moses and Elijah, two great figures of the OT whose names will often appear in Luke's narrative (and they will even appear as characters in the action! [cf. 9:28-36]), also experienced a period of forty days of solitude from other people at significant periods in their lives (cf. Exod 24:18; 1 Kgs 19:8). Perhaps Luke wishes the reader to compare the work of Jesus to the important influence of these great men of old.

The number *forty* might also allude to the forty years of testing in the wilderness experienced by Israel during the exodus. In all three temptations, Jesus' retorts to the devil consist of quotations from Deuteronomy. In the first (v. 4) Jesus quotes Deut 8:3. In Deut 8:2, Moses refers explicitly to Israel's testing for "forty years in the wilderness" and Israel's experiencing hunger and being fed with manna "in order to make you understand that one does not live by bread alone." Jesus' second retort to the devil (v. 8) quotes Deut 6:13, found in a context referring to Israel's impending possession of the land. It is emphasized that God gave Israel the land and Israel should, therefore, serve only God (cf. Deut 6:10-15). Notably, Jesus rebuffs the devil's offer to give him *all the kingdoms of the world* if Jesus will only worship him (vv. 5-7) with a quotation from the OT found in a context emphasizing that it is *God* who gives the land. It is also relevant that Ps 106, which rehearses the rebellious story of Israel in the face of God's mercy, notes that one of Israel's iniquitous acts "in the wilderness" was the false worship offered to the calf (Ps 106:14, 19-20). Jesus, unlike Israel, does not succumb to the temptation of false worship. In the final retort, v. 12, Jesus quotes Deut 6:16. Moses specifically commanded Israel, "Do not put the LORD your God to the test, as you tested him at Massah." Psalm 106:14b also states that Israel "put God to the test in the desert." Collectively, these rejections of the devil's tests show that Jesus accomplished in the wilderness what Israel could not. Such an impression cannot help but leave the reader sensing that indeed good times may be ahead for Israel. Where Israel had failed in the past, Jesus, the one who brings God's salvation prepared *for glory to [God's] people Israel* (2:32), succeeds. And yet, such reminders of Israel's failings might leave the reader feeling ambiguous. If Israel failed before, might failure come again?

Although informed readers can easily detect a comparison between Jesus and Israel, they cannot overlook the fact that this narrative is about a direct conflict between Jesus, the Spirit-anointed Son of God, and the devil. Luke does not need to introduce the devil; informed readers know who he is. He is Satan (cf., e.g., 10:18; 11:18; 13:16), Beelzebul, the ruler of demons (11:15), and even the ruler of *all the kingdoms of the world* (v. 5).

This, the last story told before Jesus begins his public ministry, makes clear that the way that has been prepared is a way that involves conflict of the most serious proportions. Jesus' nemesis will be Satan himself. To be sure, Jesus wins this round: *when the devil had finished every test, he departed from him* (v. 13). Luke has made clear to the reader that the Spirit-anointed Son of God is more powerful than Satan. But this battle is not over, for the devil *departed [only] . . . until an opportune time.* As subsequent stories will make clear, Satan, this ruler of demons, has allies everywhere.

The Galilean Ministry of the Spirit-Anointed Prophet, 4:14–9:50

This second section of Luke's narrative hurls Jesus into action and into confrontation with the allies of Satan. The first pericope sets the tone of the entire section and for Jesus' ministry: it will be a ministry of liberation, or release. In parts one (4:14–6:16) and three (7:1–9:50) of this section, Jesus' ministry of liberation comes primarily through his and his followers' actions. In part two (6:17-49) he offers his liberating word in the sermon on the plain.

Release to the Captives, 4:14–6:16

4:14-30. The rejection at Nazareth. Luke prefaces the story of the Nazareth incident with a summary statement (vv. 14-15) of Jesus' public ministry, leaving the impression Jesus has been at work for some time. This summary of Jesus' activities differs from that of Matt 4:13-17 and Mark 1:14b-15, both of which make explicit reference to Jesus' proclamation of the "kingdom of God." This has led some to believe that Luke does not wish to emphasize the eschatological significance of Jesus' work. The remainder of chap. 4 challenges this conclusion.

Luke's story of Jesus' Nazareth rejection is longer than the accounts found in Matt 13:54-58 and Mark 6:1-6a. The length of the story and Luke's use of this story to inaugurate Jesus' public ministry indicate its significance. The text from which Jesus reads (Isa 61:1-2a; 58:6) refers to familiar issues, especially *the Spirit of the Lord*, and *anointed* (having same Gk. root as the word "Christ"). Since readers already know Jesus to be the "anointed one" (2:11) and "full of the Spirit" (4:1), they will associate this text with Jesus and the work he is going to perform.

Captives and *oppressed* (v. 18) describe similar types of people. The words translated *release* and *go free* represent the same word in Greek (ἄφεσις). Reference is being made to the "setting free," the liberation, of oppressed persons. Such liberation is juxtaposed with references to bringing *good news to the poor*, *recovery of sight to the blind*, and proclaiming *the year of the Lord's favor* (vv. 18-19). Thus, several important issues pertaining the upcoming ministry of Jesus, particularly preaching and healing, are set in an overall context of liberation.

The eyes of all . . . were fixed on him (v. 20). Something significant is happening. Jesus declares that *today this scripture has been fulfilled in your hearing*. Thus, it is not surprising that *all spoke well of him and were amazed at the gracious words* (v. 22). Of course, readers know that Jesus is not merely *Joseph's son* (v. 22). Still readers share with the audience the expectation that liberation is coming, and wonder just what kind of liberation. Just who are the oppressed and the captives?

Jesus does not warmly receive the reaction of his hometown audience. He predicts that his people will quote Jesus the proverb, *Doctor, cure yourself* (v. 23), which he then interprets and applies specifically: *Do here also in your hometown the things we have heard you did at Capernaum* (v. 23). Despite an initially positive response, relations will cool. Such cooling has to do with Jesus' hometown citizens wanting to make sure that no other town receives anything that they do not. There are evidenced here hints of possessiveness and even jealousy.

Jesus' next words offer further interpretation, applying to himself the title prophet and stating that he will not be accepted by his own. Rejection, however, does not stop the prophet from doing his work. Elijah had certainly experienced rejection from his own, being the object of AHAB's and JEZEBEL's wrath requiring that he flee for his life (1 Kgs 19). Yet his prophetic work continued even in the midst of such struggle as indicated by his being sent to a non-Israelite widow (1

Kgs 17). ELISHA, upon whom the spirit of Elijah had come to rest (2 Kgs 2:15), further demonstrated that God's blessings were not reserved for Israel in that he healed the Syrian Namaan (2 Kgs 5).

The application to Jesus' own situation is clear: he will experience rejection from his own—but that will not stop him from performing the liberating work to which God has called him. He will move on from NAZARETH. In the larger setting of Luke-Acts readers may also sense something of an ominous foreshadowing: will Jesus ultimately be rejected by Israel just as he has predicted that he will be rejected by his hometown? If so, readers are assured that such rejection will not stop the liberating work of God. Elijah and Elisha went to the others—so can Jesus.

The reaction of Jesus' hometown is violent beyond reason. The very hint that God's blessings will not be halted by the rejection of his messenger drives the people to fury. Their violent protest against the prophecy that they will reject Jesus leads them to do precisely what Jesus predicted: *they drove him out of town* and tried to *hurl him off the cliff* (v. 29). Already the "rising and falling of many in Israel" has begun. Jesus' first public word to Israel has shown him to be the *sign that will be opposed* (2:34).

4:31-44. The liberating work of God's reign. Luke offers four pericopes that quickly demonstrate precisely the kind of liberation Jesus was talking about in Nazareth.

The first is 4:31-37. Jesus' word in 4:23 has prepared readers for something significant to happen in Capernaum. This pericope fulfills the expectation. The significant thing that happens is Jesus' confrontation with an *unclean demon* (v. 33), clearly an ally of the devil. The demon, speaking for himself and his band of fellow hosts of Satan, sums up the essence of the conflict: *Have you come to destroy us?* (v. 34) Jesus' answer is clear as he *rebuked him* and thereby demonstrated his *authority and power* to command *the unclean spirits, and out they come!* (v. 36) Jesus' liberating ministry has begun.

Jesus' liberating work continues as he assaults not only demons but disease (vv. 38-39). The clause, he *rebuked the fever* (v. 39), recalls how he had earlier *rebuked* the demon (v. 35). The connection with Jesus' announced ministry of "release" (4:18) is found in the statement that the fever *left her*, which literally is translated "it released her." The *service* Peter's liberated mother-in-law renders to them demonstrates that she is indeed well. A deeper meaning is suggested in that the word used for service (διακονέω) is often used of "Christian service" (e.g., Luke 22:24-27). Those liberated by Jesus are liberated for service to him and others.

The third pericope (4:40-41) again juxtaposes Jesus' healings and exorcisms. Readers are told that Jesus *rebuked* the demons, not permitting them to reveal his identity as *the Messiah* and *Son of God*. No specific clue is given as to why Jesus will not permit such revelations. Perhaps Jesus wishes to define these titles on his own terms.

In the final pericope (4:42-44) of this section, Luke uses a phrase he has not yet used: *the kingdom of God*. Finally, readers know what all this is about. The proclaiming of *good news to the poor* and *release to the captives* (4:18), the rebuking of demons and disease, even the head-to-head encounter with the devil in the wilderness—all of these come under the straightforward clause: *to proclaim to good news of the kingdom of God* (v. 43). The reign of God himself is coming—and with it comes liberation from that which has oppressed and held captive God's people. CAPERNAUM has enjoyed these blessings. Capernaum must learn what Nazareth failed to learn: these blessings are not only for them. Jesus must proclaim this good news in *other cities also*.

5:1-11. Calling disciples. Luke introduces the story by referring to the pressing *crowd*, a mass-character already introduced (cf. 4:42). This is one of the many references portraying the masses as responding favorably to Jesus (cf. 5:15; 6:17; 7:11, et al.).

The story indicates the work of Jesus will involve the help of others, of whom *Simon* and *James and John, sons of Zebedee*, are the first chosen. Luke introduced Simon rather abruptly in 4:38. It is clear that he has seen the many mighty works of Jesus, works that point to Jesus' authority and power (cf. 4:36). The miraculous catch of fish offers one more demonstration of Jesus' power, a power to which Simon responds in amazement (v. 9). *He fell down at Jesus' knees, saying, "Go away from me, Lord, for I am a sinful man"* (v. 8). The call of Jesus transcends the sinful human condition. In spite of Peter's condition as a sinner Jesus calls him to *be catching people* (v. 10), a peculiar phrase literally rendered "catching alive." Surely, the implication is that Simon will be catching people alive for the kingdom of God (4:43). Simon and his companions respond with total allegiance: *they left everything and followed him* (v. 11).

5:12-16. Healing of a leper. Luke offers another example of the liberating power of Jesus. Here Jesus heals a man inflicted with a disease that ostracized him from the community of the people, due to uncleanness (Lev 13:45-46). The leper, therefore, desires to be made clean (5:12). Jesus' concern to restore the leper to community is shown in his command that the leper go immediately to the priest to *make an offering for your cleansing*, an offering that resulted in restoration to the community (cf. Lev 14:2-9). The liberating power of Jesus has genuine communal and sociological concern.

Luke now offers a series of controversy stories, extending from 5:17 through 6:11. In these stories, Jesus will continue to manifest his power and authority through the miracles by which he confronts oppressive disease. Jesus will also demonstrate his authority through confrontation with a new set of characters, the religious authorities. These people offer a different, yet no less real, kind of oppression of human beings: scrupulous religion.

5:17-26. The forgiveness of sins. Luke sets the stage for the next story by introducing the *Pharisees and teachers of the law* (v. 17). Readers would associate them with religious authorities, an association reinforced by reference to their being *from Jerusalem*. Notification of the presence of the crowd (v. 19), whom Luke has already shown to be positively disposed to the work of Jesus, raises a question as to whether the religious leaders will also respond positively to Jesus' work.

Luke sets readers up for another healing miracle, stating that *the power of the Lord was with him to heal* (v. 17). The story then takes a strange turn. When the paralytic is presented to Jesus, he declares, "*Your sins are forgiven*" (v. 18). Two things become clear. One, the religious leaders react negatively to Jesus' word of forgiveness. Readers know the power of the Lord to be with Jesus (cf. 5:17; 3:21-22; 4:1); the leaders obviously do not. Their reaction is quite the opposite of the crowd who *glorified God* (v. 26). The division of Israel has begun! Ironically, in their skepticism the leaders ask what is a crucially important question: "Who is this man . . . ?" (author trans.) Two, readers are invited to consider that the power of Jesus to liberate from demons and disease can also liberate people from sin. The word used for "forgiveness" shares the same Gk. root as the word for "release" found in 4:18. "Release from sins" is part of a much larger ministry of liberation—the liberation from the oppressive grip of the devil from which the kingdom of God has come to release humanity. Jesus associates this dimension of the liberation with the title *Son of Man*, thereby answering his opponents' question.

5:27–6:11. Controversy with the religious leaders. Luke now offers a number of dramatic controversies. Jesus' word of forgiveness in the preceding pericope sets the stage for this story of calling a notorious sinner (a tax collector) to follow Jesus (5:27-32). The *Pharisees and their scribes* (5:30) are both equally scandalized by this act of Jesus. Jesus employs another physician proverb (cf. 4:23) to make clear that the invitation of sinners to repentance is why he has come, implying that the liberation from sin that Jesus offers requires a genuine change of heart and mind in the life of the sinner.

The following PARABLES offered by Jesus (5:33-39) make clear that this way of offering God's liberating power is something radically new. Jesus has not come to confirm the old ways of piety and religion, such as fasting, but to bring a joyful new way of life that calls for celebration. The seemingly innocuous metaphors about cloth and patches, wine and wineskins, illustrate a most ominous principle: the new and the old won't mix—indeed they cannot mix.

The incident of plucking grain on the SABBATH (6:1-5) demonstrates the *Pharisees'* brand of religiosity. Jesus appeals to the story of David (1 Sam 21:1-7) to declare that human need takes precedence over legal scruples. Speaking again of the *Son of Man* he declares himself (implicitly) to be lord even of the Sabbath. Luke seems to be presenting Jesus as the one whose authority alone as the lord of the Sabbath allows for this radically new understanding of Sabbath law, rooted in Jesus' unique and authoritative interpretation of scripture.

Luke concludes this section with one final Sabbath controversy (6:6-11). The intensity of the conflict between Jesus and the religious leaders may have led readers to wonder just how far these leaders might go to stop Jesus. Verse 11 invites readers to assume the worst. Could it be that even these religious leaders, like demons and disease, are on the side the devil? Luke leaves readers wondering.

6:12-16. Naming of the apostles. Luke concludes this section by completing the circle of those whom he is calling to "catch people." That this is to be the mission of the *apostles* (v. 13), these men whom Jesus will "send out," is suggested by the fact that Simon, whom Jesus specifically called to "catch people" (5:10) heads the list. The number twelve is reminiscent of the twelve tribes of Israel, suggesting that Jesus' liberating work does indeed involve a renewal and possibly redefinition of Israel. The statement that JUDAS *became a traitor* is particularly ominous in light 6:11. Will the leaders and Judas form some alliance?

Proclaiming the Favorable Year of the Lord, 6:17-49

In the preceding section, Jesus has demonstrated the liberating power of God through miracle and confrontation. In this section, the sermon on the plain, Jesus offers the liberating word.

6:17-19. Introduction. Here Luke introduces two important details: notification of the audience and a reminder of the eschatological context. The audience consists of the apostles (*them*), *a great crowd of his disciples* v. 17; (Jesus' followers are not limited to the circle of the apostles), and *a great multitude of people. People* is almost a technical term denoting "the people of Israel." It is often synonymous with the "crowd(s)" (cf. 5:19). Conspicuous by their absence is the Jewish leadership. The eschatological context is noted with reference to healing and exorcisms. This word of Jesus is to be heard within the context of his ministry of liberation.

6:20-26. The beatitudes and woes. Beatitudes are words of blessing that announce the happy condition of someone. They are not exhortations. The first beatitude, for example, does not say, "Be poor and God will give you the kingdom." Rather, the poor, the hungry, the sorrowful, and the despised and excluded are pronounced as blessed now because of what God will offer in the future: the kingdom, satisfaction, joy, and reward in heaven (cf. 1:52b, 53a). Present blessing on the basis of God's future action is no numbing opiate for the masses. Recall the demonstrations of Jesus' power already manifested. God's reign is already breaking in to set right a corrupt world whose *kingdoms*, *authority*, and *glory* now lay in the hand of the devil (cf. 4:5-6). For those who have no claim or stake in the kingdom of this age, the liberation of God's kingdom comes.

For those who have staked their claim in the *kingdoms of the world* (cf. 4:5)—the rich, the satiated, the happy-go-lucky, and the respected (cf. 1:51b, 52a, 53b)—God's action brings *woe*. The demonic grip on the world is already being loosened—the sandy and shifting foundation of that world is being washed away (cf. 6:49). Indeed, *woe to you* who have staked your lives on this!

6:27-42. Response to God's initiative. God's action now, serving as a foretaste of his action to come, requires response. At the heart of that response is the command, *Be merciful, just as your Father is merciful* (v. 36). The one who benefits from God's merciful reclamation of his world and its inhabitants from the grip of evil must extend that mercy to others.

Such mercy manifests itself primarily in two ways. First, one is to love radically, even one's enemies (vv. 27-31), and without the expectation of reciprocity (vv. 32-35a). The word of Jesus offers concrete (although not casuistic or exhaustive) illustrations of such radical love. It involves the love of enemies (might this be how, in God's reign, enemies are conquered? [cf. 1:71, 74]), prayer for the abusive, turning the other cheek, giving both to the one who would beg and the one who would take, and even loving the one who has no intention of returning such love. The shock of Jesus' examples is no doubt intentional, leading the reader to "feel" just how radical the expectations of God's mercy really are. Such expectations, however, are grounded in the fact that God *is kind to the ungrateful and the wicked* (v. 35b). Readers cannot help but ask whether God's mercy to them has been as radical as loving those who despise, abuse, and take advantage of them.

The second concrete way that one exhibits the mercy received is to refuse to judge and condemn, and to extend forgiveness and generosity (vv. 37-38). Being merciful as God is merciful does not justify being the judge as God is the judge. Such refusal to judge does not mean refusal to acknowledge and address the corrupting evil of the present age. To conclude this is to forget the eschatological context of the sermon (cf. 6:17-19). It does require, however, that one's concern with sin and corruption begin with the logs that obscure one's own vision, not the specks that one is so sure pervert the vision of one's neighbor.

6:43-49. Concluding parables. The first concluding parable (vv. 43-45) teaches that the kind of good *fruit* required of those called to be *children of the Most High* (v. 35) can only come from good trees. Verse 45 interprets the metaphor, indicating that Jesus is talking about *the good person [who] out of the good treasure of the heart produces good.* Transformed persons and hearts are the prerequisites to the response demanded of the kingdom. The whole of this Gospel clearly implies that such transformation is possible only in light of the merciful liberation Jesus has come to offer. In short, God is the source of this "goodness" (cf. 18:19). Nonetheless, as the second concluding parable (vv. 46-49) indicates, a life built on the solid foundation which can survive the onslaught of God's discerning judgment, is the life of one who *hears my words, and acts on them.* Obedience, not just good intentions (what many call a "good heart") is demanded.

Release to the Oppressed, 7:1–9:50

This section provides further illustration of Jesus' ministry of liberation. In this section Jesus will encounter and conquer demons, disease, and even death. As these encounters progress, characters in the story will address the central question: Who is Jesus?

7:1-10. The centurion's slave. Jesus returns to Capernaum having finished offering his words of liberation to the *people.* He hears of a *centurion,* a gentile. Simeon's words about Jesus being *a light for revelation to the Gentiles* (2:32) come to mind. Unlike Matthew's version, Jesus does not deal with the gentile directly, but through intermediaries, Jewish leaders and the gentile's friends. Perhaps Luke views this as representative of the indirect way gentiles of his time encounter Jesus. The Jewish elders appeal to Jesus on the basis of the centurion's merits saying, *"He is worthy of having you do this for him"* (v. 4). However, when the centurion speaks for himself, through friends he sent to Jesus, he says, *"I am not worthy to have you come under my roof"* (v. 6). The centurion bases his request entirely on his simple faith that the *word* of Jesus carries with it *authority*. The centurion shows by this simple statement that he recognizes what Jesus has been demonstrating since the initiation of his ministry: he is the one with the authority to vanquish the corrupting powers within the world (cf. 4:36; 5:17, 24; 6:19). Jesus' statement indicates that such recognition is exactly the appropriate response to Jesus. *Not even in Israel have I found such faith* (v. 9). Faith in the absolute power and authority of Jesus over evil is what renders such power effective (cf. 5:20).

7:11-17. Jesus confronts death. While this story offers Jesus' greatest challenge yet, Luke makes clear that compassion for the plight of a widow, now without a son, is what moves Jesus to act. This woman could now look forward only to an anxious existence in a world where orphans and widows served as proverbial models of the oppressed (cf. Jas 1:27). The story reminds readers that behind the awesome power that vanquishes evil is the love of God. Through his characters, Luke comments on the larger implications of the event. The people recognize that *a great prophet has risen among us* (cf. Jesus' own words [4:18-24]). Further, the crowd recognizes that *God has visited his people* (RSV cf. 1:78; "the dawn from on high has visited us" [author trans.]). The conquering of death shows clearly that the oppressive forces of evil and corruption are being conquered.

7:18-23. The Baptist's question. John is in prison (3:19-20), so he asks his question to Jesus through his *disciples*. The question, *Are you the one who is to come?*, is reminiscent of John's declaration of 3:16: *one who is more powerful than I is coming*. John predicted that this powerful one would separate the wheat from the chaff (3:17). John's question now can only imply that he does not recognize that Jesus is accomplishing the mission of this "powerful one" of 3:17. Jesus' response is a summary of his healing activity (v. 22; cf. Isa 35:5,6; 61:1; Luke 4:18). This summary, combined with Jesus' blessing of those who do not take offense at him, certainly communicates a positive response to John. Readers know these activities of Jesus to be demonstrations of his authority over evil. Readers also should recognize that the division Jesus is creating in Israel, manifested to this point primarily by the different responses to him by the masses and the leaders, is the realization of John's prediction that Jesus would separate the wheat from the chaff.

7:24-30. Jesus' view of John. Jesus invites his audience to consider the role of John. He is a prophet, but more than a prophet. Jesus reviews the role of John already spoken of by Luke. He is the *messenger* sent *to prepare your way before you* (cf. 1:17, 76: 3:4). John is more than a prophet, for he is a prophet whose role was itself a fulfillment of prophecy (cf. Mal 4:5). Yet John, as great as he is, pales in significance when compared to that for which his primary role was to prepare the people: the reign of God. The least of those who share in the reign of God are greater than the best of those who prepared the way for it. So much greater is the time of fulfillment than the time of promise. Verses 29-30 note the division created by John's preaching, a division between the masses and the leaders continued by Jesus. "The people . . . justified God" (RSV); the leaders "rejected the purpose of God" (RSV).

7:31-35. This generation. Luke introduces a new term to denote those opposed to Jesus and his work: *this generation*. In this pericope *this generation* denotes those who are like spoiled children who reject both the strict asceticism of John and the openness of Jesus. In this context, *this generation* denotes *the Pharisees and the lawyers* (v. 30). To be contrasted with *this generation* are the *children of wisdom*. These "children" by whom "wisdom is justified" (RSV) clearly denote the "the people" who "justified God" (7:29). *This generation* is clearly a group to which one does not wish to belong.

7:36-50. The sinner and Simon. The sinner woman and Simon the Pharisee offer concrete illustrations of the two types of people spoken of in the previous episode. No duplicity is hinted at in Simon's invitation to Jesus. Still, in the end, Simon refuses to acknowledge that Jesus is a prophet (v. 39), for Jesus allowed the sinner to touch him. By this lack of acknowledgment Simon showed himself to be one of "this generation" who rejected Jesus because he showed himself to be *a friend of tax collectors and sinners* (7:34). On the other hand, the sinner woman's act of heartfelt affection showed her to be one who "justified God," that is, "to acknowledge the rightness of [God's] call in John and Jesus and to repent and be forgiven" (Talbert 1986, 85).

Jesus' parable about the two debtors indicates that the operative principle in this story is that great forgiveness renders great love. In short, the woman is not forgiven because she treats Jesus lavishly. She treats Jesus lavishly because she has experienced the "release from sins" (v. 48). She has been a recipient of the ministry of liberation, which serves as the hallmark of Jesus' work in Luke (Luke 4:18-19). *Her sins, which were many, have been forgiven, hence she has shown great love.* The following statement, *But the one to whom little is forgiven, loves little,* can only be directed at Simon who has demonstrated "little love" for Jesus. The question of Simon's guests, *Who is this who even forgives sins?* echoes the question of other Pharisees in 5:21. The woman who has experienced "release," salvation, and *peace* shows by her *faith* in Jesus that she knows the answer to the detractors' question.

8:1-21. The word of the kingdom. Luke sets the stage by reiterating and expanding upon some themes already introduced, reminding readers that Jesus is preaching the *kingdom of God* and is accompanied by *the twelve.* Yet he also has other followers, *some women who had been cured of evil spirits and infirmities* (vv. 1-2). Talk of Jesus' healing reminds readers of the nature of Jesus' kingdom work:

liberation from the corrupting powers of evil. Inclusion of women among his followers offers an expanded definition of Jesus' followers. He has come to liberate all persons and to call all persons to follow him.

The parable of the sower and its interpretation (vv. 4-15) serves to explain how the preaching of the kingdom of God brings division among the people. Verses 9-10 offer a partial explanation. As offensive as it may appear to modern readers, these verses declare that the will of God stands behind this division. To the disciples *it has been given to know the secrets of the kingdom of God.* Such "giving" can only come from God. The others are described as *looking* although *they may not perceive* and *listening* although *they may not understand* (v. 10). Jesus is offering a loose quotation of Isa 6:9. This prophet, to whom Jesus has already compared himself (4:18-19), was called to preach to a people whom God knew would not heed his word. Jesus too has been called to preach to a people, not all of whom will perceive or understand, for Jesus has been *destined for the falling and the rising of many of Israel* (2:34).

Verses 11-15 provide further explanation as to why many reject the *seed* that is *the word of God.* Satan and his hosts hinder the planting, nurturing, and growth of the seed. For some, *the devil comes and takes away the word from their hearts.* For others faith lasts only until *a time of testing comes* and they *fall away.* Luke 4:2 and 13 imply the devil to be the source of such *testing.* Other people *are choked by the cares and riches and pleasures of life.* One who suspects the devil to be behind such life-killing concerns is correct (cf. Acts 5:1-3). The seed of the word proves fruitful only in those who *hold it fast in an honest and good heart.* Jesus here is speaking of the same kind of person about whom he spoke in 6:45.

Verses 16-18 exhort those who possess the *secrets of the kingdom of God* (8:10) to share the light of revelation that has been offered them. The world must continue to hear that God's victorious reign is breaking in. This is how one must *listen* to the word preached. A good example of the kind of persons about whom Jesus is talking are his *mother and his brothers* (v. 19), for such *are those who hear the word of God and do it* (v. 21). Readers are invited to recall how Mary responded obediently to the Lord, *according to [his] word* (1:38) and proclaimed openly his mighty works of salvation (1:46-55).

<u>8:22-25. Rebuking the forces of chaos.</u> This is the first of four miracles that make up a unit prior to the pericope of the sending forth of the twelve (9:1-6). Together they offer powerful testimony to the authority and power of Jesus over the forces of evil—a power and authority he will soon share with his followers.

This appears initially to be a story about Jesus' power over nature. Luke may wish the reader to discern a deeper meaning. The *windstorm [that] swept down on the lake* placed Jesus' disciples in *danger,* leading them to believe that they were *perishing.* In response Jesus *rebuked the wind and raging waves. Rebuked* is the same word used in 4:35, 39 where Jesus "rebuked" a demon and a fever. Luke might be intimating that even "forces of nature," which modern persons interpret in the context of the naturalistic laws of nature, can also be used by the "forces of evil" to harm people.

Jesus' question to his disciples, *Where is your faith?*, implies that if they truly trusted Jesus as the one who could "release" people from the threatening grip of evil, they would have realized that even the demonically manipulated forces of nature could be subdued by their *master*. Their concluding question, *Who then is this?*, shows that even those to whom *the secrets* have been given (8:10) can manifest a lack of perception like those of *this generation* (cf. 7:31, 49).

8:26-39. The Gerasene demoniac. Jesus has entered gentile territory, as evidenced by the presence of a *herd of swine* (v. 32). Jesus' first miracle in Jewish territory was an exorcism (4:31-37). So it is in gentile territory. This case of demon-possession seems particularly acute (cf. vv. 27, 29), suggesting that Satan's grip on the non-Jewish world was even tighter than his grip on Jesus' homeland.

The demons fear being sent *back into the abyss* (v. 31), which would spell the end of their earthly dominion. Jesus tricks them by granting their request to be sent into the swine. However, the swine *rushed . . . into the lake and drowned* (v. 33). The drowning of the demon-possessed swine in the lake results in the return of the demons to the abyss, for large bodies of water, such as lakes, were considered the entrance into the abyss (cf. vv. 22-25).

Again, Jesus offers release from the oppressive forces of the devil; as in Jewish territory, his work creates division. The *people of the surrounding country . . . asked Jesus to leave them* (v. 37). The one who had been *healed* (v. 36; lit. "saved"; cf. 7:50) wished to remain with Jesus. Jesus, however, commands that he return to his home and *declare how much God has done for you* (cf. 8:16). Luke states that he *proclaimed . . . how much Jesus had done for him.* Although anachronistic trinitarian thinking is not to be assumed, Luke clearly invites the reader to acknowledge that Jesus' work is actually God's work.

8:40-56. Jairus's daughter and the hemorrhaging woman. These two intertwined miracle stories conclude this section. Jesus has returned to Jewish territory, as evidenced by the presence of *Jairus, a leader of the synagogue*. Verse 42 indicates that the *crowds*, who have tended to respond positively to Jesus, are back on the scene as well.

On the way to Jairus' house, *a woman who had been suffering from hemorrhages for twelve years* and who had been unable to find help from doctors approached Jesus from behind *and touched the fringe of his clothes* (v. 43-44). This woman would have been considered as living in a perpetual state of uncleanness (cf. 4:12-16; Lev 15:25-27) and not welcome in the community. When touched, Jesus discerns *that power had gone out from* him (v. 46) and demands to know who touched him. In fear, the woman confesses what she had done. Jesus' statement is, in the Gk. text, exactly the same as that offered to the sinner woman who dared to approach him: "Your faith has saved you. Go in peace" (v. 48, author trans.; cf. 7:50). The trust that brings salvation manifested in "release from sins" also brings salvation manifested in being released from uncleanness. The ministry of liberation continues.

Upon arriving at the ruler's house, it is announced that Jairus' daughter is dead. Jesus can liberate from this evil as well: "Only believe and she shall be saved" (v. 50, author trans.). Again, "faith" and "salvation" are explicitly juxtaposed. The cynical skepticism of the crowd, offering notice to readers that the crowds do not fully trust in Jesus as one might hope, does not dissuade him. Taking his closest disciples and the girl's parents, he enters the house and raises her from the dead. His command to silence (v. 56) indicates that this mighty deed was in response to faith, not to convince the skeptics.

Four miracle stories have spoken clearly of "faith" (8:25, 48, 50) and "salvation" (8:36, 48, 50). The kind of salvation Jesus has come to offer is becoming increasingly clear: liberation from *all* forms of evil demonic oppression. The power that unleashes Jesus' liberating power is faith. THE TWELVE who have been with Jesus for the events of this entire chapter (cf. 8:1) are now ready to share in the work of Jesus.

9:1-6. The sending out of the twelve. *The twelve* have been with Jesus since 6:12-16. They have witnessed the mighty deeds of liberation. Now they share in that mission as Jesus gives them *power and authority over all demons and to cure diseases* (v. 1). The work that they do, like that of Jesus, is *to proclaim the kingdom of God* (v. 2). Jesus will not do his work alone. They travel without provision showing that those who accomplish the work of Jesus accomplish it by faith.

9:7-9. Herod's question. This brief notice serves three functions. One, it informs readers of the Baptist's fate—he is dead. Two, it raises the question of the precise identity of Jesus, an issue readers have seen before (cf. 5:21; 7:49; 8:25). Three, it raises an ominous note in that the one who had killed the Baptist now wants to see Jesus.

9:10-17. Feeding of the five thousand. *The apostles* have returned and *told Jesus all they had done. The crowds* are also back on the scene (v. 11). Readers are offered still another reminder of what the mission of Jesus is all about: he *spoke to them about the kingdom of God, and healed those who needed to be cured.*

Having established the audience and the eschatological setting and context, Luke narrates the miraculous feeding. One should not hunt only for symbolic meaning, as though the actual feeding of people in need of literal food is not at all the issue. Still, it seems that *the crowds* who have *followed him* (v. 11) are hungry for more than just bread—after all, one does not live by bread alone (4:4). One cannot ignore the language of the last supper (cf. vv. 16; 22:19) or the Lukan interest in the "breaking of bread" as an expression both of Christian fellowship (Acts 2:42, 46; 20:7) and recognition of fellowship with the risen Lord (24:30-31, 35). The fact that the apostles assist with the distribution of the food conjures up post-Easter images of Christian community as well. In short, a Christian reader (cf. 1:4) would recognize in this incident a foreshadowing of the spiritual nourishment that was to come in the context of the "breaking of bread." It is this spiritual hunger that the Messiah has come to fill (v. 17; 6:22). This too is a very real part of the liberating reign of God.

9:18-36. Recognizing Jesus. If in Luke's narrative world recognition of the risen Lord comes in the context of the *breaking of bread* (cf. 24:35), it is no surprise that after Jesus first breaks bread in the narrative (9:16), his disciples explicitly come to recognize who Jesus is. Readers too will learn some new things.

First, Peter confesses Jesus to be *the Messiah of God* (v. 20), something readers have known for some time. Second, Jesus, in defining his role as Messiah, talks in terms of his death and resurrection as the *Son of Man* (v. 22). Jesus' language is quite strong: *The Son of Man must undergo. . . .* The Greek word for *must* (δεῖ) is almost a Lukan code word to denote "divine necessity." The "Son of Man" has functioned in other capacities to this point (5:24; 6:5; 7:34). The implication is that this death and resurrection will play a decisive role in the work of liberation. Third, *the Son of Man* is spoken of by Jesus as the glorious judge of the end time. Fourth, after Jesus, Peter, James, and John ascend to the mount of transfiguration, the glory of Jesus is revealed even now to these men (v. 32). Luke may wish to emphasize that the glorious Son of Man to come is *this* Jesus whom the disciples are now following. Fifth, Moses and Elijah appear with Jesus and speak of his departure, which he was about to accomplish (lit. fulfill) at Jerusalem (v. 31). The OT, which these two so thoroughly embody, finds its realization in Jesus and in some significant event he is to fulfill in Jerusalem. Finally, God himself speaks to the disciples to identify Jesus: *This is my Son*. This provides the warrant for the concluding exhortation: *Listen to him* (v. 35). Readers will later learn from Acts 3:22-23 that this Jesus is the "prophet like Moses" to whom one must listen or "be utterly rooted out of the people."

The disciples also learn about following Jesus. Just as they have been called and sent out to share in his work of liberation (cf. esp. 9:1-6), so too they are called to share in his life of self-denial (vv. 23-24).

Luke has portrayed Jesus as the minister of the liberating power of the reign of God. Readers might expect that this climactic section offering the strongest testimony thus far concerning the identity (MESSIAH, SON OF MAN, SON OF GOD) and work (death and resurrection, exodus at Jerusalem) of Jesus might very well have some connection with this mission of God's liberating kingdom. Such a connection seems warranted, even if not fully explained, given the specific declaration of Jesus in the middle of this section: *some standing here . . . will not taste death before they see the kingdom of God* (v. 27).

This tantalizing declaration is followed by the experience of Peter, James, and John on the mountain where they not only behold Moses and Elijah, but experience the direct and immediate presence of God. This raises expectations that the disciples have come to the highest and best possible moment in their relationship with Jesus. Such expectations are shattered in the very next scenes.

9:37-50. Failing disciples. The conclusion to this section (4:14–9:50) ends on a low note. This disappointing conclusion is made even more noticeable by the "high notes" resonating from the preceding scenes.

The first scene, vv. 37-43, depicts the followers of Jesus as unable to use the power they had only recently been given (cf. 9:1) to heal the demoniac child. Jesus' response, *you faithless and perverse generation,* which has the disciples in view, is particularly strong for two reasons. One, *this generation* is a term already used by Jesus to denote those who *rejected God's purposes* (cf. 7:30-31). Two, the miracle stories that have preceded chap. 9 have emphasized the importance of faith in the actualization of Jesus' liberating power (cf. 8:48, 50). The disciples lack this faith and hence are unable to accomplish the ministry assigned to them.

Jesus reiterates his upcoming rejection (9:43b-45). Jesus' introduction, "*Let these words sink into your ears*" (v. 44; cf.8:18), highlights the significance of his words. *But they did not understand this saying; its meaning was concealed from them* v. 45). Not only do the disciples fail in doing what Jesus has given them authority to do, they have not at all grasped what lies at the heart of his mission of liberation. Luke does not say who or what concealed the meaning from them, but in light of the parable about the devil and his means of robbing people from the fruition of the planted word (8:12-14), one may suspect demonic foul play.

The disciples do not understand the role of self-denial to which Jesus had earlier called them (vv. 46-48; cf. 9:23-25), for on the heels of Jesus' speaking of his own rejection, they argue *as to which one of them was the greatest* (v. 46). Jesus must repeat his exhortation to self-denial, using a child as an illustration.

Finally, the disciples do not recognize that the work of Jesus is about the conquering of evil, not merely being associated with the inner circle which *follow[s] with us* (v. 49). The fact that the unknown exorcist was doing what the disciples themselves could not do (cf. 9:37-43a) and thereby accomplishing the work of the Spirit-anointed Son of God, is not within the purview of the disciples' perception.

The Anointed Prophet's Journey to Jerusalem, 9:51–19:44

The transfiguration scene of 9:28-36 sets the stage for this upcoming journey. There Moses and Elijah spoke of Jesus' "exodus which he was about to fulfill in Jerusalem" (9:31; author trans.). This section narrates the journey to that city. Later the voice of God spoke to the disciples of Jesus declaring, "*This is my Son . . . listen to him!*" (9:35; cf. Acts 3:22-23). The low notes on which Luke ended the previous section indicate that they have much listening to do. Hence, this journey section is rich with sayings material that the Son offers to his disciples, as well as the crowds and even his adversaries. On this journey, "Israel" will have opportunity to listen to God's Son, the Spirit-anointed prophet like Moses.

Beginning the Journey, 9:51–10:42

9:51-56. Rejection of the Samaritans. This pericope twice states that Jesus' *face was set toward Jerusalem*, the goal of Jesus' journey. For the prophet to "set his face against" something implies judgment (cf. Ezek. 21:2). On the surface, the Samaritans' rejection of Jesus is explained by the long-standing antipathy between Jews and Samaritans (cf. Neh 4:2-9; John 4:9). In the context of the story, Jesus' rejection by the Samaritans places the whole journey to Jerusalem under the ominous cloud of rejection. Jesus' refusal *to command fire to come down from heaven* (vv. 54-55) to destroy the Samaritans for their rejection, however, makes clear that rejection of Jesus is not unforgivable or irreversible. The fact that Jesus *rebuked* (cf. 4:35, 39; 8:24) his disciples for suggesting such irreversible judgment implies the ungodly, even demonic, character of such a sentiment.

9:57-62. Following Jesus. "Following" and its demands are the themes of this pericope (vv. 57, 59, 61). One is called to *follow* the *Son of Man*, whose mission is defined by rejection (v. II 58; cf. 9:22, 44). One is called to a thorough-going commitment to the *kingdom of God*, even at the expense of essential family duty or loyalty, such as burying one's father or bidding *farewell* to one's family. Since following Jesus involves a decision to enter into the fray against the devil himself who will stop at nothing to hinder fruitful discipleship (8:11-14), commitment must be unequivocal.

10:1-16. Mission of the seventy. As the previous pericope implied, Jesus is willing to gather new disciples as he journeys to Jerusalem (9:57), and to specify the demands of such discipleship as well. Jesus has now gathered *seventy others* as followers and is sending them out on a mission similar to that of the twelve (cf. 9:1-6).

Only Luke has a mission of the seventy (some ancient mss. read "seventy-two"). The instructions to the seventy echo the instructions Jesus gives to the twelve in Matt 9:37-38; 10:7-16. The seventy might symbolize the traditional seventy nations (cf. Gen 10), foreshadowing the mission to the nations. They may be similar to the seventy elders whom Moses appointed (cf. Num 11:16-25), comparing Jesus to Moses (cf. Acts 3:22-23). The focus of their mission is to be the same as that of Jesus and the twelve: *cure the sick* and proclaim that *the kingdom of God has come near* (vv. 9-11). The authority of the seventy is emphasized as Jesus declares that *whoever listens to you listens to me* and, ultimately, whoever *rejects you rejects me and . . . the one who sent me.*

Such an authoritative message demands response. Thus Jesus lays forth the consequences of rejecting the messengers and their message in a series of woes (v. 13) and explicit threats of judgment (vv. 14-15). The particularly harsh words directed at CAPERNAUM (v. 15) where Jesus has spent so much time (cf. 4:31-42; 7:1-10) convey that repentance is required especially of those blessed with witnessing Jesus' ministry (cf. 13:26-27).

10:17-24. Return of the seventy. Having returned, the seventy joyfully report what readers already knew: the work of healing and proclamation subjected *even the demons*. Jesus reports a vision that interprets what the subjection of the demons means: the fall of Satan from heaven (cf. Rev 12:7-9). Such a fall is not the final defeat of Satan. In fact, such a *fall from heaven* can portend intensified struggle here on earth (cf. Rev 12:10-17). In this struggle Jesus' followers have been given *authority to tread on snakes and scorpions; and over all the power of the enemy* (vv. 19-20). More importantly, Jesus' followers should rejoice in the assurance of their final salvation, their names having been *written in heaven* (v. 20; cf. Rev 3:5).

In vv. 21-22 *these things* refer to this demise of Satan. Jesus' prayer states that the impending fall of Satan is not apparent to all. Failure of the *wise and intelligent* to recognize the significance of the present time serves only to show that they are not among the *infants* (cf. 7:35) to whom God, in his *gracious will*, has chosen to *reveal* these things. The affirmation of v. 22, reminiscent of the language of John's Gospel, indicates that recognizing the meaning of *these things* is dependent on revelation from *the Son*. Apart from following Jesus in the work of the kingdom (cf. 9:57-62), *these things* shall remain *hidden*.

Verses 23-24 show *the disciples* to be among those privileged to *see* and *hear* what the worthies of old only hoped for. One, however, must "perceive" as well as *see*, and "understand" as well as *hear* (cf. 8:10).

10:25-37. The lawyer's challenge. Luke introduces this scholar of the Jewish law negatively, explicitly stating that he wished *to test* Jesus, an activity attributed to the devil (cf. 4:2, 13). Like the devil who tested Jesus, the lawyer knows his scripture. He can answer rightly what one must *do to inherit eternal life*: love God wholly and one's neighbor. The lawyer, however, wishes to limit his definition of *neighbor* (v. 29). Luke's statement that he wished *to justify himself* echoes 7:29-30, where Jesus contrasted the crowds who "justified God" with the "Pharisees and lawyers" who "rejected the plan of God."

The parable of the good Samaritan is Jesus' response to the lawyer. Two points are clear. One, Jesus substitutes the broadest possible definition of neighbor for the lawyer's attempt to offer a restrictive definition. One is to be neighbor to any who must be shown *compassion* (v. 33, RSV) and *mercy* (v. 37). Two, by making a non-Jew the hero of the parable, over even the Jewish priest and Levite, Jesus suggests that doing what the law requires to inherit eternal life is not the exclusive privilege of the Jews (cf. 3:7-8). God's offering of eternal life is for all (cf. 2:31-32; 3:6) and attempts to limit God's saving grace to one's own group will be rebuffed by Jesus (cf. 4:24-30; 5:30-32).

10:38-42. Mary and Martha. The universalistic concern of Luke extends to women (cf. 8:1-3). This story continues that theme while offering commentary on the notion of "service" (RSV; NRSV reads *tasks*, v. 40). Given the choice between "serving" and sitting at the feet of *the Lord* and "hearing his word" (lit. trans.), Mary has chosen the latter. Jesus explicitly states that she *has chosen the better part*. Women too can hear the word. Martha is described as *distracted by many things*. These many distracting things are described earlier as "much serving" (v. 40;

RSV). The word used for service is used elsewhere by Luke to denote Christian ministry (cf. 22:26; Acts 1:17, 25; 6:1-4). Luke does not wish to belittle such "service" (cf. the good Samaritan), but this story reveals that *there is need of only one thing*: "hearing the word." Service not rooted in such hearing becomes busy work. Yet, one who truly "hears" will serve (cf. 6:47; 8:21).

Understanding the Present Time, 11:1–13:35

As the Spirit-anointed prophet like Moses makes his way toward Jerusalem offering the word to which Israel should listen, he will devote a major portion of his teaching to the issue of the eschatological significance of his work and response to that work.

11:1-13. Teaching on prayer. Prayer has empowered Jesus during his ministry of eschatological liberation (cf. 4:21; 5:16; 9:18; et al.). *His disciples* need to pray as well.

The Lord's prayer. Disciples are charged to approach God even as Jesus does, as *Father* (cf. 2:49; 10:21-22), implying a direct and intimate approach to God. The prayer presents five petitions.

The first, "let your name be made holy" (author trans.), requests that God act so as to establish before all his sovereignty and holiness. An ancient Jewish prayer captures the sense: "Exalted and hallowed be his great name in the world which he created according to his will" (Marshall 1978, 457).

Two, *your kingdom come* (v. 2). This petition is no empty plea, for even now Jesus and his disciples are proclaiming and demonstrating that the "kingdom of God is drawing near" (cf. 10:9).

Petition three requests the provision of daily sustenance. Luke 9:3-5 and 10:8 inform readers that such sustenance comes from the hands of God's people. Luke 4:4 and 9:12-17 offer reminders that essential sustenance is not confined to literal "bread alone."

The fourth petition, *forgive us our sins*, (v. 4) asks God to make effective for his disciples the "releasing" benefits (cf. 4:18; 5:17-26) of God's salvation (cf. 7:48-50). Disciples must remember that God releases "because we ourselves release everyone owing us" (author trans.), for disciples must be merciful just as their *Father is merciful* (cf. 6:36).

The final petition acknowledges the reality of *trial* (v. 4; lit. "testing," cf. 4:2, 13; 8:13; 10:25) that will come the way of the disciple. "The kingdom of God is caught up in a struggle of powers. . . . This is not a struggle for humans to enter armed only with their 'free will'" (Tiede 1988, 214).

Verses 5-13 exhort persistence in prayer. The parable about the friend (vv. 5-8) is not saying that God responds only to nagging. This is an argument "from the lesser to the greater." If a friend, merely wanting to be left alone, will respond to one's request, surely God will respond to the requests of those who call him "Father." A similar message is conveyed by vv. 11-13.

The concluding statement that *the heavenly Father [will] give the Holy Spirit to those who ask him* (v. 13) is most appropriate in the Lukan context. Prayer focuses on the KINGDOM OF GOD and what is needed from God to engage in the struggle of the kingdom (cf. vv. 2-4). The greatest power for this struggle is that of the Spirit, which empowers Jesus himself.

11:14-36. Controversy over Jesus' power. Reference to the HOLY SPIRIT in the preceding verse sets the stage for this conflict over the source of Jesus' power in exorcising demons. Jesus' antagonists charge that he is in league with Beelzebul. These antagonists are *some of. . . the crowds* (vv. 14-15), which is not a good sign, since to this point the crowds have generally responded well to Jesus. *Others*, presumably from *the crowds* as well, wish *to test* Jesus by *demanding* a *sign from heaven* (cf. 4:9-12). Testing is the work of the devil (cf. 11:4) and that too does not bid well for the crowds.

Jesus rebukes their charge (vv. 17-23) and their demand for a sign (vv. 29-36). He rebukes the charge, first, by pointing out its obvious absurdity. Satan would not be casting out his own demons (vv. 17-18). Second, Jesus declares that his exorcisms demonstrate that *the kingdom of God has come to you.* Further, such works demonstrate that Satan, the *strong man, fully armed*, is being *attacked*, *overpowered*, and *plundered* (vv. 21-22). Jesus concludes his defense with an emphatic demand for total allegiance in this eschatological struggle: *whoever is not with me is against me* (v. 23).

Before responding to the sign-seekers Jesus offers a warning. Verses 24-25 assume that exorcised demons can return and make matters worse. "It is not sufficient to cast out demons if there is no acceptance of the kingdom whose presence is attested by the expulsion of demons" (Marshall 1978, 479). Hearing and obeying the word of God is the only sure cure, which, if applicable even to Jesus' mother, is surely applicable to everyone else (vv. 27-28). Such hearing and obeying of God's word is linked with hearing and obeying Jesus and his message of the kingdom (cf. 6:46-49; 9:26-27).

Jesus addresses *the crowds* demanding a sign in harsh terms (vv. 29-32). He identifies them with *this generation*, the term used by Luke to denote those who reject God' purpose (cf. 7:30). Non-Israelites, like the *queen of the South* who listened *to the wisdom of Solomon* and the *people of Nineveh [who] repented at the proclamation of Jonah*, know how to respond to God. The Jewish crowds are now confronted with something much greater than either of these OT figures or events: *the kingdom of God has come to you!* (v. 20). In the face of this, *this generation* (cf. above commentary on 7:31-35) is headed for judgment and condemnation.

Jesus concludes with a collection of sayings having to do with light, a general metaphor for that which pertains to God (vv. 33-36). He exhorts the crowds to have a healthy eye, which denotes one who "focuses his or her eye on God alone" (Garrett 1991, 99). Most especially the crowds are exhorted to *consider whether the light in you is not darkness* (v. 35), that is, whether they have a vision of life which is so perverse (such as imagining that "Satan is divided against himself" [v. 18]) that, in fact, *your body is full of darkness* (v. 34). At this juncture, the crowds stand in peril of eschatological judgment.

11:37-54. Controversy with Pharisees and lawyers. Luke has just identified the crowds with *this generation,* the generation epitomized by the PHARISEES and lawyers (cf. 7:30-31; 11:50-51 [Moessner 1989, 92-114]). Jesus has exhorted the crowds not to live in utter darkness. Now Luke uses Pharisees and lawyers to illustrate a kind of "light" that is, in fact, "darkness" (cf. 11:35).

The Pharisees (vv. 37-44) demonstrate "darkened light" in their meticulous concern for external piety, such as cleaning *the outside of the cup and of the dish* (v. 39) and tithing *mint and rue and herbs* (v. 42) at the expense of *those things that are within* (v. 41) and more important matters such as *justice and the love of God* (v. 42). Thus, *inside you are full of greed and wickedness* (v. 39), i.e., their bodies are *full of darkness* (v. 34).

The lawyers (vv. 45-48), the scholars of the Law and Prophets, show their concern for the law through their interpretations and teachings. In fact, they *only load people with burdens hard to bear* (v. 46). They claim to honor the prophets because they have built tombs for them, a boast Jesus turns on them: *you . . . approve the deeds of your ancestors* by building these tombs (vv. 47-48).

The judgment pronounced on *this generation* (vv. 50-51) is unequivocal. It will *be charged with the blood of all the prophets shed since the foundation of the world.* From the first murder recorded in Hebrew scriptures (Abel, Gen 4:8), to the last (Zechariah, 2 Chr 24:20-22), *it will be charged against this generation.* When one considers that *all,* not only Jewish leaders, but the "crowds" (cf. 11:29-32) and even the disciples (cf. 9:37-43) have been linked with *this generation,* things are looking quite gloomy indeed. In the face of this gloom, Luke's closing comment, that *the scribes . . . and Pharisees* now *began to be very hostile toward* Jesus (v. 53; cf. 6:11), borders on wry understatement.

12:1-12. Warnings to the disciples. Jesus has just offered a harsh judgment against *this generation,* epitomized by the Pharisees. Jesus has also identified both the crowds and the disciples with *this generation.* It is fitting, therefore, that as *the crowds gathered by the thousands* Jesus would tell *his disciples* to *"beware of the yeast of the Pharisees, that is, their hypocrisy"* (v. 1; see Moessner, 1990).

Verses 2-3 state that there will eventually come total disclosure of one's cover-ups, secrets, and whispers. Judgment *is* coming. Do not be associated with *this generation,* for its inner *greed and wickedness* (11:39) will be exposed. This exhortation anticipates the clear call of Peter to the masses of Jerusalem in Acts 2:40: "Save yourselves from *this* corrupt *generation*" (emphasis added).

Verses 4-7. The eschatological fray into which Jesus' followers are called to enter can bring death. Jesus calls upon his *friends* in the struggle to remember to whom ultimate allegiance, even *fear,* belongs. *Fear of him who . . . has authority to cast into hell* exhorts the disciple to stand firm before *those who kill the body.*

The realization that one's total allegiance belongs to the one who does not even forget the sparrow or who has *counted* the *hairs of your head* can bring a deeper comfort which warrants the exhortation, *do not be afraid.*

Verses 8-12. The one who calls the disciples *my friends* (v. 4) is also the one who will come as the eschatological judge, *the Son of Man.* As the SON OF MAN, Jesus will judge according to whether one has *acknowledged* or *denied* him *before others*, presumably *the synagogues, the rulers, and the authorities.* Denial of Jesus, speaking *against the Son of Man, will be forgiven* (cf. 22:31-34, 61-62). Blasphemy *against the Holy Spirit,* however, *will not be.* Clearly, Luke has a post-Easter understanding of the Spirit in view here, given the statement *the Holy Spirit will teach you [the disciples] at that very hour what you ought to say.* The disciples do not receive the Spirit until after Easter (cf. Acts 2:1-4). In this context, to blaspheme against the Spirit is to persist in rejecting and opposing the gospel message spoken by God's Spirit-inspired people. "As long as that obstinate mindset perdures, God's forgiveness cannot be accorded . . . " (Fitzmyer 1985, 964).

<u>12:13-34. Concern over possessions.</u> The word of Jesus offered in 8:14 has already warned that an improper view of riches can choke the word. Here he offers a more detailed word about possessions.

Verses 13-21. *Someone in the crowd* misunderstands the nature of Jesus' authority, thinking that Jesus is concerned to offer judgment over matters of the *family inheritance.* Rather, Jesus warns the crowd to be on guard against greed that can distort one's perception of what life truly consists. The parable of the rich fool illustrates the folly of those who think life *consists in the abundance of possessions* and the storing *up of treasures for themselves but are not rich toward God* (v. 21). In the end, he has absolutely nothing.

Verses 22-31. Using arguments from the lesser (*ravens, lilies*) to the greater (people), Jesus offers assurance that God does care about the basic needs of life. Still, Jesus requires acceptance of the principle that *life is more than food, and the body more than clothing* (v. 23). Most importantly, one is to *strive for [God's] kingdom.* The promise that *these things will be given to you as well* must be heard rightly (*pay attention to how you listen!* [cf.8:18]). This is no carte blanche. To strive for the kingdom involves following the rejected Son of Man (9:58) into the fray of battle that can lead even to death (12:4). Only when heard in such a context is this promise heard rightly.

Verses 32-34. What is involved in being *rich toward God* (v. 21) and striving *for his kingdom* (v. 31) is a radical detachment from one's possessions. Possessions only bind one to an age that is passing (cf. 1 Cor 7:31). Detachment allows one to receive "the kingdom from your Father and to make for yourselves treasure in heaven" (author trans.). What one treasures reveals what type of *heart* one has (cf. 6:45; 8:15).

12:35-59. Eschatology: future and present. This subsection offers three parables (vv. 35-48) dealing with the future and three clusters of sayings, including one parable, dealing with the significance of the present time (vv. 49-59).

The three parables dealing with the future all involve the theme of readiness. One must be ready for the future coming of the *master* (vv. 36, 43), that is, *Son of Man* (v. 40), for when he comes he will bring judgment. Luke's readers know this master/Son of Man to be Jesus and the subject to be the PAROUSIA.

Verses 41-48 show that these warnings of readiness are not just *for us [but] for everyone.* All disciples, not just the inner circle of Jesus' time, need to hear these exhortations to readiness. This last parable not only speaks of readiness, but helps to define it. Readiness consists of the disciples being faithfully *at work* when the master arrives. The *manager* or *slave*, who represents the disciple, *who knew what his master wanted, but did not prepare himself or do what was wanted, will receive a severe beating (v. 47)*. In the parable itself, doing *what was wanted* is described as giving the other slaves *their allowance of food at the proper time.* This is a metaphorical reference to responsible discipleship that is defined for readers by the teachings of Jesus in this entire journey section. The parable concludes with an explicit warning to *everyone to whom much has been given*: *much will be required* (v. 48). With the privileged call of discipleship comes responsibility.

Verses 49-59 focus on the eschatological significance of the present time. The present time is not significant just because the master or Son of Man is coming at some point in the future. The present is significant because the reign of God is breaking in even now.

Verses 49-53 offer a word on the intensity and importance of Jesus' present mission: it brings the *fire* of judgment *to the earth.* It is a mission—a *baptism*—which consumes him completely: *what stress I am under until it is completed!* (v. 50). The judgment Jesus brings involves *division* (cf. 2:34-35 [the *falling and rising of many in Israel*]; 3:16-17 [the separation of the wheat and the chaff]; 7:29-35 [the *children of wisdom* vs. those who *reject the plan of God*]). Such division reaches into the intimacy of the *household.* In the present time one must decide to gather with Jesus or to scatter, to be for Jesus or against him (cf. 11:23).

Verses 54-59. This chapter began with a warning to Jesus' disciples in the presence of the crowds to beware of the *yeast of the Pharisees* (12:1). These verses continue Jesus' warning to *the crowds.* He calls them *hypocrites*—which is the very *yeast of the Pharisees* (12:1). Apparently the crowds are being overcome by the pervasive influence of *this generation* (cf.7:31-35). They must come to see the present time as a time for radical decision. They can *interpret the appearance of the earth and sky*, but they cannot see *the present time* as a time for decision that carries eternal significance. It is the time prophets and kings had longed to see (10:24). It is the time of Satan's demise (10:18). *The kingdom of God has come to you!* (11:20).

This generation is on its way to court (vv. 57-59). One must come to terms with one's *accuser* before one gets to the judgment bench. In short, one must come to terms with Jesus now. It will be too late once one is *dragged before the judge*.

13:1-9. The need to repent. The preceding talk of judgment and decision leads to the issue of repentance. In vv. 1-5 the essential message is that all need to repent. Persons cannot take comfort in the fact that life is going relatively well for them, that they have escaped the sword of Pilate or the catastrophe of falling buildings. Jesus indicates here that such fortune or lack of misfortune does not denote one's innocence before God: *No, I tell you; but unless you repent, you will all perish just as they did.*

The theme of repentance is continued with the parable of the fruitless fig tree (vv. 6-9). Trees that do not bear fruit are cut down. Readers recall echoes of John's preaching about *bearing fruits worthy of repentance* and trees not bearing good fruit being *cut down and thrown into the fire* (3:8-9). In this parable the fruitless tree is given a brief reprieve—it is given one more year to bear fruit. The implication is that the time is short.

13:10-17. Healing on the sabbath. Two important themes are reiterated. One, Luke offers a clear reminder of what is so significant about this present time: it is time when those bound by Satan are set free from his bondage (cf. 4:1-44). Two, the story reiterates the theme of division. The *leader of the synagogue*, whom Jesus identifies with the *hypocrites*, the Pharisees and *this generation* (cf. 11:50–12:1), is trying to persuade *the crowd* to his point of view. He is spreading the "yeast" of "hypocrisy" (cf. 12:1). His view is that strict, external sabbath observance takes precedence over human need. This is the kind of religiosity Jesus has condemned in 11:37-44. In this story, *the entire crowd* sides with Jesus. Is the crowd heeding Jesus' warning and call to repentance (13:5)?

13:18-21. Parables of the kingdom. Talk of the release from the bonds of Satan leads logically *(he said therefore)* to talk of the kingdom of God. Both parables are contrast parables—the point of the parable is found in contrasting the beginning with the end result. Jesus' healings and even resuscitations, impressive as they are, hardly justify the claim that God reigns totally and Satan is now completely bound. True. What one sees now is but the beginning, the *mustard seed* which will *become a tree*; the little bit of *yeast* that will leaven the whole *three measures of flour*. The comparison of the kingdom with *yeast* invites contrast between the leaven of the kingdom and that of the Pharisees (cf. 12:1). The parable affirms that, in the end, the leaven of the kingdom will prevail.

13:22-30. Further warnings. After offering a reminder of the "journey theme" and what is so central to this journey (*Jesus* was *teaching as he made his way to Jerusalem* [v. 22]), Luke presents Jesus giving more warnings to his listeners. Verses 24-27 prevent one from being too optimistic about the ultimate response of the crowd to Jesus (contra 13:17). The door leading to salvation is *narrow* and although *many . . . will try to enter,* they *will not be able*. Reflection upon the "demands of discipleship" makes clear why (cf. 9:57-62). When judgment day comes, having been in the presence of Jesus (as are the crowds, Jewish leaders, and even disciples as he journeys to Jerusalem) will not be sufficient. When the festive banquet of the kingdom begins (vv. 28-30) *you* will be *thrown out*, while *people* from all over the world *will eat in the kingdom of God*. Jesus could hardly offer a more dire warning to his audience: some of these who have been *the first* to hear this word of the kingdom *will be last* when judgment comes.

13:31-35. The Pharisees warn Jesus. The way that Pharisees have been presented to this point (cf. esp. 11:37-44; 12:1) hardly allows readers to view their motives as above suspicion. They bear bad news. HEROD, who killed John (8:9), now wishes to kill Jesus. Jesus' work of liberation (exorcisms and cures) will not be deterred, for his mission is driven by divine necessity. (The *must* of v. 33 translates the Gk. δεῖ [see comment on 9:18-36]). The reference to *today, tomorrow, and . . . the third day/next day* should not be taken literally—that Jesus' work will be completed within the next seventy-two hours. Such wording points to the deliberateness of God's plan.

Jesus' work of liberation culminates in JERUSALEM, where the prophets are destined to die (vv. 33b-34). Jesus' "exodus" (9:31) and being "taken up" (9:51) will occur in the city which *kills the prophets and . . . those who are sent to it* (cf. Jer 26:20-23). Jesus falls short of explicitly predicting his death there, but readers will get the point. Sadly, Jesus wishes *to gather your children together* but *you are not willing*. Consequently, "your house is abandoned" (author trans.). "House" may refer either to the city, the temple, or the leadership—the meaning is still the same. The irony is that the word translated "abandoned" is the same Gk. word translated as "release" or "forgiveness" in many significant texts (4:18; 5:20; 7:48; 11:4). Jesus came to offer "release"; Jerusalem's response ensures "abandonment." Jesus concludes with a curious prophecy about what must happen before Jerusalem will *see* him. Is Jesus talking about literal sight, or more in-depth sight (cf. 8:10; 19:38)?

The Leaven of the Pharisees, 14:1–16:31

Jesus has warned his audience of disciples and crowds to beware of the Pharisees' leaven (12:1), the quintessential example of *this generation* (cf.7:31-35). This section is devoted primarily to an exposure of that corrupting yeast and some of the consequences of yielding to it.

14:1-24. Dining with the Pharisees and lawyers. Luke wastes no time in continuing his indictment of these Pharisees and their allies, the lawyers. Jesus is on his way to eat with them, but their invitation should not fool readers. They want to *watch him closely*. Such watching is motivated by sinister intentions: *to catch him in something that he might say* (see 11:54). On the way, Jesus performs a sabbath healing which again exposes the contrast between Jesus' and the Pharisees' notion of what is *lawful*. The Pharisees are not persuaded by Jesus' rhetorical question. They have learned only that they cannot successfully challenge him. Jesus' question of v. 5, reminiscent of 13:15-16, reminds readers that this healing is ultimately about liberation of people from the bonds of evil.

Verses 7-14. Noting how the Pharisees jockey for *the places of honor* (vindicating Jesus' charge of 11:43), Jesus offers a parable that puts their lack of humility into the proper perspective. On the level of social decorum, the jockeying of the Pharisees was most inappropriate (cf. Prov 25:6-7). Verse 11 gives this parable about the public humiliation of the arrogant a more general application. Yet talk of the proud being humbled and the humble being exalted gives the whole scene an eschatological application (cf. 1:51-53; 6:20-26; 13:29-30). These Pharisees show themselves to belong to the proud and mighty whom God's judgment will bring down.

Jesus presses his point further, still using the meal setting as context for his teaching. He encourages *the one who had invited him* (a Pharisee, 14:1), to invite to his *banquet* those who cannot reciprocate (*the poor, crippled, lame, and blind*). This is consistent with what Jesus taught earlier in 6:30, 34. Why should one do such a thing? Because *you will be repaid at the resurrection of the righteous*. Nothing in the story indicates that Jesus' host would consider inviting such people, implying that he does not show concern for those whom Jesus, God's Spirit-anointed prophet, shows concern. Such lack of concern further implies that the Pharisee does not belong to "the righteous" destined for resurrection.

Verses 15-24. A guest catches the eschatological allusions of Jesus and pronounces a blessing on those *who will eat bread in the kingdom of God*. Jesus' parable about *someone [who] gave a great dinner* offers a rather direct message: only those who respond positively to the invitation to the banquet of the kingdom will participate in that banquet. Jesus and his followers have thus far in Luke's Gospel made reference to the reign of God some twenty times, as early as 4:43 and recently as 13:29. Yet the Pharisees and their kind (*this generation*) have yet to say yes to the invitation. Who is saying "yes"? The kind one would not think of inviting to a banquet in the first place: *the poor, crippled, blind, and lame* (v. 21; cf. 14:13) and those who reside in the *roads and lanes* (v. 22). These social outcasts represent not only literally those whom Jesus is inviting to share in the kingdom's blessing (cf. 7:22), but the spiritual outcasts as well—the tax collectors and sinners—whom Jesus also invites (cf. 5:27-32). The concluding line of the story serves as Jesus' closing line to his Pharisaic hosts: *none of those who were invited will taste my dinner* (v. 24). Why? The parable gives the answer: they chose not to come.

<u>14:25-35. Counting the costs.</u> The audience changes from Pharisees to *large crowds . . . traveling with him*. The crowds' being with Jesus offers another hopeful sign that they will heed Jesus' warning concerning the Pharisees' leaven (12:1). Jesus refuses to soften his message, however: the door into salvation is narrow (13:24) and he does the crowds no favors not to spell out clearly the demands if they are to continue to travel with him.

Jesus demands loyalty beyond family and even self (vv. 26-27). Literal hatred of anyone is not consistent with the message of Luke's Jesus (cf. 6:27; 10:27-28). The strong language confronts the crowds (and the reader) with how thorough and radical the demand of Jesus is. Are the crowds willing to risk what Jesus ldemands? Just as one does not begin to *build a tower* unless one is sure that he can finish the project; just as a king does not go to war unless he is sure that he can successfully oppose the approaching army, one should not pick up the cross (v. 27) unless one is ready to follow through with total commitment—and that includes that one *give up all [one's] possessions*. Would-be disciples who turn back after putting their hands to the plow (cf. 9:62) are worth less than worthless salt that one would not even throw on the dung-heap (vv. 34-35). Although Luke's Jesus would want to take the masses "under his wing" as he would even Jerusalem (cf. 13:34), he will pull no punches with them to persuade them to follow.

15:1-32. Pharisees and scribes oppose the mercy of God. The Pharisees and scribes show their contempt for Jesus' association with the spiritual equivalent of those types whom they would *not* invite to *their* banquets (cf. 14:13). While the *tax collectors and sinners* wish *to hear* Jesus, the Pharisees and scribes *were grumbling and saying* that Jesus *welcomes sinners and eats with them*. They have raised this objection before and Jesus has before responded to their objection (5:29-32). Now Jesus offers three parables that not only address why he associates with such types but that challenge their attitudes as well.

The parables of the lost sheep (vv. 3-7) and the lost coin (vv. 8-9) carry the same message. Both the shepherd and the woman value highly what is lost. Such extraordinary concern is indicated by shepherd's willingness to *leave the ninety-nine in the wilderness and go after the one that is lost* and the care he shows the sheep, laying *it on his shoulders*. Concern is shown in the way the woman searches for the lost coin (lighting the lamp and sweeping the house). To be sure, the parables end with a word about repentance—but repentance is preceded by persistent searching on the part of characters who represent God. Why would God take the initiative to look for sinners in the way depicted by these parabolic characters and react with such joy over their repentance? The reader must supply the only possible answer. God is merciful (cf. 6:36).

The parable of the prodigal son (vv. 11-32) offers insight into three different characters, each easily representing characters in Luke's story. The father, so anxious and willing to forgive the erring son, provides a glimpse of the mercy and love of God. Clearly the father was mistreated by his younger son who literally could not wait until he was dead to inherit his *share of the property* (v. 12). In receiving back his son with joyous celebration—the best robe, rings, sandals, and veal (v. 22-23)—he portrays the God who *is kind to the ungrateful and the wicked* (see 6:35).

The younger son illustrates well that as much as God may take the merciful initiative (as demonstrated by the first two parables), sinners are not really passive sheep or inanimate coins. The younger son *came to himself* (v. 17) and resolved to confess his sin before his father (v. 18). The parable expresses no interest in the motives of the son. One can argue that he was seeking his own best interest—being a slave is better than eating pig slop. The father, however, is not interested in pure motives. He is interested in receiving the lost. That too is merciful.

The elder son illustrates the *grumbling* Pharisees and scribes (v. 2). He begrudges the father's forgiveness of the younger brother (whom the elder brother can only bring himself to call *this son of yours*, v. 30). What is further exposed in his conversation with his father is how baseless the elder brother's fear and jealousy is. The father loves the obedient son no less simply because he also loves the son who was lost: *Son, you are always with me, and all that is mine is yours* (v. 31). Thus his son simply has no good reason not to *rejoice* because *this brother of yours was dead and has come to life*. Likewise, the Pharisees and scribes who are opposed to God's sharing of his love with those who need his forgiveness have no good reason either.

<u>16:1-15. The dishonest manager and wealth.</u> The primary audience of this section is *the disciples*, although *the Pharisees* (v. 14) are also present. The portion of the story has three sections. Verses 1-8a present the parable of the dishonest manager. Verses 8b-13 offer general application of the meaning of the parable. Verses 14-15 offer specific application to and judgment of the Pharisees.

The parable of the dishonest manager is confusing to many because *the master commended the dishonest manager because he had acted shrewdly* (v. 8). What impresses the master, despite the fact that he will still have to fire the manager, is that the manager, when faced with the prospect of being turned out into the streets either to *dig* ditches or *to beg*, devised a plan to protect himself. He took a course of action to ensure that *people may welcome [him] into their homes* once he was dismissed. What the manager did, of course, was to reduce the amount due from his master's debtors. Whether the manager was stealing one last time from his master by fixing the books or merely writing off his own healthy commission is not clear nor that significant. The point is that he used money to lay a foundation for the future.

In vv. 8b-15 Jesus invites the disciples to use wealth as a means of laying a foundation for the future—the ultimate future. Surely if *the children of this age* can do this, *the children of light* can. Just as the dishonest manager used wealth that people might welcome him into their homes (v. 4), Jesus exhorts the disciples to use *dishonest wealth* (lit. "unrighteous mammon," used here to denote "money") *that they* [probably a circumlocution for God] *may welcome you into the eternal homes*.

Jesus continues his application in vv. 10-13. Verse 10 makes clear that the issue here is *faithful* use of that to which one has been entrusted. On this earth, God entrusted his children to deal with money (*dishonest wealth*). If they cannot deal responsibly with that, *who will entrust you with true riches?*, which probably denotes spiritual wealth. If disciples cannot be *faithful with what belongs to another*, an allusion to money that is "on trust from God" (Marshall 1978, 623), *who will give you what is your own?*, an allusion most likely to *treasure in heaven* (see 12:33). Verse 13 indicates that what is at stake in the way one uses money is the issue of whether one is truly devoted to God or something else. Unfaithful use of wealth, of which the upcoming parable offers an excellent illustration, renders one a *slave* to *wealth* and a despiser of God.

The Pharisees, described as *lovers of wealth*, ridicule such a notion. By their own response they show where their loyalties lie. They are people more concerned to *justify* themselves (cf. 10:29) than God (cf. 7:29-30). Thus, what they value *is an abomination in the sight of God* (v. 15). No wonder theirs is a leaven which must be utterly avoided!

16:16-18. The law and the prophets. Hans Conzelmann (1982, 157-69) argued that v. 16 served as the key to Luke's view of history: phase one was the period of the *law and the prophets*, which *were in effect until [and including the time when] John came. Since then*, phase two, the proclamation *of the kingdom of God* by Jesus, is in effect. Phase three, the era of the church, will begin with the outpouring the Spirit. Conzelmann drew the lines too sharply between the old and the new. As Jesus himself says in the very next verse *the law* is still very much in force; in fact *it is easier for heaven and earth to pass away* than for even one *stroke . . . in the letter to be dropped.*

Verse 18 illustrates just how much in force it is! In fact, the demand of the law, interpreted in the context of the kingdom of God, is intensified. *Adultery* is no longer confined to "sleeping with another person's spouse." It includes even the perverse legal niceties people use to justify breaking a marriage covenant.

With respect to the *kingdom of God*, Jesus says that *everyone tries to enter it by force*. Perhaps a better translation is the NRSV marginal note: *everyone is strongly urged to enter it.* This kingdom is something to which one *must* respond. The consequences for not entering the kingdom are disastrous, as the next parable clearly shows.

16:19-31. The rich man and Lazarus. This is a fitting parable to conclude this section aimed at the Pharisees' corrupting brand of religion. The audience is still the disciples (16:1), to whom the parable offers warning, and the Pharisees to whom the parable offers judgment as lovers of money (16:14).

The rich man, traditionally known as Dives (Latin for "rich man"), clearly does not use his wealth in such a way so as to be "welcomed in eternal homes" (16:9). After reading this parable, no one is left wondering just what Jesus meant by not being "faithful with dishonest wealth" (16:11). Ignoring the plight of the poor and oppressed, whom Jesus and the kingdom have come to liberate, is to oppose the liberating work of the kingdom and to be against Jesus (11:23).

The words of ABRAHAM in vv. 29 and 31 allude back to Jesus' comments concerning the law and the prophets in 16:16-17. The implication is that one who truly "hears" (*listen*, NRSV) *Moses and the prophets* will know that such contemptuous use of wealth is eternally damnable. The message of the kingdom is not adding anything new to the Law and the Prophets, nor is it diminishing this aspect of the Law's and the Prophets' demand for justice. Dives, as an example of one who embodies the Pharisees' love of money, offers clear reason to the disciples and readers why the leaven of the Pharisees must be utterly avoided.

Verse 31 offers an ironic allusion to the resurrection of Jesus. People who cannot "hear" the message of the Law and the Prophets will not be convinced even by one rising from the dead (cf. Acts 13:26-41). This concluding word offers a harbinger of the ultimate reaction of the Jewish leadership to the message of the kingdom—and an ominous warning as to what side of the eternal *chasm* they and people like them will end up on.

Persistence for the Journey to Come, 17:1–18:30

The disciples are not the exclusive focus of this section, but they are certainly the primary focus. Furthermore, many of Jesus' words concern issues that would be facing the church of Luke's time—the time of the church's journey.

17:1-10. Demands and duty. Verses 1-4 offer two difficult demands for life among disciples. Verses 1-2 acknowledge that *occasions for stumbling* will come. Jesus requires that disciples not be the ones to *cause one of these little ones* (other followers) *to stumble*. The second demand, vv. 3-4, requires disciples to forgive—offer "release" to (cf. 4:18)—those who sin against them and *turn back* (meaning "repent"). Disciples share in the liberating work of the kingdom is by the offering of forgiveness to others.

Such demands require faith (vv. 5-6), even for *apostles*. The Greek construction of Jesus' answer *does* assume such faith—little as it may be (contrary to NRSV). Only a little faith is needed to accomplish great things, such as watching out for and forgiving others.

Verses 7-10 offer a parable making clear that when disciples *have done all that [they] were ordered to do* it is not cause for self-adulation, for they *have done only what [they] ought to have done*.

17:11-19. The ten lepers. Luke offers another story of healing, the meaning of which readers are now accustomed to hearing: faith in Jesus brings salvation (v. 19, lit., "your faith has saved you"). It is important that such words are pronounced on a *Samaritan foreigner*.

First, v. 11 refers to Jesus being *on the way to Jerusalem* and *going through the region between Samaria and Galilee*, which recalls 9:51 where Jesus, on his way to Jerusalem, was rejected by the Samaritans. Here Jesus pronounces the same word of salvation upon a Samaritan that he has pronounced on Jews earlier (cf. 7:50; 8:48). The fact that this Samaritan *turned back* (v. 15, same Gk. word found in 17:4), allows Jesus to illustrate how *he* responds to those who "turn back": he offers salvation. Second, this Samaritan's *praising God* serves to foreshadow the response that Samaria would give to the gospel later in Acts (Acts 8:5-25).

17:20-37. The kingdom of God and seeing the Son of Man. The question of *the Pharisees* (vv. 20-21) concerning *when the kingdom of God was coming* lets Luke reiterate that the power of God's reign is already active in the world *among you* (v. 21). ("Within you" [NIV, NRSV mg.] assumes an inner-spiritualistic view of God's reign that does not do justice to the kind of reign Luke's Jesus proclaims.) The Pharisees' inability to see the kingdom reveals their blindness (cf. esp. 11:14-36).

Attention is turned again to the disciples and *the days of the Son of Man* (v. 22; cf. vv. 24, 26). The subject here is the PAROUSIA. The coming of the Son of Man, like the reign of God, is not something that one can localize *there* or *here*. Unlike the reign of God, whose presence in the world can be missed, the coming of the Son of Man cannot be missed, for it is like the *lightening* flash which *lights up the sky from one side to the other*. Thus disciples need not be distracted by over-zealous cries that the Son of Man is already *there* or *here* (cf. 2 Thes 2:1-2). To silence any speculation that Jesus' current ministry represents the *days of the Son of Man*, Jesus reminds the disciples that he must first *be rejected by this generation*. Such words remind readers of the severe judgment Jesus has already pronounced on this *generation* (cf. 11:49-52).

Verses 26-37 envisages the judgment on the generation that rejects the Son of Man. The judgment will fall with complete surprise as *in the days of Noah* and *the days of Lot*. Verses 31-32 offer images of persons facing catastrophe. There is no time to gather one's possessions! No time to look back! One must escape to safety! These vivid illustrations show that in the *days of the Son of Man* (v.22) there will be no escape: *one will be taken and the other left*. Only those who were willing to *lose their life* for the sake of Christ (cf. 14:26-27) and the kingdom of God (cf. 18:29) *will keep* their lives. Where will those be who are left? *Where . . . the vultures will gather*—as food for the birds (v. 37).

18:1-14. Persistent and genuine prayer. The stark images of judgment make Jesus' following comments on prayer most appropriate. Jesus' question of 18:8, *When the Son of Man comes, will he find faith on earth?*, indicates that these words on prayer should be heard in the context of the preceding words on the *days of the Son of Man* (17:22). The Greek construction implies that the question is asked in an anxious frame of mind, betraying the seriousness of the question. Only each disciple, and each reader, can answer the question for him or herself. Hard times are coming. Will the disciple endure? Only by prayer.

The parable and application of the widow (vv.1-8) offers another example of Jesus arguing from the lesser to the greater (cf. 11:5-8). If an *unjust judge . . . will grant her justice* simply not to be bothered, surely God *will . . . grant justice to his chosen ones who cry to him day and night*. Indeed, he will do it *quickly*.

The parable of the Pharisee and tax collector (vv. 9-14) is directed at persons *who trusted in themselves that they were righteous and regarded others with contempt*. Fittingly, Jesus uses a Pharisee as the example of that kind of person. Yet the words are not addressed only to Pharisees. Disciples in the journey to come need to beware of such a disposition. Jesus has come to invite sinners and the many types of social outcasts to repent and share in the reign of God (5:32; 14:21). In his mercy God is anxious to receive such persons (cf. chap. 15). The one who recognizes this, such as the tax collector of this parable, is the one who will go *down to his home justified.*

18:15-17. Jesus and the children. This story illustrates that *disciples* were not (or are not) immune from holding others in contempt, as they *sternly ordered* people not to bring their *infants* to Jesus. Jesus does not call upon *the little children* to repent or to become disciples, but he does command that people *let* (lit. "release"!) *the little children come to him . . . for it is to such as these that the kingdom of God belongs*. While the story does affirm God's love of *even infants*, it is also about the spirit with which one must receive the kingdom—*as a little child*: complete trust in the care and mercy of God—like the tax collector of the preceding parable.

18:18-30. A final word on wealth. Wealth is an important issue to Luke (cf. e.g., 6:30, 34; 8:3, 14; 12:13-34; 14:33; 16:1-14, 19-31). It is fitting, therefore, that this section, which offers teachings for the journey to come conclude with a word on the topic. This final word offers three sub-sections: the story of the rich ruler (vv. 18-23), Jesus' interpretation (vv. 24-26), and Jesus' final word to Peter (vv. 28-30).

Jesus' response to the appellation *Good Teacher* (v.18) should be viewed neither as a denial that he is good nor as a coy way of identifying himself with God. His response reminds the ruler and readers that all that is genuinely good, including *eternal life*, is found in *God alone*. The ruler wants to know what he must *do to inherit eternal life*. Jesus has heard the question before (10:25). Here, as there, Jesus looks to the law. The ruler insists that he has *kept all these [commandments] since [his] youth*. Jesus insists that *there is still one thing lacking*. This ruler is bound by his possessions. Hence, Jesus requires of him what he said in 12:33 that he requires of all disciples: *sell your possessions, and give alms. Make . . . for yourselves . . . an unfailing treasure in heaven*. The ruler counts the costs and realizes that the price of eternal life is too high.

Jesus' interpretation assumes what he has tried to make clear throughout the Gospel. *Total* surrender to him is necessary: family, life, and possessions (14:26-33). The sad fact is that the rich are too blessed for their own good. They have so much to surrender. Thus, it is *hard . . . for those who have wealth to enter the kingdom of God!* (v.24). It is *hard* for everyone. Family, life, and even meager possessions are humanly impossible to abandon. *What is impossible for mortals is possible for God* (v.26). This echoes what the angel said to Mary (1:37). God does not force his possibilities on people. One must respond to what he makes possible even as Mary did: *let it be with me according to your word* (1:38).

Peter reminds Jesus that he and the disciples *have left [their] homes and followed* Jesus (cf. 5:11). The word translated *homes* is literally "our own things" and is used in Acts to denote friends (4:23; 24:23), financial resources (4:32; 28:30), and homes (21:6). The disciples are not perfect, but they have left it all behind to follow Jesus. He promises them *much more in this age* ("perhaps a reference to the new family in the church" [Talbert 1986, 173]) and *in the age to come eternal life.* A most fitting promise to end a section offering guidance to disciples for the "journey to come."

Approaching Jerusalem, 18:31–19:44

This last portion of the "journey to Jerusalem" begins with a final prediction of the passion of Jesus in Jerusalem (18:31-34) and ends with Jesus approaching and weeping over the city (19:41). In between, some important events and words performed and spoken in Jericho are narrated (18:35-19:28).

18:31-34. The passion foretold. This is the fourth PASSION prediction in Luke (cf. 9:22, 44-45; 17:25). It is by far the most detailed and specific: Jesus will die in Jerusalem in order to accomplish *everything that is written about the Son of Man by the prophets.* As horrifying as the Jerusalem events will be, they are according to the plan of God. The disciples do not understand (cf. 9:45), and Luke seems purposefully mysterious as to the cause. More important than who or what has *hidden . . . what he said . . . from them* is whether they will ever come to see.

18:35-43. The first Jericho story: healing a blind man. It is not accidental that word of the disciples' lack of understanding sets the stage for a story about a blind man. In this story readers encounter one who can see who Jesus is and what he is all about. The blind man hails Jesus as *Son of David*, a designation of Jesus as the Messiah (cf. 1:32, 69). He also knows the mission of this *Son of David*: to show *mercy* (cf. chap. 15). He approaches Jesus with the kind of *faith* that others have demonstrated before and Jesus pronounces a word with which readers have become familiar: literally, *your faith has saved you* (v. 42; cf. 7:50; 8:48, cf. v. 50; 17:19). The blind man has come truly "to see" as evidenced by his reaction: he *followed him, glorifying God.* Perhaps *the people* as well are seeing more clearly, for *all the people, when they saw it, praised God.*

19:1-10. The second Jericho story: Zacchaeus. This too involves a man who wanted *to see who Jesus was.* Unlike the blind man, Zacchaeus is restricted by more than his physical limitations—his profession as a *chief tax collector* who *was rich* makes him an example of the rich whom it is virtually impossible to save (cf. 18:23-26). Zacchaeus, this *Son of Abraham*, however, is willing to let go of that which binds him to this age. Like the daughter of Abraham whom Jesus released from the bondage of Satan (cf. 13:16), Jesus releases Zacchaeus. Unlike the rich ruler who was *sad* (cf. 18:23), Zacchaeus bears *fruits worthy of repentance* which characterize the true *children of Abraham* (cf. 3:8). For Zacchaeus declares, *Half of my possessions . . . I will give to the poor; and if I have defrauded anyone of anything, I will pay back four times as much* (v. 8; cf. 3:12-13).

The reaction of *all who saw it*, presumably the same people who just moments ago were praising God (cf. 18:43), is identical to the reaction of the Pharisees and scribes when they saw Jesus associating with tax collectors and sinners (cf. 15:1-2). In both instances there was grumbling (v. 7; cf. 15:2). Jesus' mission as the *Son of Man* is *to seek out and save the lost*. Will the masses ever come to see this?

19:11-28. The third Jericho story: the parable of the pounds. Luke indicates that the parable is prompted by the fact that *he was near Jerusalem, and because they supposed that the kingdom of God was to appear immediately* (v. 11). The parable as a whole informs readers that the kingdom of God did not appear with Jesus' arrival in Jerusalem. Talbert is perhaps correct that "in Luke's church . . . some disciples were regarding events in Jerusalem (Jesus' resurrection and ascension) as the PAROUSIA. In response the evangelist is saying 'not yet'" (Talbert 1986, 178).

There are three main characters, *a nobleman*, *slaves*, and *citizens of his country*, all of which are open to allegorical interpretation, representing, respectively, Jesus, his disciples, and the Jews who reject him. The parable directs attention away from the false notion that the *kingdom of God* appeared with Jesus' arrival in Jerusalem and redirects attention to the future.

The *nobleman* is going away for a while *to get royal power for himself and then return* (v. 12). In the meantime his *slaves* are given equal amounts of responsibility, represented by the *ten pounds* given to *ten of his slaves*, presumably one to each. They are to *do business with these until I come back. . . . When he returned, having received royal power* (vv. 14-15), he summoned the slaves to see what they had done with the pounds for which they had been given responsibility. The overall message is clear: those who used fruitfully what the nobleman had given them are rewarded; those who did not will not be rewarded. In fact, even what they have will be taken away. The message is harsh, but it is quite consistent with the message heard throughout the Gospel: following Jesus requires total commitment and dedication.

The citizens reject *the nobleman* because they *do not want this man to rule over* them. Their punishment was most harsh *when he returned*. He calls these citizens *these enemies of mine who did not want me to be king over them* and orders that they be slaughtered in his presence (v. 27).

Luke concludes bluntly: *After he had said this, he went on ahead, going up to Jerusalem* (v. 28). This journey section is about to come to a close. Israel, consisting of disciples, crowds, and the Jewish leadership have had opportunity to hear the word of God's Son (cf. 9:35). This concluding parable makes clear the consequences of not hearing.

19:29-40. Descending the Mount of Olives. Jesus' preparation to enter the city of Jerusalem is introduced by the story of the disciples' securing a colt for him. The impression left is that some sort of supernatural prescience on Jesus' part is involved. This impression reinforces the notion that what lies ahead in Jerusalem is according to some larger plan. As Jesus descends down the Mount of Olives he is greeted by the cry of *the whole multitude of the disciples*. Their cry, *Blessed is the king who comes in the name of the Lord* (v. 38), is a clear echo of 13:35 where Jesus said that Jerusalem would not see him until it offered a similar cry.

Two things stand out. One, it is not Jerusalem that makes this cry. Only the disciples do. Jerusalem has not offered the cry Jesus says it must if it is truly to "see" him. In fact, *the Pharisees*, the closest representatives to "Jerusalem" in this story, want Jesus to rebuke his disciples into silence. Jerusalem, it seems, does not "see" who Jesus really is. Will it ever? Two, the disciples hail Jesus as *the king.* This harks back to 19:27. These disciples are not like the citizens of that parable who did not want the nobleman to be their king. Like the blind man of Jericho (18:35-43), the disciples have come to see who Jesus is. No one else seems to. This does not bid well for the citizens of Jerusalem, but it does seem that at least a portion of Israel, the disciples, has listened to the SON OF GOD during the journey to the city (cf. 9:35).

19:41-44. Jesus weeps over Jerusalem. Jesus has still not reached Jerusalem, but as he approached it *he wept over it*. Jerusalem, unlike the disciples who cried *Peace in heaven!* (19:38), does not "see" *the things that make for peace;* in fact, *these things are hidden from [its] eyes* (v. 42). The consequences are devastating: Jerusalem and its inhabitants will be destroyed. "God has visited his people" (author trans. of 7:16b) in Jesus, but Jerusalem, the city of God's people, *did not recognize the time of [its] visitation* (v. 44).

The fate of Jerusalem and its people now seems a foregone conclusion. Jesus had earlier said that *this generation* would be charged with the blood of the prophets (cf. 11:49-50), including, it seems, the blood of the prophet Jesus (cf. 13:33-35a). Luke 17:25-37 envisaged the judgment to come to *this generation* that rejects the Son of Man.

Apparently, part of the punishment of *this generation* will include judgment against Jerusalem and its inhabitants as *they will crush you [Jerusalem] to the ground, you and your children within you* (v. 44). There seems only one means of escape: to separate oneself from *this generation* and accept Jesus as king. That will not save Jerusalem, but at least one might save oneself. Upon entering Jerusalem Jesus will present the word one more time to all the people of Israel. How will they respond?

Exodus from Jerusalem, 19:45–24:53

With the arrival of Jesus at the Temple (19:45), Jesus arrives in Jerusalem. He can now fulfill the exodus from this city about which MOSES and ELIJAH had spoken (9:31). There are three steps to fulfill this exodus: one, Jesus' teaching of *all the people* of Israel in the Temple (19:45–21:38); two, Jesus' passion, the *hour of darkness* (cf. 22:53; 23:44); three, Jesus' *entrance into glory* (24:26).

The Temple Ministry, 19:45–21:38

19:45-46. The cleansing of the Temple. Before Jesus can teach from the Temple, he must possess it. He must transform this place, intended as a *house of prayer* (Isa. 56:7) but *made* into *a den of robbers* (Jer 7:11), that it might be worthy the king's (19:38) presence.

19:47-48. The opening notice of Jesus' teaching. Luke 19:47-48 and 21:37-38 mark the beginning and ending of this section. Both passages state that every day *he was teaching in the temple* and that his audience was "all the people." Luke consistently uses "people" to denote "Israel" (cf. 1:68) and, thus, in a sense Jesus, the Messiah, is teaching "Israel" in its holy Temple, calling it to a decision.

Here Luke presents a division between *all the people* and *the chief priests, scribes, and the leaders of the people.* The Pharisees have disappeared. It is clear that their role is now assumed by these representatives of Jerusalem leadership—the officers of the SANHEDRIN, or ruling assembly (cf. 22:66), who are *looking for a way to kill him. The people* of Jerusalem failed to welcome Jesus as the king. Now, if they will only remain on the side of Jesus and opposed to their leaders, perhaps they can escape the fate of Jerusalem (19:41-44) and *this generation* (11:49-52; 17:25-37).

20:1-8. Jesus' authority. The Jerusalem leadership begins its attack on Jesus by questioning the source of his *authority* to do *these things*, referring to seizing the Temple and teaching the people from it. This is a legitimate question for the religious leadership to ask, assuming they are sincere in their question. Jesus asks them to decide the source of John's authority—and, implicitly, his own. Was it human or divine? They deliberate, not because they are really interested in the issue itself (although as the leaders of Israel they certainly should be!), but only for jaded, political reasons. Is there any way to win this bout with Jesus? They decide they cannot win and retreat, exposing their insincere motives in asking the question. Having exposed their motives, Jesus is under no obligation to answer their question.

20:9-19. Parable of the tenants. Jesus goes on the offensive against his opponents (v. 19), offering a parable and interpretation. The parable, vv. 9-16, is open to allegorical interpretation, with the *vineyard* representing Israel (cf. Isa 5:1-7), *the owner* representing God, *the tenants* representing the Jewish leadership, and *the son* representing Jesus. The meaning is clear: the Jewish leadership rejects all of God's messengers, including even his son, whom they kill. As a consequence, God will *destroy those tenants [the leaders] and give the vineyard [Israel] to others* (v. 16). Israel is *not* destroyed—only its leaders! Who are the others? (cf. 22:28-30).

The people, to whom Jesus is telling the parable, react in horror (*Heaven forbid!*, v. 16), recognizing the ominous tone of his message. Jesus drives his message home, quoting from Ps 118:22 and Isa 8:14-15. He is the *stone* the *builders* (the leaders) will reject. He will be vindicated; he will *become the cornerstone.* In addition, he will become a stone that will trip up and crush those who opposed him. The option of the people seems clear: do not side with *the builders*!

20:20-26. Taxes to Caesar. The *spies*, sent from the leadership, possess the pseudo-righteousness of the Pharisees (NRSV *honest*; lit. "righteous"; cf. 18:9). They flatter Jesus (v. 21) with words they do not mean, but with words which are, nonetheless, absolutely true. Their goal is to place Jesus in the untenable position of either loosing credibility *in the presence of the people* by advocating payment of taxes, or placing himself in legal jeopardy with the *authority of the governor* by advocating refusal to pay taxes.

Jesus' answer (v. 25) does not speak of divided loyalties, but of legitimate obligations. Jesus does not deny the legitimacy of giving the Roman emperor back his due of his own money, money that, ironically, not Jesus but only his opponents carry in their pockets. One must give to God what is God's due. Readers should recall 10:27-28. God's due is total love and devotion. Such total devotion does require that when obligations to human beings conflict with loyalty to God, one must "obey God rather than any human authority" (as Peter proclaims in Acts 5:29).

20:27-40. The question of the resurrection. *Some Sadducees* now try to challenge Jesus. The *chief priests* and perhaps even some of *the elders* of 20:1 would have been aligned with this aristocratic, conservative party of Jewish society. Apparently they want to force Jesus either into rejecting the idea of resurrection, an idea to which the Sadducees did not adhere, or into advocating marital infidelities in the afterlife. Either way, he will loose credibility with the people.

They appeal to the Jewish law of Levirate marriage, wherein a widow married the brother of her dead husband (Deut 25:5-6). The Sadducees set up a comical situation, seeming to require Jesus to approve either of bigamy *in the resurrection*, with the woman now having seven husbands for eternity, or of multiple divorces, a practice Jesus has already forbidden (16:18).

Jesus responds, first, by rejecting the assumptions of the Sadducees who wrongly believe that life in *that age* is a continuation of life in *this age* (vv. 35-36). *Marriage* is a divinely sanctioned rite of *this age* to perpetuate the human race (cf. Gen 1:28). It is not necessary for the *children of the resurrection* for *they cannot die anymore*. Second (vv. 37-38), Jesus affirms the idea of resurrection by appealing to the Torah (Exod 3:6), the portion of scripture which the Sadducees recognized as authoritative. He asserts that God would not refer to himself as the God of Moses' ancestors if they were dead at the time God spoke to Moses, for God *is not God of the dead, but of the living*. Hence, the three ancestors must have been *living*. Thus, *the dead are raised*.

Even *some of scribes* had to acknowledge that Jesus was right (v. 39). Verse 40 indicates that attempts to *question* Jesus are finished. Will the leadership give up or resort to other means to kill Jesus?

20:41-47. Jesus' conclusion. In vv. 41-44, Jesus addresses the question of authority raised in 20:2. Jesus acts on the authority of *the king* (19:38) and the Messiah (2:11; 9:20), the son of David (1:32, 69; 18:35-43). How is Jesus this son of David? Ps 110:1 provides the answer. Jesus is rightly understood as the Messiah and son of David when he is understood as the one who is also David's Lord, who sits at the *right hand* of God until his *enemies* are subdued. By this kingly authority Jesus does *these things* (cf. 20:2).

Earlier Jesus warned the disciples in the presence of the crowd to *beware of the yeast of the Pharisees* (12:1). In vv. 45-47, Jesus, *in the hearing of all the people*, offers a word of warning *to the disciples* to *beware of the scribes*. His description of the scribes is similar to what he said about the Pharisees (cf. 11:43; 14:7). The people and the disciples must beware of all elements of the Jewish religious leadership: the Pharisees, the scribes, and the chief priests and elders. It is they who evict *widows* while they *say long prayers*, and who are destined for *the greater condemnation*.

21:1-4. The widow's offering. Having just spoken of widows, Luke now tells a story about a widow's offering. While the rich contribute to the Temple *out of their abundance*, *the poor widow* contributes *out of her poverty*. While Jesus may admire her devotion, readers might well wonder how this woman who *has put in all she had to live on* will now live at all. One way that the Temple has become a *den of robbers* (19:46) is by taking the last of the poor's pennies, knowing that they will soon be evicted.

21:5-38. The destruction of Jerusalem and the end of the world. This speech must be read carefully, for it is presented to two audiences *in the story* and an audience *outside the story*. The audience outside the story is Luke's readers. For them, the destruction of the Temple is a past event (70 C.E.) and they would read from that perspective. One audience in the story is Jesus' disciples (20:45). The other audience in the story is the people who call Jesus *teacher* (v. 7). In Luke's Gospel, "only non-disciples refer to Jesus by the title 'teacher'" (Chance 1988, 135–36). Hence, readers of Jesus' words cannot ignore that Jesus is speaking not only to disciples outside and inside the story, but to non-disciples, the people of Jerusalem, inside the story as well. Careful reading is required to maintain a proper focus.

21:5-7. The destruction foretold. The *some* who are with Jesus who speak *about the temple*, includes both the disciples (20:45) and *some* of *all the people* whom Luke describes as *spellbound by what they heard* (19:48). Mention of the Temple prompts Jesus to predict its destruction and to address the question *when will this be?*

21:8-19. Coming catastrophes and persecution. In the story, Jesus is presenting to his audience predictions of what will come prior to destruction of the Temple: the rise of false messiahs, predictions that the *time is near*, political, economic, and even natural upheavals as well as *dreadful portents and signs from heaven*. Luke's readers know these to be past events. The Jewish historian JOSEPHUS wrote of such things occurring before the destruction of Jerusalem (*Ant* 18.4.1; 20.5.1; 20.8.6; *BJ* 6.5.3-4).

Verses 12-19 are directed to the disciples in Jesus' story audience, for they speak of persecutions to come to Jesus' followers *before* the destruction of the Temple and the events of vv. 8-11 (cf. v. 12a). Luke will write of these persecutions in Acts.

21:20-24. The destruction of Jerusalem. These words are addressed to both of Jesus' story audiences, the disciples and the people. After the events of vv. 8-19 *you [will] see Jerusalem surrounded by armies*. Jesus then begins to talk in the third person about those who will actually experience the destruction of Jerusalem. This allows Jesus' words to apply to any who might live in Jerusalem and its environs when Jerusalem's *desolation has come near*, not just the story audiences. Jesus' words make clear that the destruction of Jerusalem exhibits the *days of vengeance* and speaks *wrath against this people*. Both elements of Jesus' audience must know that the destruction of Jerusalem is God's emphatic word of judgment against *this people*. The gentiles will trample God's holy city, but only *until the times of the Gentiles are fulfilled* (cf. Dan 8:1-14). Both elements of Jesus' audience hear that Jerusalem's trampling is of limited duration. What will happen to Jerusalem, and more importantly its people, after this?

21:25-28. The Son of Man and your redemption. From v. 25 through the remainder of Jesus' speech, Luke's readers and Jesus' story audience are on equal footing, for they are both hearing Jesus speak of things yet-to-come. Great cosmic and natural upheavals will create *distress among the nations* and *foreboding*. Then *they will see "the Son of Man coming." They* probably denotes everybody, the *people* of v. 26 (lit. "humans" [ἄνθρωποι]).

With the coming of the Son of Man comes the end (17:22-37). With the coming of this end comes *your redemption*. Hence, when *these things* [the events of vv. 25-26] *begin to take place* "you" can know that *your redemption is drawing near*. What is the antecedent of "your"? Jesus' story audience consists of both disciples and the people of Jerusalem. Is Jesus promising the people of Jerusalem, as well as the disciples, that when *the times of the Gentiles are fulfilled* (v. 24) they will experience redemption? Might this be the time when Jerusalem will declare, *Blessed is the one who comes in the name of the Lord?* (13:35b)?

21:29-33. Concluding predictions. Jesus offers *them a parable*. "Them" denotes immediately his two story audiences and implies his reading audience. In this parable the same message of v. 28 is reiterated: *the kingdom of God is near* when *you see these things taking place*. Verse 33 offers an emphatic affirmation of the sure authority of Jesus' words. Verse 32 is saying more than all these things will happen before Jesus' contemporaries die. *This generation* denotes those who reject the Son of Man (cf. 17:25) who will experience severe judgment (cf. 11:49-51). *This generation* will not escape the *days of vengeance* (21:22) or the *great distress* and *wrath* (21:23). It shall by no means disappear from the stage until all these things have come upon it.

21:34-38. A final warning. Jesus concludes with a word to his audiences to stay on the alert so that *that day* (the "day of the Son of Man," cf. 17:24; 21:27) will not be one's undoing. Prayer will not allow one to avoid the hard times that are coming, but will allow one *to escape* the judgment that will fall upon *the whole earth* and *to stand before the Son of Man*. Jesus' disciples (both inside and outside the story) must continue in their faithfulness to obey his exhortation. The thus-far uncommitted people must decide whose side they are on.

The comments on 19:47-48 also apply to 21:37-38. What opened in chap. 19 comes to a close in chap. 21.

The Hour of Darkness, 22:1–23:56

This section tells of Jesus' PASSION. The other Gospels tell broadly the same story, with the other two synoptics being most similar to Luke (cf. Matt 26:1–27:66; Mark 14:1–15:47; John 13:1–19:42). John's is much longer in part because of the great attention given to Jesus' discourses (cf. esp. chaps. 14-17). Many interpreters believe a PASSION NARRATIVE to have been one of the earliest connected narratives to be composed by Jesus' early followers. Some argue that Luke had access to two passion narratives: Mark's and an independent narrative (see Fitzmyer 1985, 1359-68).

Luke began the story of Jesus' ministry by telling of direct confrontation between Jesus and the devil (4:1-13), described as a period of "testing." Now Satan reemerges as a direct player in the action (22:3), marshaling his allies of darkness (22:53) in this final time of "testing" (22:46). During this passion story, the three sets of characters with whom Jesus has been dealing in the preceding narrative, disciples, crowds (people), and the Jewish leadership, will have to make firm choices whether they are for or against Jesus (cf. 11:23).

22:1-6. The plot to kill Jesus. *The chief priests and scribes* still seek to kill Jesus (cf. 19:47). There is no question whose side they are on in this struggle. *The people* are not on their side in this plot (cf. 19:48), for an *opportunity* must be found for the leadership to catch Jesus *when no crowd was present*. Sadly, *Judas, one of the twelve,* will provide this *opportunity*. Will all the disciples side with evil? Judas' plot offers a warning that any can be corrupted by the leaven of the Pharisees (cf. 12:1) and join forces with *this generation* (cf. 17:25). *Satan* is directly involved in creating the *opportunity* to betray Jesus—the *opportune time* he has been waiting for since 4:13. The conflict of the two kingdoms (cf. 11:18-20) is about to reach a critical moment.

22:7-13. Preparing the Passover. The time for the sacrifice and preparation of *the Passover lamb* was the afternoon of 14 Nisan (March/April). The story displays Jesus' prescience (cf. 19:29-34), implying that things are unfolding according to plan.

22:14-23. The last supper. There are some significant textual critical issues in this passage (see NRSV mg.). The commentary below follows the NRSV text.

The Passover meal was eaten the evening after preparation. The Jewish day goes from sundown to sundown, hence, sundown brought the 15th of Nisan. Verses 15-16 imply that Jesus did not share the meal with his disciples, but only led in their eating of it. He declares that he *will not eat it until it is fulfilled in the kingdom of God*. He makes a similar statement about drinking with the disciples (v. 18). Jesus has given notice that the reign of God is already here (cf. 11:20; 17:21). He recently spoke of the reign that is to come (21:31) with the coming of the Son of Man (21:27). It is this reign to which Jesus primarily refers. Jesus promises his disciples that they will eat and drink together at the kingdom's table (cf. 13:28-29).

In vv. 19b-20 Jesus offers an interpretation of the *bread* and *cup* that need not await fulfillment in the kingdom of God to be meaningful. He speaks of the giving of his body and pouring out of his blood *for you* and *the new covenant*. Jesus' mission to inaugurate the reign of God, manifested in the offering of liberation ("release/forgiveness" [cf. 4:18; 5:20] and "salvation" [cf. 7:50]), will include his dying. Jesus' many predictions of his death have implied that. Jesus' relating of his death to *the new covenant* strongly implies that this death is most significant in the accomplishment of his ministry of liberation.

In vv. 21-23 Luke conveys that the tragic plot of Jesus' enemies will succeed. But Jesus' words also make clear *the Son of Man is going as it has been determined*, assuring readers that God is in control of the action.

22:24-34. The flawed, yet faithful, disciples. Readers have read the many attempts on the part of Jesus to lead his disciples into a mature following. The betrayal by Judas (cf. vv. 21-22) reminds readers that even one of the twelve can fall away. The dispute that arises concerning who *was to be regarded as the greatest* shows that even the balance of the disciples have much to learn. Having just spoken of his own death, Jesus calls upon the disciples not to pattern themselves after gentile lords. Rather they are to take their cues from Jesus who is among them *as one who serves*.

The disciples must learn the proper way to lead, for Jesus is conferring upon them *a kingdom*. This promise assures the disciples and the readers that despite their failings the disciples will share rule with Jesus in his kingdom *judging the twelve tribes of Israel*. Why? It is because they are *those who have stood by [Jesus] in [his] trials* (lit. "testing" cf. 4:13). Jesus does not expect perfection. He does demand faithfulness in standing with him in the trials that come in the struggle with evil.

Despite their failures, the disciples have, to this point, stuck with Jesus. Following his resurrection, Jesus will ascend to his throne and begin his reign as Messiah (cf. Acts 2:34-36). It is in this context that the apostles *will sit on thrones* (v. 30) and lead Israel—at least that portion of Israel which comes to recognize Jesus as Messiah and saves itself from "this corrupt generation" (cf. Acts 2:40).

The sad dialogue with Peter (vv. 31-34) communicates that Satan will harass the apostles. Their hitherto "standing" with Jesus will begin to unravel. Even those who want to be faithful will fail. Jesus' prayer will prevent the total failure of faith. When Peter has *turned back* (cf. 17:3-4) he will *strengthen [his] brothers*. Readers will discover in Acts just how effective a leader Peter becomes.

22:35-38. Two swords. Jesus' question of v. 35 refers back to 10:4. *But now*, points to a change of circumstances. The disciples, as they "stand by" Jesus (22:28), are about to enter into the thickest flack in the fray against evil. They must take full provisions, including a *sword*. This makes clear how intense the struggle is to become. The reference to the *sword* is metaphorical, although the disciples take Jesus literally. *It is enough* is Jesus' rebuke of their philistine interpretation. Verse 37 appeals to Isa 53:12 and prepares readers for 23:32.

22:39-46. Prayer in the time of trial. Jesus and the disciples are about to enter *the time of trial* (lit. "testing"). Will the disciples stand with Jesus during the upcoming testing as they have to this point (cf. 22:28)? Testing is not something anyone should want to endure. Thus Jesus exhorts his disciples to pray that they might *not come into* such a *time* (cf. 11:4). Prayer is the best "provision" (cf. 22:36) one has for the struggle to come. Jesus himself prays a prayer of deliverance (v. 42). Verse 43 is textually questionable (see NRSV mg.), but offers a valid interpretation of why one must pray: it offers *strength*. Prayer for deliverance must include the willingness to do God's will, not one's own (v. 42). The disciples, *sleeping because of grief*, do not rise to the occasion. Satan's sifting (cf. 22:31) has begun. They may not continue to stand with Jesus. Readers recall hopefully the promise Jesus made in 22:32.

22:47-53. The arrest of Jesus. *Judas*, who has chosen to side with evil in the struggle against evil, leads *a crowd* to arrest Jesus. Verse 52 defines the *crowd*: *chief priests . . . the temple police, and the elders*. The disciples *strike with the sword* indicating that they do not grasp that prayer is how they are to engage the enemy in this present time of testing.

The Jewish leaders come to arrest Jesus *as a bandit*. Yet it is they, not Jesus, who have made the Temple a *den of robbers* (19:46, same Gk. word). Such blatant hypocrisy is to be expected, for they have assumed the role of the hypocritical Pharisees (cf. 12:1). More importantly, the Jewish leadership, being led by Judas, whom Satan is leading (22:3), are now explicitly in league with Satan, *the power of darkness* (cf. Acts 26:18). The arrest and subsequent execution of the Son of God is evil's finest *hour*. It will also be evil's undoing.

22:54-65. Peter's denial. Satan's sifting (22:21) continues. As Jesus was led to *the high priest's house* (cf. 3:2 for possible identity), *Peter was following*, but only *at a distance*. Peter's threefold denial shows that he completely fails as a thoroughly loyal disciple willing to give his life for Jesus (cf. 22:33).

Readers should recall that Jesus has promised a kingdom to his disciples because they have "stood with him" (22:28-29). They should also recall the many radical demands that Jesus laid upon those who wished to follow him (cf. esp. 9:23-26, 57-62; 12:49-53; 14:25-35). Throughout this passion narrative, one can hardly be impressed by how the disciples have "stood" or how faithfully they have devoted their lives to Jesus. If, indeed, Jesus does follow through on his promise to give the disciples a kingdom, it will be through no merit of their own. At this point readers may recall Jesus' word that he has prayed for Peter that his faith will not fail utterly. He demands repentance, to be sure (cf. *once you have turned back* [22:32]), but it is Jesus' action on behalf of his disciples that will restore and sustain them. The message of radical mercy rings through. Perhaps Peter realized this as *he wept bitterly*.

The abuse of Jesus (vv. 63-65) shows the utter contempt of Jesus' opponents as they mockingly encourage Jesus to *prophesy!* Readers catch the irony in that they have just witnessed a prophecy of Jesus come to realization as *the cock crowed.*

22:66-71. Hearing before the assembly. *The assembly* is the SANHEDRIN, the Jewish high court. This assembly as depicted in Luke has little interest in justice. In 20:20 the leadership schemed to secure politically incriminating testimony from Jesus. Getting Jesus to acknowledge his messianic status is similarly motivated. He refuses to cooperate.

Verse 68 alludes to 20:1-8, a narrative exposing the duplicity of the Jewish leadership which explains why they *would not believe* even if Jesus did answer their inquiry. He does affirm, however, that the Son of Man will assume royal power (*the right hand of God*). Readers know Jesus is talking about himself. Jesus' questioners suspect so, given the follow-up question of v. 70. Jesus' implicit affirmation gives them grounds to pursue legal action, although as the subsequent narrative will show they will have to offer a most twisted interpretation of Jesus' admission if they hope to get the governor to pass sentence.

23:1-5. The first hearing before Pilate. The charge concerning *taxes* is simply false (cf. 20:20-26). The charge of claiming to be the *Messiah* is a half-truth at best. Jesus has made no explicit claim, and certainly he has not portrayed himself as the kind of *king of the Jews* that PILATE would be interested in executing. Pilate quickly dismisses the charges before *the chief priests and the crowds*. The latter have perhaps arrived expecting to hear Jesus' teaching (cf. 21:38). The *they* of v. 5 who respond to Pilate are likely the chief priests who insist that Jesus *stirs up the people.* This charge gives Pilate further reason to execute their enemy Jesus.

23:6-12. Hearing before Herod. Readers recall that HEROD, having killed JOHN THE BAPTIST, had been wanting to see Jesus (9:9) and was seeking to kill him (13:31). Even corrupt Herod, after *he questioned him at some length* and heard *the chief priests and the scribes . . . vehemently accusing him* found nothing worthy of execution and *sent him back to Pilate* (vv. 9-11). On *that same day* they became *friends*. It is a perverted friendship, rooted in their willingness to appease the Jewish leadership. Although Herod did not recommend execution, he is held fully accountable for his complicity in Jesus' death in Acts 4:25-28.

23:13-25. The second hearing before Pilate. Again, the leadership and the people are present. Pilate, however, seems more interested in addressing his comments to the leadership, reminding them of the charges they had made against Jesus earlier in the day: *this man . . . was perverting the people.* Since Pilate cannot find - *this man guilty of any of your charges against him* he will flog Jesus *and release him* (vv.14-17).

Then they all shouted out together, "Away with this fellow!" Who are *they*? The leadership and the people, or the leadership who had been making the charges against Jesus? Luke is not clear. Whether *the people* at this juncture join the leaders of *this generation* (cf. 7:31-35) in demanding Jesus' crucifixion or simply acquiesce out of fear, the consequences are the same, as subsequent pronouncements by Jesus (23:27-31) and his followers (Acts 3:14-15) make clear: they are guilty. The implications of 11:23 become clear: *Whoever is not with me is against me.* The people have shown themselves not to be "with Jesus." Their failure, like that of the disciples, cannot be excused—it can only be forgiven. The early chapters of Acts will tell of the apostles preaching to the people offering them the opportunity to repent and be forgiven (Acts 2:38) and to separate themselves from "this corrupt generation" (Acts 2:40).

<u>23:26-31. The walk to crucifixion.</u> Luke again is unclear concerning the identity of the *they* who *led him away*. Romans? Jewish leaders? Jewish people? Luke distinguishes *a great number of the people* from those taking Jesus away to crucify him. Yet even those bemoaning Jesus' fate will not escape the punishment to befall *the daughters of Jerusalem* and their *children*. Terrible days are coming when even death would be better than life—clearly a reference to Jerusalem's destruction (cf. 19:43-44; 21:6, 20-24). The enigmatic saying of v. 31 means "If this kind of violent thing can happen to an innocent man (the *green wood*), imagine what will happen to a guilty city and its people (*dry wood*)."

<u>23:32-56. The crucifixion of Jesus.</u> This scene has three sections: the mocking of Jesus by the Jewish leaders and the soldiers (vv. 32-38); the two criminals (vv. 39-43); the death and burial of Jesus (vv. 44-56).

Verses 32-38. The scoffing and mocking of Jesus by *the leaders* (Jewish) and *the soldiers* (gentiles; cf. 18:32) centers around the spectacle of a supposed *Messiah* and *King of the Jews* not being able to *save* himself. The Jews and the gentiles share in the ridicule of the Lord's anointed (Acts 4:25-28). *The people stood by, watching,* not sharing in the ridicule of Jesus. The later sermons of Acts will condemn them, nonetheless (Acts 3:12-15).

Readers know Jesus to be the savior (1:69; 2:11) and Messiah (2:11; 9:20) and have seen him demonstrate his saving power over sin (7:48-40), disease (8:43-48), even death (8:49-50). Jesus accomplishes his saving mission through his self-giving. Luke may offer no explicit doctrine of the atonement, but the emphasis Jesus himself places upon his rejection and death as the divinely necessitated culmination of his earthly work as the Son of Man and prophet (see comments on 9:18-36; 13:33-34) allows readers to know that this death does play a role in his work of liberation and salvation. To mock him is to show that one simply does not understand "the plan of God" (cf. 7:30).

The first sentence of v. 34 may not be original (see NRSV mg.). But it is fitting here. Jesus offers ("release/liberation"; cf. 4:18)—saving others even as they mock him for saving others while he cannot save himself. It also prepares for Acts 3:17.

Verses 39-43. One *criminal* joins the scoffers. The other criminal implies his recognition of Jesus as the Messiah as he requests that Jesus remember him *when [he] comes into [his] kingdom*. Jesus' promise assures him of salvation, and even sooner than the criminal expected: *today*. *Paradise* was a common term to denote heaven and its blessings (2 Cor 12:4; Rev 2:7). The Messiah demonstrates his saving power as he dies, even as the scoffers scoff.

Verses 44-56. Reference to the failing of *the sun's light* recalls Jesus' word concerning *the power of darkness* (22:53). Jerusalem will pay a heavy price for aligning itself with darkness. The tearing of *the curtain of the temple* (v. 45) serves as an omen that the Temple will be destroyed, adding weight to what Jesus had predicted (19:43-44; 21:6). Jesus' last words show his trust in the *Father*, Jesus' favorite designation for God in the Gospel, even from childhood (cf. 2:49).

Luke narrates a number of reactions. The CENTURION, representing the mocking soldiers of 23:36, recognizes Jesus as *innocent* (Gk.: righteous). Jesus' opponents had thought they were "righteous" (18:9; 20:20 [NRSV "honest"]), but their brand of righteousness killed the one who truly was righteous. Does the centurion's response hold out hope for the gentiles?

The people react in gestures of mourning, *beating their breasts* (v. 48). The time for *weeping for themselves and their children* has begun (cf. 23:27-30). The phrase translated *returned home* is literally "turned back," sharing the same Greek root as a word Jesus has related to repentance (cf. 17:3-4), yet the verb does not actually mean "repentance." Their reaction is ambiguous. Is there hope for them?

THE TWELVE (eleven?), if present at all, are buried away in the anonymity of Jesus' *acquaintances* (v. 49). Theirs and the women's response to the scene (watching from a distance) is really no less ambiguous than that of the people. The report of the women's going to prepare spices is touching, but it also makes clear that they did not grasp Jesus' own predictions of his resurrection. Is there hope for Jesus' followers?

Joseph of Arimathea, *a member of the council*, is described most positively as *good and righteous*. His action is also the most courageous, having gone *to Pilate* to ask for *the body of Jesus*. It is made clear that he did not consent to the *plan and action* of the *council* (vv. 50-56). Readers might find some comfort in knowing that not all the Jewish leadership is utterly corrupt. Is there hope even for them?

Representatives from all groups involved in the execution of Jesus, Jewish and gentile, are present. Yet it is curious how Luke has presented them: the apostles are anonymous at best; the representative from the Jewish leadership—Joseph—is *good and righteous*. These last scenes of Jesus' passion are unsettling enough to dissuade readers from thinking that what happens in the story of Jesus is predictable. Glimmers of hope are offered for all the representative characters, especially when one remembers the prayers of Jesus on behalf of the "sifted" followers (22:31-32) and those who mocked and watched (23:34-46).

Entering into Glory, 24:1-53

For background discussion of the resurrection narratives and the resurrection of Jesus, see Fitzmyer 1985, 1533-43.

As readers reach the end of a story they look for resolution of issues raised in what has preceded (Parsons 1986, 201-204). Having arrived at the end of the story, Luke will now need to bring some closure to his story. Review of previous sections of the narrative recalls the issues of the story in need of resolution.

First, Jesus has come to offer redemption to Israel in fulfillment of scriptural promises, with clear hints of inclusion of the gentiles into God's salvation. There will be division among the people (1:5–4:13).

Second, Jesus has come to offer liberation ("release") to the captives and the oppressed. This section makes clear that Satan, later called *the power of darkness* (22:53), is behind this oppression. Jesus' shorthand expression for this liberation from Satan's power is *the reign of God* (4:16–9:50).

Third, Jesus is the PROPHET, indeed the Son of God, to whom Israel must listen (9:35). As he journeys to JERUSALEM, ISRAEL, consisting of disciples, the people, and the leadership, the last represented primarily by the Pharisees, are given ample opportunity to hear him. The leadership is hostile. The people vacillate. The disciples stay with Jesus, but they lack understanding. Despite these evidences of division among Israel, to all have been applied the negative appellation *this generation* (9:51–19:44).

Fourth, in Jerusalem Jesus called Israel to decision. No reader can be impressed by the response of any element of Israel in the passion narrative. With the death of Jesus, one must ask, will there be redemption in fulfillment of scriptural promises, liberation from the power of darkness, and a positive hearing of the word of Jesus by Israel? Readers, anticipating the resurrection, know that if resolution is to come it must come from the resurrected one.

24:1-12. The empty tomb. The women, later identified in v. 10, come to the tomb on Sunday (*the first day of the week*) morning. They have come for the wrong reason, to anoint a dead man, but *they did not find the body.* The description of *the two men in dazzling clothes* implies angelic beings (cf. 24:23). They announce the resurrection and recall the prediction that Jesus himself had made (v. 6; cf. 9:22). With Jesus alive expectations of resolution are raised. The women *told all this to the eleven* but they thought it *an idle tale.* PETER does go to inspect the tomb, however (v. 12, although this text is disputed [see NRSV mg.]). He is amazed, but does not see Jesus. So far, no resolution of any issues.

24:13-35. The road to Emmaus. It is still Sunday (v. 13). Hopes for resolution are raised as *Jesus himself* proceeds to walk with two persons journeying to

EMMAUS. *But their eyes were kept from recognizing him* (v.16); a phrase hauntingly reminiscent of what Jesus had said of Jerusalem (19:42). Hopes for resolution are quickly taken away.

The conversation of CLEOPAS and his companion reminds readers of issues in need of resolution: Will there be redemption for Israel in fulfillment of scriptural promises? They certainly do not think so (cf. v. 21). The unrecognized Jesus is emphatic that the suffering of the Messiah is part of the fulfillment of the scriptural promises, although the two do not see it and the reader is even left clueless as to exactly how. Still, it is clear that the resurrected Jesus affirms the fulfillment of scripture. This hope is not to be abandoned.

What of the work of liberation and the reign of God? The fact of Jesus' resurrection, which by the end of the story, even the characters come to recognize, affirms the effectiveness of the liberating power of God. Jesus' act of taking, blessing, breaking, and giving bread is reminiscent of 22:19. In that context Jesus had said he would *not eat . . . until it is fulfilled in the kingdom of God*. What readers are witnessing is hardly the fulfillment of the kingdom of God; Luke 21:25-33 has made clear that such will accompany the coming of the Son of Man *in a cloud with power and great glory*. Still the picture of the resurrected Jesus breaking bread with his followers instills confidence that bread will be broken again when it is fulfilled in the kingdom of God. Here one may not find the realization of the reign of God, but one does find justification to hope for such realization.

What of the response of Israel? The disciples respond affirmatively; once *their eyes were opened* (v. 31), Jesus *appeared* to them (v. 34), and *had been made known* (v. 35) to them. Response, even after being "sifted by Satan" (22:31), is possible, but it can come only at the initiation of the resurrected Lord. Will the rest of Israel have opportunity to respond to this resurrected one? Comments concerning the leadership are thoroughly negative, leaving little hope (v. 20). What of the people? They are not explicitly indicted in v. 20, but neither is any explicit word offered to indicate that they will respond to the word of Jesus. The final phrase, stating that Jesus *had been made known to them in the breaking of the bread* (v. 35), might offer a clue that recognition of Jesus apart from life in the community of faith is not possible, for in Acts "breaking bread" serves to denote Christian fellowship at the table of the Lord (cf. 22:30; Acts 2:42, 46; 20:7, 11).

<u>24:36-53. Appearance and exodus.</u> It is now Sunday evening (cf. vv. 29, 33, 36). Jesus' appearance to the group (vv. 36-42) affirms for them and the readers the reality of his resurrection. Jesus invites them to *touch* him and to see his *flesh and bones*. He even eats *in their presence* (v. 43) to confirm the reality of his resurrection.

Jesus' pronouncement of *peace be with you* (v. 36) recalls the disciples acclamation of peace when Jesus approached Jerusalem (19:38) and especially the angelic announcement of 2:14. There the angels promised peace due to the birth of the Messiah. In this scene, Jesus fulfills this hope. He had wanted to offer such peace to Jerusalem, but it could not see it (19:42). This appearance reinforces resolution of the issue concerning the response of the disciples to Jesus. At least this part of Israel sees who this Jesus is.

In vv. 44-49, numerous issues are offered resolution, although new expectations are also raised. Jesus affirms again that, indeed, *everything written about [him] in the law of Moses, the prophets, and the psalms must be fulfilled.* Jesus affirms that the story of his passion itself was *written* in the scriptures. This story readers have just read is the realization, or at least an integral part of the realization, of the fulfillment of Israel's scriptures.

Still readers are not told exactly what scriptures are fulfilled. But Jesus *opened their minds to understand the scriptures*. This assures readers that the resurrected Lord can lead believers to see to exactly how the "Jesus story" fulfills "scripture's story." In Acts, readers will have several opportunities to hear the scriptures interpreted and to see how exactly Jesus fulfills the scriptures.

The ministry of liberation, or "release," is addressed explicitly in the charge Jesus makes to his followers. This work of liberation, which included in Jesus' ministry the offering of *forgiveness* (or "release") *of sins* is to continue (v. 47). In fact, this very continuation of the ministry of liberation is itself said to be part of the fulfillment of what *is written* (v. 46). What is more, this proclamation of *repentance and forgiveness of sins* will begin *from Jerusalem*. Jerusalem and its people (even its leaders?) will hear the message of repentance and be offered the opportunity to experience the liberation they rejected just a few days before. The proclamation will not stop in Jerusalem. It shall be offered to *all the nations* (same Gk. word as "gentiles").

Will redemption come to Israel as she once again is given opportunity to hear the message? Jesus' predictions about the destruction of Jerusalem create tension. Is there a way that redemption, liberation, and forgiveness can still come to Israel if, indeed, Jerusalem must fall? Will the nations (gentiles) respond positively? These questions are not answered. But Luke approaches the conclusion with hopeful expectations.

Finally in this section, Luke raises the expectation that the mission in which he is calling his disciples to engage will be assisted by something promised by the *Father* himself that Jesus will send: *power from on high*. Attentive readers will recall such texts as 3:16; 11:13; 12:12. Less attentive readers will have to wait until Acts to find out what Jesus is talking about.

In vv. 50-53, Jesus' exodus (departure [cf. 9:31]) and "taking up" (9:51) are to be realized. The journey of Jesus is coming to an end. Before he leaves he offers his followers a priestly blessing, *lifting up his hands*. The Temple may be destined to fall someday (and from the perspective of Luke's readers it has fallen), but the blessing of God's anointed will not be impeded by the lack of a Temple and priesthood, just as the existence of a Temple and priesthood cannot insure blessing (cf. 1:22).

The brief description of Jesus' ascension *up into heaven* allows readers to experience and witness the realization of Jesus' bold claim before his oppressors in 22:69: *the Son of Man will be seated at the right hand of . . . God.* Jesus has been vindicated.

The disciples return *to Jerusalem* whence the continuing mission of liberation will commence, *continually in the temple blessing God.* Jerusalem and the Temple will fall one day. But for now, the Temple has been cleansed by the Messiah (19:45-46) and is a most fitting place for his people to congregate.

Luke ends the story where he began it: in the holy city and sanctuary of Israel, the people of God. As readers prepare to turn the page to begin Luke's second book—the Book of Acts—this closing scene calls them back to the opening scenes and to hopes raised by such characters as Mary, the mother of Jesus, and Zechariah, the father of the Baptist, but perhaps expressed best by Simeon, the righteous man longing for the consolation of Israel. *My eyes have seen your salvation . . . a light for revelation to the Gentiles and for glory to your people Israel* (2:30-32).

Works Cited

Aune, David E. 1987. *The New Testament in Its Literary Environment.*

Burridge, Richard A. 1992. *What Are the Gospels? A Comparison with Graeco-Roman Biography.* SNTSMS 70.

Chance, J. Bradley. 1988. *Jerusalem, the Temple, and the New Age in Luke–Acts.*

Conzelmann, Hans. 1982 [1960]. *The Theology of St. Luke.*

Fitzmyer, Joseph A., S.J. 1981, 1985. *The Gospel according to Luke.* Two vols. (pages numbered consecutively). AncB.

Garrett, Susan R. "'Lest the Light in You Be Darkness': Luke 11:33-36 and the Question of Commitment," *JBL* 110/1 (1991): 93-105.

Marshall, I. Howard. 1978. *Commentary on Luke*, NIGTC.

Moesnner, David P. 1989. *Lord of the Banquet: The Literary and Theological Significance of the Lukan Travel Narrative*; 1990. "The 'Leaven of the Pharisees' and 'This Generation': Israel's Rejection of Jesus according to Luke," *Reimaging the Death of Jesus*, ed. Dennis D. Sylva, 79–107.

Pervo, Richard I. 1989. "Must Luke and Acts Belong to the Same Genre?" SBLASP, 309-16.

Parsons, Mikeal C. 1986. "Narrative Closure and Openness in the Plot of the Third Gospel: The Sense of Ending in Luke 24:50-53," SBLASP.

Talbert, Charles H. 1986. *Reading Luke: A Literary and Theological Commentary on the Third Gospel.* 1988. "Once Again: Gospel Genre," *Semeia* 43:53-73.

Tiede, David L. 1988. *Luke.* AugCNT.

John [MCB 1043-82]

Gerald L. Borchert

Introduction

The fourth Gospel is one of the most fascinating books in the Bible. Its poetic-like stories have engulfed many, and a number of its verses are among the most familiar in scripture. Although its vocabulary is simple and verges on being redundant, the Gospel is one of the most complex compositions in the Bible in terms of the interweaving of theological themes. It is like a complex symphony that periodically repeats earlier themes with refreshing variations so that the reader is caught in the awe-inspiring work of a masterfully sophisticated artist.

John and the Synoptics

When one reads John after reading one of the Synoptics (Matthew, Mark, or Luke), one has the feeling of being in familiar territory. Yet, in spite of the similarities, it is strangely different. JESUS certainly performs miracles (in John called "signs"), but, except for the multiplication of bread and the walking on the water in chap. 6, the sign stories are all different. There is a great catch of fish in chap. 21 that reminds the reader of Luke 5, but it takes place after the resurrection in John so that scholars have a field day trying to work out the relationship between the two stories.

In terms of organization the Synoptics have Jesus moving from GALILEE to JUDEA to die, whereas John moves Jesus at will between the two regions. It is likely this Gospel's movement of Jesus is more reflective of what actually happened, but we are not quite sure. The question of the cleansing of the Temple points to the problem. Because the story appears in John near the beginning of the Gospel (chap. 2) and in the Synoptics in the final stages of Jesus' life, many readers automatically begin to think there are two cleansings of the Temple. But there is only one in any one Gospel. This fact raises the important question of organization in John.

Organization of the Gospel

When many readers are asked "How long did Jesus live?" the normal reply is thirty-three years. The reason is that they take the thirty years of preparation from Luke 3:23 and then go to John and count the number of Passovers recorded there.

But to count Passovers in this manner is to misunderstand this Gospel (Borchert 1993).

The Gospel of John is organized according to cycles, and PASSOVER is a key to understanding John's cycle-thinking. The Gospel begins with a prologue (1:1-18, probably written after the Gospel was finished as an introduction to the Gospel) that relates Jesus to God and to the very beginning of time. Then there is a series of short stories (1:19-52) that introduces Jesus in terms of a variety of titles including MESSIAH, SON OF GOD, and King of Israel, with the focal designation being *the Lamb of God who takes away the sin of the world!* (1:29, 36). That lamb is meant to be understood as the world's Passover Lamb.

This introductory chapter is followed by a series of three cycles in which Passover plays a significant role. The Cana cycle (chaps. 2–4) has at its heart the Passover and the cleansing of the Temple (2:13-25). The Festival cycle (chaps. 5–11) after an introduction to feast thinking (chap. 5) moves from Passover (6:4) to Passover (11:55). Chapter 12 serves as a saddle text between the public ministry of Jesus and his private ministry to his disciples. The setting is just before the Passover (12:1). The farewell cycle (chaps. 13–17) begins with an announcement of Passover (13:1), and these chapters seek to prepare the disciples for Passover and the coming of a new era.

The Passover sequence is drawn to a conclusion in the death story (chaps. 18–19) with the dying of the perfect Passover lamb on the specific day of Preparation when the Passover lambs were killed (19:14, 31). The resurrection stories (chaps. 20–21) then move the reader beyond Passover to the new era of the spirit-led community (20:22) of Jesus Christ (Borchert, *John*).

The Context of the Gospel

Behind this Gospel lies a community of faith that tradition situates in EPHESUS. Its history cannot be fully detailed but its BELOVED DISCIPLE (13:23; 19:26; 20:2; 21:20) may have been the unnamed disciple of JOHN THE BAPTIST (1:35-40).

Some time during its formative period, as J. Louis Martyn (1979, 37–62) has forcefully argued, members of the community undoubtedly encountered hostility from the SYNAGOGUE. Whether they moved from Israel first to Antioch or immediately to Ephesus is not certain. Neither is it clear whether their numbers included SAMARITANS, as might be argued from John 4:39-42.

The hostility with the synagogue seems clearly behind the story of the blind man (9:22, 34, 40) as well as the entire argument of Jesus in 8:31-59 and the warning in 16:2-4. Whether the *Birkath ha-Minim* (the curse of the heretics that was inserted into the Jewish benedictions) is directly related to this community, it is clear that the context of hostility is very similar. In this context, the reader cannot help but be reminded of the Christian evaluation of the Jews as the "synagogue of Satan" in the Apocalypse (Rev 2:9; 3:9).

The entire Gospel seems to be written from the perspective of the way Jesus filled the expectations of the OT. He is viewed, for example, as the new Temple (2:19-21), the successor to the hope of the lifted-up serpent (3:14), the interpreter of SABBATH (5:9-18), the true bread from heaven (6:48-51), the living water of Tabernacles (7:37-38), and the true shepherd king expected in Ezek 34 and Jer 23 (John 10:1-30). Such views undoubtedly raised the ire of many Jews.

Authorship

The traditional view has been that John the son of Zebedee was the author of this Gospel. Such a view was enunciated by Irenaeus in the second century C.E. (*AdvHaer* 3.1.1) and maintained until the late eighteenth and early nineteenth centuries. The theology then was challenged by some as being later dualistic and Platonic thinking (e.g., D. F. Strauss). Some began to point to the probability that the Gospel was written by a second-century disciple of the apostle (19:35; 21:25; e.g., H. Paulus). The next stage in thinking was that a school or community was responsible for the Gospel (e.g., J. B. Lightfoot) and this theory received an expanded treatment recently by Culpepper (1975).

Clearly the epilogue is suggestive in terms of authorship because three parties are there identified. The first is the disciple or witness (21:24), the second is the church or community that authenticates the work (e.g., *we*, 21:24), and the third party is the *I* (21:25) who appears to be the writer of at least the last two verses and probably more. The text itself, therefore, indicates a multiplicity of persons involved in the writing and transmission of this Gospel. The Beloved Disciple, however, is clearly viewed as the source of the tradition or basis for the message. In this commentary the designations evangelist and John are used interchangeably, recognizing the complex nature of the issue.

Date

The traditional date for the writing of the Gospel has been the decade of 90–100 C.E. This date had been called into question by some who supposed the theology was second-century. The discovery of a fragment of the Gospel in Egypt (containing 18:31-33, 37-38, and housed in the Rylands Library in Manchester), which probably dates from the early second century, has resulted in the earlier date being resubstantiated.

Theology

This Gospel was early regarded as a very special work. Clement of Alexandria designated it as the "spiritual gospel." That name has adhered to it throughout the centuries. Even before Clement, however, Gnostic mythologizers and spiritualizers found it to be a powerful vehicle for their distorted message (see Borchert 1981, 249). Indeed works like the Gospel of Truth (*Evangelium Veritatis*) found at NAG HAMMADI and reputed to have been written by Valentinus made use of the Gospel of John. Moreover, Gnostic spiritualizers like Heracleon were the first commentators on the Gospel.

Such facts have led some to suspect the Gospel to be marginally heretical. Its theology is certainly lofty and its CHRISTOLOGY is among the most elevated in the NT. The Gospel does not begin with the birth of Jesus but with the LOGOS/WORD at the beginning of time. But while the christology is elevated, it is important to see that on the basis of the purpose of John the Jesus of this Gospel cannot be an adoptionistic, nonsuffering, alien messenger from without. The Jesus of this Gospel is very real, very human but also God-directed and divinely empowered. He is truly a God-man.

His concern is for his suffering community and for leading people from one stage of believing to the next. In John, Jesus is the divine-human rescuer of faithless, doubting people. He, the creator of the world (1:3), has come to his own people and place and has been rejected (1:9-11) but he continues to build a community from those who will believe (1:12), the purpose for which John wrote his Gospel (20:30-31).

In reaching this purpose the evangelist has interwoven many great themes. Those themes include seeing, believing, knowing, light, darkness, life, death, truth, hour, signs, judgment, love, "I am," freedom, bread, water, and a host of others. Each theme can make for interesting research studies and each can be developed as windows into the nature of the Gospel.

The careful reader will also discover that this Gospel can be studied on various levels so that its wells of insight seldom run dry. It is a work that is loved by many new Christians although they may not understand what it means to *eat the flesh of the Son of Man* (6:53). It will challenge the minds and hearts of the most mature believer. It is indeed a book that is used by the Spirit of God to touch the world.

For Further Study

In the *Mercer Dictionary of the Bible*: BELOVED DISCIPLE, THE; CHRISTOLOGY; FEASTS AND FESTIVALS; GNOSTICISM; GOSPELS, CRITICAL STUDY OF; INCARNATION; JESUS; JOHN THE APOSTLE; JOHN THE BAPTIST; JOHN, GOSPEL AND LETTERS OF; LAMB OF GOD; LAZARUS; LOGOS/WORD; MESSIAH/CHRIST; MIRACLE STORY; PHARISEES; RESURRECTION IN THE NT; SIGNS AND WONDERS; WOMEN IN THE NT; WORSHIP IN THE NT.

In other sources: G. R. Beasley-Murray, *John*, WBC; G. L. Borchert, *John*, NAC; R. E. Brown, *The Gospel according to John*, AncB; D. A. Carson, *The Gospel according to John*; J. Charlesworth, ed., *John and the Dead Sea Scrolls*; R. A. Culpepper, *Anatomy of the Fourth Gospel*; E. Haenchen, *John*; R. Schnackenburg, *The Gospel according to St. John*; C. H. Talbert, *Reading John*.

Commentary

An Outline

I. Introduction, 1:1-51
- A. The Purpose, 20:30-31
- B. The Prologue, 1:1-18
- C. The Baptizer's Witness, 1:19-28
- D. Three Cameos of Witness, 1:29-51

II. The Cana Cycle, 2:1–4:54
- A. The First Cana Sign: Water to Wine, 2:1-12
- B. The Temple Cleansing, 2:13-25
- C. Nicodemus and Teaching on Salvation, 3:1-21
- D. The Baptizer and Salvation, 3:22-36
- E. The Samaritan Woman: An Unlikely Witness, 4:1-42
- F. The Second Cana Sign: Healing the Official's Son, 4:46-54

III. The Festival Cycle, 5:1–11:57
- A. The Sabbath and the Healing at Bethesda, 5:1-47
- B. Passover and the Exodus Motif, 6:1-71
- C. Tabernacles and the Motif of Deliverance, 7:1–9:41
- D. Dedication and the Motif of the Shepherd, 10:1-42
- E. A Climactic Sign and the Passover Plot, 11:1-57

IV. The Anointing and Entry into Jerusalem, 12:1-50

V. The Farewell Cycle, 13:1–17:26
- A. The Footwashing and Authentic Discipleship, 13:1-38
- B. The Question of Anxiety and Loneliness, 14:1-31
- C. The Vine and the Branches, 15:1-17
- D. The Question of Anxiety and Persecution, 15:18–16:33
- E. The Great Prayer, 17:1-26

VI. The Death Story, 18:1–19:42

VII. The Resurrection Stories, 20:1-29; 21:1-23

VIII. Conclusions, 20:30-31; 21:24-25

IX. Appendix. The Woman Taken in Adultery, 7:53–8:11

Introduction, 1:1-51

The Gospel of John is one of the most fascinating documents in the NT. While it may appear to be simple in vocabulary and style, it is one of the most highly organized and sophisticated works in the Bible (Borchert 1981, 249). Although scholars suggest some variations in detail concerning organization, most agree in the primary divisions of the book, with a major-segment break at either chap. 12 or 13. My particular contribution (Borchert 1987, 86–152; and Borchert, *John*) is the view that the Gospel was written in cycles (the Cana cycle, chaps. 2–4; the Festival cycle, chaps. 5–11; the farewell cycle, chaps. 13–17) framed by other sections that provide special developmental emphases (the prologue, 1:1-18; stories of witness, 1:19-51; transition to death, chap. 12; the death story, chaps. 18–19; the resurrection stories, chap. 20; and the postscript, chap. 21). Moreover, the book hangs together as a magnificent testimony to Jesus, *the Lamb of God who takes away the sin of the world* (1:29), and provides a model of authentic life for the community of believers.

The Purpose, 20:30-31

To understand the thought and goal of John, one would do well to begin with the first ending of the book—its purpose statement. This purpose statement is formulated to provide readers with a window into what has been written. There it is said that

> Many other signs, indeed, Jesus did before his disciples that are not recorded in this book, but these are recorded that you might believe that Jesus is the Christ, the Son of God, and that in [the genuine act of] believing you might have life by [or in the power of] his name.
>
> (author trans.)

From this statement it is evident that the evangelist expects a response from the reader. Clearly nothing less than active believing in Jesus which issues in a new way of living is adequate to encompass what this Gospel intends for its readership (Borchert 1987, 91). True life is the goal, authentic believing is the means, and relationship to Jesus (the SON OF GOD) is the basis. Furthermore, this purpose statement also indicates some of the most important themes that permeate the Gospel such as the understanding of signs, the importance of believing and life, the nature of Jesus, the importance of names and confession, and the significance of discipleship. In addition, readers of this Gospel should be alert to repetitive themes, words, phrases, and questions that arise in the Gospel. Attending to them should bring a new vitality to the study of this magnificent book. But all study should be related to the evangelist's purpose for the book and should result in a personal response involving one's own life. Only in such a context will the purpose be realized.

The Prologue, 1:1-18

The Gospel begins with one of the most profound statements concerning Jesus in the NT. The lofty CHRISTOLOGY is scarcely approximated elsewhere except perhaps in Heb 1:1-13 or Col 1:15-20. Moreover, its poetic-like style has led scholars to speculate on whether it was originally a poem or a hymn (e.g., J. Sanders 1971, 20–24; R. Brown 1966, 3–4). Some have sought to find a core document in Aramaic (Burney 1922, 40) while others like Bultmann have thought they found its roots in a gnostic logos hymn (1971, 23–28). Käsemann has countered that it was probably an early Christian hymn that was incorporated into the Gospel (1969, 138–67). Whatever may have been its roots, as it stands it has been thoroughly Johanninized in the editing process.

1:1-5. The eternal Word. In contrast to the synoptic Gospels, the evangelist begins at *the beginning* and builds upon the first and sixth orders of the creation account in Gen 1. He does not repeat those earlier presuppositions but identifies the *Word* (λόγος) with the very beginning and with God's divine selfhood, not in terms of subjugation of the *Word* but in a pattern of mutual interaction (Newman and Nida 1980, 8). The *Word* here is to be understood as a persona of God, not "a god" of subordination as argued by the Jehovah's Witnesses (see Metzger 1953).

In the prologue the contrast between the Greek verbs for "being" (ἦν) and "becoming" (ἐγένετο) is very crucial. The verb for "being" is used in vv. 1, 2, 4, 8, 9, 10, and 15 and refers to an existence without precondition, whereas the second word is used in vv. 3, 6, 10, 14, and 17, and implies moments within history. The *Word* in v. 1, however, is not a mere philosophical term to be identified simply with divine rationality as in Philonic speculation or Jewish Wisdom literature (cf. Dodd 1958, 274–75). Instead, it is to be understood as an early stage in the Trinitarian formulation concerning the various *personas* of God.

Not only is the preexistence of the *Word* here clearly implied, but it is also asserted that the *Word* has been active in the entire process of creation (v. 3). Indeed, the *Word* is here identified with the age-old quest of human beings for the essence of life (v. 4) and this pre-life-existing one is designated as the light-giver whose light is unquenchable (v. 5).

Many scholars today reject the translation of *overcome* (κατέλαβεν) in v. 5, arguing that the idea here could hardly be related to the ancient struggle between light and darkness—viewed as a conflict picture, symbolic of the warfare between good and evil (Beasley-Murray 1987, 32; Brown 1966, 8; Schnackenburg 1987, 1:245–49). My suggestion (*John*) is that there is a conflict to be understood here related to the rejection or nonreception (παρέλαβον) of the *Word* (cf. v. 11). For John the coming of Jesus divides persons and realities, and the underlying postresurrection perspective in the entire Gospel means that evil and rejection will not triumph (Borchert, *John*, and 1988, 502).

1:6-8. John the witness. The next three verses are prose and focus attention on *John* (the baptizer or *witness*). They function like a window from the lofty, poetic stance of the hymn on the *Word* down to the human context of witness, which is the first subject of concern following the lofty prologue. As such these verses provide a clear contrast: namely, John the witness is not to be considered in the same category or on the same level as the *Word* (cf. also 1:15), a view some of John's disciples apparently could not accept (John 3:25-30; see Borchert, *John*). Yet the designation of John as a witness is not to be considered a minor matter because witness, as J. Boice (1970, 31–38) argued, is a major theme in the Gospel. John the witness, like many persons in the Gospel, is more than an ancient person. He is an exemplar or representative.

1:9-13. Receiving the light. The *Word* is next identified as authentic light and linked to the idea of "the coming one," a designation derived from OT texts such as Zech 9:9 and used to identify the coming of the Messiah (cf. 4:25). According to the evangelist, however, although the *true light* entered the world in the midst of those who should have been expecting him, the tragic reality was that the *Word* encountered rejection rather than reception. This theme of rejection is often repeated in the Johannine stories of Jesus. But the evangelist is quick to assert that, despite rejection by many, those who believed are named the children of God not because of human lineage, desire, or power but because they have received the active *Word* of God.

1:14-18. The Incarnation and its implications. The second appearance of λόγος (*Word*) in the prologue signals the changed state of the *Word*'s work. In the first stage the emphasis was upon creation. The second stage, the work of the coming one, is redemption. In the language of the TENT OF MEETING in the EXODUS story, the evangelist describes the "enfleshment" of the *Word* in "tent" (σκηνόω) terminology. The *Word* is said to have actually "presenced" itself among humans. The idea of tent here implies no mere gnostic appearance theology. Instead, the meaning is that the *Word* actually entered the historical context and *became* (ἐγένετο) *flesh* or truly human. INCARNATION theology is one of the basic theses of historic Christianity.

As Israel experienced the glory of God at the wilderness tent (Exod 40:34), so both John (*we*, v. 14) and the early witnesses experienced divine glory in the enfleshed *Word* (Borchert, *John*). This sense of divine presence and glory was given to the world in God's "only" (μονογενής, see Moody 1953, 213–19) son. In him was vested divine "fullness" (πλήρωμα), a term later used by the Gnostics to describe their godhead. But here the fullness of the *Word* is said to be the source for the Christian experience of abundant *grace* (v. 16). Such grace (a term used only in the prologue of John) is contrasted directly with the divine gift of law that came through Moses (remember: law is also gift).

Then in v. 17 the *Word* is finally named: *Jesus* Christ, the divine-human agent of grace and truth. Truth or authenticity is one of the major themes in John and is a mark of both Jesus and his genuine followers. Clearly no one has ever seen the full semblance of God. But Jesus—the only SON OF GOD, whose intimacy with God the Father is described by the term "bosom" (v. 18; *heart* NRSV)—has portrayed, detailed, or narrated (ἐξηγήσατο) the nature of God for the world. With this idea of portrayal, the evangelist concludes the prologue of his Gospel (see Borchert, John) and sets the stage for the introduction of Jesus by John, the witness.

The Baptizer's Witness, 1:19-28

Each of the canonical Gospels focuses on John the Baptizer prior to introducing the ministry of Jesus. This means that for the early Christians the work of the Baptizer was seen as a strategic signal for the beginning of the Gospel (cf. Mark 1:1). In this Gospel the Baptizer almost appears to be an intruder into the prologue. Yet for the evangelist the Baptizer is no intruder. Everything in this Gospel treats the Baptizer as an ideal model of witness. There is no suggestion here of doubt concerning Jesus by the Baptizer (as in Matt 11:3). His disciples may have doubts (3:26), but not John.

1:19-23. Questioning of John. Without further introduction, John is set in a defense posture by the investigating committee of Jews (the term *Jews* in this Gospel is applied primarily to adversaries; see Freeman 1991). In successive questions he is asked whether he is MESSIAH (cf. 1QS 9.1), ELIJAH (cf. Mal 4:5), or the *prophet* (cf. Deut 18:15). When these questions fail to elicit the anticipated response, the next question posed is a demand for self-definition. As a former lawyer, I usually ponder both such questions and their answers. Many scholars have noted that these questions reflect the confusing nature of the messianic expectations of the time. But it is also important to draw attention to the fact that the first two of John's answers are similar to Peter's first two answers in his denial, namely, *I am not* (οὐκ εἰμί, v. 21). As such these answers are a direct contrast to the constant affirmation in this Gospel of Jesus as "I am" (ἐγώ εἰμι, see Borchert, *John*). The clarity of the final "no" gives rise to John's self-definition as a non-self-centered "voice" of witness. Using Isaiah's reference to the unevenness of Israel's natural geography, the Baptizer calls his hearers to prepare a new highway of reformation.

1:24-28. Criticism and John's response. Undeterred by the Baptizer's call for preparing a new way, the PHARISEES questioned his right to testify. To set this story in the context of the time of writing it is important to remember that the Pharisees were major opponents of Christian witnesses. Other parties such as the SADDUCEES are not mentioned because they had vanished with the destruction of Jerusalem. The Baptizer's response then can be viewed from two perspectives: the time of Jesus and the time of the early Christians. Moreover, the Baptizer's words are a proclamation of the presence of true authority in their midst and an assertion of his own personal unworthiness even to be a slave (one who touches feet) of this worthy one.

Three Cameos of Witness, 1:29-51

The next three witness stories form a unit that emphasizes seeing and finding the Messiah who is identified by a series of names such as the LAMB OF GOD, SON OF GOD, teacher or RABBI, CHRIST, King of Israel, and SON OF MAN. Each segment begins with the notation *the next day* indicating the interrelationship of these three pericopes.

1:29-34. Witness to the Lamb. The Passover in John is not merely a time designation. It is a theological organizing principle for the Gospel (see Borchert 1993) and it is introduced by the Baptizer/Witness when he identifies Jesus as *the Lamb of God who takes away the sin of the world* (v. 29). To his earlier statements of self-humiliation or unworthiness the Baptizer here added his admitted lack of full understanding by his confession that he did not know the Lamb until he gained insight through the descent of the Spirit upon Jesus.

Some scholars take pains to seek a harmonization with Luke's infancy accounts of the relationship between the mothers of Jesus and the Baptizer by suggesting that the latter's solitary life may explain the text (see e.g., Brown 1966, 65). But "knowing" in John is not mere acquaintance. Recognizing Jesus for who he is takes spiritual insight (Borchert, *John*). When spiritual insight comes then there follows both the ability to distinguish between mortal and spiritual realities (baptism with water vs. the Holy Spirit) and the willingness to confess that Jesus is the *Son of God* (v. 34; a better translation than "elect of God" as in some texts).

Readers of John should not interpret the descent of the Spirit upon Jesus as an adoptionistic view whereby Jesus becomes Son of God, but as a divine witness to the Baptizer concerning the existing divine nature of Jesus. Readers should also note that the confirming voice from heaven at the baptism in the Synoptics (e.g., Mark 1:11 and par.) is reserved in John for the personal confirmation of Jesus' Passover death (John 12:28-30). They should likewise note that nowhere in John is the Baptizer said to baptize Jesus. Such a reference would have run counter to the evangelist's goal of arguing against the views of the remaining disciples of the Baptizer who had not understood the Baptizer's mission of witnessing to Jesus (see John 3:25-30).

1:35-42. Witness to the first disciples. The next stage of witness involved the turning over of the Baptizer's disciples to Jesus by the announcement to them that Jesus was God's Lamb. ANDREW and an unnamed disciple (some suggest Philip) responded and followed this Lamb. Bultmann reminds us that upon seeing them, Jesus began his transforming invitation with a simple question: "What do you want?" (Bultmann 1971, 99–100). This dialogue, I would argue, is crucial because "Where are you remaining [abiding]?" (v. 33, author trans.) initiates one of the great themes of discipleship in John and the response *come and see* (v. 39) identifies another of those themes (Cullmann 1953).

What this Gospel teaches us concerning the making of disciples is that witness and invitation are far more important than argument and apologetics. That is the pattern with Andrew who found PETER. It was the same with PHILIP who found Nathaniel in the next pericope. The theme of finding is important in these two pericopes because the witnesses not only find the prospects but also say they have found the expected one. The irony in the stories is that while disciples may say they find Jesus, it is not Jesus who is lost or unknowing.

Readers will also note in this pericope several interpretive statements: Rabbi means teacher, Messiah means Christ, and Cephas means Peter (today, we would probably say "Rocky"). These and other notations in the Gospel indicate that the intended readers were probably unfamiliar with Jewish or Hebrew/Aramaic terminology and needed guidance from an interpreter.

1:43-51. Witness to Nathaniel. The theme of finding again forms the background of this story. But here Nathaniel is introduced with a protest or argument: *Can anything good come out of Nazareth?* The response of Philip is not argument but witness: *Come and see* (v. 46).

Jesus recognized in Nathaniel (v. 47) as he did in Simon (v. 42) that which was authentic, and he named him an Israelite without guile (a contrast to the pre-Jabbok Jacob, Gen 32:27-28). In answer to Nathaniel's puzzlement—*Where did you get to know me?* (v. 48)—Jesus identified him as a serious student seeking God's way (for studying under a FIG TREE, cf. Str-B 2:371).

When Nathaniel responded to Jesus with some exalted titles of messianic expectation (*Son of God* and *King of Israel* v. 40), Jesus virtually said that you are just at the beginning of understanding who I am. Instead of prediction, however, Jesus pointed back to the strategic dream of JACOB (Gen 28:10-17) and identified himself both as a new BETHEL ("house of God") and as *Son of Man* (a favorite self-designation of Jesus which involves a number of theological possibilities from the embodiment of humanity to an apocalyptic figure). With this self-witness of Jesus these cameos both reach their conclusion and provide an introduction to the actions of Jesus in the Cana cycle.

The Cana Cycle, 2:1–4:54

The five stories that form this cycle move the reader's mind from Galilee and Cana to Jerusalem, then with ever widening ripples of the darkness of the Judean context to the acceptance of Jesus by the rejects of SAMARIA, and then back to the more open setting of GALILEE (4:47, 54). The cycle also moves from the first (beginning) sign to the second sign, both of which take place in Cana and are the only signs in the Gospel designated by numerical order.

The First Cana Sign: Water to Wine, 2:1-12

The attentive reader should learn quickly that this wonderful little wedding story which is cited in some wedding services is fraught with a number of interpretive pitfalls that can easily distract from the main points of the pericope. Briefly reviewing some of these traps, the reader should note that *the third day* (v. 1) is not a sequential time designation following the three "next days" of chap. 1. Moreover, Jesus did not mistreat his mother when he called her *Woman* and added "What is it between me and you?" (v. 4, author trans.). And for those troubled by Jesus turning water into wine (οἶνος), it is a non sequitur to argue that such wine has no alcoholic content. It is also illegitimate to use this text as an authorization by Jesus for or against drinking alcohol today or as an authorization for or against a certain kind of wedding pattern.

2:1-4. A troubled wedding ceremony. In this story the mother of Jesus apparently had an important relationship with those in charge of the wedding party in which embarrassment was on the horizon either because of something such as inadequate planning or lack of funds to cover the long celebration (perhaps a week or longer, cf. Tob 8:19; 11:18). Typical of any Jewish mother in such a tense situation, the mother of Jesus began to use her parental relationship to solve the crisis of another relationship. It was at this initial stage that Jesus reminded her that he was not to be some magical solution or amulet to prevent disaster from striking, nor was she the one who directed his life. He was directed by a divine purpose or *hour* (v. 4, a theme of John).

2:5-10. Water to wine. His mother (she is not called Mary in this Gospel) quickly caught his meaning and redirected her attention from Jesus to the servants with the words *Do whatever he tells you* (v. 5). The message is clear: humans, including his mother, cannot use Jesus (or God) for their purposes. Instead, God uses persons to bring about the divine purpose.

The six large *stone water jars* used for purification in this story probably contained nine gallons each (Newman and Nida 1980, 59). A great deal of water! When the changed water was carried to the banquet master (who was responsible for keeping the guests happy), he was confused by the quality of the wine at this late point in the festivities. He *knew* nothing of the involvement of Jesus and could only judge that something strange had occurred.

2:11-12. The sign. While the banquet master viewed the results as strange, the evangelist reflected that the incident served as a *sign* (not "miracle" as in KJV) to the disciples. Indeed it was the beginning (or a key) to signs because in it Jesus *revealed his glory* (v. 11 a Johannine theme) and the disciples believed. In this strange act, the disciples saw something more than water and wine, and it led to commitment.

The pericope ends with a brief pause in the action as Jesus spends a few days with his family (mother and brothers—not cousins) and friends before the storm of the next pericope.

The Temple Cleansing, 2:13-25

Many persons with mindsets focused on chronology become sidetracked with comparisons here between John and the Synoptics and argue either for the priority of the Synoptics or of John, minimizing the theological concerns of both (cf. Brown 1966, 117–19). The alternative is to argue for two cleansings of the Temple, but such an approach is a construct of the interpreter, and no Gospel has two such cleansings. The problem is a presupposition that insists on turning the Gospels into pedantic prose/chronological reports and fails to allow a great literary figure like the Johannine evangelist to write the way he wishes. Instead, this story seems to serve the evangelist in a way similar to the literary or dramatic vehicle called *in medius res* ("in the thing's middle") where decisive moments are transported to the beginning of a story to involve readers immediately in the trauma of the story (see Borchert, *John*). Such does not minimize history and chronology but allows both to serve the purpose of theology and witness.

2:13-17. Jesus' confrontation in the Temple. The story opens with the strategic notation that it was PASSOVER time (see Borchert, *John*) *and Jesus went up to Jerusalem* (always "up" in the minds of the Jews). The time was the significant celebration of God's deliverance or salvation. Rather than being focused on God and worship, however, the Temple here is pictured as a combination of a noisy bank or exchange ("tables," the Greek term for banking) and a farmer's market. This misuse of God's house irritated Jesus, and he reacted with zeal by forcefully stopping all business transactions (not a "namby-pamby" Jesus).

2:18-22. The meaning of the act. The attack on the Temple business brought a demand from the Jews for an explanation or *sign* (a Johannine theme). Jesus' response was a three-day prediction concerning his death and resurrection. The Jewish reaction of forty-six years in building the Temple is significant because this story would then be dated at ca. 27 C.E., since the Temple rebuilding began ca. 20–19 B.C.E. (Josephus, *Ant* 15.11.1).

The entire conversation is important because it is packaged in a play on words for Temple. In vv. 14 and 15 ἱερόν means the "Temple complex" with its courts, whereas ναός (vv. 19, 20, 21) means "sanctuary" and is here used not of a building but of Jesus' body. This text also supplies an important post-resurrection perspective for this Gospel (v. 22), a fact that should be remembered by all readers of John (see Borchert 1988, 502–503).

2:23-25. The nature of believing. The evangelist adds a crucial postscript to this Temple confrontation by referring again to Passover and by reminding readers that Jesus does not accept everyone's believing because he knows human nature. The distinction about true and authentic believing is not a linguistic nicety of Greek, as some have suggested, but a matter of commitment to Jesus (cf. Carson 1981, 249–50n.37).

This postscript or summary statement is, like the entire Gospel, written from a holistic or post-resurrection view of the work of Jesus. The responses to him are reckoned from such a perspective. Thus, when one encounters the plural word *signs* (v. 23; cf. 3:2) before the *second sign* at 4:54 and when one meets a variety of believing responses so early in the Gospel, one should be alerted to the necessity of reading this Gospel from a holistic or post-resurrection point of view.

Nicodemus and Teaching on Salvation, 3:1-21

The pericope involving Nicodemus contains some of the best-known verses in the Bible. It is also the first of John's longer units that combine to form superb teaching vehicles.

3:1-4. The opening exchange. In the introduction Nicodemus is described as a significant Jewish Pharisee who was recognized as a ruler (ἄρχων) or member of the Jewish high council (SANHEDRIN), composed of the high priest and his seventy advisers (cf. 7:44-52). He came to Jesus by night (not merely a time notation in John but also a reflection of a spiritual state).

His polite assessment, based upon his supposed knowledge of Jesus' role with God, received a startling response. He was told in no uncertain terms that he needed to be born ἄνωθεν ("again" or "from above") or he would not experience the KINGDOM OF GOD. His initial knowledge vanished with his question: how could he as an adult re-enter the tiny womb of his mother? It was illogical.

3:5-10. Clarification and confusion. Jesus' response to Nicodemus' question of logic was to present two levels of discourse based on the word ἄνωθεν. Nicodemus understood the term to signify *again* (implying an earthly context), while Jesus meant that the newness or birth was *from above* (a spiritual context; cf. 3:31). *Spirit* and *flesh* are thus regarded as different realms.

Spiritual (new) birth here is identified with the combination symbol of water and the spirit. *Spirit* should not be capitalized in v. 5 as in NRSV because it usually results in the "and" being treated disjunctively (cf. Harris 1971, 3:1178, and Carson 1991, 191–96). This combination reflects the interconnection between the water of cleansing and newness of heart or new spirit in the OT (e.g., Ezek 36:24-27). Some scholars would argue that this verse reflects a baptismal concern and I have so argued, but the major focus of the text is not on an event or a sacrament/ordinance but upon spiritual life. Bultmann dismisses the baptismal question completely by attributing the words "water and" to a later ecclesiastical redactor (1971, 139). But such is unnecessary, if one understands the OT roots.

Flesh (σάρξ) in John refers to the realm of humanity with all its weakness and mortality. The word here is not per se antagonistic to God as is the expression "according to the flesh" in Paul, which implies that a person has made this existence the center of life (cf. Rom 8:4-8). Here the spirit (πνεῦμα) is used to designate the empowerment of weak humanity by the Spirit of God (v. 6).

The expression "spiritual birth" thus should not lead the believer to puzzlement (v. 7) because an enlightened person should perceive the two levels of discourse, illustrated here by the fact that spirit and wind are the same word (πνεῦμα). Yet a teacher like Nicodemus, if he could not perceive the two levels, would remain confused (vv. 9-10).

3:11-13. The witness of the Son of Man. Clarification of human confusion concerning divine realities is possible only through the in-breaking of Jesus as the divine witness who descended to earth from the heavenly realm. No one else than the SON OF MAN, according to John, has been able personally to bring such a first-hand account of heaven to the realm of earth. This Son of Man figure, however, is *not* to be identified as a nonhuman, nonsuffering gnostic alien messenger from outside our realm but as the divine one who truly became human and suffered the passover death for the world.

3:14-15. Jesus and the Mosaic serpent. The work of this Son of Man is thus identified as a healing agent, like the bronze serpent that Moses had fashioned and set on a pole in the wilderness epic of the poisonous snakes (Num 21:4-9). When the bronze snake was raised and the people looked upon it, healing came to the stricken. So believing in the *lifted up* Jesus (cf. also John 8:28 and 12:32, a symbol primarily of his death but not unrelated to his resurrection/exaltation) provides the agency for healing or salvation, here called eternal life.

The expression *eternal life* (ζωὴ αἰώνιος) is a particularly important Johannine theme that is used only once in the LXX (Dan 12:2) to render the rare OT idea of "life to the end of the age" or possibly "life of eternity." In John the qualitative nature of such life is stressed, although the long duration of such life is not to be dismissed.

3:16-18. Eternal life and judgment. These three verses contain one of the best known theological summations concerning salvation in the Bible. While many have memorized 3:16, however, I have consistently insisted that the three verses belong together in providing a proper theological balance (e.g., Borchert 1987, 104–105). The middle verse (17) states God's intention or purpose in sending his only son: not for destruction but for salvation. In v. 16 both the encompassing, self-giving love of God for the world is asserted and the necessary human response of believing is defined. Then in v. 18 the harsh reality of the situation is acknowledged: namely, believing provides the rescue whereas failure to believe means condemnation—not merely in the future but already in the present. This dark side of the gospel is an *integral part* of the message of salvation.

In sending his "one and only Son" (3:16; cf. Moody 1953), however, God made clear that his intention was not destruction. The God of the entire Bible is a loving and caring God whose concern is acceptance and salvation (v. 17). But there is pathos in the divine sacrifice that was illustrated beautifully on the human level in Abraham's near sacrifice of his "only" son Isaac (Gen 22:1-14). Yet the cost of human salvation was far more significant because the price was the life of God's only Son.

3:19-21. Actions, the measure of life. Love and hate, like believing and unbelieving, are action words in John. They define the nature of a person's life like the motifs of obedience and disobedience. Accordingly, as in the Book of James, this Gospel is concerned about the evidence of Christian life (v. 21). The one who acts authentically is associated with light, but the one who does evil hates light because it reveals the dark side of one's life.

The Baptizer and Salvation, 3:22-36

The Baptizer, as witness, here takes center stage for a final time. Scholars often debated the sequence of events in this Gospel, particularly since in the Synoptics the Baptizer was imprisoned before the Galilean ministry began and Jesus had in the Gospel of John performed a sign in Cana at 2:1-11. Unlike the Synoptics, however, Jesus in John moves with regularity between south and north, leading some like Bultmann to posit displacements in segments of the Gospel. Schnackenburg (1987, 1:380–96) places 3:31-36 before 3:13 to combine the salvation discussions, but I find most displacement theories including this one unconvincing because of the failure to recognize the evangelist's totalistic perspective of time.

3:22-24. Jesus and John's baptizing. The notations at v. 22 and 4:1-2 are the only places in the Gospels where Jesus and his disciples are said to be associated with baptism prior to the resurrection. Many questions therefore arise as a result of these statements, including the question of the significance of such baptism at this stage and its relation to the baptism of John.

The assertion that John had not yet been imprisoned in v. 24 indicates that the evangelist is clearly aware of chronological issues and is making a point. Perhaps the reference to the two baptisms of Jesus and John is here made in the context of John's forthcoming imprisonment because some of his disciples (vv. 25-30) had not understood the differences in the two baptisms indicated in 1:33. In any case, Jesus is said to have been baptizing in the territory of Judea and John is identified with Aenon meaning "a place of springs" near a town called Salim meaning "a place of peace." The identification of these places is not certain, although some possibilities include a northeast DEAD SEA site and a place near SHECHEM.

3:25-30. Concerns of the Baptizer's disciples. A dispute over water purification arose between the disciples of the Baptizer and a Jew (Loisy 1921, 71, speculated that the original may have been "and of Jesus"). The reason was consternation over the popularity of Jesus. Seeking consolation, John's disciples confronted their teacher with his diminishing status. True to his earlier stance, however, John reminded them of his former witness (cf. 1:19-28) and asserted that Jesus' calling was given from heaven (a typical Jewish circumlocution for God). Then he confirmed his witness by identifying Jesus symbolically with a bridegroom and his own role as the friend of the bridegroom, whose task was to listen for the bridegroom's expression of joy in the marriage (for marriage customs see Str-B 1:45–46 and 500–502).

Acts 19:1-5 (cf. 11:16) provides evidence that the Baptizer's disciples apparently were still active at a later time. It is doubtful, however, as some have suggested that a direct connection can be made between the Baptizer and the later Mandeans (cf. Borchert, John).

3:31-36. Summation concerning the Son. The evangelist then unites the stories of Nicodemus and of the Baptizer in a reaffirmation of two levels of discourse. Only the one from above can provide authentic witness concerning divine reality. The tragedy is the general lack of acceptance (*no one*, a literary hyperbole) of this witness from above (v. 32). But fortunately some do accept (cf. 1:11-12) and by their acceptance here have confirmed, sealed, or certified the authenticity of this divine witness.

While God has sent many on missions (including the Baptizer), the Son is God's model for mission (having the Spirit without limitation v. 34). Into his hand the Father "has given" (a timeless perfect) all things (v. 35). Such an assertion does not mean that the Father has abandoned the world but that in the love of God there is epitomized the unity of purpose between Son and Father. Accordingly, believing (πιστεύων εἰς) the Son provides the assurance of life eternal, whereas disobeying (ἀπειθῶν) the Son guarantees the horrifying reality of God's abiding (μένει) wrath (v. 36). There is thus no room for sitting on the fence concerning Jesus because of the present reality of judgment (cf. also 3:18).

The Samaritan Woman: An Unlikely Witness, 4:1-42

This pericope is one of the most fascinating in the Gospel. It not only challenges certain set prejudices of some religious people but it offers insights for ministry such as evangelism (Borchert 1976, 62).

4:1-6. Transition and introduction. This section may provide some rationale for the departure of Jesus to GALILEE via SAMARIA, namely: Pharisaic suspicion because of his popularity (4:1-3, cf. 4:44). But the use of ἔδει ("It was necessary" [author trans.], 4:4) in John may suggest once again that Jesus was moving according to the divine plan (cf. the use of *hour* in 2:4). This section certainly serves to correct any possible misconception that Jesus was a baptizer (only his disciples did so). In addition, it supplies a general description of the setting for the encounter. The meeting place was at the ancient town well near *Sychar* (a site not identified but probably on the slope of Mt. Ebal across from Mt. Gerizim) and near land owned by Jacob and Joseph (Gen 48:22). Sources of water were often places of meeting (cf. Gen 24:10-15; 29:1-12). The time was *about noon* (v. 6).

4:7-9. The meeting and the first exchange. The unusual circumstances are quickly defined: a Samaritan woman seeking to draw water during the heat of the day and a tired Jewish man asking her for a drink. It was the kind of setting that would cause heads to turn.

In fact, the encounter was unusual for the woman. Jesus did not fit the pattern and she sought an explanation to his request for a drink. SAMARITANS were rejected by Jews as half-breeds, a people with mixed origins (cf. Ezra 9–10), resulting from the settlement patterns of the Assyrians after the fall of SAMARIA in 722 B.C.E. (2 Kgs 17:6, 24). Their temple was later ruthlessly destroyed by the Jewish Hasmonean king John Hyrcanus (128 B.C.E.) and relations with the Jews continued to deteriorate until a major engagement in 52 C.E. (cf. Josephus, *Ant* 20.118–136). Although the temple was not rebuilt, Samaritans have continued even today to hold their Passover celebrations on that site.

While Jesus was resting, the disciples were engaged in a shopping tour. The quest was for food, acceptable food in Samaria. They probably settled on some bread and fruit (allowable items) after their search.

4:10-15. The second exchange: on water. Picking up the water themes from previous chapters that focused on baptism and water into wine, water now becomes the subject of the two levels of discourse. The woman was concerned with water and Jesus offered her *living water* (v. 10). Her mind, however, remained fixed on the earthly plane but her question in v. 12 (*Are you greater than our ancestor Jacob?*), although anticipating a negative response, provided Jesus the necessary opening to move the conversation back to the eternal realm.

The point is that water here temporarily quenches thirst, but the water of Jesus results in *eternal life* (v. 14). Yet the woman was stuck in the concerns of worldly tasks and asked for help to ease her burden (v. 15). She was in for a surprise.

4:16-19. The third exchange: the woman's life. The response of Jesus was to address her life and relationships. Although she tried to bypass the issue, Jesus spelled out her story in greater detail. The only way to avoid the issue was to change the subject to Jesus and focus on his perceived wisdom (*a prophet*), then ask him some questions. It was a sure way to discussion.

4:20-26. The fourth and fifth exchanges: ecclesiastical and theological issues. What better way is there to create religious tension than to ask which is the best place to worship, especially since the Jews had destroyed the Samaritan temple? Carson, however, apparently thinks such an explanation is too psychological (1991, 221–22). But I think there is more to the story than Carson sees because Jesus did not fall into the trap of a changed subject. Instead, he once again turned the discussion from the level of earthly institutionalism (v. 21) to the realm of the divine goal (*hour*) for worship and to God who is the subject of such worship (v. 23-24). Moreover, he reminded the woman that proper worship, like salvation, is a matter of divine revelation (*from the Jews*) and not a human construct concerning a God who is unknown (v. 22). It was a stinging rebuttal of Samaritan worship.

The woman's next response (v. 25) is intriguing because she has been moved in her concern to speak of the future era. Yet it is not entirely clear if she is using messianic talk to counter the rebuttal of Jesus by reminding him of a higher source for information (i.e., the Messiah) since she had already politely acknowledged him as *a prophet*. Or is this statement her honest anticipation? One thing seems clear: she had not yet connected Jesus with the Messiah or the coming of the messianic age.

That connection Jesus quickly made is an important self-identification. English readers of most translations may not recognize that the Greek at v. 26 is ἐγώ εἰμί (*I am*), the primary thematic self-designation of Jesus for his role as God's anointed one (Messiah) in this Gospel.

4:27-30. The disciples' interruption and the woman's witness. The return of the disciples signals the end to this part of the story. Their surprise which is indicated by their confused thinking (v. 27) only confirms the unusual nature of Jesus' conversation with the woman. Jewish men seldom talked to women in public. Yet here he was speaking with a Samaritan woman, and one not having the best reputation.

But the evangelist wanted readers to understand that the woman's concern had shifted from the mundane realm of the water pot (she left it) to the realm of messianic visitation. The Greek text says she sought out the "men" of the town and informed them she had met a man *who told me everything I have ever done* (v. 29). I wonder if *people* (v. 28) in the RSV and NRSV is the best translation? It seems that some of the implications for the initial interest which the men had in Jesus may be lost in these versions. But her question—*He cannot be the Messiah, can he?*—certainly had its desired effect because they left the city to meet Jesus (vv. 29-30).

While Craddock (1982, 36–37) makes a point that her believing was hardly ideal, I would insist that her story must be seen in the context of how John organized the Cana cycle through increasing stages of more adequate patterns of believing. Here she carries her understanding of Jesus to the point of telling others what she is thinking.

4:31-38. The disciples miss the point. While the woman had moved from the mundane level in her thinking to that of messianic expectation, the disciples were stuck in the physical realm of food (vv. 31, 33). So Jesus tried to raise the level of their thinking from the mere search for food to the quest for nourishment that comes by fulfilling their calling of doing the will of God. He modeled for them the concern that satisfied his hunger (v. 34) and he challenged them to accept their role of harvesting *fruit for eternal life* (v. 36).

The *four months* mentioned in the proverbial statement of v. 35 is generally regarded as the shortest time between the last of the seeding season and the start of harvest. Jesus was thus calling for his disciples to recognize that the messianic era of reaping had dawned. The evangelist, as Morris argues (1986, 150–51), undoubtedly considered this message also to be an urgent call for the church to evangelization, especially since he included the notation for the disciples that reaping is a crucial task even when the reaper had not been the sower (v. 38). Yet both sower and reaper can rejoice together at the harvest (v. 36) because the division of labor here does not exclude the sower from the returns of harvest as many ancient proverbs might suggest (cf. Beasley-Murray 1987, 64 and Brown 1966, 182–83), but both laborers are seen as partners with God in this important work of ingathering.

4:39-42. The Samaritans' belief and confession. The conclusion to this magnificent story indicates both the openness of Jesus to the rejects of the world (he stayed with them for *two days*, dispensing with proprietary living patterns of status and purity) and the fact that such rejects could make the most important confession in the Cana cycle. The Samaritan rejects came to discover Jesus through the witness of a rejected woman and then to confess him as *the Savior of the world* through direct encounter (v. 42). The motif of Savior in the OT is used of God (e.g., Isa 12:2 and 43:3, cf. Luke 1:47) and not elsewhere in the Gospels of the preresurrected Jesus, except in the prediction of the angel (Luke 2:12). It is a familiar Christian confession following the resurrection (e.g., Acts 5:31; Phil 3:20; 2 Pet 1:11). Since the designation was used by Jews of God and by others of Hellenistic deities and even the Roman emperor, the Christians' use of the term for Jesus was probably one of their identifying marks.

This confession signals for readers of the Gospel the great scope (i.e. *the world*) of the mission of Jesus and agrees with the intention of God in blessing Abraham (Gen 12:3). While Jesus told the Samaritan woman that *salvation is from the Jews* (v. 22, the historical womb of God's blessing), this village of rejects discovered that God really loves *the world* (3:16) and *all who receive* Jesus can become children of God (1:12).

4:43-45. Transition to Galilee. These verses serve as one of the typical "saddle" or "shoulder" texts between pericopes in a similar way that "saddles" unite mountain peaks in a mountain chain. The evangelist uses this saddle to move attention from Samaria to Galilee and to remind readers that Galileans are not unaware of what had been taking place in Jerusalem at the Passover.

The Second Cana Sign: Healing the Official's Son, 4:46-54

By focusing on Cana in Galilee for the second sign (only two are numbered by John) the first and second signs serve as an INCLUSIO (contrary to Beasley-Murray) whereby the stories in chaps. 2 to 4 form a unit. The first story identifies the role of signs in believing (2:11) and the second argues for a new level of believing that questions the very need for signs (4:48).

The second sign is in the form of a healing story with a twist. A person (a boy) is seriously ill and a request is made for healing (in this case by the father). Jesus then responds and the person is made well. But unlike the healing of the centurion's servant in the Synoptics (Matt 8:5-13; Luke 7:1-10), the royal official here (probably an administrator or soldier in the service of the Herodian dynasty or the Roman Caesar) begs for Jesus to come to his home. In the synoptic story the centurion begs for healing but he tells Jesus it is not necessary to come to his home. There Jesus greatly commends such gentile faith (e.g., Luke 7:9). Here, however, Jesus must tell the father to go because his son is living (v. 50). This word of Jesus then engenders believing in the father, even though he is unable to see the reality of the healing. But when the father confirms the healing, he again and for the first time his house are said to believe (v. 53).

This pericope thus is important because it may suggest a Johannine view of stages in believing. Certainly when people in John believe, they are usually called to the next stage of believing (Brown and Carson think they can distinguish such levels by variants in the Greek form of "believe," but such linguistic distinctions should not be pushed in John). This story also seems to foreshadow the kind of believing without seeing to which Thomas is called at the end of the book (20:29).

The Festival Cycle, 5:1–11:57

Many patterns of organization have been suggested for chaps. 4–12 of this Gospel. Bultmann has chaps. 7–10 as a unit; Brown has chaps. 5–10; Carson has two segments involving chaps. 5 to 7 and 8 to 10; and Sloyan has chaps. 5 to 7 and 8 to 12. Beasley-Murray, Morris, and Schnackenburg eschew finding a unit principle and settle for much smaller sections from chaps. 4 to 12. Bultmann and Schnackenburg are impressed by some topical and geographical variations in the stories and advocate theories of displacement to settle their uneasiness with these chapters.

Aileen Guilding proposed a theory that the Gospel had been organized as a festival lectionary (1960). While her overall theory found little acceptance, her focus on the Jewish festivals sparked renewed attention by some commentators on the festival context of several chapters. Brown in particular highlights the festivals in chaps. 5 to 10. I suggest (Borchert 1993) that chaps. 5–11 are a festival cycle with an introduction involving the overarching Jewish festival of Sabbath (chap. 5) and a cycle running from Passover (chap. 6) to Passover (chap. 11). The focus of this cycle is on the growing hostility that led inevitably to the Passover death of Jesus.

In this section the Jews are frequently mentioned. It is important for the reader to realize that the context in which this Gospel was written was one of persecution of Christians by the Jews, similar to that suggested by Rev 2:9 and 3:9. But such historical realities must not be made the basis for hatred of any group today.

The Sabbath and the Healing at Bethesda, 5:1-47

The festival cycle opens with a notation concerning a feast of the Jews (v. 1) but it remains undesignated except that it soon becomes evident that the issue focuses not on that unnamed feast per se, but on a SABBATH conflict. This conflict quickly touches many other underlying concerns like Jesus' authority, identity, and relationship to the Father as well as themes such as hour, judgment, life, and witness. As Sabbath became for the Jews a pervasive, haunting factor in their lives (witnessed by its importance in the Mishnah), so the Sabbath controversy was important for the evangelist. Yet it is used only in the festival cycle and serves the evangelist as one of the factors leading to the inevitable death of Jesus.

Some scholars are not satisfied here to discuss Sabbath alone and seek to posit possibilities for this feast such as PENTECOST, TABERNACLES, etc. I think the focus here falls on Sabbath, but it is intriguing to note that the evangelist speaks of "the great day of the Sabbath" (19:31, author trans.) in connection with Passover. The problem for most commentators is that they are concerned with filling in the chronology of John and fail to realize the cyclical pattern of John that focuses on Passover.

5:1-9a. The healing of the paralytic. When Jesus went up to Jerusalem he visited the pool area below the Temple where the helpless dregs of society existed in a pathetic state. While most people avoided the area, Jesus went out of his way to visit the place and found a paralytic who had experienced the wilderness of abandonment for thirty-eight years (equal to the time of Israel's wilderness experience from Kadesh to the brook Zared, cf. Deut 2:14).

The man's response to Jesus' question concerning healing revealed his hopelessness. His only expectation was a trust in a myth concerning angelic visitations to the pool (vv. 3b-4 are later additions to the text). His hopelessness was highlighted by the fact that he thought God was not interested in the most helpless. Jesus did not argue with his erroneous presupposition or his theological perspectives about receiving healing. Instead, Jesus merely told him to get up, pick up his bed roll, and be on his way. Healing was the immediate result.

5:9b-16. Sabbath controversy. The next statement that this day was the Sabbath strikes the reader with the force of a bomb. The opponents pounce on the helpless man who has just experienced the unbelievable joy of entering the promised land of a new existence. They focus not on his healing but on his breaking of their carefully articulated Sabbath rules, formulated to support the TORAH principle in Exod 31:12-14. The bewildered man can only defend himself by quoting his healer's words, even though he did not know who he was (vv. 12-13). The evangelist, however, reminds us that Jesus did not simply leave victims to the wolves but *found* them (v. 14, cf. 9:35; cf. also the theme at 1:41ff.).

The warning of Jesus not to *sin any more* is not to be understood here as a reference to a direct cause and effect relationship between sin and illness. That issue is treated at 9:2ff. Here Jesus is alluding to sin and judgment, which are treated in the next section (5:24). While Jesus had evidenced a self-giving-healing spirit, the healed paralytic (in contrast to the healed blind man of chap. 9) may have displayed a spirit of self-preservation in reporting to the Jews. In any case, the result was that Jewish sabbatarians turned their hostility on Jesus.

5:17-18. Jesus' first response: Sabbath. The response of Jesus confronted these sabbatarians and led to a new charge. Carson (1991, 247–48) notes that the rabbis would basically agree with Jesus that providence demands that God should continue to work on the Sabbath. The issue for the rabbis is that humans are not God. That, of course, is the question. So, if God continues to work positively on the Sabbath and Jesus' works are the works of God, then why are his works not legitimate? The battle was joined when Jesus called God his Father. The Jews recognized the equation immediately. Now the charge was not merely Sabbath breaking but also blasphemy.

5:19-24. Jesus' second response: relationship to the Father. The double ἀμήν (*truly*) signals again that two crucial statements are being made in this section. While the Jews have focused on equality, Jesus had highlighted his dependency on the Father. That dependency would be the means by which humans would come to understand the Son's role in the giving of life and the rendering of judgment. In that context there would come a recognition of the relationship between Father and Son. Moreover, obedience is not defined by Jesus in relation to rules such as observation of the Sabbath, but in terms of dynamic life patterns involving honoring the Son (v. 23) and believing (v. 24). Such obedient response is the basis for gaining the assurance of eternal life and avoiding judgment.

5:25-29. Jesus' third response: the two resurrections. In these responses the questioners have almost faded into the background as the evangelist's interest is directed only to the words of Jesus. The double ἀμήν once again announces a significant statement. The previous response identified a division between life and judgment. In this response the announcement is sounded concerning the coming of the decisive hour and the future eschatological separation between life and judgment represented in the idea of two resurrections.

Bultmann (1971, 258–61), who is committed to a perspective of realized eschatology, finds such futuristic suggestions to be "dangerous" editorial additions to the early message. But the perspective of the text is that both present and future are genuine realities. Yet these realities are intertwined because present hearing (obedience) leads to the resurrection of life. Moreover, the idea of resurrection from the evangelist's understanding was hardly a mere spiritual experience. For Jews the resurrection meant dealing with dead bodies and that is the reason why John has no hesitation in including a reference to persons emerging from tombs (v. 28). The point of the discussion is that Jesus' opponents and the evangelist's hearers are being clearly warned that relationship to Jesus has immense eschatological consequences.

5:30-47. Jesus' fourth response: witnesses to his authority. The statements in vv. 30 and 31 seem to presuppose challenges both to Jesus' authority in judgment and the validity of his God-directed claims. The responses on the part of Jesus are a forthright denial of his self-seeking and the articulation of a four-fold testimony supporting his claims.

The first witness he called was John the Baptizer. He chose John not because he wished to rely on human testimony but because such a testimony might help lead humans to salvation (v. 34). The second testimony is rated by Jesus at a higher level than the first, namely, his works. These works he was doing in accordance with the Father's will and the Jews could hardly deny their existence (v. 36).

The third witness he called was the Father. What does the evangelist mean by such a statement? It was a type of shorthand. Was it some voice from heaven (e.g., 12:28) or a sense of divine presence (e.g., 11:41-42)? Greater clarity would help. But the difficulty of using the Father as a witness for them was immediately apparent to Jesus and he highlighted it. They could not accept such a witness because, unlike the prophets, they had not heard God speak. Moreover, unlike Isaiah (Isa 6:1) or Jacob at Jabbok (Gen 32:30), they had no vision of him or sense of his form. But perhaps most devastating of all was that they who claimed to uphold the Torah did not have God's *word* inwardly resident in them (vv. 37-38).

The mention of God's word provides the fourth and final witness: *the scriptures*, to which they by profession had committed themselves (v. 39). Here Jesus forthrightly condemns them because of their refusal to accept him (v. 40) and recognize the testimony of the texts they supposedly defended. Human religious confirmation of his role, however, was not required by Jesus (v. 41) because humans are confused in their offering of praise (vv. 43-44). So Jesus asserted that the religious leaders should clearly realize that he did not need to play the roles of both accuser and judge concerning them. Their accuser would be none other than Moses on whom they said they relied but failed in fact to believe (vv. 45-46).

Passover and the Exodus Motif, 6:1-71

The crossing of the sea (v. 1) and the coming of people out to a lonely mountainside (v. 3) formed a picture-perfect setting for reflecting about Jesus and the EXODUS. Accordingly, it should be no surprise that in this chapter the linkage of a miraculous feeding and a control of the sea is compared to the experience of MOSES in the wilderness.

It should also be no surprise that in such a context the evangelist announces it was PASSOVER time (v. 4). Even within the Passover Haggada today, in the introduction before the pronouncing of the "three words" and the "Halelya," two of the great "benefits" that are rehearsed are the control of the sea and the feeding of manna (see e.g., Fisch 1965). Likewise, when detailing God's great mercies both the Psalmist (Ps 78:13-30) and Paul (1 Cor 10:1-4) link these two events of water control and food supply as crucial for remembrance.

It is most likely, therefore, that as the early Christians told the stories of their Lord, bread and water miracles from his earthly life were also recited. Thus, when Mark first set the gospel in written form, it was quite natural that these two events would be narrated in a related context (Mark 6:30-52). Another highly significant event for Mark was the decisive point of discipleship in which Mark includes a confession by Peter (Mark 8:27-30). John brings all of these elements together in his development of this strategic Passover chapter and hints at the fact that the death of Jesus (flesh and blood) will be a key to eternal life (v. 54).

6:1-13. The distribution of food. In the unfolding of the text, following the crossing of the Sea of Tiberias (the Roman designation usually called Galilee, but also Gennesaret in Luke 5:1 [from the Heb. *kinnereth*], because it had the outline of a lyre), Jesus is pictured as sitting on a mountain side (v. 3), reminiscent of an ancient dispenser of divine wisdom. The linkage with the Mosaic experience at SINAI may be in mind (cf. Matt 5:1).

The feeding is introduced by Jesus questioning PHILIP (the company logician) concerning resources. Philip's answer was that the crowd was so large (5,000) that even 200 days' pay would have been insufficient to feed them. ANDREW (the company helper) found a small amount of food among the crowd (five barley loaves and two dried fish), but for Jesus it was sufficient (total, seven; cf. also the seven loaves and a "few" fish in feeding 4,000 of Mark 8:6-7). Thus, when Jesus acted, everyone had enough (v. 11).

Indeed, there was so much remaining that the disciples (Brown 1966, 233, wonders whether they are synonymous with the Twelve) collected twelve baskets of bread. The number twelve is symbolic for the people of God. This story was of such significance to early Christians that it is the only miracle per se reported in all four Gospels. The sea miracles vary, but their impact is the same. For John the bread miracle served as an important sign and became the basis for the following discourse.

6:14-15. The people's messianic expectations. In the minds of the Jews awaiting the MESSIAH, this act of feeding spurred the people's messianic hopes. Their immediate reaction was that this Jesus had to be the long expected *prophet* like Moses (Deut 18:15; cf. John 1:21). The additional reference to the one *who is to come* (v. 15) was, as Mowinckle has argued, also viewed as a messianic designation (1954, 213–41, 295–321, 385–93).

The expectations of the people were ignited to such an extent that they were ready to give Jesus the throne of DAVID and force the realization of their hopes (v. 15; cf. Jer 23:5; Ezek 34:23). But Jesus instead took to the mountains again because their understanding and timing were both skewed.

6:16-21. Walking on water. This pericope begins with a note that night and darkness fell. Such designations in John are usually theologically instructive (cf. 3:2 and 13:30), especially here since a storm arose and the disciples were caught in the middle of the sea (which was between five and seven mi. wide; cf. Josephus, *BJ* 3.10.7; 506). Despite the conditions, Jesus calmly walked on the sea. The Exodus symbolism is hard to miss.

No doubt the evangelist regarded this appearance as a Christophany (like the appearances of God in the OT) for here are present both the familiar sense of fear and the calming words, *Do not be afraid* (v. 20). While the expression "I am" (ἐγώ εἰμι) may be interpreted as a simple self-identification (*It is I*, as in many translations), the reader familiar with John cannot help but connect these words with God's revelation to Moses (Exod 3:14).

The joy of the disciples then replaced their fear as Jesus entered the boat. Moreover, their goal of reaching a safe harbor was immediately realized. Jesus thus is like the God of the OT who brings his people from a stormy sea to a safe haven (Ps 107:23-32).

6:22-25. The people sought Jesus. While the geography is a little vague, these stories suggest that the feeding may have taken place on the east side of the sea where there are hills (less likely is the traditional northeast side). The boats came from the west side (TIBERIAS) and the people took their boats from *near* the feeding place and found Jesus on the northwest side (CAPERNAUM). The people's query of Jesus concerning his coming to that place set the stage for a discourse on the sign of bread.

6:26-34. The sign of bread. The familiar Johannine double ἀμήν (*truly*) formula once again introduces a key perspective. The people were following because of the physical food, not because they recognized the *signs* (v. 26). The KJV incorrectly reads "miracles" here. The nature of the sign is to point beyond miracle to the one who nourishes to eternal life. When one understands such a sign, one should perceive the relationship of the acts of the *Son of Man* (Jesus' self-definition, cf. 1:51) to the works of the Father.

The response of unperceiving Jews, however, was tragic. Their request for a sign that would lead them to believe thus inspired yet another double-level Johannine insight framed, as Borgen (1965) has argued, like a midrashic interpretation of Exod 16:15, etc. They missed the point because their desire was for a return to a physical preservation model like that of manna in the wilderness (v. 31). But the bread was not merely a gift from a deliverer like MOSES; it had been given by God. The real gift of God's bread was not physical; it was life *come down from heaven* (v. 33). The misunderstanding inherent in their subsequent request for continual supplying of such bread (6:34) introduces an "I am" discourse.

6:35-40. Jesus' proclamation: the bread of life. The self-identification of Jesus as *I am the bread of life* (v. 35) is made here, but the motif of eating is expanded to include drinking (important for the next section). This affirmation merges into a discussion of separation and preservation. The opponents of Jesus are judged as unbelieving. But those whom the Father gives to Jesus will not be castaways (vv. 37, 39). Instead, they will have eternal life and experience resurrection in *the last day* (vv. 39-40). This concept of the resurrection on the last day is defuturized in Bultmann (1971, 233) but would have been perfectly understandable to a futuristically oriented Jewish Christian audience of the first century.

6:41-48. Reaction and defense. The reaction of the Jews is by John defined in Exodus terminology: "murmured" (NRSV, *complained*). The text implies they understood that he was claiming divine descent and mission. As a result they launched into a discussion of his family tree, which they said they knew (v. 42). The irony is obvious. Jesus responded in terms of his relationship to the Father and the eschatological hope of those drawn to him by God (v. 44). His response was based on the proclamation of the prophets that in the messianic era God's people would be instructed by God (cf. Isa 54:13; Jer 31:33-34).

Employing another double ἀμήν saying, he then identified their concern for physical bread and their earthly messianic hope with the hopeless state of those who perished in the wilderness even though they ate physical MANNA. But those who are nourished by *the living bread*, Jesus said, would have eternal life (v. 51). The problem for them was that such bread was his *flesh*.

6:52-59. Identification of flesh and blood. This identification of bread and flesh was too much for the Jews to swallow. The response of Jesus was another double ἀμήν saying that linked the inward acceptance (eating) of his sacrificial death (flesh and blood) to the reception of eternal life and resurrection on the last day (v. 54). The Jews, however, were stuck in the physical realm of reality with their fathers who ate manna and died (v. 58).

This section has been the focus of much theological discussion concerning the relationship to the LORD'S SUPPER. Brown (1966, 287–93), for example, sees it as the Johannine "institution," whereas Carson (1991, 295) thinks that the use of "flesh" rather than "body" argues against such a primary eucharistic sense. It is impossible in this space to detail the arguments on this matter but our attention should be kept on the major focus of the passage: namely, the familiar Johannine theme of receiving Jesus (cf. 1:12). That the evangelist probably saw in the supper a symbolic representation of the reception of Jesus is quite likely. But it is a question of what gives birth to what in John. This Gospel is certainly very symbolic. The issue is: Is sacrament a primary focus here?

6:60-71. Reaction of the disciples. The reader of John may be confused here by the designation *disciples* in this passage because disciples are said here to be troubled by Jesus' saying and, like the wilderness people, they murmured (v. 60). Indeed, Jesus said, they did not believe (v. 64) and in fact they departed and no longer walked with him (v. 66).

The insertion of the distinction between flesh and spirit in this context (v.63) is a reminder that the evangelist frequently employs words with two levels of meaning as he did when he used the term *believe* at 2:23-24. The confession of Peter and the mention of Judas is here a clear indication of this double level in discipleship.

The mention of Jesus choosing Judas Iscariot (vv. 70-71) must not be made the basis for a theology of reprobation (election or determinism to destruction). The text does not say that Jesus determined Judas to be a devil-man. The designation Iscariot is not totally clear. He may have been a man (*ish*; or the son of a man) from Kerioth or one of the "sicarii" (revolutionary knife men). But John will not let the reader forget the dark side of this disciple in contrast to the self-sacrifice of Jesus.

Tabernacles and the Motif of Deliverance, 7:1–9:41

This section of the Festival cycle involves the popular (Josephus *Ant* 8.100) post-harvest Feast of Booths or Tabernacles. If the Messiah were to come, it would be expected that he would put in an appearance in the month of Tishri, the most celebrated month of the Jewish year. The month started with the joyous celebration of the New Year on the first and second. It was followed on the tenth by the most sacred day of *Yom Kippur* (Day of Atonement) and it was climaxed with the joyous celebration of Tabernacles on the fifteenth to the twenty-second when the faithful devotees left their houses and dwelt in booths as a reminder of God's preservation and deliverance.

This section, which highlights controversy, begins with the issue of timing concerning the adoption of Jesus' messianic role (7:1-13) and the reaction he engenders (7:14-36). The focus then moves to Jesus as water (7:37-39) and returns to the question of Jesus' messiahship (7:40-52). It moves next to Jesus as light (8:12) and returns again to his messiahship in terms of the question of his origin and purpose (8:13-29). Then it moves to the question of freedom (8:31-32) and leads to an outright confrontation on lineage and bondage (8:33-59). The evangelist then illustrates the importance of both light and deliverance in the story of the blind man (9:1-34) and concludes with Jesus' verdict about the parties in the dispute (9:35-41).

The pericope of the adulterous woman (7:53–8:11) is a fascinating story that wound up as a somewhat disconnected segment in the framework of the message of Tabernacles, and will be treated in an appendix at the end of the commentary. This style of treatment is no reflection on the worthiness of the story or its legitimacy to be regarded as a canonical pericope.

<u>7:1-13. The brothers' question of messiahship at Tabernacles.</u> The mood of this section is set by the opening notation of hostility. The issue is focused by the demand of the brothers (Mary's other children, not cousins) that Jesus adopt their time frame for his messianic revelation at Tabernacles (v. 3). The dialogue that follows is somewhat reminiscent of Jesus' rejection of his mother's timing (2:4).

Many readers become confused by the fact that Jesus said he was not going up to the feast (v. 8) when he did so almost immediately (v. 10). Like many other issues in John, the reader needs to recognize the two levels of discourse that are taking place. Jesus' timing is PASSOVER not TABERNACLES, and his role is not that of conquering hero but of dying Messiah. It was not Jesus' time for public show (v. 4) but for personal ministry (vv. 4, 10). Expectation concerning Jesus was obviously very high at this feast (vv. 11-12) although fear muted some open expression of it (v. 13). That Jesus could not help but engender public reaction (v. 26), however, does not change the fact that for John the actual public work of Jesus is his hour of glorification (12:31-32; 17:1).

<u>7:14-36. Reactions to Jesus' messiahship.</u> The appearance of Jesus in a teaching mode raised a question immediately. The *am ha'erez* (the "people of the land," who worked with their hands like carpenters and fishermen) were not trained in the technicalities of religious dialogue. Their insecurity in religious discussion would be obvious. Yet to the surprise of his hearers, Jesus (who was one of them) assumed the authority to teach (v. 15). Indeed, he claimed divine authority (v. 16) and criticized his opponents (the Jewish leadership) for not obeying Moses.

Their intention was to kill him (v. 19) because he healed on the Sabbath (v. 23; cf. 5:18). Of course, the argument could have turned on the rabbinic interpretations of the priority of Sabbath laws (Exod 31:12-17) over murder laws (Exod 20:13) but here they denied any intention to kill him. Indeed, they categorized him as a misguided, demon-possessed lunatic (v. 20). But Jesus did not accept their designation and attacked their motives and their Sabbath law logic by reference to circumcision (v. 22). The point was to critique their lack of tenderness for hurting people (vv. 23-24).

This open confrontation on religious logic with the religious elite raised for the people the issue of his role and their theories of an unknown origin for the Messiah. The questions of *where?* (origin, v. 27) and *where?* (goal, v. 35) are an undercurrent in this Gospel and once again John employs an ironic double-level meaning for the word *know* (v. 27) to focus attention on who Jesus is.

The leadership's answer to this threat was an attempt to silence this religious interloper by dispatching their guard to seize him (7:32).

7:37-39. Jesus and the water ritual. When the Jewish people moved in large numbers from the rural areas to the cities, the festive experiences of harvest were not as significant. But following long dry summers, cisterns were usually depleted and urbanites prayed for the coming of rain. The PHARISEES (mostly urbanites) promoted the addition of rain prayers in the celebration of Tabernacles (cf. Zech 14:16-19; *m. Sukk.* 5:1). The SADDUCEES generally had resisted this insertion as revisionist and conflict over this matter came to a head in the time of the Sadducean high priest and king, Alexander Janaeus, who poured the water offering at his feet. A rapprochement with the Pharisees was gained by his successors and the water ritual was retained. While the festival was eight days in length (including a Sabbath climax) the water ritual was conducted for seven days. On the seventh day the priests brought water seven times from the pool of Siloam. It may be that the evangelist means this seventh day by his designation *the last day* (v. 37) or perhaps he means the solemn Sabbath that followed.

The evangelist here draws together several themes in reflecting on Jesus at this event. Water in the OT is linked with the people's expectation of salvation (Isa 12:3; 55:1). Also, as life-sustaining water flowed from the rock (Exod 17:6), so life-giving water comes from Jesus (v. 38; cf. the visions of the future in Ezek 47:9-12 and Rev 22:1-2). Moreover, the evangelist notes that such a life-enhancing experience is to be connected with the coming of the Spirit following the glorification of Jesus (v. 39).

There is a minor textual variation in vv. 37 and 38. The NRSV, which links believing and drinking and forms a parallelism, is to be preferred over the earlier RSV rendering.

7:40-52. Evaluations of Jesus' messiahship. Division of opinions followed. Some affirmed him and answered positively the questions directed at John the Baptist (cf. 1:20-21). Some were frustrated by their theories concerning his origin.

Others wanted to be rid of him. The guard returned empty-handed, stunned by the power of his words (v. 46). But the authorities and Pharisees remained undeterred. Their arrogant question (Had any of them believed? v. 48) was for the evangelist a double-edged irony when compared to their opinion of the stupid *crowd* (v. 49). Even the logic of fairness proposed by *Nicodemus* (v. 50-51) was rebuffed by their intolerance and name-calling. The issue for them was closed.

8:12. The light. The joyousness of the ritual of lights, which was accompanied by singing and dancing and which permeated the seven festival days of Tabernacles, was a reminder of God's leading of the people by fire in the darkness of the wilderness (Exod 13:21). Here the *I am* saying affirms the role of Jesus in lighting the darkness for his followers.

8:13-29. Return to the conflict: A legal argument. The rejection of Jesus' messiahship is again raised by a Pharisaic charge of bearing witness to himself, a charge Jesus preemptively argued in 5:30-47. In this passage, however, the issue of "whence" and "whither" (origin and goal; v. 14) are brought to center stage in the context of truth or authenticity.

The scene here is reminiscent of a legal argument. The opponents have rendered their verdict by rejecting Jesus (v. 15). His rebuttal was that he was not yet at the judgment stage (cf. v. 26), but if he were to render a verdict, it would be true because of his divine connection (v. 16). Instead, he was at the witness stage and while he provided the required two witnesses (cf. Deut 19:15) their problem was that they did not know the Father who functioned as his confirming witness. Moreover, their failure to regard him made it impossible for them to know the Father (v. 19). This testimony is certainly a tight one, but it is not necessarily convincing to the unconvinced.

On the other hand, the opponents were unable to carry out the sentence attached to their verdict because of a fundamental Johannine thesis: the *hour had not yet come* (v. 20). So the conflict continued.

There is no question, however, that Jesus understood that the opponents' desire for his death would be fulfilled. But it was not to be interpreted as their victory. Rather it was a divinely directed departure (v. 21) or "lifting up" (v. 28) that would bring a verdict on them: namely, they would die in their sin (v. 21). Yet Jesus did supply a verdict. They would not be able to join him in his realm above (vv. 22-23) because the basis for entrance to that realm was believing that he was the *I am* (v. 24; cf. Exod 3:14).

The dialogue that follows confirms the fact that Jesus and the Jews were operating on different wave lengths (v. 27). While the text of v. 25b is not entirely clear, the remaining verses indicate that recognition and condemnation would follow upon his death.

8:30-59. The conflict continues: truth and freedom. The notation in the midst of the conflict that many believed (v. 30) is followed by a statement that to those who believed Jesus issued his famous logion concerning truth and freedom (v. 32).

The result was an immediate defensive response on the part of those addressed, involving both an assertion of kinship with father Abraham and a denial of any bondage experience (v. 33). These verses thus provide an illustration or commentary on 2:23-25 and the fallacy of much human believing.

Because the logion in v. 32 is frequently removed from its context and used as a justification for academic education, it is well to remember that knowing truth here is not related to academic information. The point is knowing Jesus. Moreover, freedom is not mere liberty; it is freedom in Christ and freedom from sin (vv. 34-36).

These "believers" are thus not to be categorized as legitimate disciples because their reliance for acceptance was built upon human descent patterns (father Abraham, vv. 37, 39) and their style of life was linked to those who would kill Jesus (vv. 37, 40). True believing in Jesus and true children of God would reflect the attitude of loving Jesus (v. 42). Instead, Jesus judged them harshly as *liars* and as children of the *devil* (v. 44). Accordingly, Jesus asked them to respond to two underlying questions: (1) Who can bring a verdict of sin upon Jesus? and (2) Why did they not in fact believe (v. 46)?

Their reaction was predictable. Like the priests and Pharisees who dismissed Nicodemus with a name (cf. 7:52), these "believers" categorized Jesus as a despised Samaritan (cf. 4:9) and as one possessed of a demon (v. 48). This interaction between Jesus and the so-called "believers" raised the issue of honor and shame (v. 49) in that society (for discussion, see e.g. Malina 1981, 25–50), a reality that runs extremely deep, particularly in many non-Western cultures.

The response of Jesus was another double ἀμήν (*truly*) saying, this one concerning obedience and death (v. 51). The promise of no death was for his opponents the proof of his authenticity. Even Abraham died. Who did he think he was? *Greater than . . . Abraham* (v. 53)? This question, like the woman's concerning Jacob (4:12), was seen by the evangelist to provide the coup de grace for his argument. Abraham acknowledged the priority of Jesus and not the reverse (vv. 56-58). The second double ἀμήν saying here (v. 58) is fascinating because it explodes our natural reasoning concerning time and reminds the reader that Jesus is the *I am*.

Such a response was too much for his opponents and although they would have stoned him, he departed and left them with their frustrations (v. 59).

9:1-12. Healing a blind man. The Tabernacles motif is brought to a climax with the story of the blind man. The connection with Tabernacles and chap. 8 is assured by the repetition of the *I am* saying concerning the light of the world (v. 5; cf. 8:12). The story is thus to be regarded as an illustrative outworking of earlier issues.

The question of theodicy (God's goodness and power in the face of evil) serves as the starting point of the story. It was raised by the disciples who sought a simplistic rationale to the problem OF BLINDNESS (v. 2). They were not unlike the pessimistic friends of JOB and they certainly had hardly digested the message of Ezek 18:20 concerning blame and the role of parents. But here was a man born blind.

Who was to blame for this tragedy? Rather than agreeing to their easy solutions of blame, Jesus shifted the discussion to the grace of God in the face of human need (v. 3) and called attention to the shortness of his mission by reference to the theme of light and darkness (vv. 4-5).

Then he put mud cakes on the man's eyes and sent him to wash at Siloam ("sent," vv. 6-7). Following his healing the neighbors were filled with questions (vv. 8-9) and he was called upon to answer their queries concerning this strange happening (vv. 10-12).

9:13-34. A predetermined controversy. Verses 13 and 14 serve as early warning signals in the story that trouble was on the horizon. Bringing the man to the Pharisees had all the earmarks of a kangaroo court and the notation that it was Sabbath is like a prediction of doom (cf. 5:9b).

The interrogation began with a simple question about what happened (v. 15). It quickly led to a division of opinion concerning the relative weights to be attached to Sabbath and healing in the evaluation process (v. 16). So the man was asked for his judgment about the healer. His response that the healer was a *prophet* would seem on the surface to be a minimally safe assessment (v. 17). But for judges who have predetermined the case and who are unimpressed by a caring, merciful spirit, such logic carries little or no casuistic force in an argument.

Instead, the interrogation sought for a reason to debunk the impressive miracle. First, they questioned the authenticity of the man's former blindness. So they called for a confirmation from his parents about his blindness and for an explanation of his transformed state (vv. 18-19). The parents were of little help in the debunking process. Moreover, in seeking to avoid excommunication from the synagogue the parents refused to become involved and referred the interrogators back to their son as fully capable of answering for himself (vv. 20-21).

Next the interrogators tried to set the parameters for the man's answers so they could accept his present state and reject the healer (v. 24). But the man refused their theological gymnastics by reminding them of the legitimacy of the miracle (v. 25). So they began their questioning again. The exasperated man then questioned both their motives (v. 27) and their evaluation (vv. 30-32) concerning the healer. His logic proved impeccable because healing and a good God belong to the same side of reality and are not opposites as the interrogators were trying to make him believe.

These teachers (who relied on Moses and did not know who sent this healer) refused to accept correct teaching, called the man a name (sinner), dismissed his testimony, and excommunicated him (v. 34). The relationship of this story to the early Christians who were designated heretics (*minim*) and excluded from the synagogue would hardly be missed by the early readers.

9:35-41. The verdict of Jesus. The verdict of the interrogators and their dismissal, however, was followed by the searching Jesus who *found* (v. 35, cf. 1:43 and the ironic uses in 1:41, 45) the abandoned man and began a brief, alternative interrogation geared to his acceptance.

The man's witness to the Pharisees had been firm although he had not seen his healer. Now he had the chance to behold the *Son of Man* and confirm his belief (vv. 35-37). Forged in the context of deliverance and defense and faced with his God-sent healer, his confession became a firm *I believe* and his worship of Jesus (v. 38) has stood as unique in this Gospel's pre-resurrection stories of Jesus. He is a model of faith and commitment to the fulfillment of the messianic hope (cf. 4:23-26).

Accordingly, Jesus as judge judged the parties. In his coming as light to the world the blind were enabled to see and those who thought they saw became blind (vv. 39-41). The verdict was clear.

Dedication and the Motif of the Shepherd, 10:1-42

The Gospel is filled with many symbolic ideas, ironic statements, and double-level presentations. But in this long symbolic or parabolic chapter the evangelist for the first time identifies his treatment as figurative (παροιμία; cf. 16:25, 29). This mashal or extended parable provides several insightful portrayals of who Jesus is and his relationship to his followers. Moreover, he is symbolically contrasted with his opponents and the pseudoservants of God.

The chapter begins with a portrayal of Jesus as shepherd (vv. 1-6) which merges into a more involved picture of him as both door or gate and shepherd (vv. 7-18) which then leads to a familiar theme of division (vv. 19-21). In the heart of the discussion the note is sounded that it was the feast of Dedication at the Temple (vv. 22-23) that celebrated the cleansing of the defamed altar and Temple in the time of Judas Maccabeus, who himself became a messianic symbol. The discussion, accordingly, moves to the messianic role of Jesus as shepherd and his relationships with both believers and unbelievers as well as with the Father (vv. 24-30). It concludes with the attempt to stone Jesus which results in his departure across the Jordan (vv. 31-42).

10:1-6. Jesus the shepherd. The double ἀμήν introduces a new section and a new series of *I am* sayings focusing on the role of Jesus as the Messiah (cf. 10:24). The first picture is of Jesus as a shepherd leader, who fits the prophetic picture of the coming messianic shepherd-king like DAVID (Jer 23:5-6; Ezek 34:23-24). To watch shepherds leading (cf. vv. 3-4) sheep in Israel today with a song or tune even in urban areas points to the intimacy of relationship between shepherd and sheep that is often missed in the hard driving patterns of much contemporary life. Thieves and strangers cannot participate in such a close relationship and the evangelist points his judgmental finger at the opponents of Jesus with the words *they did not understand what he was saying to them* (v. 6).

10:7-18. Jesus as door and shepherd. The second double ἀμήν saying adjusts the focus slightly to describe Jesus as *the gate* or door of the sheepfold (v. 7). Many sheepfolds were built of rock walls but without gates. So once the sheep were safely inside, the shepherd took his position at the entrance serving as the guard.

The shepherd who is thus symbolized as the means of safety and security for the sheep is contrasted to thieves (v. 10) and wolves (v. 12) who plunder, devour, and devastate the flock. The implication would have been very clear in that day because the prophets likened the leaders of God's people to such destructive portraits (cf. Jer 23:12; Ezek 34:3-5).

The shepherd is likewise contrasted to the hired servant (v. 12) who received pay for work but was hardly invested in the sheep. Thus, when danger threatened, the paid worker was more concerned with payment and self-survival than with the security of the sheep (v. 13; cf. Ezek 34:8b-10).

The good shepherd, however, was invested so much in the sheep that he was ready to die for the sheep (vv. 11, 17). The picture of the dying shepherd is clearly to be associated in John with the dying *Lamb of God that takes away the sin of the world* (1:29), an image that coordinates with the fact that the goal of the death and resurrection for Jesus reaches beyond the Jews to the whole world (v. 16). The death and resurrection are here clearly implied (vv. 17-18) and the death is to be understood as Jesus' authoritative self-sacrifice and certainly not in terms of the power of world authorities over Jesus. The meaning is one of divine control and timing even in death.

10:19-21. Division. By now the reader is familiar with the theme that Jesus caused division (cf. 1:11-12). His words brought hostile reactions so that he was identified by many as demon possessed (v. 20; cf. 7:20; 8:48; etc.). Yet his works often caused others to evaluate him differently (10:21, 32-33; cf. 2:23; 4:48; 7:31; 9:32-33; etc.).

10:22-30. Dedication and the messianic question. On the twenty-fifth of Kislev 164 B.C.E., a new festival of Hanukkah (Dedication) was inaugurated into the Jewish year that celebrated the rededication of the Temple after the Syrians of Antiochus IV (Epiphanes) desecrated the Temple by slaughtering a pig on the altar and by setting up a statue of Zeus in the Temple. The defeat of the Syrians, the liberation of Jerusalem, and the cleansing of the Temple under the Maccabees electrified Jewish messianic dreams. These dreams of a messianic state bubbled into sporadic uprisings until they were crushed by the Roman destruction of Jerusalem in 70 C.E. and finally put to rest by the defeat of Bar-Kochba (135 C.E.).

These dreams were undoubtedly behind the question of the Jews concerning the possibility of Jesus being the *Messiah* (Christ, v. 24). But a shroud may be cast over the question by the fact that John announced it was Dedication and *it was winter* (v. 23). Obviously, Dedication came in winter time, but time designations in John often have theological import. Could it be that John was again thinking on two levels? In any case, their request that he should speak *plainly* (v. 24) is set in contrast to the "figurative" nature (10:6) of most of this chapter.

The response of Jesus to their request has the earmarks of frustration with their unwillingness to accept his words and to recognize the divine origin of his works (v. 25). The issue was not one of having information concerning Jesus but of being his sheep and believing the reality to which his words and works witnessed (vv. 26-27).

The reintroduction of the shepherd motif serves an important function in this argument. After operating on the thesis that his sheep knew him and heeded his voice (cf. 10:3-4, 14), Jesus moved their thinking from the level of safety in the sheepfold to safety and security in terms of eternal life of the believer and security from the powers of destruction (v. 28). This verse has often been used as a proof text in discussions of the security of the believer and sometimes linked with theories of predestination (here *given me* v. 29) to advocate concepts like "eternal security." It is important to recognize both that the term "eternal security" is a multi-meaning construct that does not appear in the Bible, and that any theory of security must take seriously the warnings of God and the idea of "following" the shepherd (v. 27—see Borchert 1987).

For the believer, life and security are gifts of God which are vested in the unified leading of the shepherd and the Father (vv. 27-30).

10:31-42. The hostile reaction. The identification of Jesus with the Father (10:30) once again raised the ire of the Jews (v. 31; cf. 5:18). Stoning for them was the answer (cf. 8:59). The Romans were in charge of capital punishment cases, but mob violence was frequent in the uneasy context of Judea. The charge here of blasphemy (v. 33; using God's holy name) was not technically satisfied (*m. Sanh.* 7:5) but mobs are hardly concerned with technicalities.

Jesus' defense (v. 34) was to cite a passage from Ps 82:6 where others are called gods (the meaning of that text is not clear but it may refer to sons of God at Sinai, corrupt judges who act like gods, or angelic beings). The purpose of the citation was to challenge their judgment patterns by reference to their indisputable source of argument, *the scripture* (v. 35). The reference to *law* here (v. 34) is obviously not to be understood technically as the written five books of Moses but as a general reference to scripture.

Jesus' concern was to help them understand his role in the overall work of God. So in the context of Dedication he referred to himself as *the Father's* consecrated (or *sanctified*) one, *sent* on mission by the Father (v. 36; cf. 17:17-19). He then turned to remind them that he was not blaspheming as the Son of God. He called them to think about his works as a basis for understanding his words of identification with the Father (vv. 37-38).

His defense, however, failed to convince them because they could not accept the premise of the relationship of Jesus and the Father (v. 38). Instead, they once again attempted to arrest him, but they were unsuccessful (v. 39). Accordingly, he left Judea and crossed the Jordan. He stayed in the area where John the Baptizer began his witness. People there, in contrast to Judea, *believed in him* (vv. 40-42).

A Climactic Sign and the Passover Plot, 11:1-57

In this strategic chapter the Festival cycle has come full circle. Beginning with a SABBATH introduction (chap. 5) the evangelist leads the reader from PASSOVER (6:4) to Passover (11:55) and from a desire to kill Jesus (5:18) to the decisive death plot (11:47-53). As the earlier Cana cycle began (2:11) and ended (4:54) with miraculous signs, so this cycle that has five signs begins (5:8) and ends (11:43) with miraculous events.

Unlike the portraits of Jesus in the Synoptics where the cleansing of the Temple is viewed as the last straw for the Jewish opposition, the event in John that welded the opposition into its climactic verdict (v. 50) is the raising of LAZARUS. The story of Lazarus (vv. 1-44) and the Passover plot (vv. 45-57) are thus intimately bound together in a stirring conclusion to the Festival cycle.

11:1-16. The setting: The death of Lazarus and reactions of the disciples. The story begins with the introduction of a sick man, Lazarus, and his two sisters from BETHANY (probably a town on the eastern ridge of the Mount of Olives, a short distance from Jerusalem). Mary is further identified, prior to the event, as *the one who anointed* Jesus (v. 2; cf. 12:3). This note provides perspective later when the reader learns that the anointing was for his burial (12:7).

The message the sisters sent to Jesus, *he whom you love is ill* (v. 3), has led Filson (1963, 22–25) to speculate that the BELOVED DISCIPLE and thus the author of this Gospel was Lazarus. While this argument is intriguing, it has been accepted by very few scholars. However, it does point out that speculation is always with us.

The reaction of Jesus that the sickness is *not to (πρός) death* but *for God's glory* (v. 4) may seem to the reader to conflict with the statement that *Lazarus is dead* (v. 14). But the author, who is in control of the story, employs the earlier statement as a window into the development of the story so that the reader will realize that Jesus is in control of the situation and that the events of the story will lead to the glorification of the *Son of God* (v. 4).

This window can be helpful in understanding both the actions of Jesus and the reactions of his followers. It may seem from a modern perspective that Jesus' love for Lazarus and his sisters (v. 5) cannot be coordinated with his delay of *two days* in coming to them (v. 6). Indeed, later Martha and Mary seem to express such a feeling (11:21, 32).

The disciples on the other hand were relieved to be outside of Judea and had no desire to return. So when Jesus announced to them an intention to return (v. 7), resistance seized their minds and they reminded him of the Judean threat of stoning (v. 8). The sermonette of Jesus about walking in the daylight hardly calmed their troubled hearts (vv. 9-10). When, therefore, Jesus told them he was going to awaken the sleeping Lazarus, they pled that he would not do anything rash because sick and sleeping people recover and wake up (v. 12).

His announcement that Lazarus was dead stunned them and they failed to hear his words that the situation would ultimately support their believing (v. 15). THOMAS, the model of earthly realism, voiced their hopelessness in the decision. But it was hardly the perspective of a coward. It was the voice of resignation in the face of a perceived reality, the acceptance of hopelessness for what it seemed to be. It was a willingness to die (v. 16). History has generally treated Thomas superficially.

But the foundations for the major confession in this Gospel (20:28) can already be seen in the realism of the man popularly called "doubter."

11:17-44. The dialogues with the grieving and the work of Jesus. This scene opens with Lazarus already *in the tomb four days* (v. 17). Hope even for any word from the deceased was thus totally gone because, in popular thinking, the spirit no longer hovered around the tomb but departed for SHEOL (the place of the dead) on the third day.

As Jesus made his way towards his friends, a grieving Martha met him with the emotion-filled words *if you had been here . . . but even now . . .* (vv. 21-22). Those words indicate her strong belief in the power of Jesus but also reflect her sense of hopeless resignation. The words of Jesus, *Your brother will rise again,* were met with a strong affirmation of her trust in Jewish resurrection theology (vv. 23-24). The rejoinder of Jesus that he is the resurrection and the agent against death was met by Martha with an affirmation of belief in his messiahship and his descent from God.

The last statement represents the third time within a few verses that the title SON OF GOD is used (10:36; 11:4, 27) and indicates a definite movement in the Johannine message that earlier employed SON OF MAN as Jesus' self-designation (cf. 9:35). The linkage was of course already suggested in the Nathaniel pericope (1:49, 51).

Because the confession of Martha is such a strong theological statement, preachers using this chapter may tend to conclude their sermons with the high note of 11:27. But that is not the end of the story. Indeed, when one adds Martha's reaction at the tomb "Lord . . . he stinks" (NRSV, *there is a stench,* v. 39), it becomes quite clear that Jesus and Martha have been talking on two different levels of reality. Confession and belief do not always match.

Sandwiched between the two segments of the Martha story is a pericope about the hopeless state of Mary and the mourners. In spite of Martha's theological assertions nothing had changed. Indeed, Mary repeated the first hopeless statement of Martha *if you had been here* (v. 32; cf. 11:21). The text says that when Jesus saw her and the mourners weeping and beheld the situation at the tomb of Lazarus, "Jesus wept" (RSV, cf. NRSV, *Jesus began to weep,* v. 35).

Many interpreters accept the mourner's view of the weeping Jesus (vv. 36-37), but I am not so sure that an interpretation of mere "love" for Lazarus is fully sufficient to explain the weeping of Jesus. The mourners thought that all was lost (*kept this man from dying,* v. 37) but Jesus was hardly a helpless mourner. It is, therefore, not unlikely that their lack of comprehension (failing to understand the power that could open blind eyes could also touch a dead man) greatly contributed to the emotion of Jesus. Indeed, the next event begins to confront their puny presuppositions.

The events that followed are a study in contrast. Jesus' command to remove the stone (it is not clear here whether the tomb stone was a slab or a roller) brought forth Martha's protest against the stench. But Jesus was undeterred. In fact he gently censured her for her lack of believing in his role of bringing the glory of God (v. 40). The prayer of Jesus here begins with the typical Johannine address, *Father,* and moves to Jesus' concern for his mission (vv. 41-42; cf. 12:27-28 and esp. comments at chap. 17). But his prayer is not for his benefit (10:42). The cry of Jesus to the dead man and the command to release the resuscitated Lazarus was a stunning example of the power of Jesus to deal with human presupposition and doubt and at the same time to give incredible meaning to the theological formulations of Martha.

The story is a masterpiece of narrative writing. It is a reminder that theological answers can be very shallow in life application. It is, moreover, a story that moves the reader to the conclusion of the Festival cycle and towards the end of the public ministry of Jesus. Unlike the other stories in the cycle, however, most of the theological dialogue here precedes the act of Jesus.

But it must be added that not all the dialogue precedes because the Festival cycle has a major focus on conflict and up to this point the story has involved only the friends of Jesus. The foes of Jesus and the conflict dialogue are introduced next as the raising of Lazarus is seen as the climactic event that stirred the Passover plot (v. 53).

While many believed, some reported the event to the Pharisees (v. 45). The council members (SANHEDRIN) were frustrated by the implications of Jesus and they sought to avoid the possibility of confrontation with the Romans and the loss of their power and devastation of the nation (vv. 47-48). This section of the story is filled with irony (cf. Duke 1985, 86–89), especially when the reader remembers that the Gospel was written after the fall of Jerusalem (70 C.E.). The protective efforts of the Jews, from the Johannine perspective, proved to be futile.

Indeed, the argument of the high priest (which for the evangelist was the equivalent of an *ex cathedra* statement, v. 51) was also laced with irony. The high priest declared that saving the people would take the death of one man (10:50). It was a typical argument of the end justifying the means but for the evangelist it was an insight into the gospel of salvation. Moreover, the words of Jesus were not limited to the nation but were for all of God's scattered children (v. 52).

This section like several others in John may raise for readers questions of historicity: e.g., how did the author know the mind of the high priest? Such a question has been answered both skeptically and positively. Some posit a witness such as Nicodemus reporting the incident. In general, however, such discussions are attempts to use silence and are best recognized as speculation.

The Passover, the time of cleansing, was on the horizon (v. 55). The orders for the arrest of Jesus had been issued (v. 57). Jerusalem was in a state of upheaval and excitement (v. 56), but Jesus had departed from there and stayed with his disciples on the edge of the desert (v. 54). It is not entirely clear where this town of *Ephraim* was located. It may have been in the hill country between Jerusalem and the Jordan River but in spite of speculation, no archaeological confirmation has yet been made.

The Festival cycle is thus concluded. The remainder of the Gospel involves the outworking of Passover in the death and resurrection of Jesus.

The Anointing and Entry into Jerusalem, 12:1-50

Positioned between the Festival cycle and the Farewell cycle is the strategic chapter which announces the forthcoming death of Jesus. For mountain climbers it functions like a saddle that unites peaks of mountains and provides the opportunity to move from one place to another. In that sense this chapter contains elements of both what has been said and what is yet to be said. It is one reason why scholars have sometimes wrestled with the relationship of chaps. 11–13.

Most scholars begin a new section with chap. 13 because of the summary type section at 12:44-50, but chap. 12 should not be totally divorced from chap. 13 any more than it should be completely segmented from chap. 11. Chapter 12 is a literary conjunction and should be treated as such. But it is more than a conjunction between chaps. 11 and 13; it also is a preparation for chap. 18 and the death story.

This chapter is the work of a literary genius because of the multiplicity of cords that are being struck. In this chapter is the familiar story of the entry into Jerusalem and the several reactions that are raised by it (vv. 12-22). But the entry story is sandwiched between the anointing scene (vv. 1-11) and the Johannine Gethsemane-like scene (vv. 23-36a), both of which give the entry scene the ominous sense of a dirge. The chapter then concludes with two summations, one on believing (vv. 36b-43) and another on judgment (vv. 44-50).

12:1-11. The anointing for death. The opening announcement that it was six days before Passover sets the stage for the interpretation of this chapter as a window into the death of Jesus. Verses 1 and 10, which refer to Lazarus, underline the fact that the raising of Lazarus was viewed by the evangelist as a crucial event in the coming death of the Passover lamb.

The mention here of Martha and Mary together with brief references concerning their activities (vv. 2-3) is intriguing because the Johannine statements are quite consistent with the picture presented in Luke 10:38-42, the only other pericope in the NT where the sisters are mentioned together. In the Lukan context Martha is busy in the serving role and Mary is at Jesus' feet listening to his teaching. Here Martha is serving a meal and Mary is at the Lord's feet anointing him. In both stories Mary is commended for her activity (v. 7; cf. Luke 10:42).

It is also intriguing that the name Lazarus appears elsewhere in the NT only in the Lukan pericope with the rich man (Luke 16:19-31), although in Luke he was not a dead man but a helpless beggar who was full of sores. Dual texts like these involving the sisters and Lazarus make scholars ask questions concerning possible links between Johannine and Lukan traditions, at least at the oral or pre-canonical stage of the texts.

The anointing material has been variously translated into English as an "ointment" (KJV, RSV) or perhaps better a *perfume* (NRSV, TEV) since the emphasis seems to fall on its smell (v. 3c). The vial of *nard* or "spikenard" (KJV) used here was probably a plant oil extracted from the root (and "spike") of the Indian nard plant. The point here is its expensiveness (v. 3a) since the vial was valued by Judas as the equivalent of a year's wages (v. 5: *three hundred denarii* is of course one denarius per day for about six working days per week for a year, less the festival days).

The contrast here is between the self-giving Mary and Judas Iscariot (see comment at 6:70-71), whom John designates as the thieving treasurer of the band. While it could be argued with Judas that the anointing was a waste of resources that could have been used on the poor (v. 6), in censuring Judas Jesus was not rejecting the needs of the poor (v. 8). Instead, Jesus regarded the breaking of the fragrant vial as a symbol of his forthcoming burial (v. 7; cf. the commendation at Mark 14:8-9). It was an anointing fit for a king (cf. the elaborate burial spicing of the body at 19:39-41).

The scene closes with an expanded death plot that includes Lazarus (v. 10) because of the dead man's living testimony. The reference to departing and believing (v. 11) may have been viewed by the evangelist as a foretaste of the conflict which the early Christians would have with the synagogue and the subsequent departure of believers from their Jewish cradle.

12:12-22. The entry to Jerusalem and the reactions. While many Christians refer to the Palm Sunday event as a "triumphal entry," the designation scarcely does justice to the Johannine perspective. There is no question that the crowd was excited. The people shouted *Hosanna!* (v. 13), which is either an exclamation of salvation or an emotional petition for salvation (cf. Ps 118:25). The attached blessing makes it clear that the people were ready to install Jesus as *King of Israel* (v. 13; cf. Nathaniel's similar messianic exclamation 1:49). *The one who comes* (v. 13) from Ps 118:26 was viewed as a messianic designation and the early Christians regarded the entrance on a donkey to be a fulfillment of Zech 9:9. It was for the crowd the hoped-for beginning of the messianic age and the Lazarus event seemed to confirm their hope (vv. 17-18).

The disciples are pictured as being in the event but as those who were trying to piece together the strange puzzle of Jesus. Their problem was that they did not yet have the key of his death and resurrection (his glorification) so it did not yet make sense (v. 16).

The Pharisees were exasperated. The world seemed to be changing around them and they could not integrate Jesus into their socio-theological structures. The events were passing them by and they did not like it (v. 19).

The Greeks (Ἕλληνες, not merely Greek-speaking Jews) are next introduced (v. 20). The obvious implication is that the gentiles are interested in meeting ("seeing") Jesus. Andrew, the helper, and Philip, the programmer (cf. 14:8), are called upon to deal with this new situation (vv. 21-22; cf. 6:5-9). The mission of Jesus was expanding and they needed his direction (v. 22). The request of the Greeks, however, was not in fact answered in this story. Instead, it is as though the coming of the Greeks is merged into the Gethsemane-like experience recorded in the Synoptics (cf. Matt 26:36-39 and par.). Did the evangelist view it as the signal for the next stage of the story and part of the overall purpose of the gospel? It certainly seems so because Jesus declared in John 12:23 that his hour had come.

12:23-36a. The agony of Jesus and his purpose. The evangelist drew together the anointing and entry scenes into an integrated focus with the announcement that the hour had arrived for the glorification of the *Son of Man* (v. 23). Moreover, he provided another double ἀμήν *truly*) saying involving the dying of a grain of wheat to make it absolutely clear that the glorification of Jesus had to involve his death (v. 24).

But the metaphor of the seed contains an important Johannine statement of reversal. The dying of seed brings multiplication of life (v. 24). In the same manner losing or gaining eternal life actually is rooted in a reversal (v. 25) and following Jesus is indelibly linked to being a servant (v. 26).

Nevertheless, such reversal is often costly for it can be an agonizing experience, one that involved pain for Jesus. Avoidance of pain is a human desire and even Jesus wrestled with such avoidance (v. 27, *save me from this hour*). Yet, recognizing God's hand in pain was the method and model of Jesus. His prayer of yielding to the will of the Father and accepting his divinely given purpose in life (see also Borchert, "Prayer") was answered by an assuring voice from heaven.

Because the Synoptic scenes of the BAPTISM of Jesus (cf. Mark 1:9-11, and par.) and the TRANSFIGURATION (Mark 9:2-8 and par.) have been eliminated in John, the evangelist employed the confirming voice from heaven as an assurance that Jesus' acceptance of his death was affirmed in heaven (v. 28). The statement that the voice was not for his sake (v. 30), however, is somewhat confusing in the light of the fact the crowd thought it thundered (v. 29). It is a little speculative to argue that the evangelist was here making a distinction between the crowd and the disciples who heard. But it seems clear that he is once again clarifying for the reader that Jesus was not in danger of choosing the wrong way.

With this decisive moment concluded, Jesus declared that judgment-time had arrived together with the defeat (driving out) of the world ruler (v. 31), the deeper mystery about which C. S. Lewis wrote in his tale of Aslan (1950). The lifting up of Jesus (his death) was the hope of life for all (vv. 32-33; cf. 3:14-15). But the death of the Messiah did not fit the crowd's messianic expectations (v. 34) because they did not understand the deeper mystery of victory beyond death. Light was now with them for a short while. Their task was to believe the light so that they might become the children of light (vv. 35-36a).

12:36b-50. Summations: believing and judgment. The seven signs of the two cycles have been concluded and the final sign (the death and resurrection of Jesus) has been unequivocally introduced. But the reality was that the people would not believe (v. 37) and so the evangelist brings his story of Jesus' public ministry to a close with Jesus hiding himself from the people (v. 36b; cf. 8:59).

This rejection must have been hard for John to accept but he provided a rationale for such a rejection by including a composite text from sections of Isaiah (vv. 38-40; cf., e.g., Paul's use of such a florilegium in Rom 3:10-18).

The rationale here began with the haunting questions of who and why earlier addressed in Isa 53:1, a text frequently used by early Christians (cf. Rom 10:16). The answer, as Isaiah reflected in his call (6:6-9), was understood and determined by God alone. While Isaiah referred to both hearing and seeing problems of the people, the focus here is on seeing (v. 40), undoubtedly because of the Johannine emphasis on signs (v. 37).

The concept of God's hardening in this proof text (v. 40), as Beasley-Murray (1987, 216) has well observed, should not be made a basis for a view of reprobation (see notes at 6:70-71 and 10:27-28). The OT can speak at the same time of God hardening Pharaoh's heart (e.g., Exod 7:13) and of Pharaoh hardening his own heart (Exod 8:15, etc.). The tension between God's work and human reaction is never fully resolved in the Bible and must remain a mystery. Here John says *they did not believe* (v. 37) and at the same time *many, even of the authorities, believed* (v. 42). The broad sweep of Johannine categorizations may disturb some Western readers but the point is that the tension must always be understood in John.

But the evangelist added that believing by itself is not adequate because some believed yet failed to confess openly their loyalties to Jesus because they yielded to human pressures and affirmations rather than seeking divine acceptance (vv. 42-43; cf. 2:23-25). Such a situation brought forth a concluding analysis from Jesus: believing in him is the equivalent of believing in the one who sent him (v. 44) and such believing is enlightening in a dark world (vv. 45-46). Failure to hear and keep (obey) his word will result in judgment (v. 48), although that was certainly not the purpose of Jesus' coming (v. 47; cf. 3:17). Both the Father and Jesus have been of one purpose, namely the provision of eternal life (vv. 49-50).

The Farewell Cycle, 13:1–17:26

Scholars have long recognized that in chaps. 13–17 Jesus was preparing his disciples for his departure. Moreover, Leon Morris (1971, 610) and other writers have designated these chapters as the "Farewell Discourses," but these chapters are clearly more than discourses.

The cycle begins with the reminder that it was almost time for the PASSOVER and that Jesus' hour of destiny had come. This cycle is therefore epitomized in an act that has become the model of the self-giving love of Jesus for his disciples (chap. 13). The cycle ends with a prayer that epitomizes both Jesus' self-giving love for his disciples who must live and witness in a hostile world and the assuring expectation that his followers would be with him (chap. 17). Between these two "book-end" segments the evangelist placed some very tender discussions concerning the disciples' perceived sense of abandonment (chap. 14) but also Jesus' promise of the supportive Paraclete (chaps. 14–16). These three middle chapters then frame a central magnificent mashal or parable concerning the vine and the branches (15:1-11) and a crucial reminder of the importance of the love command (15:12-17) introduced earlier (13:34-35). This central segment thus forcefully illustrates the relationship between Jesus and his followers.

The Footwashing and Authentic Discipleship, 13:1-38

This chapter is regarded by many as a model of Christian discipleship. It is also a strategic introduction to the farewell cycle.

13:1-11. Jesus, the footwashing, and Judas. The story opens with the notation again that it was almost Passover. The dull ring of those words is joined by the reminder that the hour of darkness had arrived. Judas, the devil's agent, was about to act (vv. 1-2). The evangelist makes sure that the reader knows that the events were not unexpected for Jesus.

In the midst of this fateful time one would expect a dirge, yet a melody of "love" is sharply sounded (v. 1). Love is a theme used in chaps. 13–21 four times more frequently than in chaps. 1–12. Here love is portrayed by Jesus in the moving scene of laying aside his clothes and taking up the slave's towel. He assumed the demeaning role of washing the disciples' feet (a role usually reserved for the lowest gentile slaves, women, and people of little status; cf. Str-B 1:121).

This act was undoubtedly repulsive to the disciples. Peter voiced the common shock in his halting words (v. 6) "Lord, *you* are washing my feet?" (author trans.) Peter's response to such an idea was equivalent to "Stop!"

The reply of Jesus was virtually: "No washing of your feet, then no part in me!" That answer sent another shock wave through Peter. He did not know the meaning. Understanding would come later because the act was a symbolic prediction (v. 7).

Peter immediately changed his tune from refusal to a request for a bath or a shower (vv. 8-9). It is a humorous note of good intention that misses the point. A bath was not the issue (v. 10). Bath terminology is here symbolic of the OT concern for CLEAN/UNCLEAN (purity). In many OT contexts uncleanness is linked to sinfulness (cf. Lev 16:16-30; Ps 51:2; Isa 1:16, 64:6; Zech 13:1).

It was not, therefore, the amount of water nor the number of body parts being washed that counted with Jesus. He was concerned with the nature of a person. Moreover, the issue is probably not even BAPTISM as some have thought, although it may be a related idea. The cleansing of Christ is the issue.

The disciples were cleansible, but one of them was not (v. 11). The evangelist never whitewashes Judas. He was the devil's agent, and the verdict was firm (vv. 2-18, 26-27). For John, Judas was bad news because as a friend he *lifted his heel against* Jesus (v. 18; cf. Ps 41:9). He was certainly numbered among the *chosen* (v. 18; cf. 6:70), but he was, nonetheless, a traitor.

13:12-20. The meaning of the event. The actions of Judas like the denials of Peter (cf. 13:38), however, did not take Jesus by surprise. For John all these events are within Jesus' messianic mission. They are viewed as fulfilling scripture and said to have contributed to believing that Jesus was indeed the *I am* (v. 19; cf. Exod 3:14).

The disciples' designations of Jesus as *Teacher* and *Lord* (v. 13) were fundamentally correct but incomplete. Jesus was their master and instructor, but they also needed to understand that self-giving humility was a mark of Jesus. Indeed, it was also to be a mark of his followers (vv. 14-15).

Accordingly, two double ἀμήν (*truly*) sayings were added to remind readers of the need to accept this servant role (vv. 16-17) and to receive both Jesus and anyone sent by him (v. 20). In these sayings the evangelist has again developed a dual level of discourse. Here one can sense John has in mind both the settings in the life of Jesus and that of the readers of this Gospel. Receiving a sent one is clearly an illusion to the post-resurrection work of Jesus' followers.

13:21-30. The painful tragedy and Judas. This section opens with the pain of Jesus (v. 21; cf. 12:27) and with a double ἀμήν saying concerning betrayal (v. 21). The announcement created confusion among the disciples, and Peter sought clarification (vv. 22, 24).

The evangelist uses the event to introduce one of his famous contrasts between PETER and the BELOVED DISCIPLE. Here the Beloved Disciple reclines next to Jesus at an oriental style meal (vv. 23-24; cf. 20:4; 21:7, 20-22). As in other cases Peter seems to emerge "second best," perhaps reflective of some struggle between the early Johannine community and others. But these statements in John are not a denigration of Peter as much as a positioning of him.

The identification by the dipped morsel (probably bread or perhaps some Passover herbs, v. 26) was also the effective signal for Judas to accept his role as the instrument of the devil (v. 27). The restraining power of God was removed from him and Satan took over. Therefore, there was no necessity for further delaying his tragic work (v. 27). The meaning of the signal, however, was not yet clear to the other disciples who assumed he was engaged in some economic enterprise (v. 29). But the evangelist understood that this event was decisive. Judas' departure finally brought the tragedy of "night" (v. 30; cf. 12:35-36).

13:31-35. The new command. Segovia (1991, 59) and others think the first unit of the discourses begins at this point. Perhaps, but this section also serves as a summation of the introduction to the farewell cycle and as a window into the discourses.

The coming of the hour (v. 1) had brought the imminent glorification of the SON OF MAN (v. 31). The departure of Judas signaled the coming "departure" of Jesus (v. 33). In this context Jesus enunciated for his disciples (*little children*, v. 33; cf. 1 John 2:1) one of his most famous statements: the new commandment of love. Love was to epitomize his followers and was to be the means by which everyone would recognize them as disciples of Jesus (vv. 34-35).

This command is one of the core statements of Christianity because the mark of discipleship was not formulated in terms of a statement of faith but in terms of a way of living. In the history of the church the last day of Jesus with his disciples is remembered in the celebration of MAUNDY THURSDAY (a name derived from a defective form of the Latin *mando*, "I command," in honor of this crucial saying of Jesus). The mandate of discipleship applies more than once a year.

13:36-38. Peter's denial foretold. The announcement of Jesus' departure (13:33) drew from Peter the question: *Where are you going?* (v. 36). This question formed the foundation for Peter's strong assertion of faithfulness and Jesus' prediction of Peter's threefold denial (vv. 37-38). It also served the evangelist as the introduction to the next chapter with Thomas's question and Jesus' discussion of going away (14:1-11, 18). Moreover, it undoubtedly influenced the second-century C.E. story of the return of Peter to face death in Rome when according to one tradition Jesus appeared as Peter was fleeing and asked, *Quo vadis?* ("Where are you going?"; see *ActsPet* 35; cf. Brown 1970, 607–608).

The Question of Anxiety and Loneliness, 14:1-31

Chapter 14 is the first of the three central discourse chapters of the farewell cycle. The focus in these chapters is on the disciples' relationship to God and to others. In this chapter the evangelist seeks to confront the disciples' fear and anxiety from loneliness. Also woven into the discussions here are the first two of five Paraclete sayings.

This chapter breaks naturally into four sections involving the departure of Jesus (vv. 1-3, previously introduced in 13:33 and 36), questions of Thomas and Philip concerning the way to the glorified Jesus and the Father (vv. 5-11), the relationship of believing, working, and asking through Jesus (vv. 12-14), and the promise of the Paraclete's presence in loneliness and frustration (vv. 15-31).

14:1-3. Departure and preparation for the future. The chapter begins with two crucial commands: one negative—"Don't let your troubled hearts (wills) control you"—and one positive—"Commit yourselves to (believe in) God and me" (author trans., v. 1). The reason given for heeding these exhortations is that in God there is security. God's home has many secure dwelling places, and the role of Jesus was to prepare for our future (vv. 2-3).

14:4-11. Questions of our destiny. Jesus' comment that the disciples now know their destiny with him (v. 4) brought utter confusion among them. Thomas, like Nicodemus, had difficulty in thinking about the realm of God (v. 5; cf. 3:12). He wanted a road map to his destiny. The *I am* saying of Jesus concerning *way, truth,* and *life* (v. 6) failed to clarify the situation because the disciples really did not understand the relationship of Jesus to the Father. Philip's practical request for a genuine vision of the Father (v. 8) revealed that the key to their understanding was still missing. Later Thomas would know the key (20:28), but not before the resurrection.

Seeing Jesus did not yet mean for them having a vision of God (vv. 9-10). So Jesus once again reminded them of his works (v. 11).

14:12-14. Elements of discipleship. Having mentioned his works, Jesus turned the conversation to discipleship. Believing was basic to accepting the disciples' work on behalf of Jesus. Indeed, they would expand his ministry (*do greater works*;

v. 12) after his departure if they were properly attuned to him (*ask in my name*; v. 14). Such asking was not merely repeating Jesus' name in prayer, but asking according to his nature. God would thus be glorified in their working for Jesus (v. 13).

14:15-31. The coming of the Paraclete. While talk of Jesus' departure left them feeling empty and lonely, Jesus was not abandoning them (v. 18). He had been their companion; now they would have *another Advocate* (v. 16; one who would stand alongside of them). This term *Advocate* (or Paraclete) includes various meanings such as support, counsel, comfort, and exhortation. The disciples would not be orphaned because the authentic Spirit (of Truth) would be an internal resource for them (v. 17).

The distinction between *with* and *in* (v. 17) must not be made the basis of two levels of Christian life, as argued in some charismatic discussions concerning the Spirit. Rather, it is to be related to John's historical view of the coming of the Spirit and John's understanding of transformation (e.g., the nature of external and internal knowing and believing God). *On that day* (v. 20) they would understand (*know*) internally the relationship between Jesus and the Father and the true meaning of obedience (keeping Jesus' commands) which is rooted in love (vv. 20-21; cf. the love command in 13:34).

Living in the love of God and obediently loving others (cf. the two great commands of Mark 12:28-31 and par.) is the basis for sensing the divine presence in one's life. Such presence dispels loneliness (vv. 18, 21-24). The purpose of the first ADVOCATE/PARACLETE saying is thus to clarify the nature of God's presence in the disciples' life.

The second Advocate/Paraclete saying is built upon the first. In theophanies (appearances of God), angelophanies, and christophanies of the Bible, the presence of God usually brings a sense of fear and the need for a calming word of assurance (cf., e.g., Judg 6:22-24; Matt 14:26-27; see Thornton and Borchert, 1989).

The word of assurance normally is "Don't be afraid," or "Peace/Shalom." Here Jesus offers his shalom—a peace unlike that which the world can offer. It is a message not to be afraid or troubled by this new sense of presence and the departure of Jesus (vv. 27-28).

The role of the Advocate/Paraclete in the lives of Jesus' followers would be that of instructor to help them live in a hostile world (vv. 26, 30). The idea of instruction is deeply rooted in the OT faith. The Torah or Law was the center of instruction (Deut 6:4-9). Paul then argued that the Law's instructional value was to lead to Christ (Gal 3:24). Here the Spirit's, i.e., the Advocate/Paraclete, instructional role is to remind the disciple of Jesus (v. 26).

The pain of Jesus' departure was not to be magnified. Instead, the disciples were to rejoice at this new stage in God's unfolding work and in the fact that God's enemy (*the ruler of this world*) is not ultimately in control (vv. 28-30). Indeed the departure would turn out to be a witness to the world (v. 31).

The chapter ends with a note *Rise, let us be on our way* (v. 31). Some scholars have suggested that this note indicates that chaps. 15–17 are an insert. Others would argue that 15–17 take place in the garden (18:1) or somewhere between the site of the last supper and the garden. Perhaps the easiest answer is that it was a note retained from an earlier stage in the editing process and is one of the few literary seams in the Gospel (cf. Brown 1970, 656–57).

The Vine and the Branches, 15:1-17

In the midst of the painful discussion of farewell involving the disciples' fears and Jesus' promises of the Paraclete, the evangelist has inserted the captivating *mashal* or allegory of the vine and the branches together with the powerful reminder of the love command, both of which focus on the intimate relationship between Jesus and his followers.

This beautiful poetic passage contains the second *mashal* of John. The other in chap. 10 also focuses on Jesus' relationship to his disciples and pictures Jesus as the good shepherd. The opponents of Jesus are there likened to thieves, wolves and hired servants. Here are portrayed various aspects of authentic (true) and inauthentic discipleship in vineyard terminology.

Scholars hold varying opinions on the relationship of this section of the Gospel to the Lord's Supper or Eucharist. Its placement within the farewell cycle certainly is related to the death (glorification) of Jesus. The linkage of the love command here (v. 12) with the command in the footwashing scene (13:34) is hard to miss. But it is probably safe to conclude that the *mashal* per se was probably not eucharistic in orientation and should only be seen secondarily as such (for the contrary see: Beasley-Murray 1987, 269 and Brown 1970, 672–74).

15:1-11. Discipleship and the allegory of the vine. The vineyard had long been a symbol of Israel, God's people (cf. for example Isa 3:14; 5:1-7; Ps 80:8-18). Here the vineyard keeper is pictured as God the Father. Jesus is the authentic vine and his followers are branches (vv. 1-2). Genuine disciples know they are utterly dependent on Jesus and his word for cleansing (v. 3), fruitfulness (vv. 4, 8), and a proper understanding of their identity (v. 5). Failure to live in the vine is devastating in its implications (v. 6) but abiding in the vine is the key to prayer (v. 7, cf. 14:13), the glorification of God, and authentic discipleship (v. 8).

Such abiding is defined in terms of love (v. 9) and obedience (v. 10). Both are modeled on the relationship between Jesus and the Father. Indeed, such abiding should lead to the joy of the Lord becoming evident in the life of the disciple (v. 11).

15:12-17. Love and chosen disciples. The command to *love one another* announced at 13:34 is forcefully repeated here and identified with a call for the sacrificial death of the disciples (vv. 12-13). The strong summons undoubtedly reflects not only the circumstances in the farewell of Jesus but also the evangelist's context of a persecuted community. To love one another is the glue that enables the Christian community to stand together in times of suffering.

But this love is more than comradeship. It is rooted in the identification of the disciple with Jesus. Therefore, the evangelist includes the reminder that dying disciples are not merely obedient slaves but are participating friends in the mission of Jesus (vv. 14-15). Moreover, they are not self-directed actors but chosen and appointed agents of Jesus. Their mission is to bear fruit that lasts (v. 16).

Two important principles emerge in this central section of the cycle. First, divine chosenness or election in the Bible is not to privilege but to mission. God chooses not for the person's own benefit but to serve God's desire to bless the world (cf. Abraham's call in Gen 12:1-3). To reject the mission is tantamount to rejecting the call.

Second, the theme of "abiding," "remaining," or "lasting" is foundational in the Bible for inheritance or salvation texts. Accordingly, all assurance texts have a stated or implied warning or condition attached to them (cf. John 15:4, 6; 3:18). Thus, the promises made to successive patriarchs or kings are renegotiated between God and each generation. Moreover, each warning text has a stated or implied promise or assurance attached to it because God's intention is not the destruction of the world but the hope of salvation for all humanity (cf. 15:7, 10-11; 3:17).

It is in this context of the tension between assurance and warning that texts concerning asking God (or prayer) must be understood (15:7, 16; 14:14). God is not an unthinking Santa Claus-like figure supplying endless human desires or prayers. If such were the case, he certainly would have supplied the request of Jesus to avoid "the cup" of death (cf. Mark 14:36). God loves us and desires to commune with us but to pray in the name of Jesus is to accept the Lord's nature in our lives when we pray (cf. Borchert 1970).

The Question of Anxiety and Persecution, 15:18–16:33

This second major section dealing with the anxiety of the disciples is like a reversal or mirror image of chap. 14, except that the focus shifts from loneliness to world hatred. The earlier section ended with an announcement of the world ruler's limited power (14:30) and this section begins with world hatred and persecution (15:18-25). The earlier section began with Jesus confronting the anxiety of the disciples' loneliness over his departure (14:1-11) and this section ends with Jesus confronting their anxiety over his departure, the forthcoming persecution, and their superficial understanding of the implications of what was to happen (16:16-33).

Embedded in both sections is a reminder that they are to pray or to ask for divine help concerning their situations (14:13; 16:23-24). Both sections also contain Paraclete sayings: two in the first part (14:16-17; 14:26-27) and three in this second part (15:26; 16:7-11; 16:12-15). These three chapters thus form an INCLUSIO framed around the central *mashal* and love command (15:1-17).

15:18-25. World hatred and persecution. The world in this farewell section is viewed from a negative, anti-Jesus perspective (cf. 3:16 where the world was viewed as the place of mission). Because the disciples have become identified with

Jesus' select group, they stand over against this orientation of the world and thus receive the same hatred that was directed at Jesus (vv. 18-19).

The dual setting of the Gospel is once again in mind—for example, the life of Jesus and the early church. The maxim concerning *master* and *servant* is again used to recall the pattern. Not only were the disciples to be like their teacher in their life of service (13:13-16; cf. Luke 6:40), but here it is clear that the disciples would also not be able to avoid the hostility directed at their Lord (v. 20; cf. Matt 10:24). Persecution of the disciples and the church was therefore inevitable because the enemies would not accept (*do not know*) Jesus (v. 21).

Moreover, the hatred of Jesus meant the enemies also despised and did not know God the Father (vv. 21, 23). But they would not be excused for their sinful actions because their rejection of Jesus and his works preempted any defense on their part (vv. 22, 24; cf. the testimony section in 5:30-47). The unjustified nature of their hatred is supported here by a quotation from Ps 69, which early Christians viewed as messianic (v. 25 and Ps 69:4; cf. Ps 35:19. Note also the use of Ps 69:9 in John 2:17). *Law* (Torah) is the general use of the term for the OT. The enemies in mind here are Jewish persecutors but the early Christians would have expanded this negative orientation of world to include other persecutors as well (see Brown, 1979).

15:26–16:15. Three more Paraclete sayings. To face the world's hostility Christians are again reminded of their resource: the Paraclete or Spirit (cf. 14:15-31). The disciples' task was/is that of witness in the midst of hostility, but their witness was not self-induced or self-motivated. They had been with Jesus from the start of his ministry and were to bear witness to him (v. 27). In this third Paraclete saying Jesus indicated that their support for witness would be the Paraclete or Spirit of truth that was to be sent by Jesus and to come from the Father.

During the centuries when Christians were formulating the early creeds a dispute arose between the Eastern and Western churches about whether the Spirit proceeds from the Father "and the Son" (Lat. *filioque*). While much ink has been spilled over this Trinitarian formulation, it is best not to view the statement in v. 27 as involving a concern for relations within the Godhead per se. As Schnackenburg (1987, 3:118-19) has argued, it is a mission statement of the Spirit that in parallel form involves both Jesus and the Father. The point is that the Paraclete is intimately involved in the witness of Christians.

The concern of the evangelist was that Christians who were faced with persecution, death, and exclusion from the synagogues would be tempted to "abandon," "stumble," "fall away," "become scandalized" (σκανδαλίζω) by the persecution (16:1-2). Such persecution was in the time of the evangelist not merely a vague threat; it was a reality. In the Apocalypse of John one can sense the scope of that threat because there the synagogue is called "a synagogue of Satan" (Rev 2:9 and 3:9; cf. the *birkath ha-minim* or so-called Jewish curse of the Nazarenes and heretics in the twelfth benediction [see Martyn 1979]). The Christian community was under attack and the evangelist wanted to remind the members (16:4) that Jesus understood their plight and that, like their Lord, Christians also would have their hour. But in that hour of danger they had a God-given resource to prevent their capitulation.

The fourth Paraclete saying is introduced by another statement concerning Jesus' departure, the disciples' accompanying sorrow (16:5-6; cf. 14:1-11), and the promise of consolation (16:7; cf. 14:18). Here the coming of the Paraclete is said to be an advantage. Certainly the statement does not suggest superiority of the Spirit to Jesus but the meaning probably implies that the extent of the personal ministry of Paraclete in the world is to expand the implications of the coming of Jesus.

In this fourth saying the threefold role of the Spirit in the world is outlined. The governing term (ἐλέγχω) that introduces *sin and righteousness and judgment* is multidimensional (16:8). Its meanings include "expose," "convict," demonstrate," "correct," and "convince." Obviously in using such a word with these three roles, the evangelist implies that the Paraclete is prepared to use Christians in confronting all orientation to evil in the world. In so doing the Paraclete will expose the world's sinfulness, identify the standards of righteousness in Jesus, and judge all sin as connected with Satan, the prince of evil (16:9-11). The role is a powerful one.

The fifth and final Spirit statement (Paraclete is not used here but follows by implication) involves future counsel or direction for the disciples. Recognizing that it was impossible to spell out everything, the function of the Spirit in relation to the disciples themselves was to be that of guide (16:13). But the guide would not operate independently of the revelation in Jesus. Indeed, in all communication the Spirit would glorify Jesus and in so doing affirm the unity between Jesus and the Father (16:13-15).

16:16-33. Confronting the implications of Jesus' departure. Following upon the sorrow of the disciples (16:6) and the last two Spirit sayings, Jesus' mention of *a little while* in reference to both not seeing him and seeing him, especially in the context of going to the Father, left the disciples confused (vv. 16-18). In response Jesus replied with the first of two double ἀμήν (*truly*) sayings. Sorrow would come to them, but it would be followed by joy (v. 20).

The combination of pain followed by joy is like the delivery process for a woman concluding in the birth of a child (v. 21). The mention of birth pangs immediately brings to mind the idea of the birth pangs of the Messiah. Israel developed a sense of hope and an expectation of deliverance in the midst of their experiences under foreign rulers. Grist for the idea was supplied by important texts such as Isa 66:5-14 and Mic 4:9-10; 5:2-3. In v. 22 the event does not signify joy at the birth of the Messiah but joy at the resurrection of Jesus and his ascent to the Father (cf. v. 17) following the painful experience of the crucifixion.

In the light of such an anticipated victory the second double ἀμήν saying is employed to remind the disciples that the Father takes seriously the prayers of Jesus' followers (v. 23). God's desire is to respond to Christians so that they will be filled with joy (v. 24; but for further perspective on asking in the name of Jesus see the discussions at 15:16 and at 14:14 and 15:7).

The pattern of Jesus in his ministry was to describe his life and work in word-pictures. With the coming of the hour, however, the disciples would have the key to understanding Jesus' mission and such figurative patterns would be unnecessary (v. 25). They would understand prayer and the relationship between Jesus and the Father at that point (vv. 26-28).

But the disciples jumped to the conclusion that they had the key before the crucial events (v. 29). Clearly they perceived that Jesus was God-sent (v. 30). Yet they still did not have the kind of perception that Jesus was seeking. Accordingly, Jesus announced that they would abandon him (vv. 31-32). While Jesus would not abandon them (cf. 14:18), their perception did not result in commitment. Yet Jesus did not give up on them. He reminded the disciples that he (*in me*) was the source of authentic *shalom* (*peace*; v. 33). The world was not the basis for peace. It provided the opposite, namely persecution or trouble. But the disciple should not despair because the disciples' Lord has *conquered the world* (v. 33).

The Great Prayer, John 17:1-26

In recent years many scholars have commented on this great prayer (see Borchert, "Prayer"). Some (such as Schnackenburg, Malatesta, and Black) have emphasized structural analysis based on theological or linguistic studies and many have focused on the theme of unity. Some have divided the text into three parts following Westcott, and others have opted for a four-part division.

In an earlier study on prayer, I showed that chap. 17 breaks naturally into seven petitions all except one of which follow the Johannine formula of invoking the *Father* (πάτερ). This formula is also present in other prayers in the Gospel (cf. 11:41; 12:27, 28). Also similar is that each of the petitions, no matter what the context, deals with some aspect of Jesus' mission. Although the invocation *Father* is used only six times (vv. 1, 5, 11, 21, 24, and 25), there are actually seven petitions because of the interconnection of the prayers. Taken as a whole the chapter is a magnificent summary not only of the farewell cycle but of the entire Gospel.

17:1-3. The first petition. The lifting up of Jesus' eyes and the announcement that the hour had come following the first *Father* signals the conclusion to the farewell cycle. The emphasis in vv. 2 and 3 is really a restatement of the mission of Jesus and the purpose statement for the Gospel in 20:30-31.

17:4-8. The second petition. The emphasis on *finishing the work* and "the glory before the world began" (author trans.) is a clear reminiscence of the "Word" who was "at the beginning" intimately related to God (1:1) and was the "only" Son who came to make God known (1:14, 18). The petition in 17:5 for the restoration of glory (cf. 1:14) is striking. Also striking is the fact that 17:7-8 concerning the disciples' receiving, knowing, and believing Jesus and his words echoes the key verses of the prologue (1:10-12) as well as the major emphasis of the Cana cycle—seen in the disciples at Cana (2:11), the crucial perspective on believing after the Temple incident (2:23-25), Nicodemus (3:12), the Samaritans (4:42), and the official (4:48-49).

17:9-19. The third and fourth petitions. *I am asking* or "I pray" (v. 9) begins a new emphasis on the situation of the disciples in a hostile world. The strong invocation *Holy Father* (v. 11) together with the repeated request for protection (vv. 11-15) in the *name* of God appears to be an allusion to the OT idea of power in the name of God and to the idea that God's name must never be spoken irreverently (e.g., Exod 20:7). The perceived hostility in these verses echoes the repeated hostility to Jesus in the festival cycle with the paralytic (5:18), the bread of life (6:41 and 70), the statement on truth (8:41-48), the blind man (9:24), the good shepherd (10:31-33), and Lazarus (11:45-50). Evil or *the evil one* is real (v. 15) and the disciples need the protection of God to survive.

The fourth petition, which does not include the invocation "Father," is a prayer for holiness or sanctification (v. 17) that picks up the holiness idea in the earlier invocation (v. 11). The use of *holiness* terminology is exceedingly rare in this Gospel and the only other use is in the good shepherd *mashal* (10:36; it is also used in 1 John 2:20 in a conflict situation). The purpose of the disciples on mission here (v. 18) is similar to that at 10:36.

17:20-26. The fifth, sixth, and seventh petitions. Again the words *I ask* signal a shift of emphasis (v. 20). These last three petitions are related to the farewell cycle but in fact go beyond them.

The prayer for oneness (v. 21) immediately reminds one of the central *mashal* of the vine and the mission of fruit bearing (15:5), which is mirrored in the purpose of the world believing in the one who was sent (vv. 21, 23). Moreover, the *through their word* reminds one of the post-Thomas expectation concerning those who will have to rely for believing on testimony (v. 20; cf. 20:29). The theme of love is also very significant here (v. 23) and reminds one of the command to love (13:34; 15:12) and the questions to Peter (21:15-17; cf. Peter's earlier scene in 13:37-38).

The sixth petition is the wish for the disciples to share in the glory of Jesus. The words *where I am* (v. 24) are exactly the same words as in 14:3, which emphasize the future the disciples can expect.

The final petition begins with the invocation *Righteous Father* and forcefully distinguishes the world from Jesus and his followers (vv. 25-26). The petition is intriguing because it remains unexpressed, but the interpretation seems clear. The only two places in the entire Gospel where the righteousness motif is used are here and at 16:10 of the farewell cycle where the role of the Paraclete is again introduced because Jesus is going *to the Father* (13:1; 14:6, 12, 28; 16:10, 17, 28; 20:17).

The task of the Paraclete there (16:8-10) was to define for the sinful world the nature of righteousness in and through the followers of Jesus. It is significant, therefore, that the nature of the community that should provide the standard for the world's judgment is here (v. 26) defined not in theological formulas but in terms of the love of the community.

Thus in bringing the farewell cycle to a close the evangelist ends where he began in chap. 13 with the model of Jesus' love lived out in the lives of his followers.

The Death Story, 18:1–19:42

The death story of John is one of the most fascinating pieces of NT literature. Throughout the story Jesus is portrayed as serenely in control of everything from the betrayal and arrest (18:1-11) to the mock trial before Annas (18:12-14, 19-24), the denials of Peter (18:15-18, 25-27), the skillfully crafted seven scenes before Pilate that move in and out of the praetorium (18:28–19:16), the crucifixion and death scenes (19:17-37), and finally the burial (19:38-42).

All the actors in the story pale in comparison to the king of Israel (Jesus). He is in charge of his own death and everyone connected with it. The skill of the evangelist is evident throughout the story; irony is a great tool that makes the portrait of Jesus stand out in bold relief when compared to the hollow characters who think they are in charge of his death.

In this story there is no kiss of Judas (cf. Mark 14:45), no washing of the hands of Pilate (cf. Matt 27:24), no carrying of the cross by Simon of Cyrene (cf. Mark 15:21), no identification of the two who were crucified with him (contrast Mark 15:27 and Matt 27:38 with Luke 23:32, 39-43), no acknowledgement of sin by Judas and report of his death (contrast Matt 27:3-10 with Acts 1:16-20), no cry of forsakenness or tearing of the Temple veil (cf. Mark 15:33-38, etc.), and no centurion's confession of the Son of God (cf. Mark 15:39). It is not that these events did not happen, but that for John the focus is upon Jesus' control of his death and the guilt of all the world before the enthroned king on the cross. Jesus as king is the central figure in this story and everything points towards his yielding of his spirit in death as the sacrificial LAMB OF GOD.

18:1-11. The garden scene. Separating the Mount of Olives and the Temple Mount runs the Kidron Valley. At the base of the Mount of Olives still today lies a garden that tradition marks as the place of the arrest of Jesus. But in John the scene is pictured in a unique manner.

The soldiers are there with Judas. Indeed, the *detachment* is designated by John (vv. 3, 12) in Greek as a σπεῖρα, normally used to refer to a battalion or cohort of at least 600. The leader is called a χιλιάρχος, a rank just under that of a general in the Roman army (v. 12). The picture is clearly intended to be one of imperial force coming out against Jesus, and to this political force was added the power of the religious establishment (v. 3). But the irony is that with all their human weaponry this great force needed lanterns and torches to find their way (v. 3), a reminder that night had come (13:30) and they did not know where they were going (cf. 12:35; 11:9-10).

The story is ironic in another way because it was Jesus who asked them: "Whom do you seek? (v. 4, author trans.)" The powerful ones were on a search-

and-seize mission but it was Jesus who identified himself. And the identification words of Jesus echo the identification of God to Moses (Exod 3:14): "I am." The devil-man, Judas, is merely mentioned (vv. 2, 5) and then melts into the background. He does not identify Jesus in John. The evangelist wanted the reader to realize that Jesus was in control, even of his arrest. When therefore the religious leaders and powerful soldiers heard the self-identification of Jesus, they were rendered absolutely helpless in his presence (v. 6). Worldly power met supreme power, and human power faded.

It was Jesus who then gave the human pawns permission to arrest him but not before he cared for his disciples (vv. 8-9). Yet brash Peter had to act for the disciples. Impressed with these events, Peter determined he would try to rescue Jesus (only in John do we learn that the disciple is Peter, v. 10). The puny sword of Peter could damage a human ear but it could not deter a divine mission. The cup of death was the will of God. Inconsistent Peter was in the way of the divine mission and Jesus censured him. But Peter would still have his chance to prove his commitment.

<u>18:12-27. The mock priestly trials and Peter's denials.</u> For John the verdict had already been delivered by CAIAPHAS, the reigning high priest. The verdict was death, a sacrificial death (vv. 13-14; cf. 11:49-52). The trial therefore was a sham.

It was conducted by *Annas . . . the father-in-law of Caiaphas* (v. 13) whom John also designates as *the high priest* (v. 19). While Annas was no longer technically the high priest because he had been deposed in 15 C.E. by the Roman general Valerius, he continued to be the power broker of the high priestly family, acting through his sons, son-in-law, and grandson. The power-hungry corruption of the high priesthood was well known at this time and Ananais, the high priest at the time of Paul (cf. Acts 23:2), was so despised that the Jews themselves assassinated him before the fall of Jerusalem.

The arguments before Annas in John are little more than a late-night interrogation and are a contrast to the openness of Jesus' teaching in the synagogues and Temple (v. 20). The blow to Jesus by the high priest's servant could be explained as a defense of God's prince (Exod 22:28). But such a defense was firmly challenged by Jesus' own question concerning unjust punishment and false witnesses (v. 23). The interrogation became a standoff between justice and injustice so Jesus was shuttled to Caiaphas, the high priest (v. 24).

Alternating with these interrogation scenes, the evangelist inserts Peter's denial scenes. Both scene-patterns take place at night—the interrogations are inside while the denials are outside. The denial scenes take place in the context of *a charcoal fire* (ἀνθρακία, a term used only here at v. 18 and at 21:9). The threefold denial of Peter will later be paralleled in chap. 21 by a threefold question of love and service.

The responses of Peter in these denial scenes are striking when contrasted with the response of Jesus in the garden. Jesus had responded *I am* (ἐγώ εἰμι, vv. 5-6), but Peter responded to his question of commitment and identity with *I am not* (οὐκ εἰμί, vv. 17, 25). The implications are enormous. The disciple was ready to fight but would not accept the way of Jesus. But in his third response even his willingness to fight is shown to be a mere shadow, for Peter, when confronted with his own slashing of the servant in the garden, denied even that involvement. The denial was thus complete and the cock immediately crowed (v. 27), fulfilling Jesus' prediction indicating that Peter's commitment was a matter of hollow words (13:36-38).

18:28–19:16. The mock trial before Pilate. The setting was the praetorium or Roman judgment hall, and the scenes once again alternate between inside and outside. The Jewish leaders, who had already determined Jesus' guilt even before the trial (v. 31; cf. 11:50), desired to maintain their ritual purity by remaining outside the gentile court at PASSOVER time (v. 28). The irony for John is clear because the lamb was being readied for Passover and the leaders were responsible for the fact that he was delivered (παραδίδωμι, v. 30; the same word frequently used of Judas, the betrayer) to be killed (v. 32).

The next scene shifts as PILATE, the procurator or prefect, entered the praetorium to question Jesus. Judea was a subdivision of the imperial province of Syria and unlike the senatorial provinces imperial provinces were viewed as hostile to Rome. The question of treason and rebellion was always a concern in such provinces.

From Pilate's viewpoint the question *Are you the King of the Jews?* (v. 33) was directed at determining the possibility of such a treasonable situation. The dialogue that ensued over Jesus' kingship left Pilate asking *What is truth?* (v. 38) and Jesus affirming his kingship but redefining the nature of such kingship (v. 37).

The third scene moves outside again and reveals a frustrated Pilate who found that Jesus was hardly a political rebel as Pilate had been led to believe. Accordingly, he sought to release Jesus because in his judgment Jesus was innocent. Realizing the determination of the Jews to condemn Jesus, however, Pilate tried the gimmick of a tradition or custom established for the Jews at Passover in releasing a confirmed criminal (v. 39). He gave them what seemed an easy choice—a hardened criminal BARABBAS, a thief who had no doubt robbed some of them, or the seemingly facile preacher Jesus. His strategy failed, and they chose Barabbas.

The fourth scene reveals Pilate's next strategy. Inside the fortress his troops whipped Jesus and played their mocking kingly game with him. Then in the fifth scene Pilate brought Jesus out to the hostile crowd, hoping that the sight of the beaten Jesus ("Behold the man," 19:5 KJV) might engender sympathy. But the crowd had tasted blood and wanted more. *Crucify him*, they shouted, to which Pilate finally responded, *Take him*. Yet he added his evaluation of innocence (v. 6; cf. 18:38; 19:4). Political expediency was carrying the day.

But the Jews countered Pilate's declaration of innocence with their own judgment that he was guilty of blasphemy because he declared himself to be the *Son of God* (v. 7). That announcement stunned Pilate who wanted a "time-out." Yet as

Garland (1988, 491) and others have indicated, the Jews' reliance on the law to condemn Jesus set the stage for their own condemnation. They broke the law in their unjust pursuit of Jesus' death and ultimately in their affirmation of Caesar as their only king (v. 15).

Pilate's time-out forms the sixth scene. At this point his fear at the breach of the Roman peace by a mob uprising was countered by his fear of the unknown, and he reentered the praetorium to requestion Jesus (v. 8). His question, couched in the Johannine theme of origin, brought nothing but silence from Jesus. Pilate retorted by reminding Jesus of his power to condemn and to free, but Jesus finally broke the uneasy silence with a reminder that Pilate was not the source of power. Dispensing power was in the hands of God but guilt was the result of human action. So the theme of the deliverer is once again brought to focus and it serves as a forewarning to Pilate (v. 11).

The seventh and final scene took place before the Jews. It began with Pilate's renewed attempt to release Jesus but it was countered by the Jewish threat to identify Pilate as a foe of Caesar and a supporter of treason (v. 12). The threat proved effective and brought Pilate to the judgment seat to render the verdict.

Scholars today debate whether the *Pavement* (*lithostratus*, v. 13) was at the Herodian Palace on the west side of Jerusalem near the Jaffa Gate or at the Tower of Antonio to the north of the Temple (see Mackowski 1980, 91–111). While a few translations suggest that Pilate sat Jesus on the judgment seat in a defiant act, most translations correctly have Pilate seated to begin the final phase. To think that a Roman puppet would turn over his seat to a Jewish peasant seems highly unlikely.

The time of this event is duly noted by the evangelist, namely, *the day of Preparation . . . about noon*. The time is significant for John and it is repeated (19:14, 31) because the *day of Preparation* was the day for killing the Passover lambs. In the Synoptics the day of crucifixion is merely related to Passover, but theologically for John the death of Jesus has to be related specifically to the slaying of the lambs. Because of the apparent differences in such time statements, scholars have sought to reconcile John and the Synoptics by a number of arguments, including an argument based on the differences in the calendar of official Judaism and the calendar of the ESSENES. Such attempts usually prove to be fruitless. What is clear in John is the theological nature of the time designations.

In the final trial scene Pilate made one last attempt to free Jesus, but he was rebuffed by the ultimate Jewish hypocrisy: *We have no king but the emperor* (i.e., Caesar, v. 15). Throughout Israel's history it was God that was to be their king (cf. 1 Sam 8:7). So finally Pilate also joined the deliverers and handed Jesus over to be crucified (v. 16). Judas, the Jews, and Pilate are all guilty.

19:17-27. The crucifixion of the king. John simply notes that Jesus bore his own cross to the place of the skull and was crucified between two others. While Luke mentions Simon of Cyrene and the death confession of one of the criminals (Luke 23:26, 40-42), John's focus is on Jesus and the cross itself. Charges of condemned victims were nailed to their crosses. The charge against Jesus was treason because he was *the King of the Jews* (v. 19).

For John two facts were important. The charge was written in three languages: Hebrew, the language of the chosen people; Latin, the language of Roman authority and government; and Greek, the language of international commerce (v. 20). So the evangelist regards the charge as in fact a confession to the whole world concerning the kingship of Jesus. Moreover, while the Jews sought to modify the charge/confession to that of a pretender, John sees the weakling Pilate as finally having a backbone (vv. 21-22).

The conclusion is obvious: Pilate is not in control of this death. He has indeed finally received strength to stand against the Jews so that the integrity of the death scene is maintained. Jesus was indeed *the King of the Jews*.

The evangelist highlights two groups around the cross for attention. The soldiers in disposing of the clothing of Jesus are seen as fulfilling scripture (cf. Ps 22:18).

The women are briefly mentioned as a means to introduce Jesus' mother and *the disciple whom [Jesus] loved*. Traditionally that disciple was regarded as John. The thesis of Filson (1963, 22) that the disciple was Lazarus has little support. As the eldest son, Jesus cared for his mother and in this text Jesus made his choice (vv. 26-27). The implications were significant. The Johannine community was special and Jesus cared for his own.

19:28-37. The death of the lamb. Two more statements from the cross bring to a conclusion the death of the lamb. The *I am thirsty* (v. 28) reminds the reader that the death scene was real and the *It is finished* (v. 30) accentuates the fact that the death was part of God's intention to bring Jesus to this hour. With this last statement Jesus *gave up his Spirit*. The point is clear: people were not ultimately in charge of the death of the lamb.

With the ending of *the day of Preparation* (and the killing of the Passover lambs), the Jews sought to ready the land ritually for SABBATH by having the crucified ones quickly dispatched. But surprisingly, the soldiers found the Passover lamb was already dead and there was no need to break Jesus' legs. John sees that fact to be very significant because the lamb died without blemish (Exod 12:46; Num 9:12). Yet he was appropriately stabbed, a fact that must have reminded the evangelist of some allusions to a pierced Messiah (cf. Zech 12:10).

But when he was pierced there came out *blood and water* (v. 34). Some writers and preachers who are opposed to ideas of Johannine symbolism have often been tempted to interpret blood and water as mere signs of death. But to a symbolic writer like John *blood and water* carry multifaceted meanings related to salvation, including but not limited to the ordinances or sacraments of the church.

The fact that the evangelist makes a special note to the effect that these symbols or signs are testimonies and are important for believing (v. 35) immediately reminds the careful reader of the purpose statement of the Gospel (20:30-31).

19:38-42. The burial of the king. The picture presented in this burial is that of a king. He was buried in *a new tomb* (v. 41) with the appropriate bindings and a hundred (Roman) pounds of spices (seventy-five by modern measure), sufficient to bury a king. The attendants, Joseph and Nicodemus, were undoubtedly among the PHARISEES who believed in the resurrection but who were still somewhat fearful of the Jewish leadership. With the burial of the king, the story seemed to be finished. But everyone was in for a big surprise.

The Resurrection Stories, 20:1-29; 21:1-23

The great PASSOVER had taken place; the lamb was slain; the king had died. No more would the theme of Passover be mentioned in this Gospel. A new day was ready to dawn. The night was ready to pass away. The stories of the resurrection in John are thus the stories of the transition into the new era.

In the Synoptics the appearance stories are set either in Galilee (in Matthew, except 28:9-10, and apparently in Mark) or in the Jerusalem area (in Luke). In John the main appearances occur in Jerusalem (chap. 20) but in the postscript the context is Galilee (chap. 21). The stories in John are unique although they are not different in kind from those in the Synoptics.

Chapter 20 contains three stories: the story of Mary Magdalene (20:1-2, 11-18), the episode of the two disciples visiting the tomb (20:2-10), and the appearances to the disciples and Thomas (20:19-29). Chapter 21 is a threefold story of the miraculous catch of fish, the breakfast, and the restoration of Peter (21:1-23).

20:2-10. The visit of the two disciples to the tomb. Although the resurrection stories begin with the note that Mary is the first one to the tomb, the story quickly shifts to the two disciples: Peter and the disciple whom Jesus loved (v. 2). The comparison between the two disciples that began at 13:23-24 is peculiar to John.

After being informed by Mary that the tomb was open, the BELOVED DISCIPLE outran Peter and first saw the tomb with the empty grave wrappings (vv. 4-5). Why he did not enter has been variously interpreted by commentators from a sense of reverence to waiting for Peter. Ecclesiologies often determine perspectives. But in spite of the order of entrance the text indicates that other disciple *saw and believed* (v. 8). This text is the only statement in the canonical Gospels where it is said that the empty tomb was a sufficient basis for belief. In all other cases the basis was the appearance of Jesus. What stage of believing was implied here is not quite clear because the evangelist seems anxious to move the people in the narratives from one level of belief to the next. Clearly he suggests that they did not yet fully understand the scriptural warrant for Jesus' resurrection (v. 9).

20:1-2, 11-18. Mary Magdalene. After her initial visit to the tomb and the notification to the disciples that the tomb was empty (vv. 1-2), Mary returned to the tomb weeping (v. 11). Then after the appearance of angels in the tomb she conversed with someone (who seemed to be a gardener, v. 15) about her sorrow and the missing body. But all the pain vanished with one word: *Mary!* He spoke her name and everything was changed (v. 16).

She grabbed at him and uttered the intensive word *Rabbouni!* But Jesus stopped her with the words, *Do not hold on to me* (v. 17). The reason given by the risen Lord is that he had not yet ascended. This statement has led a few commentators and preachers to pose an ascent and then a descent so that Jesus could be later touched. Such thinking is a complete misunderstanding of the text. Assurance of Christ's presence and support does not come via his physical presence (see Borchert 1987, 142). Mary wanted to hold on to him but such was not possible. Instead she had to leave him and carry her testimony to others (v. 18).

20:19-29. The disciples and Thomas. It was again *evening* and fear still plagued the disciples as they gathered on the *first day of the week* (v. 19). But they were in for a shock. Locked doors like a shut tomb did not deter the risen Jesus. He entered their room and like the theophanies or angelophanies of the OT the appearance of Jesus was accompanied by his word of *Peace* (vv. 19, 21) and followed by a commission to carry the message of forgiveness to others (v. 23).

Interpreters of this text must not concentrate on the "retaining" aspect here any more than they should concentrate on the "binding" aspect of the Matthean statement at Caesarea Philippi (Matt 16:19; 18:18). The role of the authentic rabbi (and believer) was to bring persons into a proper relationship with God.

The breathing on the disciples and the command to receive the Holy Spirit is the Johannine summation of the pentecostal promise (v. 22; cf. Luke 24:49, 51; Acts 1:8, etc.). Interpreters of these stories should avoid detailed, Tatian-like (as found in the DIATESSARON), Western attempts to fit these stories into neat packages. The testimonies are authentic messages concerning God's Son and our faith. They stand as faithful statements of the evangelists. For this reason Tatian was never accepted as a substitute for the Gospels.

While the disciples who were gathered on the first day of the week received a blessing, Thomas missed the first church service. When he heard the report, he stoutly refused to accept the word of testimony from others without the authentication of the nail holes and the stab wound (v. 25).

But the next Lord's Day, that is, *the first day of the week* (v. 19), he was at the service. Eight days later is one week later according to our system of reckoning where the first day is not counted (v. 26). Again Jesus entered and gave his "peace" or "shalom to those gathered. The ecclesiastical implications are obvious. The church meets each Lord's Day to receive the peace of the risen Lord.

Thomas had challenged the other's testimonies. At this gathering his failure to believe was challenged by Jesus' offer to touch his wounds. The experience was more than convincing for Thomas, and he uttered what has come to be Christianity's premier confession of faith: *My Lord and my God!* (v. 28). But the doubter turned confessor was nonetheless reminded that the church that would thereafter be built upon testimony would not have the same opportunity for verification. Thus a blessing was issued by the risen Lord to those who would believe "without seeing" (v. 29).

21:1-23. The epilogue, a triple story. The first segment of this story once again begins at night but this time it is in Galilee. The disciples decided to return to fishing and as in Luke 5:1-11 they toiled all night without success. At daybreak Jesus appeared on the shore and suggested to these seasoned fishermen that they try the other side of the boat (v. 6). The result was a large catch of fish. The BELOVED DISCIPLE first recognized the Lord and informed Peter (v. 7). Once again the comparison is made. And once again Peter, the second best, impetuously dashed off to see Jesus.

This story has been the subject of considerable form analysis and comparison with the Lukan story. These two texts are the only two places where a miraculous catch is recorded. Some argue that it is the same story with Luke being a transposed resurrection narrative. But some also suggest that part of the story is not unlike Peter walking on the water in Matt 14:28-33. Such suggestions have led to speculation that the entire story may be a construction from segments of other stories.

Others have asked about the significance of the number of fish. Some have suggested that maybe the author thought there were 153 varieties of fish in the sea or 153 language patterns at the time of the evangelist's writing, both of which might be the symbol of the worldwide scope of the Christian mission. Clearly this text is the subject of a great deal of speculation and analysis. While the story can stand on its own, further reflection may be helpful (see Brown 1970; Bultmann 1963; Schnackenburg 1987, v. 3).

The second part of the story takes place on land. The *charcoal fire* (v. 9) is a reminder of the one burning when Peter denied Jesus three times (cf. 18:18). In this story the risen Lord had prepared a meal of fish and bread (clearly reminiscent of the feeding of the five thousand at Passover time in the pre-resurrection era; cf. 6:1-14). The statement that Jesus *took the bread and gave it to them* as well as *the fish* (v. 13) is related to the words of the church's supper. The point is that in this event the disciples recognized that it was *the Lord* (v. 12), a theme related to the breaking of bread in the Lukan EMMAUS story (Luke 24:30).

The third part of the story involves the threefold question to Peter in his restoration. That threefold question of the Lord involved Peter's love. Would his relationship to others get in the way of his love for Jesus? It had done so on the horrible night of his betrayal. It was therefore review time. When Peter answered three times that his love for Jesus was primary, Jesus gave him a commission to feed the flock (vv. 15, 16, 17), a commission that Peter faithfully passed on to subsequent church leaders (cf. 1 Pet 5:2).

In preaching on this text some ministers become enamored with linguistic discussions about *love*. But the point of Peter's grief is not primarily a linguistic nicety. The text indicates that Peter was grieved because Jesus asked *the third time, "Do you love me?"* (v. 17). The third time was a haunting reminder that Jesus was right and he was wrong in his boast of commitment to Jesus (cf. John 13:37-38).

But when Peter's restoration was completed, the story was not ended because his boast of dying for Jesus (13:37) was accepted by the Lord. He would indeed die for Jesus, the stretched out death of crucifixion (v. 18).

Yet like all of us Peter was still Peter. If he were to die, what about the BELOVED DISCIPLE (vv. 20-21)? That question, Jesus told Peter, was totally irrelevant to him. His task was to follow Jesus (v. 22).

But that question was relevant for the Johannine community because some thought that Jesus said the Beloved Disciple would not die (v. 23). Obviously that disciple was either dead by the time the Gospel was being circulated or very near death. So the correction of false theories needed to be made.

Conclusions, 20:30-31 and 21:24-25

This Gospel contains two conclusions, the first at the end of chap. 20, which originally was intended to serve as the conclusion to the book, and the second at the end of chap. 21, which concludes the epilogue and expands the force of the earlier conclusion.

20:30-31. The first ending. As indicated earlier, these verses in fact contain a summary purpose statement for the entire book and tie together a number of the major themes of the Gospel. So complete did Loisy consider the work to be at the end of chap. 20 that he wrote: "The book is complete, quite complete" (1921, 514). The first twenty chapters—despite the displacement theories of Bultmann, the organizational weavings of MacGregor and Morton, and the structural arguments of Fortna—appear to be a continuous theological argument of the evangelist. This conclusion is therefore a masterfully tied knot that encircles these twenty chapters.

21:24-25. The second ending. While the epilogue should definitely be viewed as an afterthought or a postscript, it is important to recognize with Westcott (1889, 359) that there is no textual support for thinking that the other twenty chapters ever circulated without this epilogue. It was from the earliest times an attachment to the text. In theology and style the epilogue is truly Johannine.

In form this ending has two parts: an authentication and a conclusion. The authentication is a community-written testimony (*we know,* v. 24) that this Gospel represents the genuine witness of the disciple who stands behind the written text. The conclusion is an affirmation of the selective nature of materials included in the Gospel and the hyperbolic statement reflects the writer's (*I*, v. 25) grand opinion that the selection is drawn from a vast resource of material concerning Jesus.

The *I* of v. 25 may imply that the writer is a recorder who differs from the witness of v. 24. But this final verse stands as a striking invitation to discover the magnificent testimony of John that is drawn from an immense storehouse of information concerning Jesus, the word of God come in human flesh (1:14).

Appendix. The Woman Taken in Adultery, 7:53–8:11

This pericope has been regarded by most textual analysts as an insertion into the Johannine Gospel. In style, form, and content it was hardly written by the author of the other parts of the Gospel. But that does not mean it should not be considered canonical. Early Christians were convinced that it was a reflection of an authentic Jesus tradition.

The major question seemed to be where it should be placed. Some manuscripts contain it here in the context of Johannine conflict stories but other manuscripts have it after Luke 21:38 and before the plot to kill Jesus. While it is more like the Lukan stories that emphasize the care of the Lord for the unfortunate, the setting at the end of Luke 21 is also a misfit. The best solution is to regard the pericope as an independent story going back to Jesus.

Adultery was regarded as a violation of the will of God in accordance with the seventh statement of the TEN COMMANDMENTS (Exod 20:14). But a double standard had emerged that held women more liable than men. This story reflects that same double standard because the woman's partner was not brought forward by the condemning men.

Jesus recognized the double standard and the Pharisees' attempt to entrap him in his care for the helpless (v. 6). His response therefore was aimed at the self-righteousness of the accusers (v. 7). When he disposed of those self-righteous ones and was alone with the woman, he addressed her in a forgiving spirit without dismissing the reality of her sin (v. 11).

The pericope is thus an excellent example of Jesus' firm confrontation of hypocritical self-righteousness and caring salvation of sinners who need to find transformation.

Works Cited

Beasley-Murray, G. R. 1987. *John*. WBC.

Black, D. 1988. "On the Style and Significance of John 17," *CTR* 3:141–59.

Boice, J. M. 1970. *Witness and Revelation in the Gospel of John.*

Borchert, G. L. 1981. "The Fourth Gospel and Its Theological Impact," *RE* 78:249–58. 1987. *Assurance and Warning*. 1988. "The Resurrection Perspective in John," *RE* 85:501–13. 1993. "Passover and the Narrative Cycles in John," *Perspectives in John*, ed. M. Parsons and R. Sloan, 303–16. Forthcoming. *John*. NAC. Forthcoming. "Prayer in John 17," in *Prayer in Biblical Research.*

Borgen, P. 1965. "Bread from Heaven," NovTsup.

Brown, R. E. 1966, 1970. *The Gospel according to John*. AncB. 1979. *The Community of the Beloved Disciple.*

Bultmann, R. 1963. *The History of the Synoptic Tradition*. 1971. *The Gospel of John.*

Burney, C. F. 1922. *The Aramaic Origin of the Fourth Gospel.*

Carson, D. A. 1991. *The Gospel According to John.*

Craddock, F. 1982. *John.* Knox Preaching Guides.

Culmann, O. 1953. *Early Christian Worship.*

Culpepper, R. A. 1975. *The Johannine School.* SBLDS 26. 1983. *Anatomy of the Fourth Gospel.*

Dodd, C. H. 1958. *The Interpretation of the Fourth Gospel.*

Duke, P. 1985. *Irony in the Fourth Gospel.*

Filson, F. 1963. *John.* LBC.

Fisch, H., ed. 1965. *Haggada.*

Fortna, R. 1988. *The Fourth Gospel and Its Predecessor.*

Freeman, C. H. 1991. "The Function of Polemic in John 7 and 8," Ph.D. diss., The Southern Baptist Theological Seminary.

Garland, D. E. 1988. "John 18–19: Life through Jesus' Death," *RE* 85:485-99.

Guilding, A. 1960. *The Fourth Gospel and Jewish Worship.*

Harris, M. 1971. "Prepositions and Theology in the Greek NT," *NIDNTT*, 1171–1215.

Haenchen, E. 1984. *John.* Herm.

Käsemann, E. 1969. "The Structure and Purpose of the Prologue to John's Gospel," *NT Questions of Today*, 138–67.

Lewis, C. S. 1950. *The Lion, the Witch and the Wardrobe.*

Loisy, A. 1921. *Le Quatrieme Evangile.*

MacGregor, G., and A. Morton. 1961. *The Structure of the Fourth Gospel.*

Mackowski, R. M. 1980. *Jerusalem, City of Jesus: An Exploration of the Traditions, Writings, and Remains of the Holy City from the Time of Christ.*

Malatesta, E. 1971. "The Literary Structure of John 17," *Bib* 52:190–214.

Malina, Bruce. 1981. *The NT World: Insights from Cultural Anthropology.*

Martyn, J. L. 1979. *History and Theology in the Fourth Gospel.*

Metzger, Bruce M. 1953. "The Jehovah's Witnesses and Jesus Christ: A Biblical and Theological Appraisal," *TT* 10:65–85.

Moody, D. 1953. " 'God's Only Son': John 3:16 in the RSV," *JBL* 72:213–19.

Morris, L. 1971. *The Gospel according to John.* NIGNT. 1986–1990. *Reflections on the Gospel of John.* 4 vols.

Mowinckle, Sigmund. 1956. *He That Cometh.*

Newman, B., and E. Nida. 1980. *A Translator's Handbook on the Gospel of John.*

Sanders, J. T. 1971. *The NT Christological Hymns.* SNTSMS 15.

Schnackenburg, R. 1987. *The Gospel according to John.*

Segovia, F. 1991. *The Farewell of the Word.*

Sloyan, G. 1988. *John.* Interp.

Thornton, Edward E., and Gerald Borchert. 1988. *The Crisis of Fear.*

Westcott, B. F. 1887 [1954]. *The Gospel according to St. John.*

Mercer Commentary on the Bible.
Volume 6. ***The Gospels.***

Mercer University Press, Macon, Georgia 31210-3960.
Isbn 0-86554-511-1. Catalog and warehouse pick number: MUP/P138.
Text, interior, and cover designs, composition, and layout by Edd Rowell.
Cover illustration (*The Evangelists*) by Fr. Gregory Kroug (see p. ii, above).
Camera-ready pages composed on a Gateway 2000
via dos WordPerfect 5.1 and WordPerfect for Windows 5.1/5.2
and printed on a LaserMaster 1000.
Text font: TimesNewRomanPS 10/12.
Display font: TimesNewRomanPS bf and bi,
plus University Roman titles (covers and title page)
and ATECH Hebrew and Greek.
Printed and bound by McNaughton & Gunn Inc., Saline MI 48176,
via offset lithography on 50# Natural Offset and perfectbound into 10-pt.
c1s stock, with 4-color-process illustration and lay-flat lamination.
Individually shrinkwrapped and bulk packed in cartons on skids.
[February–March 1996]